SEXUALITY COUNSELING

A
TRAINING
PROGRAM

Kay Frances Schepp, Ed.D.
Counseling Psychologist
Counseling and Testing Center
The University of Vermont
Burlington, Vermont

 **ACCELERATED DEVELOPMENT INC.**
Publishers

Muncie,   Indiana

SEXUALITY COUNSELING
A TRAINING PROGRAM

Library of Congress Catalogue Card Number: 86-70572

International Standard Book Number: 0-915202-47-6

Technical Development: Tanya Dalton
                         Judy McWilliams
                         Sheila Sheward

Cover Photography: Tony Keppelman

Cover Design: Kate Pond

Ms. Pond is a sculptor who lives and works near Lake Champlain, Burlington, Vermont. The sculpture on the cover and her other recent stainless steel works reflect the feeling of water and movement of wind.

The author interprets this sculpture as reflecting reciprocity in relationships and harmony between counselor and client.

Order additional copies from

AD ACCELERATED DEVELOPMENT Inc., PUBLISHERS
3400 Kilgore Avenue, Muncie, IN 47304
(317) 284-7511

DEDICATION

For Ron and our children. I wish the actual writing had taken less time, but know that the counseling and supervision experience on which this training program is based has made me the person I am.

ACKNOWLEDGEMENTS

The hundreds of clients with whom I have worked in the last twenty years taught me the subtleties of sexuality counseling which are included here. As each person improved, he/she was very good at telling me what was really important. The constant questions and insights of graduate students from all the human service professions contributed to the final form. Being a counselor educator led me to keep recording the skills for the use of other counselors.

Most of us in human services received our sexuality counseling education outside of graduate school. I am indebted to fine trainers like the following who structured my thinking as I worked with clients: Lonnie Barbach, Terry Beresford, Hak Coplin, Ed Donnersteen, Lyman Gilmore, Sol Gordon, Nicholas Groth, Eleanor Hamilton, Virginia Johnson, Helen Singer Kaplan, Winifred Kempton, Robert Kolodny, Barry McCarthy, Brian McNaught, David McWhirter, James Maddock, William Masters, John Money, Carol Nadelson, and Patricia Schiller. These people and dozens of others have presented their experiences at conferences and in-service training programs, and have written books and articles to follow through.

Resources are an important aspect of sexuality counselor training, because of the breadth of the field. I'm indebted to Gary Kelly, Editor of AASECT's *Journal of Sex Education and Therapy,* for appointing me Resource Review Editor. The position puts me at a crossroads of information on what new books, films, videotapes and software are really useful to practitioners in this fast moving field.

The following people are colleagues who have generously talked about their work with me and possess great understanding of human sexuality: Jim Barbour, Ellen Cole, Roddy (Mary Frances O'Neill) Cleary, Sam Dietzel, Susan Donnis, Bob Fine, Armin Grams, Bob Moore, Trisha Rose Moore, Eric Nichols, Alice Outwater, Lyman Gilmore in New Hampshire, Dan Richards in Maine, and my cousin Phil Connell in California. My other friends and family have been truly supportive too, even when my professional interests seemed a little unusual to them. They have all helped broaden my perspective on sexuality.

When this book was just an idea, Keith Miser, Associate Vice President for Student Affairs at the University of Vermont, supported my request for a sabbatical leave. Joyce Slayton Mitchell shared her knowledge of the publishing process when the text got to the prospectus stage. The clinical staff at Planned Parenthood of Northern New England and their librarian, Jan Fuller, shared their expertise and resources with me. And finally, Joseph Hollis, President of Accelerated Development, Publishers, did the editing which turned the manuscript into a book. Joe's experience as a veteran counselor educator at Ball State University makes him ideally suited for understanding how to communicate the complex mix of skills which is sexuality counseling.

Thank you all.

Kay Frances Schepp

January 29, 1986

Burlington, Vermont

SEXUALITY COUNSELING: A TRAINING PROGRAM

CONTENTS

SECTION I
SELF ASSESSMENT OF FOUNDATION SKILLS

SECTION II.
SKILLS FOR SEXUALITY COUNSELING

SECTION III
INTEGRATING SKILLS

FIGURES

FORMS

INTRODUCTION

Welcome to an extension of your counseling skills. Since all people are sexual beings, they need counselors, social workers, specialized teachers, psychologists, health care personnel, and clergy who are comfortable with sexual concerns. Everyone in our society receives mixed messages about sex, so to find helpers who are informed and at ease is a relief.

This program is about professional counseling and assumes that the reader has training, or intends to obtain it, in an established helping profession. Usually this means graduate work in counseling, social work, pastoral care, health or special education, nursing, mental health, psychology, or related fields. Sometimes individuals with less professional education provide sexuality counseling for specific populations, such as reproductive health clinics, alcohol and drug treatment centers, or college peer programs. In order to protect the consumer, a sexuality counselor needs to have a "home base" in a recognized helping profession, or be part of a team supervised and trained by professionals.

If people who read this training manual met in groups to discuss "what is counseling?", probably each individual would develop a different answer. Fortunately, agreeing on a narrow definition of counseling is not necessary in order to add to one's skills. This program takes the position that counseling can be placed between the personal growth processes of education and psychotherapy, and partakes of the best of both.

Sex Education—SEXUALITY COUNSELING—Sex Therapy

Sex education is a necessary component of sexuality counseling. A practitioner needs to be a sensitive, effective educator in order to help people remedy sex-related problems and prevent future ones. Some practitioners minimize their education courses, and yet knowing how to sequence information, to engage in a teaching dialogue, and to design an individual learning program is invaluable in sex counseling.

The word "counselor" is used in this training program to refer to any trained professional who utilizes counseling skills as part of the treatment of a client/patient. In most instances the term "sexuality counseling" is used instead of "sex counseling," to describe work with sex-related issues rather than sexual satisfaction alone.

Differences exist among practitioners over the dividing line between counseling and psychotherapy, and the terms are used interchangeably in many instances. Some techniques developed for use in sex therapy have been modified by counselors and used with great success in treating less entrenched sexual problems. The approach taken in this book is that severe sexual dysfunction requires a trained sex therapist, but that sexuality counseling is appropriate for many people. Every effort has been made to indicate when referral for psychotherapy or sex therapy is preferable to sexuality counseling.

Counseling is a satisfying skill, because it encourages personal development and helps the client cope with pressures, problems, and decisions as a way of becoming stronger. Counselors in schools, mental health agencies, family planning clinics, private practice, health care facilities, churches, community service agencies, and residential facilities reach the broad general public. Counselors can personalize sexual information for a client more than the educator can, and see more people earlier than does a sex therapist.

BALANCE OF SKILLS

Sexuality counseling is a specialty area which should not be practiced without professional level knowledge in both general counseling and human sexuality. In addition to self instruction, graduate level course work in the two areas is needed as well. Also, an important requirement is to have objective feedback from others through professional supervision of one's sexuality counseling before offering this service to the public. HOWEVER, once balanced training is achieved, sexuality counseling is one of the most gratifying, effective, helpful services a counselor can provide.

People who attend sexuality counseling courses and workshops seem to belong to one of two major groups:

1. They have a strong background in health and/or sex education, but have less training in mental health or counseling. Health personnel and sex educators usually are in this category.

2. They are well trained in counseling skills, but have less knowledge about sexuality. Social workers, school and pastoral counselors are often in this group.

When individuals from the different groups are in the same course they can become impatient with one another. But after working together they come to see the importance of knowing about both the physiology of puberty or the stages of sexual arousal, and techniques of empathy or dealing with resistance. Of course many professionals belong in neither group exclusively, and simply need to add skills in one or both. In order to help the trainee locate where further work needs to be done, self assessment checklists and learning exercises are included throughout the first section of this program.

VALUE OF SEXUALITY COUNSELING

Are any more specialists in human sexuality needed? People talk about sex; they view sexual movies, home video and television; they find a barrage of material at supermarket checkout counters; they can buy pornography which is available almost everywhere. Vividly written sexual self-help books are sold by the millions, and surveys continue to report increased rates of sexual activity for all age groups. Perhaps because of the cultural climate, confusing as it is, some seminars are now being given for professionals entitled: "Where Have All the Easy Cases Gone?" Many people have undoubtedly worked through sexual problems by talking to friends, through experience, and by obtaining information.

The blatant and conflicted sexual messages are not serving all the public well, however. A strong need continues for competent sexuality counselors, and the literature supports the effectiveness of good counseling. Some of the valuable aspects are as follows:

1. Reliable information is not easy to obtain; clients report reading newspaper advice columns and watching television talk shows to learn about sex. Counselors can apply their knowledge of sexuality to the individual case, and find that clients are grateful for good information.

2. Sex is both a high interest and a high anxiety area for most people. Clients welcome the opportunity to discuss sexual concerns with an informed professional. In doing so the counselor can help make sexuality a normal part of living in a manner acceptable to the individual.

3. Socialization has made honest communication about sex difficult even though every person has sexual feelings, experience, ideas, and values. Counseling is uniquely suited to provide the individual with a safe place to integrate diverse impressions, work out language, and practice more effective sex-related communication.

4. A bewildering wealth of sexual resources are for sale in the marketplace, of varying degrees of quality. The counselor is in a good position to help the client sort out what books and sexual aids are useful.

5. Techniques which work to facilitate appropriate sexual development and responsible sexual expression are available to counselors. Many are not self-help and therefore a professional is needed to structure a personal treatment program.

6. Sexual pleasure is a powerful reinforcer to help the client succeed. Personal integration (body, feelings, mind), increased self confidence, and a decrease in anxiety, guilt, and confusion are further rewards which facilitate sexuality counseling.

7. Complete failures in sexuality counseling are few. Almost every client can be helped toward more positive sexual attitudes or behavior, and the results are satisfying because they are tangible.

8. Individual sexual problems often coincide with important life stages. Helping the client resolve the sexual aspects (even in a developmental crisis), facilitates overall growth.

9. Society has begun to address criminal sexual problems, and effective interventions are being developed. To be part of positive social change is rewarding.

10. Human sexuality is closely connected to intimacy, wellness, family, reproduction, creativity, and the quality of life; helping people in this area enriches society.

PERSONAL FACTORS

When a person in a helping profession reads this training manual with the serious intention of becoming proficient in sex-related counseling, that person needs to commit to becoming open about his/her own sexuality. Counseling is frequently described as an art as well as a science, and needs more than "dry," cognitive insights. The "alive" material, such as the counselor's feelings, breadth of awareness, prejudices, present lifestyle, and the mix of good and bad experiences which all human beings have in their sex history, is required.

The pressures which led to ignorance, guilt, and negative experience for others also have been felt by the counselor. Just as no book alone can provide the skills needed to become a competent counselor, or a fully knowledgeable sexologist, this training program cannot create full awareness of one's own sexuality. The reader is encouraged to use the suggested resources to design a personal program of self growth in sexuality.

Individuals need not have accomplished perfection in their own sexual expression, nor have had an "ideal" sexual development to become a good sexuality counselor. To have experienced victimization or sexual inhibition and to have faced the problem are sometimes assets. Just as in other helping situations, however, the counselor must have substantially worked through the alcohol problem, the crisis of faith, or the grieving process before practicing in those areas. A practitioner can obtain help and make progress on sex-related problems in order to be authentic when working with clients on sexual issues.

CAUTIONS

Sexuality counseling can accomplish many things. At the same time one must recognize a number of things sexuality counseling is NOT:

Impersonal information on topics such as venereal disease, abortion procedures, or rape trauma syndrome. Counseling implies individualized, therapeutic use of information.

Exclusively problem-oriented (impotence, incest, painful intercourse). Sexuality counseling is health oriented in the holistic sense, and suited to early intervention and prevention as well as remediation.

A way of controlling other people's behavior or imposing morals. No counselor is value-free, and yet each has a professional obligation to respect the client's world and the integrity of freedom of choice.

A substitute for psychotherapy to treat serious mental health problems, or for therapy for chronic, severe sexual dysfunction. These are better referred to a specialist.

A substitute for medical treatment. A competent sexuality counselor refers a client for health care immediately when there is any indication of a possible medical problem.

Sexual interaction between counselor and client. The counselor can not exploit the privileged counseling position to gratify his/her own sexual needs; professional ethical codes are clear about this.

USE OF THIS TRAINING PROGRAM

One of the best uses for this text is as part of a course, practicum, or other training. If no formal opportunity exists, several people can form an ongoing study group with a commitment to attaining competence in sexuality counseling. Many of the exercises require involvement with others and benefit from dialogue with objective feedback. Active learning is especially necessary for a professional who is not in a regular training context, and who is working on a self-study program.

Section I, "Self Assessment of Foundation Skills," can be read and the checklists completed fairly quickly. The Learning Experiences will and should take time, however. These activities will give the trainee an idea of strengths and indicate where more work is needed. Those aspects discovered as requiring more work need not be completed in sequence. For instance a plan to participate in a SAR (sexual attitude restructuring) weekend, to do interview tapes for a Learning Experience in Chapter 3, and to attend a seminar on adolescent sexuality, all complement one another. The important goal is to strengthen one's background skills.

With the foundation attained, or in good progress, Section II, Chapters 5 and 6, focus on specific sexuality counseling approaches. These chapters present an overview of types of sexual concerns expressed by clients to counselors, and many resources are listed in each section. No one can be equally proficient in all areas of sexuality counseling, nor will many counselors expect to work with every type of client since the field is so broad. As a basic standard a reasonable approach would be to offer competent counseling for the range of sexual issues likely to be presented by one's usual client population, and then make appropriate referrals when necessary. The professional has the responsibility to define the extent of his/her practice, and to expand it with due care.

In Section III, the reader has the opportunity to read sample cases as they appear in practice in Chapter 7, to expand brief client statements and to recognize the key issues. Ideas are presented in Chapter 8 for further application of the counselor's training to larger units of society. Creating opportunities for early intervention and prevention are encouraged.

Counselors are familiar with the concept: BECOMING. Becoming a competent sexuality counselor is a significant step in self actualization for many professionals in human services. Trainees first have to let themselves be vulnerable, to risk resistance from others, to admit areas of ignorance, to recall suppressed experiences, to spend considerable energy learning difficult material, and to dig into personal values. When all things come together and the counselor is practicing skilled sexuality counseling from all levels of self, the words "becoming, holistic, self actualizing, belonging, freeing" seem naturally appropriate.

SECTION I

SELF ASSESSMENT
OF FOUNDATION SKILLS

Much of the emphasis in this training manual is on self assessment of skills, based on the belief that professional people are good at learning by the time they reach levels of advanced training. Section I, consisting of Chapters 1 through 4, focuses on the foundation skills, many of which the trainee already possesses and should find interesting to review and polish. In the diagram (Figure 1) are illustrated relationships among foundation skills.

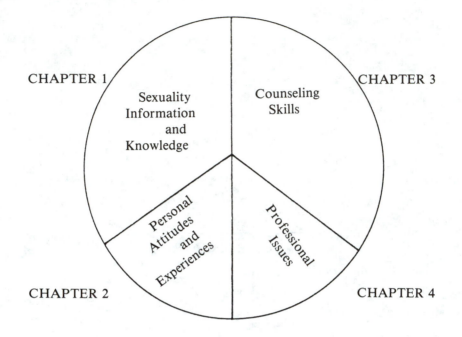

CHAPTER 1

Sexuality
Information
and
Knowledge

Counseling
Skills

CHAPTER 3

Personal
Attitudes
and
Experiences

Professional
Issues

CHAPTER 2

CHAPTER 4

Figure 1. Foundation Skills.

TYPICAL CASE EXAMPLE

In the following interview segment is illustrated how sexuality can be a significant aspect of a situation even when the client does not present it as such. Some counselors would treat Ben as having a "dependency problem," or depression, and just try to help him get back on his feet. The practitioner in this case picks up on the possibility of sex-related aspects and is willing to explore them without exaggerating their importance. Sexual issues often come to the counselor's attention in similar indirect ways.

A young man, Ben, has referred himself to a counselor in an agency, school, private practice, church, drop-in center, or other service because of insomnia and declining performance in job/school. He is clearly very upset. The counselor uses good listening and focusing skills to encourage Ben to express his grief and hurt over a broken relationship with Linda. It seems like a predictable reaction to the breakup of a person's first serious relationship until he says:

Ben: *"What I can't get over is that Linda's not the same .... she acts funny, cries all the time, and never goes out alone. She looks terrible."*

Counselor: *"Linda could be feeling bad about the relationship too, even if she did end it. But this kind of reaction has been going on for a while?"*

Ben: *"No, it was sudden. Things were great until two weeks ago. I visited my parents for the weekend to get my car fixed, and when I came back Linda was all strung out and picked a fight with me. I can't figure out why she made me tell her that I kind of pressured a couple of girls for sex back in high school. You know, nothing serious. But then she started to cry and made me leave, and won't see me."*

Counselor: *"You think everything was fine with Linda, and between you, until the weekend you were out of town?"*

Ben: *"Yes, and I'm not saying that just to make myself look better. Linda's roommate told me yesterday to keep calling .... that Linda has to get over something. I asked her if it was my messing around in high school and she said no. I just don't know what happened."*

Counselor: *"The hardest part is losing Linda, but at least you would like to know why?"*

Ben: *"Right! Maybe I did something. How do I know this won't keep happening to me?"*

Counselor's Thoughts: Linda's behavior has changed, she cries a lot and doesn't want to go out alone, she brought up an apparently remote sexual issue to fight about, and Ben seems genuinely bewildered.

Possibilities

1. Perhaps Linda just wants to drop this relationship but is still upset about it.

2. Could Linda have discovered she was pregnant, perhaps had an abortion, but doesn't want Ben to know?

3. Linda could have had a value conflict with Ben about sex in their relationship, and ended it after deciding he was pressuring her.

4. Could Linda have been seeing someone else without Ben's knowledge, and that reached a crisis while he was away?

5. Perhaps Linda contracted a vaginal infection or a sexually transmitted disease like herpes and is ashamed and upset?

6. Maybe Linda was sexually assaulted, or become aware of earlier pressured sex which she had suppressed, and is experiencing a trauma reaction?

Suggestions for This Case

Now that rapport is strong enough and Ben has explored what he is upset about, the counselor could focus with him on two possibilities for clarifying the uncertainty:

1. Linda wants to end the relationship (possibility No. 1 of those listed) and isn't assertive enough to let Ben know why. If that is the case, Ben must eventually accept it and go on with his life in a positive manner. The counselor could help with that process whether or not Ben gets feedback on what went wrong.

2. The other five possibilities listed previously can be discussed with Ben, with the recognition that completely different factors may have been involved. Ben can offer other possibilites and in so doing may learn more about what happened.

Ben might be able to help narrow the alternatives:

"I know Linda takes the pill faithfully every day, and we agreed I'd go with her for an abortion if she ever got pregnant."

or

"She wasn't pressured. We had a great sex life .... she usually initiated. Linda even teased me about how she was more daring about making out than I was."

Resolving the Uncertainty

Ben must be prepared that the chances are he will find out that Linda really wants to break up. She has given him no other message. But there is a possibility that she needs help now, even though that would not guarantee a continuing relationship. Ben can put himself in a frame of mind to try to talk to Linda in a genuinely supportive way, without criticism or blame.

Encouraging Ben to ventilate his own hurt and anger in counseling, rehearsing what he might say, and possibly talking to an empty chair called "Linda" would help him clarify what he wants. Possible Ben: "Linda, I feel rotten, but you seem really upset. Has something bad happened to you lately?" or "Are you going out with someone else? I won't try to tell you what to do or criticize. I just need to know what happened." Counselors never feed words to clients, but since Ben is upset about the sudden change he could be helped to express himself.

Follow-up with Ben would be extremely important:

1. If Linda communicates little beyond wanting to end the relationship, Ben can come to a sense that he has done all he could in a difficult situation. Rebuilding self confidence might then become the counseling focus.

   or

2. Ben could discover a different reason such as Linda went to a party while he was away for the weekend and was raped by someone she used to date, her family found her contraceptives and refuse to allow her to see him, or an entirely different problem. The counselor can help Ben clarify what went wrong and then cope with whatever reality presents itself.

Regardless of what is occurring with this couple the counselor's role is not to "fix" the relationship or manipulate Linda to explain, but to consider Ben's mental health. Helplessness and confusion are known contributors to emotional states like Ben's. Therefore whatever the counselor can do to help him clarify, face, and deal with his relationship should help Ben regain a more positive self concept and work/school adjustment. In addition, if possible, the counselor may help obtain some assistance for Linda if she needs it.

Foundation Skills Needed

This case of Ben makes the point that a knowledge of sex-related counseling is useful in many client situations, and not just with obvious sexual issues like teenage pregnancy or premature ejaculation. The trainee can scan the following list of skills presented in Figure 1, and go back through the dialogue to locate particular points where each is needed.

> Knowledge about Sexuality
>   (Chapter 1)
> Comfortable Attitudes and Values about Sex
>   (Chapter 2)
> Counseling Skills
>   (Chapter 3)
> Knowledge of Relevant Professional Issues
>   (Chapter 4)
> Possibly Later
>   Specific Sex Counseling Approaches
>   (Chapters 5 and 6)

GUIDELINES FOR LEARNING EXPERIENCES

Real gain in counseling skill can only come from honest self assessment combined with active involvement. The checklists, resources, and learning exercises within this book provide a directional map for the counselor to use.

1. Only those exercises with which the counselor is comfortable should be completed. Modification by the trainee is recommended to fit individual circumstances.

2. Where others are involved, people should be selected who are completely free to participate or not. Any hint of emotional pressure or use of an authority role must be avoided.

3. Honesty with others will help them understand that their cooperation is requested as part of the counselor's professional development, and that treatment is not being offered.

4. After a Learning Exercise is completed, the next step is to process what occurred in the interaction. The counselor has the responsibility to leave the person in as good a place or better than when they began.

5. In the rare instance when a Learning Exercise inadvertently triggers a negative response, the counselor must follow through with support and offer a referral if necessary.

Trainees can expect to spend more time on some Learning Experiences than others. In an area where the counselor's preparation is weak, he/she first should read some of the suggested resources. In this way the counselor will be better prepared for the learning activity and able to get more out of it.

THE TRAINING PLAN

In Section I, "Self Assessment of Foundation Skills," Chapters 1 through 4, a systematic overview of the cognitive, personal, and professional skills needed for competent sexuality counseling is presented. By working through these next four chapters the reader will focus on obtaining the necessary background for the full spectrum of concerns presented in real life by clients. Sections II, "Skills for Sexuality Counseling," Chapters 5 and 6, and III, "Integration," Chapters 7 and 8, then will enable the reader to learn specific sexuality counseling methods. The individual is responsible for self assessment so that his/her personal training plan allocates energy and effort as needed to attain professional competence.

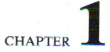

ESSENTIAL SEXUALITY
INFORMATION

One of the most challenging aspects of sexuality counseling is that the professional is constantly presented with something new. Clients bring up original situations, and almost every conference/book/workshop contains fresh issues, even for the well informed. In the most basic areas such as anatomy, research continues to reveal new knowledge. For instance, popular ob-gyn (obstetric-gynecology) textbooks of the 1940s stated that women were not capable of sexual pleasure, and yet by the 1980s publications abound on the role of the clitoris, vaginal sensitivity, and on multiple orgasms.

Much continues to be learned. Basic science researchers are currently studying the complex physiology of arousal, and searching for effective male and female contraceptives. Since the interpersonal and social aspects of sexual behavior change even faster, sexologists work in a constantly developing field.

A very practical question to ask is "When does a person have sufficient background knowledge to practice sexuality counseling?" One approach is to read through several basic texts such as the following until one is well enough informed to explain their contents to others.

RESOURCES FOR BACKGROUND KNOWLEDGE

Carrera, M. (1981). *Sex: The facts, the acts, and your feelings.* New York: Crown Publishers.

Crooks, R., & Baur, K., (1983). *Our sexuality,* 2nd ed. Menlow Park, CA: The Benjamin/Cummings Publishing.

Francoeur, R., (1982). *Becoming a sexual person.* New York: John Wiley and Sons. Brief edition (1984).

Geer, J., Leitenberg, H., & Heiman, J. (1984). *Human sexuality.* Englewood Cliffs, NJ: Prentice-Hall.

Haeberle, E. (1983). *The sex atlas* (rev. ed.). New York: Continuum Publishing.

McCary, J., & McCary, S. (1982). *Human sexuality* (4th ed.). Florence, KY: Wadsworth Publishing.

Masters, W., Johnson, V., & Kolodny, R. (1982). *Human sexuality* (2nd ed). Florence, KY: Wadsworth Publishing.

These materials are a few of many which can give a good overview. In each part of the training program will be suggested more specialized resource materials.

SELF ASSESSMENT

The checklist in Form 1.1 is provided to help focus further study, after the importance of an overall education in sexuality is clear. Each of the topics in Form 1.1 has a section of this chapter devoted to it, within which are listed further resources and learning experiences. Eventually a sex counselor can have accurate answers to all basic questions about sexuality.

Form 1.1. Individual Needs Assessment

DIRECTIONS: For each of the topics listed, indicate by a check mark your present level of understanding.

Necessary Background Information	Know Enough	Need More	Unsure
1. Sexual development over the life-span (childhood, adolescence, young adult, midlife, aging)	___	___	___
2. Interpersonal, couples and family dynamics	___	___	___
3. Methods/timing/effects of sex education	___	___	___
4. Variety of sexual language/slang	___	___	___
5. Sexual response/anatomy/pleasure curve	___	___	___
6. Contraception, physical/emotional	___	___	___
7. Pregnancy, abortion, birth	___	___	___
8. Gender identity/sex roles	___	___	___
9. Lifestyles: Celibate, heterosexual, bisexual, homosexual	___	___	___
10. Cultural attitudes and values about sexuality	___	___	___

Another measure of how much background study is needed is to take the *Sex Background Knowledge Quiz* in Form 1.2 and check the number correct. (Correct answers are found at the end of Chapter 1.) This informal checklist provides a self-analysis and can help identify areas where more effort is needed. Individual differences in the validity of pencil and paper testing, and the relatively few items to represent a sample of the field are recognized, so no "cut off" score is provided. However, people who miss one-half or more should consider taking a course in human sexuality at a college or university. Motivation is stronger when learning a wide range of material if it is presented through lectures, AV materials, readings, and discussion. Individuals who missed one-quarter or fewer can probably fill in the necessary background information by reading and self study.

Form 1.2. Sex Background Knowledge Quiz

SEX BACKGROUND KNOWLEDGE QUIZ

DIRECTIONS: Mark each statement with T (true) or F (false). Check your response against answers provided at the end of Chapter 1.

1. Studies show that most people obtain the majority of their sex education from books and movies.　　T　or　F

2. The United States has more liberal laws regarding homosexuality than do most developed Western nations.　　T　or　F

3. The cause of impotence is more often psychological then physiological.　　T　or　F

4. During menstruation it is healthier to avoid intercourse and substitute other forms of sexual expression.　　T　or　F

5. Sexual intercourse before marriage is condemned by most of the world's religious and moral systems.　　T　or　F

6. A large majority of parents want their children to receive sex education in school.　　T　or　F

7. Men are less likely to experience multiple orgasms than women are.　　T　or　F

Form 1.2. Continued

8. If married people masturbate, it is an indication of a poor sexual adjustment by one partner or both.   T or F

9. Fertilization of the human egg (conception) usually takes place in the uterus, after the sperm travels through the cervix.   T or F

10. Orgasmic experiences cannot be experienced until the hormonal changes of puberty have occurred.   T or F

11. The majority of women infected with gonorrhea have no clinical symptoms of the disease.   T or F

12. Mouth-genital sex play is experienced by less than half of all married couples.   T or F

13. Socio-economic class is closely related to the frequency of child sexual abuse.   T or F

14. A pregnancy which is terminated by natural causes is called a spontaneous abortion.   T or F

15. Impotence in men over 70 is nearly universal.   T or F

16. A woman's body temperature increases during the ovalutory phase of her menstrual cycle.   T or F

17. Vasectomy often increases the refractory period (time after orgasm   when   further   ejaculation   is impossible).   T or F

18. Taking birth control pills for more than 5 years tends to delay the onset of a woman's menopause.   T or F

19. For men and women, the basic physiological responses to sexual stimulation are vasocongestion and a generalized increase in muscle tension.   T or F

20. Pedophiles usually victimize children whom they do not know, in order to avoid possible recognition.   T or F

21. Hysterectomy involves the surgical removal of the uterus, fallopian tubes and ovaries.   T or F

22. The majority of sexually harrassed women do not file a grievance or take action against the offender.   T   or   F

23. Many more men have had homosexual experiences than identify themselves as gay.   T   or   F

24. During masturbation, the time required for experienced men and women to reach orgasm is about the same.   T   or   F

25. There is great variation across cultures in the proportion of adult women who are orgasmic.   T   or   F

26. Most lesbian women have had no heterosexual experience.   T   or   F

27. As with many crimes, between one fourth to one third of sexual assault (rape) charges are false.   T   or   F

28. Sperm cells are produced in the prostate gland.   T   or   F

29. Most male transvestites prefer to dress entirely as females and would change gender if they could.   T   or   F

30. Blisters from both types of herpes virus can be found on either the mouth or genitals.   T   or   F

SEX EDUCATION SKILLS

Skill in communication is also important for the counselor. Practice in expressing information about sexuality can be gained through interaction with others, as outlined in the following exercise.

LEARNING EXPERIENCE NO. 1

A. Set aside some definite time with another person and ask what sexual questions he/she has heard. Practice giving accurate information that would be a basis for changing a myth or sufficient information for understanding the sexual issue. Feel free to say to the person at time, *"I will need to look up specifics and will give you more information the next time we meet."* Continue to ask what facts or knowledge about sexuality the other person might question and try to answer, indicating your degree of certainty. Be sure to get back to the person if later study brings up contradictory information.

Example

Counselor: *"Can you remember some question about sex that you wonder about, to give me practice in finding out what more I need to study?"*

Interviewee: *"Well, there's this one about men hit their sexual peak at 18, and then it's downhill all the way ....."*

Counselor: *"You picked a good one—I'll give it a try."* (your answer)

_____

_____

"Can you think of another one?"

Interviewee: *"I've often heard that a person can get stuck on masturbation. Why are so many people against it?"*

Counselor: *"There are two questions there and I'll take the second one first."* (Your answers)

_____

_____

_____

_____

B. If the sex knowledge dialogue starts to become a counseling situation, limit yourself to the content of the question, support, and refer the person.

Example

Counselor: *"We agreed to talk about sexual myths and now you have said you are worried about your period being late. It would seem a good idea to talk to the nurse, or have a checkup at a woman's health center or by your physician. Would you like to discuss who you will see next? I don't like to leave you worrying about this all alone, now that it has come up."*

C. Repeat Learning Experience No. 1 with 5 to 10 people of different ages and experiences. Notice which kinds of questions are difficult to answer so you can plan further study and practice.

Possessing an in-depth knowledge of broad areas of human sexuality allows the counselor to hear what the client doesn't know, and discover where the problem is. Sex education requires answers to questions so a good library is a necessary resource, but sexuality counseling requires more than books. A strong background is necessary while talking to the client, and then small details or technical information can be obtained between sessions. Fortunately the material is available and interesting to learn.

Chapter 1, Part 1

SEXUAL DEVELOPMENT
OVER THE LIFESPAN

Sexuality counselors recognize that people's concerns about sex involve their present cognitive, physical, moral-ethical, emotional, and social functioning, and that this develops with the individual. Sexuality is not a fixed attribute but changes with the person's history and age. Therefore counselors must know the particular challenges and stresses of different developmental stages, both the sexual and nonsexual ones, to understand what their clients are experiencing.

> No one can counsel a child about upcoming changes at puberty or after a sexual assault, unless they first know a great deal about child development and childhood sexuality.

> No one can counsel a teenager about a negative body image or premarital sex, unless they are familiar with many important aspects of adolescence.

> No one can counsel a couple at midlife about sexual problems unless they are aware of both the usual stresses of that period, and sensitive to the sexual ones.

> A person would not be effective doing sexuality counseling with an elderly person until considerable background about this period of life was attained.

Developmental information not only clarifies present status but also gives the counselor perspective. Knowledge about the integration of sexuality with life stages helps the counselor to understand the client's previous experience, and to anticipate what problems could be encountered later.

LEARNING EXPERIENCE NO. 2

A. In order to get a better grasp on the concept of people as sexual beings from birth to death, draw the following timeline on a large sheet of paper:

3   5   10   20   30   40   50   60   70   80   90...

(lifespan in years)

B. Allow time in a comfortable, quiet spot to recall events and experiences of sexual significance in your own life. Jot down as many as you can, in your own shorthand above the timeline. Include self-stimulation, same and other sex experiences, times of celibacy, important partners, fantasy, and negative and positive sex-related events. Then fill in for the future what sexual experiences and lifestyle you would like to have.

C. Put the timeline aside and then return to it a week or two later. Add anything else that occurs to you. Notice the positive and negative areas and any patterns of development over your lifetime. If you are uncomfortable with anything you are remembering, you can make integration about your own sex history an important part of your training.

D. Utilize the timeline concept later when taking sex histories for Learning Experience No. 32 in Chapter 3.

An advantage to discussing many of these Learning Experience Activities in a group is the discovery that "I was blank on sex until I was 23" is not unusual, nor is the person who was molested by a family member throughout childhood, nor is the person who "married at 18 and took it all for granted." No one typical or perfect sexual development occurs, and as a result the counselor has a major task to understand many individual developmental patterns.

LEARNING EXPERIENCE NO. 3

In order to see commonalities as well as differences, begin to focus on the possible sexual experiences of different age groups.

A. Initiate a discussion with two or three people of the same age about the sexual attitudes and experiences of their peers. By talking about what they think others do, and in a group of 2 to 4 people, you should be able to avoid getting into intense personal issues. Start with the age group you know best and then work up and down. In this way it should be possible to learn about the sexual concerns of various life stages at first hand.

B. Before you interview children, be sure to ask their parents for permission to initiate discussions. Explain that you will limit inquiries to what other kids know about sex and how they learned it. Also ask the family whether you should answer any questions raised by the discussion, or whether they would prefer to. You could suggest a joint follow-up session for doing so if the parents are interested.

You may be amazed at how willing people are to generalize about the sexual attitudes and behaviors of people in their age category, and in the process reveal quite a bit about themselves. Of course no sample can inform you about "all teenagers" or "all attitudes and experiences of people in their thirties." However the interviews will broaden your awareness far beyond your own experience, and allow you to see where you need to understand human development and sexuality better.

RESOURCES FOR LEARNING SEXUALITY DEVELOPMENT

Brecher, E., & the Editors of Consumer Reports. (1984). *Love, sex, and aging.* Boston: Little, Brown.

Calderone, M., & Johnson, E. (1981). *The family book of sexuality.* New York: Harper and Row.

Chilman, C. (1983). *Adolescent sexuality in a changing American society: Social and psychological perspectives for the human services professions* (2nd ed.). New York: John Wiley and Sons.

Coles, R., & Stokes, G. (1985). *Sex and the American teenager.* New York: Harper and Row.

Constantine, L., & Martinson, F. (Eds.). (1981). *Children and sex: New findings, new perspectives.* Boston: Little, Brown.

Gordon, S., Scales, P., & Everly, K. (1979). *The sexual adolescent.* (2nd ed). Fayetteville, NY: Ed-U Press.

Kirkpatrick, M. (Ed.). (1980). *Women's sexual development.* New York: Plenum.

Roberts, E. (Ed.) (1979). *Childhood sexual learning: The unwritten curriculum.* Cambridge, MA: Ballinger.

Sarrel, P., & Sarrel, L. (1984). *Sexual turning points: The seven stages of adult sexuality.* New York: Macmillan.

Voda, A., Dinnerstein, M., & O'Donnell, S. (Eds.) (1982). *Changing perspectives on menopause.* Austin, TX: University of Texas Press.

Weg, R. (Ed.). (1983). *Sexuality in the later years: Roles and behavior.* Orlando, FL: Academic Press.

Wolman, B., & Money, J. (Eds.). (1980). *Handbook of human sexuality, part I.* Englewood Cliffs, NJ: Prentice-Hall.

Chapter 1, Part 2

INTERPERSONAL AND FAMILY DYNAMICS

Every baby is born a sexual being and can be celibate throughout life, or enjoy private sexuality such as fantasy, erotic media, and self pleasuring (masturbation). In addition, however, individuals are presented with opportunities for sexual interaction with and influence from others. A knowledge of interpersonal dynamics, communication, and social/relationship/family patterns are essential for competent sex-related counseling.

FAMILY INFLUENCES

The family has been a powerful medium through which racial, cultural, ethnic, religious, sex role, and other sexual norms have been transmitted to individuals. Generalizations about sex were easier when expectations for couples and family systems were clear and stable (although of course many people did not conform). Some regret the passing of that time, and that influences other than family now have a strong impact on sexual attitudes and behavior. Meditating while leafing through the children's picture book on today's families entitled *Your Family, My Family* by Drescher (1980) may be a more sophisticated form of learning about present reality than dry demographic articles.

Most professionals in education, health, and human services have had courses on the topic of family-social systems and dynamics. A helpful procedure is to pull personally significant books and course notebooks from the shelves and review sex-related chapters. Sometimes only a few direct sexual references are scattered throughout, or else a brief section is given which deals with obvious problems.

TRANSFERING THEORIES
TO SEXUALITY ISSUES

An interesting and creative task is to transfer theories of social structure and interpersonal dynamics to a wide range of sexuality issues.

For instance:

In using Transactional Analysis, how adequately is sexuality included in developing a life script?

When employing Reality Therapy, how skillful and sensitive are the sex-related inquiries?

In utilizing Gestalt techniques such as role-reversal or "empty chair," how confidently is sexual dialogue included?

When family sculpting (Satir) is done, or a Palo Alto/Milan style of family intervention technique is used, are the counselors as matter-of-fact and alert to sexual themes as to power ones?

When parent or teacher effectiveness is taught, is sex-related communication included as routinely as task accomplishment?

When using Rogerian deep empathy, or Gendlin's "focusing," are topics like low self worth responded to more accurately than subtle sexual references?

Do most Adlerians consider the effect of the family constellation on sexuality as well as on achievement? Note the Ansbacher's contribution (1982).

Are some practitioners of behavioral methods better at developing goals and programs for enuresis and non-smoking than for positive sexual development?

Note the positive model set by Albert Ellis' Rational-Emotive Therapy, where the influence of interpersonal interaction on individual sexual development is expertly integrated.

Look at the interpersonal and family counseling theories and techniques which are personally meaningful, and practice applying them consciously to sexual concerns. A vast literature exists on the dynamics within couples, but often the focus is on communication, power issues, sex roles, or the capacity for emotional intimacy. Searching for extra resources may be necessary because many counseling texts on social, interpersonal, and family dynamics are short on sexual applications.

LEARNING EXPERIENCE NO. 4

A. Observe a family, couples, or group counseling session on film or videotape. Then, if possible, make the same kind of observation at a family education center through a one-way mirror. You will need to obtain permission to do so.

B. Jot down your observations about possible sexual concerns of the participants and discuss those concerns later with other professionals. Some things to look for are whether any reference to sex is made, if so how comfortable is the verbal and body language of clients and counselors; the type of language used; the knowledge level about sexuality which seems present; any double meanings; the openness and communication patters about sex; any sexual attitudes, values, or expectations expressed; and the sexually well adjusted members and those with apparent sexual problems, if any. Attend to how the counselor facilitated sex-related discussion.

C. Note where you might have expected exploration from a sexual viewpoint and it didn't occur.

D. Repeat the experience by observing other counseling interactions, looking for how interpersonal sexual aspects are treated.

INFLUENCES ON SEXUALITY EXPECTATIONS

Beyond awareness of social change in couples and the family, also consider the effect on sexuality of institutions. Think about the potential influences that might occur living in a foster home, a summer camp, an alternate care facility, military service, a homogeneous neighborhood, a day-care center, a crowded housing development, a college or boarding school, a shelter for abused or homeless persons, or a correctional center. These institutions can strongly influence personal sexual style. When working with clients in any setting, make a special effort to discover what the explicit and implicit guidelines for sexuality are in their family or environment, and then what the actual sexual experiences tend to be. The sum of all messages and modeling received by clients contributes to their expectations for interpersonal sexuality.

As recommended in Learning Experience 4, continue to observe counseling with as many kinds of individuals, couples, families, and groups as possible. Regardless of social/personal change, the significant people and systems which affect a person while growing up are vitally important to his/her sexual attitudes and expression. Understanding the influences will enable the counselor to think of creative ways to help clients explore and clarify the impact of family/interpersonal sexual issues. In addition, when doing or observing counseling, notice when material is being handled well or badly in the interviews. With practice the counselor can find creative ways to help clients clarify the effects of family and relationships on their sexuality.

RESOURCES FOR FAMILY INFLUENCES

Adler, A., Ansbacher, H., & Ansbacher, R. (Eds.). (1982). *Cooperation between the sexes: Writings on women and men, love and marriage, and sexuality.* New York: Norton.

Dodson, L., & Kurpius, D. (1977). *Family counseling: A systems approach.* Muncie, IN: Accelerated Development, Publishers.

Drescher, J. (1980). *Your family, my family.* New York: Walker.

Gagnon, J., & Smith, B. (1977). *Human sexualities.* Glenview, IL: Scott, Foresman.

Gordon, S., & Gordon, J. (1983). Raising a child conservatively in a sexually permissive world. New York: Simon and Schuster.

Horne, A., & Olsen, M. (1982). *Family counseling and therapy.* Itaska, IL: Peacock Publishers.

Maddock, J. (Ed.). (1985). *Human sexuality and the family*. New York: The Haworth Press.

Rogers, C. (1961). *On becoming a person*. Boston: Houghton Mifflin.

Satir, V. (1972). *Peoplemaking*. Palo Alto, CA: Science and Behavior Books.

Whitaker, C., & Napiv, A. (1980). *The family crucible*. New York: Harper and Row.

Periodicals offer the most current information on sexuality and changing family/social patterns, as well as on specific counseling approaches.

Chapter 1, Part 3

METHODS, TIMING, AND EFFECTS OF SEXUALITY EDUCATION

An individual's sexual world is made up of ideas, impressions, images, and experiences from countless sources. To call this gestalt a result of a person's "sex education" is a broad definition, but correct. For most people the formal kind of sex education is limited to a small number of classes, texts, or talks. The informal sources of sex education are usually far more significant and the sum of both can be referred to as sexual learning.

Consider the sources identified in Figure 2 and add to it any other possible input of sexual information. The counselor can look back on all the ways he/she obtained sexual learning and check to see whether all are covered here.

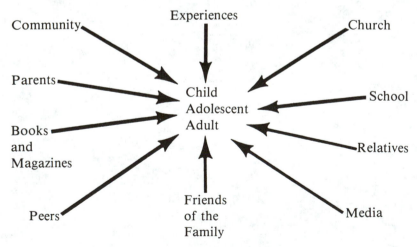

Figure 2. Sources of sexual information.

The ideal sexual learning is positive and informative about sexuality and is appropriately timed for the developing individual. Good sexuality education which is continuous and integrated with other knowledge can be expected to contribute to responsible, comfortable, sexual development. Although doing so can be hard to achieve, formal kinds of sex education planned by parents, school, and community are more effective if coordinated with the informal sexual learning coming from peers, media, and culture.

Most people seen by counselors were not exposed to any kind of planned, integrated sex education (formal or informal). Sexual knowledge does not necessarily parallel a person's level of education. This is important for the counselor to understand, so that individual needs for information may be unobtrusively filled in. Important values may be based on partial or incorrect sex education, so the counselor must listen carefully to learn from where these attitudes came.

EXAMPLE: Individual Differences

A counselor may be working with victims of the same multiple rape, or with several recent mastectomy patients, and notice how differently the experience effects the sexuality of individuals within each group. The crime of sexual assault (or the necessary surgery) may have been objectively similar for the people involved, but the individual experience is completely different. Often when doing counseling the meaning of the event, more than the experience itself, determines the impact on sexuality. Therefore the cumulative sexual learning received by each person sets the stage for the work which the counselor has to do.

INTERVIEWING SKILLS

For purposes of assessment and the planning of treatment programs, the counselor needs skill at drawing out the general outlines of a client's sexuality education. Interviews are the best way of obtaining competence in putting past learning into perspective for a client.

Interviews can become a counseling type of interaction if a person says something like: "Most of my sex education came when my parents found me fooling around with my sister; she was 11 and I was 14. They really came down hard on me and threatened to throw us both out of the house. I think their main order was to keep it in my pants, and to tell you the truth that's all I've ever been able to do since.'' It would be destructive to acknowledge only the content related to the learning exercise while ignoring the deeper implications of the statement.

When problems are brought up, and they will if one is a good interviewer, respond with empathy. For instance: ''Discussing sex ed makes you think of that really painful time when you were a teenager.'' Then clarify: ''We've been talking to help my training, but now that this topic has come up, would you like to discuss it with me or someone else? Or is it just too sensitive?'' Usually the person is interested in continuing, but putting the discussion in context allows some breathing room. If the person needs more than support and continues to describe ongoing sexual problems, the trainee can summarize that a continuing difficulty seems to be present. Referral sources and the guidelines for good referral procedures are then needed.

In the following key learning experience be alert to the significance of sexual learning such as soap operas, what a teammate said about condoms, what the home economics teacher taught about tampons, or how a parent punished masturbation. These are often more important than classes or facts-of-life talks.

LEARNING EXPERIENCE NO. 5

A. Interview a person with whom you are comfortable and whom you believe will be cooperative in discussing with you his/her sex education. The majority of people will say ''I didn't have any,'' and then laugh and begin to recall a number of formal (planned by someone) and informal sources of sexual learning.

B. Repeat Learning Experience 5 with a person you do not know. Do so to gain practice at seeing a variety of sex education patterns.

C. Repeat Learning Experience 5 until you can effectively interview any willing person about their sex education and obtain a clear picture. This could mean 5 to 20 individuals.

D. Take notes during or immediately after each interview, without last names or identifying data, and put the notes aside in a secure place.

E. Read over your notes when you have completed several interviews and analyze whether or not you have considered the following:

1. Sex education verbally delivered to the person by others (formal and informal)?

2. Sex education obtained by the person through reading, TV, movies, observation?

3. Sex education through the individual's personal experiences. Because these are often nonverbal, ask occasionally: "Did any important sex-related experiences happen at that age, from which you learned a lot?" Then concentrate on what was learned rather than the details of the experience, because this exercise is focused on sexuality education.

4. Did you reassure/support each interview subject? This exercise requires a person to look over a lifetime of sexual learning, and often brings up embarrassed feelings or apologetic remarks. Let the person know that almost everyone's sexual education was inadequate, and that whatever happened is perfectly understandable.

5. Look for patterns to see what was left out. For instance if none of your subjects mention masturbation, same-sex partners, sexual fantasy, birth control, sex-role stereotypes, religious values, or another common topic, maybe you need to examine how you responded to subtle references or whether you block some areas.

6. Begin to draw your own conclusions. What makes a good, an average, or a poor sex education/sexual learning? What are some characteristics and consequences of each?

7. During the discussion did you find yourself occasionally contributing some sexual information? If so, perhaps you are learning to integrate sexuality education into your discussions naturally, without dominating or interrupting the flow of an interview.

EDUCATIONAL SKILLS

Having attained deeper insight regarding sexuality education for individuals, one of the best experiences for a counselor is to participate as a co-teacher in a group. The simplest way is to locate an ongoing program in a health class, church, or college and then volunteer to assist. Excellent preparation would be studying the kit by Calderwood entitled *About Your Sexuality,* 1984 revision, a comprehensive program with teaching materials available from the Unitarian Universalist Association, 25 Beacon St., Boston, MA. The experience of teaching in a good program adds immeasurably to understanding individuals and in building ease of communication about sex. Nothing else will adequately substitute for doing it.

Numerous excellent resources summarize the growing data on the effectiveness of various kinds of planned sex education programs. Even more interesting are the numerous special curricula, handbooks, group leaders outlines, annotated guides for resource materials, and creative programs which may be ordered at reasonable cost. Also far more sexuality education material is available on a local level than many people realize; family living teachers, youth counselors, family planning clinics, and others usually have current resources. From the following list the counselor can find excellent ideas for presenting sexuality education and for understanding the effects of sexual learning on clients.

RESOURCES FOR SEXUAL EDUCATION

Brown, L. (Ed.). (1981). *Sex education in the eighties: The challenge of healthy sexual evolution.* New York: Plenum.

Bruess, C., & Greenberg, J. (1981). *Sex education: Theory and practice.* Florence, KY: Wadsworth Publishing.

Calderone, M., & Ramey, J. (1983). *Talking with your child about sex: Questions and answers from birth to puberty.* New York: Random House.

Calderwood, D. (1983). *About your sexuality.* Boston, MA: Unitarian Universalist Association.

Cook, A., Kirby, D., Wilson, P., & Alter, J. (1984). *Sexuality education: A guide to developing and implementing programs.* Santa Cruz, CA: Network Publications.

Dickman, I. (1982). *Winning the battle for sex education.* New York: SIECUS.

Dumont, J. (1979). *A guide to values clarification in sex education.* (2nd ed.). Cleveland, OH: Preterm Cleveland.

Halling, L. (1983). *Sexuality and family life education: An annotated bibliography of curricula.* Available for purchase. New York: SIECUS.

Hartman, B., Quinn, J., & Young, B. (1981). *Sexual expression: A manual for trainers.* New York: Human Sciences Press.

Kaplan, R., Neebs, L., & Segal, J. (1978). *Group strategies in understanding human sexuality.* Dubuque, IA: William C. Brown.

Parcel, S., & Gordon, S. (Eds.). (1981). "Special issue: Sex education in the public schools." *Journal of School Health.* Kent, OH: American School Health Assn.

Wilson, P. (1984). *Sex education: An annotated guide for resource materials.* Santa Cruz, CA: Network Publications.

Creative new curricula and material is constantly available from organizations such as The Sex Information and Education Council in the United States (SIECUS), the Planned Parenthood Federation of America and its many regional affiliates, the American Association of Sex Educators, Counselors, and Therapists (AASECT), the National Family Life Network Publications, and Ed-U Press. An extensive bibliography of teaching materials published by religious groups is available in the March 1985 *SIECUS Report.* Journals listed elsewhere in this training program contain regular articles on all aspects of sexual learning and education.

Chapter 1, Part 4

SEXUAL LANGUAGE/SLANG

When counselors respond to the language topic on the background information check list, their comments range from one extreme to the other. Some people shake their heads and say they have heard every word in the book and will hear a new one tomorrow. These people often work in residential treatment centers, in the criminal justice system, or with a particularly outspoken clientele. Other trainees admit that talking fluently about sex in a non-joking manner is very difficult for them. People agree, however, that the use of a vivid sexual vocabulary does not necessarily mean a person is comfortable with sex. In any case a counselor needs both sexual word knowledge and flexibility in order to be effective.

Language itself can be a problem; in many ways English has a limited sexual vocabulary. Sex-related language can be divided into five kinds. The first four of these were described in the September, 1980 *SIECUS Journal.*

1. *childish:* words such as pee pee, tushy, ladyplace

2. *euphemisms:* phrases such as sleeping together, that time of the month, and in the family way

3. *street talk:* includes terms like cocksucker, cunt, fuck

4. *scientific terms:* words such as clitoris, testicles, coitus

5. *private jargon:* words created by a specific group for their own needs. Original words for sexual ideas may be invented by preteens in a school, by a couple, or by people in a particular subculture.

Each language type has advantages and disadvantages, strengths and weaknesses. Some words are vague, some have arousal potential, some mask embarrassment, while others convey subtle shades of emotional meaning. Clients often skip from using one category of sexual language to another, depending on the context and their perception of counselor reactions. They may imitate the counselor's choice of words, as well as the pitch, tone, and volume, and this will disguise the client's genuine communication. In addition, so much of sexual learning is nonverbal that clients frequently say "you know" or resort to gestures, because they have no terms readily available.

ATTAINING FLUENCY

The usual kind of learning experience provided at training workshops to stretch professionals' sexual language skills is the following: "How many words can you think of for these terms (written on blackboard or handout sheet): intercourse, breast, penis, menstruation, nocturnal emission, non-marital sex, vagina, semen, homosexual, condom, oral sex, masturbation...?" Often a large group is divided into small groups which compete to provide the longest lists. Persons in each group record and later read out the lists for one term at a time, giving opportunities to say, hear, and discuss a large quantity of sexual words. Then not only is the meaning of terms like "poon tang," "giving head," or "self abuse" discussed, but also the affect, body language, and connotations which go with them for different people.

LEARNING EXPERIENCE NO. 6

A. **Find a way to analyze your own sex-related language for content, style, and comfort level. If possible do the previously explained exercise in a small group. Consciously look for scientific and informal words to describe every kind of sexual body part or behavior. Because this is a professional training program, you don't need to be given a checklist to complete; however, do find a creative way to chart your language limitations for yourself.**

B. Then record two different words for ten sexual terms and have a dialogue with another person about the difference conveyed by each. For instance "pregnancy" and "getting knocked up," or "frigidity" and "orgasmic dysfunction," or "muff diving" and "cunnilingus." See whether either of you can find a third term or expression which you prefer.

C. Then repeat the exercise using the same words with 2 or 3 other people in order to note individual differences.

Interviews assigned for all learning experiences in this book provide opportunities for expanding sexual language competence. A skilled counselor can supply an appropriate sexual term if the client is searching, within the style of language being used. When possible, be the least disruptive by using a client's natural terms, or perhaps by providing a word and asking a client for his/hers: "The formal name for that part is the 'clitoris' but many people just say 'clit.' Do you have your own word for it?" The goal is helpful communication and fluent expression, and not vocabulary building.

OFFENSIVE LANGUAGE

Very often slang terms are used as insults when sexual messages are not the main intent. Calling someone a "bastard," "fag," "fuckhead," or "on the rag" is largely meant as a put down. The target usually sees them as such and responds with general anger rather than saying: "My mother was married to my father," or "I prefer women partners." Counselors respond to the widespread abusive use of sexual terms just like other people, but may need to take a neutral stance when counseling.

"Screw" may be an insult (as in "go screw yourself") or a crude word for intercourse for some people, but a matter-of-fact term for other clients. In a non-judgmental way one can clarify what a client means: "When you said you wanted to screw her but nothing happened, was that because she wouldn't cooperate, or did you mean you couldn't get turned on?" Trying to help a client express a sensitive idea is not the time to criticize the style of verbal expression.

As in any kind of helping, listen with that third ear for the meaning and make sure not to read into or over-react to the content. Sexual words have more potential for being misunderstood than do other areas of communication, in both their literal and subjective meanings. By adding terms and discussing shades of meaning, the counselor can help clients express a more differentiated, personal sexuality. People will often use varied terms with relief, once they hear them, as long as they do not feel diminished in the process.

Either the counselor or client may offend one another by the use of language, even to the extent that rapport is damaged; then negotiation is needed. A shy, carefully brought up or sex-avoidant client may react negatively if the counselor uses explicit sexual terms too soon. A gradual familiarity (desensitization) may be needed. For instance: "When you speak of 'doing it' with your husband, we need to find a comfortable way to talk about what you like or don't like sexually..." The purpose of the dialogue is partly to develop a working vocabulary for counseling, but it also gives an opportunity to note the client's body language and level of cooperation. At the same time empathy is demonstrated for the client's discomfort/embarrassment without letting it block progress.

Another kind of negotiation happens when the client uses such rough street language that the counselor (even with work on expanded vocabulary) cannot honestly share it. Being genuine is more important than being "with it," so that self disclosure may be required.

EXAMPLE: Sex-aggressive Language

A counselor has been seeing a 17 year old boy who follows girls, leaves suggestive notes, and has taken underwear from lockers. Sex is a logical subject on which to focus. The counselor might need to say:

> *"When you use 'bang' or 'tear off a piece' for wanting to have sex, I tend to react. We used to say 'have at it' or 'get it on,' so I know everybody doesn't use book terms. There is something about bang and tear off that bothers me—it's not the idea of wanting sex, you understand, but those words sound like trouble for everybody. Would you say 'have sex with' or something like that?*

But if you mean you want to hurt, rip, bang, or harm someone I want you to say that, so I will understand what you mean.''

Take extra care to make sure that the client is not put down while the counselor is being genuine, because feelings of rejection or inadequacy may be a large part of the client's problem. By being direct in a respectful way the counselor will model honesty and set the stage for looking at underlying sex-aggression confusion.

EXPANDING FLUENCY: VERBAL AND NONVERBAL

When a counselor is comfortable with the active use of a wide range of language to discuss sexuality, a further step is to become fluent with the language used by special populations. Children, urban Hispanic men, lesbians in a woman's community, or religious groups, for instance, may have specialized communication about sex. The best source of information is probably the client, other professionals who work with them regularly, or non-client members who are willing to share their attitudes and expressions. Even though a person is influenced by group membership, however, their communication is unique. The counselor must listen carefully for individual connotations.

The single easiest measure of progress in sexuality counseling is the appropriateness and range of a counselor's communication skills with clients about sex. Almost everyone begins with some awkwardness, but after training most helpers are able to talk to anyone about any sexual subject. With practice the counselor can "hear" many more sexual concerns than previously from the same client group. This hearing, in part, is a result of greater comfort with sexual communication.

LEARNING EXPERIENCE NO. 7

A. Identify small groups where you can volunteer to teach and discuss sex-related topics. Or you may want to get together some

people to teach and discuss sex-related topics. For this exercise the dialogue part is more important than simply presenting information.

B. Ask them to interact with you about the topic. Start with a subject you know well, and then expand to an area where you need more practice communicating about sex.

Examples

Begin with a small group discussion on "changes at puberty" then add a discussion on "sexual decision making for teens"

or

begin with a small group discussion on "myths about menopause" then add a discussion on "lovemaking concerns at midlife."

Group work is especially useful for observing nonverbal signals, since everyone cannot be heard at once and yet communication is ongoing. Remember that while nonverbal communication is important, body language meanings are not universal. Just as with words, individuals adopt their own particular style of body language meaning, and in some cases nonverbal messages conflict with the verbal ones.

In order to broaden understanding, become comfortable communicating about sex in a matter of fact way with non-clients too. Stretching to talk about sex to less familiar people such as the elderly, sex offenders, an alcohol treatment staff, gifted teenagers, or disabled persons, helps a counselor continue to increase professional communication skills. This in turn results in quicker rapport with all kinds of clients where sexuality is an issue.

RESOURCES REGARDING SEXUAL LANGUAGE

Sex education materials by Sol Gordon, Jean Gochnos, Winifred Kempton, and others contain a variety of language styles and sections of dialogue.

Nancy Friday has written books on sexual fantasy which contain creative expression, such as

My secret garden (1983), New York: Pocket Books. *Men in love: The triumph of love over rage,* (1981). New York: Dell Publishers.

Interview based books and articles, such as the following, often contain extensive quotes which reveal unique styles of sex-related communication.

Barbach, L., & Lenine, L. (1980). *Shared intimacies, women's sexual experiences.* New York: Anchor Press.

Hite, S. (1982). *The Hite report: A study of male sexuality.* New York: Ballantine.

Movies, television, and popular music.

Popular literature: magazines, best sellers, paperbacks.

Chapter 1, Part 5

PLEASURE CURVE
BIOLOGICAL BASIS
HUMAN SEXUAL RESPONSE

Sexuality is a universal human experience and yet the purposes and goals people have for it differ widely. One's great grandparents may have thought of sex largely in terms of reproduction, whereas the importance of sex in relationships became more prominent in mid-20th century America. During the 1970s and 80s an increasing number of people expected pleasure as their primary interest in having sex. All of these, the Reproductive, Relationship, and Recreational purposes of sex are important to listen for in counseling. Of course other motives can be present as well, such as money, revenge, duty, power, approval, popularity, fear, or security.

The recognition that sex has many purposes is a necessary introduction to learning more about the ''mechanics'' of sex. Although all humans have essentially similar sexual equipment, their expression can be totally different. A surprising number of clients are physically normal, sexually active, and yet find little or no pleasure/fulfillment in sex. A simple question like: ''How has sex been going lately?'' may reveal negative experience, if the person chooses to be candid. The counselor who has a clear understanding of the ''why'' of sex and discusses motivation and expectations with a client, is in a good position to then explore the ''how.''

PLEASURE CURVE

Information about the "how" of sex is available from one's own experience, textbooks, popular books, films, and other people. One of the most frequently repeated concepts is that sexuality is not limited to penis-in-vagina thrusting. Sex does not necessarily equal intercourse. Therefore an important concept with which to work is the pleasure curve, Figure 3.

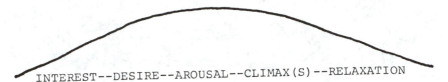

INTEREST--DESIRE--AROUSAL--CLIMAX(S)--RELAXATION

Figure 3. The pleasure curve.

The counselor can use the pleasure curve as a guide for conceptualizing any sexual experience, and then refer to the diagram to discuss it with a client. This includes fantasized sex, self-stimulation, the whole range of possible erotic experiences with partners of the same or other sex, nongenital sex, multi-partner sex, or atypical sex. Some writers have 2, 3, and 4 stage models of human sexual response, but a pleasure curve concept seems applicable to counseling. Separate "stages" are an artificial construct and can lead to overanalysis and labeling, rather than perceiving sexual response as a whole.

EXAMPLE: Pleasure Curve Used To Clarify

Counselor: *"Last week we discussed your recent marriage and some sexual problems, and you have recalled more details this week. So now that you've seen this sketch of the pleasure curve, how would you describe making love with your present wife?"*

Client: *"Well it's pretty much the same thing as with my first wife before our divorce. I'm way over here at the top of the curve, all turned on, and she's back here still thinking about tomorrow's weather report or something, and then I come too soon."*

Counselor: *"So it seems you both have trouble coordinating your timing? Lean back, relax, and think about what happens. You are near climax over here while Jeannette is still getting into the interest stage. What kinds of things would you enjoy which could slow you down, and help her get into the mood?"*

COMMENT: As the counselor helps the client explore his own sexual patterns, underlying assumptions can be expressed. One possibility among many is that he is concerned about "not keeping an erection," and actually rushes and concentrates on his own stimulation in order to "perform well." Teaching clients the pleasure curve automatically redefines the goal away from performance, allowing for discussion of what the person is feeling and thinking in coordination with actions. This leads to willingness to modify lovemaking and builds support for understanding counseling suggestions.

LEARNING EXPERIENCE NO. 8

A. Jot down your last 5 sexual experiences. If possible, include partner sex, self pleasuring, and fantasies.

B. Then draw a pleasure curve and write down specific behaviors for each phase of the curve for one experience at a time. For instance: "asked to be held," "rubbed partner's feet and thighs," "directed shower massage between buttocks," "got interested by anticipating nude partner in new position on the porch," "enjoyed trading jokes while eating pizza in bed after," "two moderate climaxes with fluttery feelings between," or "had honey rubbed on my penis."

C. Analyze the pleasure curves from Step B to discover which parts of the pleasure curve you know most and least about, and begin to look at sexual pleasure as a complex sequence of flexible events.

SEXUAL RESPONSE

Counselors who spend time studying the sexual response cycle have reported feeling embarrassed or guilty, and may wonder about the appropriateness of their behavior. Reading about, discussing, or viewing pictures and films of sexual behavior are part of training, but a person can feel like a voyeur. Also, a counselor is likely to respond sexually to some of the material even though the overall purpose is educational. Counselors need an awareness of broader sexual experience than most people get in one lifetime, but the goal is knowledge and not personal arousal. The skill to attain is the ability to listen to clients without shock or excess curiosity, to visualize their problems, and to help regardless of what are their sexual concerns.

An important point is the distinction between an erotic stimulus and destructive pornography. Current researchers are studying the differential effects of what is harmlessly arousing and what is violent, debasing, or exploitive sex. While everyone has a right to private fantasy, lab results show that sexual behavior can be readily influenced by watching/hearing about violent, aggressive sex. Human beings learn and are suggestible. While counselors need to view enough sexual material to be clear about the difference, they should influence themselves in the direction of healthy arousal too.

LEARNING EXPERIENCE NO. 9

A. Collect a folder of sexual reading, movies, photos, and music.

B. Match the sexual behaviors which are pictured or described to the pleasure curve. For example, an oriental pillow book might have colorful plates showing couples in elaborate intercourse positions (late arousal phase), whereas a magazine picture which displays a woman stroking her breast with a feather could fit in an earlier arousal phase.

C. Repeat Step B by fitting movie love scenes to the pleasure curve, and some sexual interchanges described in books or magazines.

You may find that only part of a sexual interaction is depicted. Begin to think of most sexual activities as a flow of feelings and behavior, and try to visualize what went before and after the particular event you are watching, hearing, or reading about.

D. Note that some sexual material does not depict a person enjoying any phase of sexual response, but instead the model is posed to arouse the viewer. Do you find yourself reacting? What cues are arranged to accomplish this? What have you learned about your own erotic preferences?

BIOLOGICAL BASIS

Studying the erotic aspect of sexual response should come first, because one can easily become cognitive and "scientific" about sex. While recognizing the cultural, erotic, psychological, and social, however, one also must know the biological basis of sexual response thoroughly.

LEARNING EXPERIENCE NO. 10

A. Draw the external genitalia of the male, and then of the female. Label all the parts you can.

B. Draw the internal reproductive/sexual system of the female and then of the male. Label all the parts you can.

C. Look up accurate pictures in any of the resources listed and compare them with yours. Drawings are a good way to convey information to clients, so correct yours as necessary and practice. Talk out loud and become skilled at explaining the physiological in terms people can understand. While working with the diagrams, read descriptive sections such as "The Physiology of Sexual Response," in Munjack and Oziel's *Sexual Medicine and Counseling in Office Practice* (1980). Many other texts listed so far also contain excellent summary chapters of the anatomy and biology of sexual response.

D. Explain the mechanism of erection when a man is looking at arousing pictures.

E. Describe to another person the changes in sex-related anatomy of a woman from childhood through old age. Include how her sexuality is affected.

F. Show some textbook diagrams to another person(s) and suggest that they ask questions which you can practice answering.

G. Make up some challenging questions for yourself about the biological basis of human sexual response. Look up the answers.

INTEGRATION

Somehow the clinical diagrams of physical response and the erotic expression of sex have to come together in the counselor's mind, so that one always refers back to the other. To help training groups achieve this integration, show a film such as ''The Sexually Stimulated Female (or Male) in the Laboratory'' on one side of the screen, with a film like ''A Quiet Afternoon'' on the other half. Or one lab film can be shown concurrently with a partner film and the other with a self stimulation one. The partner films can be other-sex or same-sex couples. The purpose is to remove any barrier between knowing the facts of biology and the real ways humans actually experience sex.

LEARNING EXPERIENCE NO. 11

A. Choose a colleague in a helping profession and explain the importance of your knowing both the erotic and biological realities of the sexual response cycle.

B. Show him/her some of your collected erotic material (pictures, poems, stories, films, photos) from Learning Experience 9; explain where each is in the pleasure curve and integrate that with some of the underlying anatomy and physiology. Then discuss the difference between erotica and pornography.

C. Repeat this with another person using the same material, and note your increased skill and confidence when describing sexual behavior. Avoid the stereotype of sex equal intercourse and look for the wide range of activities in which people of all ages express their sexuality.

D. As you study sexual expression, continue to translate from the biological to the erotic and vice versa, so that the integration becomes automatic. Relate both to the phases of the pleasure curve so that sex is perceived as a process.

RESOURCES REGARDING HEALTHY SEXUAL ACTIVITIES

Books like the following can enrich the counselor's understanding of the infinite variety of possible sexual expression and pleasure. Of course in addition to those listed, dozens of other sex manuals and self-help books are available with quality varying considerably. Diverse reading, from scientific research to the exotic, is helpful. Explicit films which are erotic rather than idealized or pornographic are also enlightening.

Barbach, L. (1976). *For yourself: The fulfillment of female sexuality*. New York: Doubleday.

Barbach, L. (1982). *For each other: Sharing sexual intimacy*. New York: Anchor Press/Doubleday.

Comfort, A. (1974). *The joy of sex: A cordon bleu guide to love-making*. New York: Simon and Schuster.

Hartman, W., & Fithian, M. (1984). *Any man can: The multiple orgasmic technique for every loving man*. New York: St. Martin's Press.

Heiman, J., & Lopiccolo, J. (1976). *Becoming orgasmic: A sexual growth program for women*. Englewood Cliffs, NJ: Prentice-Hall.

Kelly, G. (1979). *Good sex: A healthy man's guide to sexual fulfillment*. New York: Harcourt Brace Jovanovich.

Kitzinger, S. (1983). *Women's experience of sex.* New York: G. P. Putnam's Sons.

Levine, L., & Barbach, L. (1983). *The intimate male.* New York: Doubleday.

Lumiere, R., & Cook, S. (1983). *Healthy sex and keeping it that way.* New York: Simon and Schuster.

Masters, W., & Johnson, V. (1966). *Human sexual response.* Boston: Little, Brown. A condensed version, *An analysis of human sexual response,* by Brecher and Brecher was also published in 1966.

McCarthy, B., & McCarthy, E. (1984). *Sexual awareness.* New York: Carrol and Graf, Publishers.

Munjack, D., & Oziel, J. (1980). *Sexual medicine and counseling in office pratice.* Boston: Little Brown.

Perper, T. (1985). *Sex signals: The biology of love.* Philadelphia, PA: ISI Press.

Zilbergeld, B., & Ullman, J. (1978). *Male sexuality: A guide to sexual fulfillment.* Boston: Little, Brown.

Chapter 1, Part 6

CONTRACEPTION: PHYSICAL AND EMOTIONAL ASPECTS

Considering all the sexual activity which takes place in any given region in a 24 hour period, only a very small percentage results in pregnancy. However, the possibility of conception significantly affects many sexual interactions. A woman releases an average of 400 ova in her lifetime, men have millions of sperms in each ejaculation, and a heterosexual couple experiences 3,000 to 5,000 acts of intercourse in a lifetime. Not surprisingly, over the centuries the connection between sex and reproduction has resulted in many restrictive cultural attitudes, and the well recognized "double standard" for women and men.

Studying the history of attempted fertility control is interesting and only very recently were effective means available. Even with better methods, the fact that one out of three women in the U.S. becomes pregnant in her teens calls into question the adequacy of today's contraceptive use. At one time in the mid 1970s, "the pill" and IUD were used by millions of women and seemed to be the answer to avoiding unwanted pregnancy. Now however fewer people are using these contraceptives due to concerns about side effects, and women no longer have a total answer for the more than thirty five years they are fertile.

Contraceptive counseling is a field which never stands still. A counselor may need to educate a client about uses of a lubricated condom, explore the appropriateness of tubal ligation, or discuss the sexual implications of the "fertility awareness" approach. Even counselors who do not intend to work directly with contraceptive treatment will need to know as much as possible, in order to educate and help clients who are not being responsible about contraception. Fortunately, considerable reproductive health information is available, such as in family planning clinics or women's health centers. The provider who works in a health/medical setting will have access to this information, and to monthly journals with new studies, but other practitioners will need to make efforts to stay current.

LEARNING EXPERIENCE NO. 12

A. **Leave your study or office and travel wherever you need to go in order to visit a family planning, vasectomy, or health clinic for women. Talk to the educational-training coordinator and explain your need to be brought up to date on contraceptive counseling. Ask to see their kits of sample materials and the accompanying literature, their anatomy models and charts, their interview forms, their referral lists, and if possible, be a participant in a group education session.**

    Choose your setting carefully if you are a male counselor; one where men interns already work and where male partners are treated is more comfortable. This exposure to contraceptive problems is extremely important for a man's realistic, overall view of birth control issues. Both women and men counselors should study more than one clinic if possible, because different providers reach very different patient populations.

B. **Make an appointment to talk to a gynecologist, nurse practitioner, or physician's assistant about problems encountered in the contraceptive interview and pelvic examination. If the office employs health educators, they can share many insights about the kinds of issues raised when clients come for birth control, pregnancy tests, and group information sessions.**

CONTRACEPTIVE USE

To have a good understanding of the physical/health aspects of contraception is necessary and also to know the success rates and possible side effects of all the various methods. However, equally important is becoming aware of the emotional and interpersonal aspects of birth control. Studies have shown that even when people have knowledge about contraceptive techniques, they often do not use them.

Moral aspects of using contraception results in ambivalence for some sexually active people. For many it brings the issue of sexuality out in the open where they have to deal with it. After acknowledging sexual behavior, a person must recognize the possibility of pregnancy and how it would affect his/her life. He/she has to seek out information which is not readily available. The drugstore methods are the most advertised, and while better than nothing, they have substantial failure rates. The person who is interested in a prescription method needs to go to the trouble of finding a medical provider and having an examination, and then obtaining the material.

Even when all the preceding steps are taken, for many people the most difficult tasks lie ahead. Using a contraceptive properly and consistently requires planning, and often utilizing self control. Even more difficult for many is the partner communication required by many methods. Seldom does sexuality education teach a young man how to inquire in this area, or show a young woman how to be assertive about it. Knowing about and properly using birth control are two very different things.

The media frequently inflates studies which question the safety and efficacy of various contraceptive methods, which further discourages potential users. Unfortunately, the U.S. has the highest rate of adolescent pregnancy, birth, and abortion of any industrialized nation. A recent Guttmacher (1981) study also found the lowest rates were in countries with good sex education and ready access to birth control. Because of all the real problems with controlling fertility, the counselor needs to bring up the subject with heterosexually active clients of any age, but especially those under 25.

For counselors who work with a population which has a high rate of unintended pregnancy, an excellent project is to learn more about why and how it occurs. A large quantity of literature is available on the subject, and the important point is not to over-generalize by making assumptions. For instance, in some subcultures young women may accidentally-on-purpose seem to get pregnant to establish a place of their own with a public assistance check, whereas in other subcultures, women may avoid birth control because of a belief that it would make them look "easy." Within these groups will be individual differences as to why particular women have unwanted pregnancies, so careful listening is necessary. Countless other factors are useful to understanding many motivations that lead to problems with contraceptive use, and one must be aware of these in order to be more sensitive to a specific client's conflicts.

Medical professionals often do more patient education about health, effectiveness, and side effects than on how the birth control method effects sexual pleasure. Therefore many people could be helped if the counselor becomes expert in the quality of life aspects. Making a chart of available methods and the sexual implications of each, while reading and interviewing, creates a valuable resource.

LEARNING EXPERIENCE NO. 13

A. **Practice doing interviews focused on contraceptive histories. Ask each person to describe all the methods he/she has used, including worrying and keeping their fingers crossed. Try to estimate what proportion of his/her heterosexual intercourse experiences was unprotected in situations where conception was not wanted.**

B. **Sound out each person on his/her beliefs and motivations at the time of use or non-use of a contraceptive, on the advantages and disadvantages, and what effect if any, on sexual pleasure. Then discover what advice they might have for other people using each method.**

C. **Repeat this type of interview with people of different ages, sexes, and degree of sexual activity. Be aware that personal secrets may come out, such as unwanted pregnancy or hidden sexual partners. Focus on birth control, but of course be supportive and refer if ongoing conflicts emerge. Clarify in the beginning that everything is completely confidential, and never reveal who any interview subjects are, even in a training group.**

Change has occurred rapidly in birth control methods and attitudes, even beyond the accelerated "future shock" rate considered so stressful in modern culture. Many people with whom the counselor talks will be anxious and angry. They had confidence in the pill, an IUD, or a particular barrier method, and expected further improvements, only to be disillusioned and scared. Some react with suppressed guilt: "Maybe the moralists were right," while many turn to sterilization, risk taking, accept repeated abortions, or use multiple methods which they feel inhibit lovemaking. The counselor cannot solve all the technical contraceptive problems, but can assist the client in sorting out what is needed and help find effective health care.

RESOURCES REGARDING CONTRACEPTIVE METHODS

Asso, D. (1983). *The real menstrual cycle.* Somerset, NJ: Wiley.

Byrne, D., & Fisher, W. (1983). *Adolescents, sex and contraception.* Hillsdale, NJ: Lawrence Erlbaum Associates.

Cook, C., & Dworkin, S. (1981). *The MS guide to women's health.* New York: Berkeley Publishers.

Federation of Feminist Women's Health Centers. (1981). *A new view of a woman's body: A fully illustrated guide.* New York: Simon and Schuster.

Guttmacher, A. (1981). *Teenage pregnancy: The problem that hasn't gone away.* New York: The Alan Guttmacher Institute.

Holmes, H., Hoskins, B., & Groth, M. (1980). *Birth control and controlling birth.* Clifton, NJ: Humana Press.

Lieberman, E., & Peck, E. (1981). *Sex and birth control: A guide for the young.* New York: Harper and Row.

Kass-Annesse, B., & Danzer, H. (1984). *Patterns: National family planning & fertility awareness methods for women and men.* Claremont, CA: Hunter House Publishers.

Madaras, L., & Patterson, J. (1984). *Womancare: A gynecological guide to your body*. New York: Avon Books.

Los Angeles Regional Family Planning Council, Inc. *Training manual for natural family planning and fertility awareness method instructors training program.* (1982). 3250 Wilshire Blvd., Suite 320, Los Angeles, CA 90010.

Magazines and journals publish frequent articles with contraceptive information for women and men. Check each author's credentials.

Texts and sexuality resources already listed usually contain excellent chapters which summarize current information on contraceptive methods.

Chapter 1, Part 7

PREGNANCY
CONCERNS

A large number of sexual interactions occur every day and a small percentage do result in conception. The 23 chromosomes from a single male sperm and 23 from one released ovum unite and an embryo develops. Of these conceptions, not all will result in a baby:

> a large number never become implanted in the uterine wall due to natural causes, medication, or a contraceptive.

> for many a pregnancy begins but a spontaneous (natural) abortion occurs to interrupt it. This also may be called a miscarriage when the pregnancy has been recognized.

> for another large number, an induced (therapeutic) abortion terminates the pregnancy.

> for some a birth results. The closer to term (nine months) and the healthier, the more likely the infant is to survive.

The subjective response of a client varies greatly when conception is suspected. A number of people will be relieved if they find they are not pregnant, while a number will be overjoyed if they are. Some will be devastated to find themselves pregnant but others will feel hopeless if they do not conceive. Sexuality counselors cannot lose sight of all the possibilities, and must anticipate great individual differences concerning the reproductive aspects of sex. To complicate the situation still further, the same individual may hold deeply mixed feelings about a possible pregnancy, or have conflicting reactions at different times.

PREGNANCY CARRIED TO TERM

Pregnancy and birth are topics which counselors frequently check as "know enough," and yet upon discussion they find that much information is based on a small sample of memories. Actually the average person may know more about this aspect of sex-related experience, because it is the one which people have felt somewhat free to discuss in family/friend settings. However to be up to date on such things as new methods of prenatal care and delivery is important. Controversies about the use of technology during pregnancy and labor, Caesarian section, circumcision of male infants, amniocentesis, the local practice of midwives, alternate birthing centers and home birth should be understood. Often clients need help clarifying these and other issues, so they can seek appropriate health care and ask the right questions.

LEARNING EXPERIENCE NO. 14

A. Arrange to watch in a group setting a film or videotape like "Gentle Birth." During and following the film people usually share reactions and tend to self disclose, both those who have been present at births (or given birth), and those who anticipate the experience. A person can obtain practice in listening and being sensitive to varied concerns, while increasing one's own understanding and sensitivity.

B. If possible, attend a birth. Students frequently are present, and a counselor or other helping professional doing this kind of training can make arrangements to attend. To prepare yourself beforehand, study text books and collect information through interviews. Again it is important to discuss the experience afterwards and to put your own feelings and reactions into words.

The counselor who is knowledgeable about pregnancy and delivery will be helpful to a wide range of potential clients. Some who might have questions or fears are younger individuals, those with infertility problems, those in high risk pregnancy groups, and couples with concerns about lovemaking during and after pregnancy. In addition the counselor will be more responsive to people who have had negative experiences in pregnancy or delivery which could have affected their later sexual functioning.

Health care books are regularly available on every aspect of pregnancy from fitness to nutrition, and on preparaton for labor, delivery, and for after the birth. Information is especially helpful for clients during pregnancy in that they are empowered to feel more secure, confident, and healthy. When the counselor reads these books, positive attitudes are formed.

RESOURCES REGARDING PREGNANCY

Ashford, J. (1984). *Birth stories: The experience remembered.* Trumansburg, NY: The Crossing Press.

Bing, E., & Coleman, L. (1982). *Making love during pregnancy.* New York: Bantam Books.

Ingleman-Sundberg, A., & Wirsens, C. (1977). *A child is born.* New York: Delacorte Publishing.

Gansberg, J., & Mostel, A. (1984). *The second nine months: The sexual and emotional concerns of the new mother.* New York: Tribeca Communications.

Guttmacher, A. (1984). *Pregnancy, birth and family planning.* New York: New American Library.

Hotchner, T. (1984). *Pregnancy & childbirth: The complete guide to a new life.* New York: Avon Books.

Jones, R. (1984). *Human reproduction and sexual behavior.* Englewood Cliffs, NJ: Prentice-Hall.

Lesko, W., & Lesko, M. (1984). *The maternity sourcebook: 230 basic decisions for pregnancy, birth, and baby care.* New York: Warner Books.

ABORTION

All conception does not end in birth. For the counselor to be knowledgeable about pregnancy termination is important. Each year over a million and a half legal abortions are reported in the U.S. Some people find that learning about this topic is difficult and the counselor can be of great assistance by having an adequate knowledge base. Both pro-choice and pro-life groups are strongly committed, but the majority of people have opinions which fall between the extremes. Regardless of one's personal values about abortion, a counselor needs to study all the different viewpoints.

Most of the references already cited on women's health give the physiological facts and the timing for various induced abortion procedures. The counselor must realize that at a few weeks after conception a fingernail-sized cluster of cells exists which requires a simple vacuum procedure to evacuate, whereas at six months the fetus is near being able to survive in an intensive care nursery. This is one kind of counseling where time pressure is very real, in contrast to most sexual issues where more time is available for reflection.

Even if the counselor is completely comfortable about the ethical issues involved in abortion, a comprehensive study of the psychological aspects also must be completed. More than fertility control is involved, since larger issues of lifestyle, personal rights-religion-authority, and sex roles are intensely involved in the issue. As in other value decisions, all clients need not share the counselor's exact views; however, the counselor must be very clear so as not to impose his/her views on others.

Reading is an excellent way to begin. A person can choose from the resources listed at the end of Chapter 1, Part 7, and from news magazines and good popular literature for timely summaries. Counselors are primarily interested in the psychological aspects of pregnancy termination and may be surprised to discover how culturally influenced any "trauma" is. In countries where abortion is considered an acceptable way to limit families, women simply do not experience or expect negative emotional reactions. However where women are exposed to orthodox Freudian views of womanhood, or to religious guilt, a proportion do have depressed or other negative responses. Because cultural-social aspects are so important and are closely tied to religious/moral/meaning systems, the helper must recognize the connection.

Carol Gilligan (1982) in a book entitled *In a Different Voice* described a development model for moral-ethical choice which is based in part on women's decisions about abortion. Underneath all the women's deliberations, Gilligan found a concern for responsibility, connectedness, and relationships. The study by Gilligan and Belenky (of. cit.) found that women who struggled with their balance of values and came to a decision for their own reasons were in a far better place a year later than women who did not work with the decision.

The counselor will appreciate that with maturity a person progresses from making decisions based on pleasure-pain (survival stage), to going by rules (traditional stage), to a more global, inclusive kind of moral balance of self and others. Where and in which stage each client is cannot be rushed, and the counselor must recognize the right each client has to interpret his/her own life position. The counselor can help the female client to see the unexpected pregnancy dilemma as part of her development in life, while working out the best possible solution for the circumstances.

LEARNING EXPERIENCE NO. 15

A. **Identify all the abortion services in your area and select one or more to visit. On the first contact you can read the literature available, perhaps ask about their professional library, and speak informally to some staff. Ask to make an appointment to interview a counselor and a nurse practitioner or gynecologist at their convenience. Busy professionals are more likely to make the time when they can see your sincerity in person.**

B. **Have references if possible or have a colleague who knows someone on the staff make the initial contact for you, because abortion providers have reason to be concerned about disruption and safety. If you are comfortable in doing so, request permission to be present during a procedure. This is an excellent means of gaining information and you as a counselor may serve as a support person for a client who needs one; observe in an unobtrusive way with a patient's permission. Most health centers want counselors to be knowledgeable and will help if time is taken to work out the arrangements.**

People in general do not find any solution completely satisfactory for an unwanted pregnancy. Activist members of pro-life and pro-choice groups have volatile differences about life style and values which show no sign of a quick resolution. Clients are likely to be exposed to intense, emotional debate from others and the media while they are trying to make a decision. What the counselor can do is keep the client focused on her reality since the choice is too important to be swayed by the latest letter-to-the-editor or magazine article. The counselor can become aware of the myths and rhetoric so as to help a person arrive at a balanced judgment.

Professionals need to try to understand others' views, whether or not they would choose the same outcome for themselves. For example, professionals may have difficulty understanding the views of a depressed client who is the sole supporter of several children, who has a back injury, and who has just been accepted into a suitable job training program, and who decides to continue another pregnancy. A very different view is expressed by an ambitious couple who decide to abort their first pregnancy in order to have a child the following year. Yet these clients must be helped to carry out whatever decision they make, when they have explored all alternatives. Some find abortion the best solution in difficult places, whereas others always would carry a fetus to term; each person has the right to sensitive professional help.

Counselors can search out people whom they respect to practice talking comfortably about abortion. To speak to people with varied opinions is helpful. The purpose is not to hold a debate; at this point understanding the other person's beliefs and underlying values is essential. The goal is to sound out other people in depth, and then summarize their opinions carefully to their satisfaction. Is "goodness" seen as obeying someone's rules or sacrificing for others? Is concern for the self assumed to be mature or selfish?

Also important is to interview a woman who has had an abortion in order to understand her experience, and her partner's if possible. By focusing on her recollection of the experience as it developed, she can communicate the process she went through and her subsequent reactions. Of course the purpose is understanding and not analysis. To interview more than one person is useful, to avoid overgeneralizing from a single instance. Someone for whom abortion was a recent decision is likely to have had a different experience than a woman who went through it some years ago.

Because abortion has become a political issue, the counselor will need to keep current about laws, rules, and regulations. Professionals are being asked for opinions more often with the underaged, where partners disagree, where one is emotionally disturbed, when funding is in question, and for the disabled. Also, as prenatal technology advances and genetic testing is more common, people seek help with difficult termination decisions about possible birth defects. Finally, since no completely safe and certain contraceptive seems immediately available to all, professionals doing sexuality counseling must become competent in helping others make pregnancy decisions.

RESOURCES REGARDING ABORTION

Batchelor, E. (Ed.). (1982). *Abortion: The moral issues.* New York: The Pilgrim Press.

Callahan, S., & Callahan, D. (Eds.). (1984). *Abortion: Understanding differences.* New York: Plenum Press.

Francke, L. (1978). *The ambivalence of abortion.* New York: Random House.

Gilligan, C. (1982). *In a different voice: Psychological theory & women's development.* Boston, MA: Harvard University Press.

Harrison, B. (1983). *Our right to choose: Toward a new ethic of abortion.* Boston: Beacon Press.

Howe, L. (1984). *Moments on Maple Avenue, the reality of abortion.* New York: Macmillan.

Luker, K. (1984). *Abortion and the politics of motherhood.* Berkeley, CA: University of California Press.

Petchesky, R. (1984). *Abortion and women's choice.* New York: Longman.

Shostak, A., & McLouth, G. (1984). *Men and abortion: Lessons, losses, and love.* New York: Praeger.

Tietze, C. (1983). *Induced abortion: A world review.* New York: The Population Council.

Chapter 1, Part 8

LIFE STYLES:

CELIBACY
HETEROSEXUALITY
BISEXUALITY
HOMOSEXUALITY

Is sexual preference an "orientation" (determined), or a "decision" (chosen)? Key issues about the ethics and acceptability of partner choice revolve around this point, but because no conclusive data on the subject are available the counselor can not take a rigid position. While many researchers acknowledge the possibility of biological components, evidence also exists concerning some developmental and psycho-social forces which influence sexual life style. This does not settle the question of "given" versus "optional," because the interaction of forces can be both within and beyond a person's conscious awareness.

CELIBACY

The important background insight for a counselor is to be aware of the many possible sexual life styles. For instance, why is a particular person non-sexual? Definitions for celibate often cover two meanings: "chooses not to marry" and "eschews sexual relations." Language is limited or vague in this area. A portion of the population is not sexually active at any given time, and their motivations range from the religious to the practical, from distaste for sex to grieving. Many of these people experience self stimulation, fantasy, or an occasional sexual encounter, some with guilt and some without. Others remove every aspect of sex from their lives, with widely different motivations and success. Helpers skilled at sexuality counseling need to counter the assumption that everyone must be sexually active, just as they challenge other authoritarian dictates about sexual life style.

LEARNING EXPERIENCE NO. 16

A. Choose a period of time to be sexually less active or inactive, depending on your present forms of sexual expression. Allow it to be long enough so that you experience some definite feelings and see how the change affects you. Look for a range of reactions from changes in fantasy, physical sensations, dreams, and sensitivity to stimuli, to relief at having extra time, loneliness, less stress, and different communication with others.

B. Talk to others informally about your experience and ask them to share information regarding times when they have been sexually inactive. Listen not only for different kinds of motivation, but also to the degree of satisfaction with those times in their lives.

C. If you are hearing many negative comments such as, *"After I was raped,"* *"When I was taking medication for depression,"* *"Before, during, and after my divorce,"* then deliberately seek out positive experiences. Look for people who can help you understand: *"During my missionary year with the Church,"* *"When I was studying Eastern philosophy and decided to simplify my life,"* or *"When I moved to another city and put all my energy into the anti-nuclear movement"* (or marine biology). Notice the great inter- and intra-individual differences in the occurrence of less sexually active periods in people's lives.

RESOURCES REGARDING CELIBACY

Brown, G. (1980). *The new celibacy: Why more men & women are abstaining from sex and enjoying it.* New York: McGraw Hill.

Foster, L. (1981). *Religion and sexuality: Three American communal experiments of the nineteenth century.* New York: Oxford University Press. Contains case studies of celibacy.

Joyce, R., & Joyce, M. (1970). *New dynamics in sexual love: A revolutionary approach to marriage and celibacy.* Out-of-print but available in some libraries.

Most of the texts and interview-based resources already listed contain references to celibacy, but this life style is infrequently studied.

HETEROSEXUAL LIFE STYLE

Expressing one's sexuality with members of the other sex, both in fantasy and behavior over the life span, appears to be the experience of about half the population of the U.S. Many other people are largely heterosexual in behavior, with an occasional experience or recurrent fantasy about people of their own sex. Certainly the dominant, approved cultural mode in much of the world is for men to select women as sexual partners and vice versa.

Historically one of the strongest reasons for heterosexuality has been the establishment and maintenance of families. A female and a male parent are assumed to provide a balanced model of adult behavior and share the tasks needed to give children a secure family life. This was especially the arrangement when men were breadwinners and women were the bearers of children and homemakers. However, more recent population statistics show fewer families fitting that pattern. Absolutes, if they ever existed, are gone, but the concept of complementary roles and characteristics still holds true for many. The phrase "vive la difference" refers to the very real male-female sexual attraction which exists for most people.

The first reaction of individuals whose experience is largely heterosexual is that "you have to have" a man and a woman for natural sex. With this life style the tendency often is to focus only on penis-in-vagina intercourse as the sexual act, rather than seeing it as part of sexual expression. More knowledgeable heterosexuals have learned some of the many other ways of giving and receiving sexual pleasure, and find it also natural. A wealth of erotic literature, theater, art, films, magazines, and tradition exists which illustrates the infinite variety and potential beauty of heterosexual experience and relationships.

LEARNING EXPERIENCE NO. 17

A. **View three or more current movies (or TV films, home video, plays) with a heterosexual theme, looking for different lifestyles: casual sex, serial relationships, committed couples living together, adolescents, the married, divorced, and remarried. Watch them with one or more other people and spend some time afterwards discussing:**

What was the essential attraction between the people?

Did the women and men seem believable/authentic, or did the actors play stereotyped sexual roles?

Was the sexuality explicit or subtle? Realistic? Erotic for the viewer?

What were the advantages and disadvantages to the heterosexual life styles portrayed?

B. **After seeing several, compare and contrast them in discussion with knowledgeable friends, a study group, or colleagues. Spend some time focusing on the potential problems of heterosexual relationships, so as to learn more about those issues which clients usually bring up. Adopt the interested curiosity of a cultural anthropologist in order to gain new insights into the variety of heterosexual experience and assure yourself that no one form of it is taken for granted.**

RESOURCES REGARDING HETEROSEXUAL LIFE STYLE

Barbach, L. (1982). *For each other.* New York: Anchor Press/Doubleday.

Blumstein, P., & Schwartz, P. (1983). *American couples: Money, work, sex.* New York: William Morrow.

Comfort, A. (1975). *The joy of sex.* New York: Simon and Schuster.

Gebhard, P., & Johnson, A. (1979). *The Kinsey data: Marginal tabulations of the 1938-1963 interviews conducted by the Institute of Sex Research.* Philadelphia, PA: Saunders.

Hite, S. (1978). *The Hite report.* New York: Dell.

Hite, S. (1981). *The Hite report on male sexuality.* New York: Ballentine.

McCarthy, B., & McCarthy, E. (1982). *Sexual Awareness.* New York: Carroll and Graf.

Journals listed elsewhere contain regular articles, but more focused ones may be found in the following :

The journal of sex and marital therapy. New York: Brunner/Mazel.

Alternative lifestyles. New York: Human Sciences Press.

The journal of social work and human sexuality. New York: The Haworth Press.

BISEXUALITY

Very often an individual's early sexual experiences with others are not planned. A few boys may be playing, become aroused, and enjoy masturbating one another. Two girls may "practice kissing" at a sleepover party and be surprised by their intense physical reaction. Sometimes a sibling, cousin, or friend may initiate sexual acts they have seen or heard others do. An older adolescent or adult of either sex may seduce or persuade a younger person to become sexually involved. Any of the above may be single episodes or repeated many times.

Because sex is such a suppressed subject and often is impulsive or not clearly chosen behavior, same-sex early experiences are common and recollection is hazy. They may or may not result in guilt or anxiety, and they do not necessarily determine later behavior. The counselor can be helpful by encouraging a client to explore and accept confusing earlier experience.

At some age the sex of the partner usually becomes an issue for a person. In general about 10% of Americans define themselves as homosexual at a given time, with still others declaring themselves bisexual. Many people consider themselves heterosexual or sexually inactive but have significant homosexual experience. Research by A. Kinsey, P. Gebhard, and A. Johnson (1979), A. Bell (1981), S. Hite (1976, 1981), and many others show that a quarter to one half of all adults have had one or more sexual experiences to orgasm, after puberty, with a person of their own sex. Because same-sex sexual expression is so common, the taboos and condemnation surrounding it are puzzling.

Some of the most insulting words in the language refer to homosexual experience. In the elementary school, counselors shake their heads over the common reversal of "prevert" when the child means "pervert." Helpers in many settings can attest to the use of insults like "lezee" and "fag," which appear before children can clearly define their meaning. Everyone is aware of numerous non-verbal gestures and signs of a negative nature as well.

One cause of the homophobia and confusion around same-sex partners seems to be the stereotypes about sex (gender) roles. Although many researchers have found that only 10 to 15% of homosexuals dress or act like the other sex to a greater degree than does the general population, an infinite scorn exists for the "queer" male who is effeminate, or the woman who is "butch." To check this out, a counselor can ask a group of young men whether their parents would be more upset if they wore effeminate clothing, giggled, and acted "girlish", or if they reported "getting it on with another guy when I was drunk". Usually far greater aversion is expressed toward cross-sex imitation than to impulsive same-sex activity. To a lesser degree the same is true for women, so that assumptions about partner preference are often made if a "masculine" manner is judged.

A professional sexuality counselor will keep in mind that hetero-bi-homo sexual refers to the sex of the partner(s), and will need to recognize that confusion often exists in regard to sex role and about promiscuity. Many clients will present issues which are upsetting, such as having trouble understanding their developing sexuality, their social/sex/gender role, and attraction to partners. For instance, pubescent boys may watch pornographic home video together in secret, talk about it later and become aroused, think about the other during self stimulation, and become confused about their "manliness." Much pain is revealed with am implied "Am I normal?" theme, and it often refers back to fantasies, desires, and experiences where the sex of the partner was only part of it, and self critical conclusions were drawn.

LEARNING EXPERIENCE NO. 18

A. Study the following diagram to understand the many possible combinations of gender (male/female), sex role (masculine/feminine), and partner (men/women).

PARTNER	WOMEN		MEN	
	Fem. Role	Masc. Role	Fem. Role	Masc. Role
Female Partner	"femme" Lesbian	"butch/dyke" Lesbian	"sensitive" man	traditional preference
Male Partner	traditional preference	"liberated" woman	"effeminate" homosexual	"rough trade" gay male

B. Place the first names of some people whom you know well in the eight cells of the diagram of item A. The purposes for doing this are (1) to discover those kinds of life styles with which you are most familiar and (2) to realize that people often do not fit in categories.

In doing Item B, recognize that no person really fits in this diagram, but we all have some ways of grouping people. As a sexuality counselor, you need to be honest about how limited your experience is and to seek out individuals with different sex roles, life styles, and partner preferences in order to avoid stereotyping.

C. Consider the following questions: On which crossbars would you place "androgynous" people you know? Where would you put yourself? What about bisexual individuals? Where would you place a person who had a same-sex partner in high school or college but is now monogomous and married? Or someone who was married 15 years but is now widow(er)ed or divorced and has a same-sex lover? How do you decide what is "liberated," "masculine," "effeminate," or "traditional"?

D. Keep thinking of people and jotting down first names, trying to cover the spectrum. Modify the diagram as necessary.

E. Circle the names of people whom you especially like and underline the names of those on your diagram whom you dislike. Add some more, if needed, to obtain more "dislikes." Do the likes and dislikes fall into a pattern?

F. Look at the boxes where you have few people or none. Try to meet persons who might represent that life style.

G. Become genuinely interested and knowledgeable about all the possibilities so that you will not be tempted to "sell" your own partner preference or life style to a client.

Counselors will tend to find labels of very little usefulness in life style counseling, and yet the term bisexual might be helpful when working with a client who genuinely prefers partners of either sex, and has had significant experiences with both. Those people who have had rare, unsatisfactory, experimental, or pressured sex with one of the sexes aren't really bisexual. Sex role is also not a defining issue, because a man or woman can be bisexual and any part of the continuum of socially defined masculinity to femininity.

Some authors have suggested that individuals who can love and be sexual with people, regardless of gender, may be more evolved than those who are exclusively focused on one sex or the other. This is a philosophical and values issue which a counselor and client may find meaningful to discuss. Certainly such a dialogue is more fruitful than is pointless analysis about whether the client "really" is gay or straight when he/she relates well to both women and men. The very same human questions about lovemaking, communication, and partner issues come up with bisexuality as with homo-or hetero-sexuality.

RESOURCES REGARDING BISEXUALITY

Bode, J. (1976). *View from another closet, exploring bisexuality in women.* New York: Hawthorne Books.

DeCecco, J. (Ed.). (1984). *Bisexual & homosexual identities: Critical clinical issues*. New York: The Haworth Press.

Fast, J., & Wells, H. (1975). *Bisexual living*. New York: M. Evans.

Klein, F. (1979). *The bisexual option: A concept of one-hundred percent Intimacy*. New York: Arbor House.

Klein, F., & Wolf, T. (1985). *Bisexualities: Theory and research*. New York: The Haworth Press.

Journal articles and interview-based studies, such as those already cited by Kinsey, Hite, and Bell reveal the large proportion of people who have experience with both sexes.

HOMOSEXUALITY

Several books devote whole chapters to definitions and discussions of what homosexuality is and is not. For the counselor, the essential point is simply that a person prefers members of his/her own gender as sexual partners for a significant period of time. Just as in other life styles, a wide variety exists within the gay community(s), from committed partners to recreational singles, from conservative roles to exaggerated ones ("prep", queen, punk, sedate, or flamboyant). Recognizing that people choose many ways to express themselves helps understand individual clients.

An important area for the counselor to learn about is the pressure against open acknowledgement of homosexual preference, and the counter pressure to "come out". Most individuals have reality-based concerns about family reactions, housing, employment, admission to training programs, military service, and organizations. Some individuals choose never to come out, believing that sexuality is a private issue which need not be announced, while others find great peace in openly acknowledging their homosexuality.

Different degrees of openness and stages of coming out are likely to be experienced by a client and may require working through. This is difficult when the person has some uncertainty within him/herself, which is very common since pressure against same-sex is so common. When the counselor is free of stereotyped, homophobic assumptions, hearing the client's issues and assisting in reaching the most appropriate accommodation to the pressures of being gay are possible.

LEARNING EXPERIENCE NO. 19

A. Look in the telephone book of a large city and locate names of Gay and Lesbian organizations. Contact/visit them to obtain newsletters, information about meetings, bookstores, locations of other groups (i.e., Parents and Friends of Gays, 5715 Sixteenth St., Washington, DC 20011), campus hotlines, social events, bars, and religious or counseling services.

B. Make a resource folder for your area. If you are bisexual or homosexual, you may already be knowledgeable, but you can benefit from collecting information in one place, including brochures, new phone numbers, bibliographies, meeting places and contact persons for new groups. A counselor who has little or no knowledge of the gay community(s) will find the resource folder invaluable to learn from, and to use in working with clients. To focus on both men's and women's resources, and to look for informal friendship/acquaintance networks as well as the more public/politically oriented ones are extremely important. The best way to shed stereotypes is to talk to many people with homosexual preferences in the process, and encounter a wide range of life styles.

RESOURCES REGARDING HOMOSEXUALITY

Batchelor, E.,(Ed.). (1982). *Homosexuality and ethics (rev. ed.).* New York: Pilgrim Press.

Bell, A., Weinberg, M., & Hammersmith, S. (1981). *Sexual preference: Its development in men and women.* Bloomington, IN: Indiana University Press.

Borhek, M., (1983). *Coming out to parents: A two-way survival guide for lesbians and gay men and their parents.* New York: The Pilgrim Press.

Fairchild, B., & Hayword, N. (1981). *Now that you know: What every parent should know about homosexuality.* New York: Harcourt Brace Jovanovich.

Martin, D., & Lyon, P. (1983). *Lesbian/women* (rev. ed.). New York: Bantam Books.

Marmor, J., (Ed.). (1980). *Homosexual behavior: A modern reappraisal.* New York: Basic Books.

McWhirter, D., & Mattison, A. (1984). *The male couple: How relationships develop.* Englewood Cliffs, NJ: Prentice-Hall.

Paul, W., & Weinrich, J. (Eds.). (1982). *Homosexuality: social, psychological and biological issues.* Beverly Hills, CA: Sage Publications.

Sexuality periodicals listed elsewhere carry regular articles but the following are more specialized:

Journal of Homosexuality. New York: The Haworth Press, quarterly.

Gay Books Bulletin. Gay Academic Union, Box 480, Lenox Hill Station, New York, NY 10021, biannual.

CONCLUSION

Many clients whom a counselor sees will not fit into only one life style or partner preference. Sometimes this is because the person is still developing or searching, and other times no category is adequate. Most people eventually develop some consistent preferences which they can express and with which they are comfortable. A counselor may be consulted when a change or a challenge to established life style is present, or when the question has never been resolved.

The opportunity to explore individual issues and the simple reassurance that sorting out life style is an important task can ease the strain enormously. Even when partner choice is not a presenting problem, counselors are in a good position to clear up many guilts and fears which lead to feeling of personal inadequacy or self disparagement. Security in the area of life style and partner preference is a major component of mental health for most people.

Chapter 1, Part 9

SEXUALITY AND STEREOTYPES

(Groan)...*"We heard too much about stereotypes like the pink and blue color line in the 1970s."* Certainly the subject of sex roles has been belabored so much that people wince at the heavy handed gag lines in situation comedies, and the constant flow of newspaper and magazine references to male/female differences. In a similar way stereotypes about Black Americans, Hispanics, and many racial, religious, national, and other groups may have been overtalked. Because professionals honestly think they know about general stereotypes, they may underestimate their real sexual implications.

The origin of stereotyped roles is often debated; yet whether they are rooted in myth, prejudice, biology, or culture is less important for counseling than the fact that people are highly influenced by them. Counselors have to be aware of and must avoid two pitfalls when dealing with stereotypes—dismissal and complacence.

1. *Dismissal.* Because counselors may genuinely know a great deal about stereotypes and feel personally open to all kinds of people, jumping to the conclusion that they will have no problem in sex counseling is misleading. The helper needs to dig deeper to find his/her own hidden assumptions about how gender, ethnicity, and other factors affect sexuality. Unconscious prejudices about what is OK for men sexually or vulgar for women, what is "wimpish" or brazen, who is untrustworthy or uptight, a "good" lover or a good girl, all color the ways client's sexuality is perceived. Dismissing the subject is naive, or can be a defensive form of denial.

2. *Complacence.* Another problem is that because counselors themselves have worked through stereotypes, they may overlook the ironclad ways some clients accept roles for

themselves and others. With awareness, publicity, and mobility, many people are in the process of questioning, but the counselor will find that the sexual aspects are among the slowest to change. Even more confusing is when the client talks in an enlightened way about gender, race, or ethnicity, while assuming operational sexual roles different from the vocabulary level.

In 1970, only a few researchers were aware of the impact of gender stereotyped "masculine" and "feminine" socialization, and they went ahead to measure how the mass of the population were heavily influenced by it. Within a decade the culture has changed so that the experts writing up their articles struggled to stablize just the definitions: "sex, sexuality, sex role, sex-coded role, sexual identity, gender, gender role, gender identity" and so forth. The effects of other kinds of group membership on sexuality also is being studied, but as change occurs, confusion reigns, so that even research categories don't remain stable.

Stereotyped attitudes about race, gender, social group, and ethnic background have been shown to change with education and familiarity, but this takes time. For the remainder of the century, at least, unfounded assumptions about male/female differences in sexuality probably will persist. The counselor can expect to encounter all stereotypes in a state of flux, which means that rapid and bewildering individual differences in attitudes and behavior are to be expected. Narrow assumptions are impossible.

STEREOTYPING

What can a counselor expect will be the perceptions about roles and sexuality of the following children when they grow up?

1. A Mexican-American boy lives with his parents to age eight in a working class neighborhood of a Texas city. He moves with his mother to a student housing unit at the University of Wisconsin; his mom has occasional long relationships with men but never remarries.

2. A girl born to a single woman lives in a lesbian household for eight years; her mother then marries a divorced man who has a daughter and two sons and the children attend a suburban school.

What happens if these two people have a relationship at 26 and come in for sexuality counseling? Will they be different to work with than a couple who grew up attending the same temple (synagogue) on Long Island? Perhaps the second couple will present just as deep conflicts about their expectations for one another. With any client the counselor has to be careful not to make unwarranted assumptions, but to be open to the possible effects of learned roles on sexual expression.

One of the most harmful misconceptions is that any group of people who are disadvantaged in some way are intrinsically less moral or more dangerous than the dominant culture. Women in immigrant populations have been particularly exploited, from Irish servant girls, to black slaves and oriental women. Of course, statistically those groups with less education and little money/employment do have higher rates of teenage and unplanned pregnancy, disease, prostitution, and crime than does the more advantaged population. The counselor needs to be especially careful not to stereotype clients and yet to understand how their ethnic or social status may have influenced their sexuality.

As role stereotypes are modified and people's thinking goes ahead or lags behind their behavior, to generalize from any aspect of a client to his/her sexuality is difficult. For the purpose of counselor training, it is best to be descriptive rather than categorize, and to assume that no one fits any label. Counselors can become deeply aware of their own hidden assumptions and then look for how learned roles may effect their clients' self concept, mental health, and sexuality.

QUESTIONS OF GENDER AND SEXUALITY

Studies of sexual attitudes and behavior always consider the gender of the participants, and often the effects of race, social class, religion, and other factors. Regardless to what other groups any human being belongs, maleness/femaleness has been shown to have a definite effect on sexuality, so counselors must be especially aware of gender. The question is not whether generalizations or stereotypes are true, either in general or for individuals, but rather what effect gender could have on the client's sexuality.

The basic expectation is to assume that most people have a definite idea of whether they are female or male. The usual categories for determining the gender of an individual are external genitalia (penis, scotum, clitoris, vulva), internal reproductive organs (ovaries, uterus, prostate gland, testes), hormone balance (androgens, estrogens), sex chromosomes (XX, XY, variants), sex of assignment and rearing ("It's a boy/girl"), and self identity (I'm a girl/boy"). Amazingly, after about age 3 an individual can more easily adjust to modifying the physical characteristics (the first three), than to altering the psycho-social identity as male/female (the last two).

Only a very small percentage of people give mixed answers to the criteria for determining gender, since most clients are very sure whether they are a man or a woman. Occasionally a client will be concerned about an atypical characteristic, such as a woman with curly, blond hair on her chest, or a very late developing adolescent. These clients need anxiety reduction and support, and often a medical referral for reassurance or treatment, but are clearly either male or female.

Beyond basic gender only a few certainties exist. Most people can give their conscious perception of social roles of masculinity and femininity, but much is suppressed or not readily available. With careful interviewing, clients will compare their perceptions with those of society as they see it, and point out the differences. They also may quote significant others about gender roles and show where they are similar or different: "My father says I'm a tomboy because I hate makeup and am on the track team, but no one at my high school works at going steady anymore." The sexual aspects of gender roles are seldom spelled out or discussed clearly, so clients are less fluent in relating gender to sexual behavior.

EXAMPLE: Sexual Stereotyping

The popular and professional press have focused on how women have been stereotyped sexually, but the counselor needs to be aware of the enormous pressure about what is "masculine" as well. A counselor can collect recent copies of five popular magazines of different types and tear out a large sample of advertisements with men in them. These can be grouped by theme, according to whether the males pictured appear to fit role stereotypes of masculinity. The following are some aspects for which to look:

the narrow spectrum of traits sanctioned as masculine

a stress on material goods, winning, achieving, competing

caricatures of male/female relationships

encouragement of toughness, aloneness, aggression, dominance

exploitation of male sexuality

body language, hard eyes, posture, height, muscle, emphasis on genitals

possible non-stereotyped behavior and appearance.

If the counselor finds some old magazines and compares pictures of men in ads and illustrations, the result can be surprising. For a decade stereotypes of women have been used to sell goods, with less awareness of how sexual images of men have been regimented. To compare notes with others is useful, in order to practice communicating about sex roles and sexuality. The point is not to decry how cigarettes or cars are sold, but to realize the collective image of sexuality which the media reflects. Most of the impact is non-verbal, and a great many clients will be having sexual problems because their self image is shaped by or feels inadequate to these popular stereotypes.

In addition to a deeper insight on sex roles and sexuality, studying how racial, ethnic, or any other group is pictured in the popular mind is beneficial. Because of the threat of lawsuits, not many blatantly prejudiced materials are being published, but this covert aspect makes the sexuality stereotypes about particular groups harder to reach.

When working with clients, expectation for men and women can be discussed in depth without mentioning sexuality at first, in order to understand the person's overall values. The counselor who has done career counseling or couples communication will be familiar with the importance of bringing gender roles out for the client to consider. Usually a client can more easily modify learned gender role rigidities in one area if he/she already has in another. A person can become less performance oriented in lovemaking if he/she has already modified competetive, "Type A," behavior at work.

Many client concerns about sexuality have some area of gender role conflict, but sexual role is not necessarily identical with overall gender role. A man could be an "androgynous" lover because of modeling or sexuality education, but tend to believe in a stereotyped male work role as "boss". Or the reverse could be true; a man could be "liberated" in most ways and still adhere to a stereotypical sexual style of pressuring women for sex. In a similar way, a woman could choose a non-traditional work environment and retain a stereotyped female pattern of other-directed sexual behavior, or the reverse.

Because sexual behavior is largely private and restricted to one's chosen sexual partners, modifying the sexual aspect of gender roles is usually possible even for people who have not questioned stereotypes. For instance, a woman can learn to ask her partner for what feels good, even if assertiveness is difficult for her in the world at large. Or a teenage boy can be encouraged to speak up with his girl friend about needing birth control, even if he is not otherwise comfortable talking about emotional, personal things. The counselor thus helps the client modify negative aspects of learned social roles without creating anxiety about overall values.

Another problem is that the congruence between what clients say they should be like as men or women, and how they actually behave is complicated. Feelings of guilt, inadequacy, and defensiveness surround the whole area. People are having a hard time trying to mesh with old and new standards, or rebelling against a perceived norm. One of the most painful feelings in this society is not to fit because one isn't "masculine" or "feminine" enough. Today everyone is the target of mixed messages, so to be "appropriate" sexually and also spontaneous is difficult.

LEARNING EXPERIENCE NO. 20

A. Try to understand the influence of gender by acting the sex opposite your own, i.e., if you are a woman, act like a man sexually,

or if you are a man, behave like a woman sexually. This exercise is best to do in one's private life and then discuss in a group with others. Try it wholeheartedly for an hour, and then longer if you can. The effect of gender on sexuality is universal, because everyone has been exposed to the role of being either a male or a female in society.

B. Creatively analyze gender and sexuality so as to understand what kinds of changes are required to do Item A. Don't alter your partner(s), but do alter the way you think, feel, talk, and behave sexually. Modifying dress and mannerisms even a little is impactful. You will need to do some communicating with others about this, and honestly try to switch rather than "camp it up".

C. As much as you can, be aware of the resistance within yourself and others as you accept the challenge to change the "ultimate aspect" of socially learned roles.

D. Recognize that some behaviors, jokes, language, fantasy and attitudes just can't be imitated, because some aren't known by the other sex. To role play the other sex in terms of achievement or household tasks is far easier than sexual role reversal.

E. Consider how your sexuality would be influenced if you were different from your present self in another way than gender? Try on the idea of a different race, region of the country, national/ethnic background, religion, disability, or other difference. Many stereotypes which apply to sexuality are so covert that they are seldom verbalized, and this adds to their powerful influence.

F. Discuss the possibilities from Item E in a group, not from the point of view of proving how your sexual expression actually would be different as a Cambodian man, a Morman woman, a white Southerner, or a Black person in Boston, but to get out your presumptions. Reactions within the group to stereotypes being aired should not be to debate whether they are "true" or not, but rather "oh yes, that's another one."

Although most people in the latter part of the twentieth century are profoundly influence by gender roles, a small number of people are conflicted about both their biological gender and social role. A term for this is gender dysphoria, and one solution is to have hormonal and surgical treatment to change the basic male or female identity. Many of these people, however, work out their conflicts with counseling and psychotherapy, and may utilize some less radical medical assistance. Gender-questioning clients (''I'm a woman in a man's body''), often bring up their conflicts around sexual expression, and the counselor needs to be able to distinguish these clients from other clients who have issues of sexuality and gender role (What is appropriate feminine/masculine sexual expression?). Because all of this is a fluid area of social change and research, a counselor should become familiar with gender roles and stereotypes as they apply to sexuality, and comfortable helping people sort out sexual identity questions.

No human service person can be alive at this time without having some questions about self, gender, sex role, and sexuality. Occasionally this study leads to a rejection of maleness/femaleness, whether these differences are seen as nominal or great, largely learned or biologically determined. A counselor needs to like his/her style of masculinity/femininity, without imposing it on others. This is especially necessary when working with client issues around gender stereotypes, partner choice, couples conflict, identity, self esteem, and sexuality.

LEARNING EXPERIENCE NO. 21

A. Explore all the good things about your being a biological, social-sexual male/female. Read a sexual self-help book written for your gender, talk to same-sex friends about it, read novels and see films that express your gender's pleasure in being female/male.

B. Be sensitive to where the role issues (What is feminine/masculine?) intrude in an arbitrary way, and develop a plan for working out any conflicts in either the sexual or non-sexual area. Part of this learning exercise is to find resources for gender-pride, from individuals, groups, books, films, articles and experiences. Discussing these will obtain the other sex's input, so as to fill out the remaining half of the human condition.

RESOURCES REGARDING GENDER AND SEXUALITY

Franklin, C. (1984). *The changing definition of masculinity: Perspectives on sexuality series*. New York: Plenum.

Giddings, P. (1985). *When & where I enter: The impact of Black women on race and sex in America*. New York: Bantam.

Miller, A. (Ed.). (1982). *In the eye of the beholder: Contemporary issues in stereotyping*. New York: Praeger.

Money, J., & Tucker, P. (1975). *Sexual signatures: On being a man or a woman*. Boston, MA: Little, Brown.

Oakley, A. (1980). *Sex, gender and society*. New York: State Mutual Bank.

Safilios-Rothschild, C. (1977). *Love, sex and sex roles*. New York: Prentice-Hall.

Stimpson, C., & Person, E. (Eds.). (1981). *Women: Sex and sexuality*. Chicago, IL: University of Chicago Press.

Sexual aspects of stereotypes and roles can be found as a separate chapter in most of the general texts listed, and dozens of journal articles can be located on specific aspects.

Chapter 1, Part 10

PERSONAL ATTITUDES
AND VALUES

Clients bring two general kinds of sexuality-related issues to counseling:

1. The "how" and "what" questions.

2. The "who" and "why" questions.

In time most sexual problems are seen as having both a "how to" (practical) and a "why" (meaning) aspect. Counselors need to be skilled at drawing out and responding to both, and understanding their interaction.

If one's training has been oriented toward careful exploration of people's motivations, needs, purposes, goals, and "scripts", then the who and why sexual questions will call for a familiar approach. A client who asks: "Why can't I respond to my spouse but feel fine sexually with someone else? And I keep getting headaches lately," will be easier than: "What can I do to get over my erection problem?" A helper trained in behavioral methods, health treatment, or outcome-oriented casework, may find the latter presenting problem a clearer one with which to work. Yet this problem also may have an attitudinal/ethical dimension.

The study of cultural attitudes is essential for sexuality counseling because very few sexual issues are value free. Even the "how" questions which would seem to respond to practical, technical discussion of the mechanics, are strongly affected by cultural expectations. Often the client is not aware of attitudes and values absorbed over time, from family, friends, and the media, which are maintaining present sexual difficulties. The counselor cannot "mind read" and then know the mind set of the client; however, he/she can be so knowledgeable about cultural variables that subtle clues reveal the "meaning" a particular sexual issue has for a client. The more one knows about the sexual values of a subculture, whether Native American men, subfertile women, or a rural ethnic minority, the more accurately individual differences (both from the subculture and general culture) can be understood.

LEARNING EXPERIENCE NO. 22

A. Go back to the notes of an interview which you conducted for an earlier section of this chapter, such as the contraceptive histories. Think about one person and their sexual experiences. Write out a few sentences which express your perception of that person's "philosophy of sex." Your perception of another's values based on a topic interview are not objective reality, of course.

B. To check your accuracy, arrange to meet with the person again and ask how he/she would express the meaning sexuality has in his/her life. Few people have verbalized that consciously, and most enjoy formulating an answer; they may need some exploration time with a good listener. Try not to let your impressions intrude. The better your interview skills, the deeper and more thorough will be the total picture developed by the client. At the end of the interview, summarize the major meaning which sexuality has for the person in a manner satisfactory to him/her.

C. Later, compare the person's comments with your original impressions and note the difference(s). Very often first impressions of a client's sexual philosophy of life, based on selected behaviors, are distinctly inaccurate.

D. Repeat this kind of interview with people who are likely to have very different philosophies of sexuality. Notice the varying levels of skill and comfort that you bring to exploring different cultural, religious and personal roots of sexual behavior. If this is easy for you, remember later to pay particular attention to the "how" issues with clients. If exploring motivation, meaning, and ethical issues are less familiar for you, be sure and practice with many interviews and expand your reading for this section. The more resistant and difficult counseling cases often require skill with personal values before sexual technique interventions will work.

CULTURAL INFLUENCES

All clients' behavior will be influenced by their learning history, not only in their own lifetime but also that transmitted to them from earlier beliefs of family and community. Anthropology, sociology, and psychology researchers have shown that human sexuality is highly variable and influenced by culture and learning. Fortunately this means that sexuality is responsive to education and counseling, because otherwise learning about the effect of cultural values would only inform about fixed determinants.

Hundreds of examples could be given but the following are typical of the impact of cultural influences:

> The great majority of men in the U.S. are circumcized as infants.

> The great majority of men in Europe are never circumcized.

> The same religious and ethnic groups live on both sides of the Atlantic, and each holds many myths about the "rightness" of their custom. However, only cultural practice and not health dictates this rather significant sexual difference.

> The feet of Chinese women were bound for centuries into the crippled "lotus" position, which was considered erotic by men but caused women great pain. Women in some Moslem societies continue to have their clitoris cut or removed as a way of limiting sexual pleasure.

> Sexually mature Western women in the latter 20th century are expected to be quickly aroused and multi-orgasmic.

Even women's basic physical experience of sex has been profoundly shaped by cultural expectations, and yet this pales in comparison to the overall cultural pressure put on women's sexual activity.

The previous section on learned roles and stereotypes is one example of the overwhelming effect of cultural on sexuality. The counselor must be aware of the overall importance of gender, race, religion, ethnic, or social group, and open to its influence without judging or stereotyping the person. The client can often be helped to challenge or modify a sexual attitude or value which no longer fits for him/her.

Reading about the amazing variability of sexual behavior, which is due to cultural influence, will help understand a particular client's complex attitudes and values about sexuality in more depth.

RESOURCES REGARDING CULTURAL INFLUENCES

Beach, F., & Diamond, M. (Eds.). (1976). *Human sexuality in four perspectives.* Baltimore, MD: John Hopkins University Press.

Bullough, V., & Bullough, B. (1977). *Sin, sickness and sanity: A history of sexual attitudes.* New York: New American Library.

Cassell, C. (1984). *Swept away: Why women fear their own sexuality.* New York: Simon and Schuster.

Feldman, H., & Parrot, A. (Eds.). (1984). *Human sexuality: Contemporary controversies.* Beverly Hills, CA: Sage Publications.

Money, J. (1985). *The destroying angel.* Buffalo, NY: Prometheus Books.

Rosenweig, N., & Pearsal, P. (Eds.). (1978). *Sex education for the health professional: A curriculum guide.* Orlando, FL: Grune and Stratton. Contains an excellent short summary on culture.

Tannahill, R. (1980). *Sex in history.* New York: Stein and Day.

RELIGIOUS VALUES

Religion is an aspect of culture which can be either over stressed or underestimated by a counselor, depending on personal experience. Religious thinking has addressed sexuality even more than the legal, political, or educational systems. Sexuality is one of the most controversial areas in religious study today. Because of the varied types of religious teachings, and the wide spectrum of client involvement-non-involvement in religion, the helper needs to be open to understanding the relevance of religious values for each client.

EXAMPLES: Religious Influences On Sexuality

Without question people and groups can be powerfully influenced by religious ideas, as is well illustrated by the sexual aversion of the Shakers, the polygamy of early Mormons, the long history of celibate Christian orders, the association of menstruation as unclean and untouchable, the containment of ejaculation in Tantric Yoga, and the historical persecution of women as witches. Counselors are urges to read one of the 28 editions of Maleus Malleficarum (the Witches' Hammer), which contained widely accepted views of "devil" inspired female seductiveness, written by monks over a period of 200 years. Replete with the sadistic torture and killing of women for their sexuality, such reading can give an appreciation of the social and political power of ignorant, distorted religious thinking about sexuality.

Wider reading also will show where religious and cultural values came together, such as early 20th century medical "treatments" for masturbation, based on fears of moral pollution. The legal/judicial system also has reflected religious attitudes about sexuality and influenced people's behavior, such as when contraceptives were illegal (or only available to married people), variable laws about extra-marital sex (adultery), and extended sentences for anal intercourse (sodomy). The educational, health, political, human service, and other systems also have been heavily affected by what is "moral" in human sexual behavior, as interpreted by religious groups.

To realize that over the centuries people have been positively influenced by religious ideals about sexuality also is important. Teachings such as "love one another," and "two in one flesh," have been encouraging. Many laws and regulations are intended to protect people from harm. However, even a sympathetic review of Judeo-Christian tradition will find it to be restrictive and repressive regarding sexuality, and must be taken into account in working with clients influenced by them.

People are exposed to many religious ideas during development, regardless of actual church membership, and as they mature may hold conflicting moral and ethical views at once. This is further complicated by the fact that although religions differ from one another, factions within each group stress varied sexual teachings, often forcefully. National polls show that followers of all the major religions select what guidance in sexual practices they will accept, and often do not differ from non-religious people in their actual sexual expression.

All this becomes painful for individual clients who may be confused about what is right, and find that some teachings are in opposition to their desires or behavior. The counselor should explore delicately when a client says: "I can't touch myself/talk to my husband about sex/get married after a hysterectomy/use a diaphragm/spare the rod or my daughter will go bad/ejaculate/because of my religion." This is possibly a form of resistance or an unnecessarily strict interpretation of a religious idea, especially if others in their group work out solutions. Skill in understanding the importance of religious beliefs for a particular client will allow the counselor to help the person integrate religious/cultural/ethical issues into a positive life style.

LEARNING EXPERIENCE NO. 23

A. Talk to representative clergy from religious or ethical groups important to your clients and yourself. Ask their views on how sexuality was treated by their denomination in the past, and what dialogue on these topics is occurring now.

B. Look for clergy and informed lay members with vision, to learn ways of helping troubled members. This will also provide you with a good list of referral sources for resource people in the various denominations. However, becoming acquainted with very conservative or sex-negative religious positions is important, in order to better understand the pressures on people who are influenced by them.

C. Locate and interview several people whose philosophy of life is not related to a religious orientation. Learn how their values about sexuality developed and what part sex plays in their meaning system.

D. Allow time to sift through the various philosophies of sexuality and then discuss your interpretation/integration of them with colleagues. Describe what your strengths are in regard to values counseling, and clarify where you need to work through problem areas. Make a plan to become helpful to any client with sexuality-value conflicts.

RESOURCES REGARDING RELIGIOUS VALUES

Bullough, V., Brundage, J. (Eds.). (1984). *Sexual practices in the medieval church*. Buffalo, NY: Prometheus Books.

Gittelsohn, R. (1980). *Love sex and marriage: A Jewish view*. New edition. New York: Union of American Hebrew Congregations.

Kosnick, A. (Ed.). (1977). *Human sexuality: New dimensions in American Catholic thought*. Ramsey, NJ: Paulist Press.

Nelson, J. (1979). *Embodiment: An approach to sexuality and Christian thinking*. Minneapolis, MN: Augsburg Publishing House.

Nelson, J. (1983). *Between two gardens: Reflections on sexuality and religious experience*. New York: Pilgrim Press.

Parrinder, G. (1980). *Sex in the world's religions*. New York: Oxford University Press.

CHAPTER SUMMARY

The sexuality counselor needs really expert background knowledge of human sexuality on which to build. Then integrating new information is enjoyable, whether from a news article, a workshop, a TV talk show, or a professional journal. Even so, because no two clients are alike and the field is developing, a counselor may need to seek further information. Often no other person is more expert than the counselor; therefore, he/she must be able to locate good information and relate it to a sound base. Because sexuality is inherently interesting, and many resources continue to be available, the knowledge base for sexuality counseling is very comfortable to achieve.

ANSWERS TO SEX BACKGROUND KNOWLEDGE QUIZ

The following answers apply to the Sex Background Knowledge Quiz provided in Chapter 1, Form 1.2.

1. F	11. T	21. F
2. F	12. F	22. T
3. T	13. F	23. T
4. F	14. T	24. T
5. F	15. F	25. T
6. T	16. T	26. F
7. T	17. F	27. F
8. F	18. F	28. F
9. F	19. T	29. F
10. F	20. F	30. T

CHAPTER

PERSONAL ATTITUDES AND EXPERIENCE

A major prerequisite for sexuality counseling is comfortable acceptance of one's own sexuality and that of others, however different. In contrast to knowledge or skills, this combination of attitudes and experience is not usually acquired systematically. A person who has begun training must have already faced some confrontation with personal biases, however, and become aware of new sexual styles through involvement with others. One of the reasons for the learning exercises in this text is to encourage structured experience rather than abstract study. In spite of the importance of the subject, this chapter is brief, because one's entire professional education involves the counselor as a person.

SIGNIFICANCE FOR COUNSELING

"What do my personal sexual attitudes and experiences matter to a client?" a counselor may well ask. The answer is that one of the most essential professional counseling conditions is congruence, which is the unity between the helper's deep inner experience and his/her outward expression of it. Because much of the communication between human beings is non-verbal, a helper can say one set of words and yet communicate something entirely different through body language. The mixed message causes the client to experience less empathy, become defensive, or censor material.

When an interview can't seem to get beyond the surface level of exploring, one point to look for is the helper's comfort level with the client or topic. An observer or a videotape will identify more about counselor genuineness than can an audiotape, but all are preferable to counselor self-report. Objective feedback in this area of training is vital, because seeing what one is doing is difficult when feeling threatened or in conflict.

Sending honest accepting signals is the result of going deeply into personal sexual attitudes and exploring any conflicts. Two examples are provided to illustrate the point.

1. While no one can experience everything, counselors can recognize many fragments of universal human behavior within themselves.

   Client: *"My lover (husband, wife, friend) thinks I'm crazy when I get really turned on and want him/her to bite me at a crucial moment during sex. And I mean bite, not a kiss on the shoulder."*

   COMMENT: This is not likely to be every counselor's preference, nor need one enjoy biting or S-M to empathize. If the counselor has ever been in touch with the fine line between pleasure-pain which can exist in sex, and with control/intensity/letting go issues, the client's preference will not seem so bizarre.

2. Expanded self knowledge also allows the helper to respond genuinely to what is suggested or alluded to by a client.

Client: *"So sometimes maybe I'm too strong, but after all, what do they expect in that bar?"*

Counselor: *"From the way you've been talking and checking out my reactions, I'm thinking that you push hard for sex when you get a chance..."*

Client: *"You could put it down as determined. I've been picked up and questioned a couple of times, but nobody ever made a real case."*

Counselor: *"Don, you seem to have mixed feelings ... glad that no one ever hung anything on you, but maybe you are beginning to have some questions about the way you've been getting sex?"*

COMMENT: For a counselor to be comfortable talking to a non-convicted rapist (whose numbers are legion), legal knowledge and clinical experience with victims won't help. Getting in touch with one's own desire (however fleeting) to be in control, to win, to just "have" someone sexually, will be useful. In order to hear this client therapeutically, counselors also can recognize their own tendencies to distort what they think another person wants, and to give in to stereotyped sex roles. In this way the helper can have some sense of the client's world without ever having pressured another for sex.

A person cannot "hear" what they cannot fathom, so acknowledging all parts of oneself broadens the counselor's effectiveness. Until the client feels somewhat understood and trust is built, the focusing and work required to develop a real program for change isn't possible. Counselors not only need to integrate their more accessible sexual memories and values, but also must uncover deeper attitudes and experience in order to become personally congruent. Understanding a client's world, however, does not in any way mean condoning behavior or giving permission to continue destructive acts.

UNDERSTANDING VS. EXPERIENCING

People often attend sexuality counseling training sessions away from familiar home territory, and some immerse themselves in a variety of new sexual experiences. While of course any person has a right to do that, it is not the approach recommended here. Personal development and sexual experience which occur naturally seem to become integrated more comfortably into one's life style.

Counselors, like anyone else, can have sexual problems which they have been meaning to improve. A course of training in sexuality counseling would seem a good time to work on these issues through personal counseling. Even a satisfying sexual life style can be enriched, and this too will contribute to sexuality counseling effectiveness. Whereas enhanced sexual experience is not specifically prescribed here, a definite training goal for counselors can be expanding their awareness and understanding of all aspects of sexuality.

LEARNING EXPERIENCE NO. 27

From the list of *Suggestions for Sexual Enhancement* given as **A through J**, select several which will be helpful to you. Feel free to modify them for your own personal growth. Of course you may select those which involve sexual behavior, or simply choose those which affect attitudes and understanding.

Please note that nothing in this outline is intended to encourage or persuade a person to become more sexually active than he/she freely chooses. The purpose is to help discover, explore, and express sexuality appropriately, so as to attain a positive sense of the sexual self.

A. Carefully examine your body at leisure. Use mirrors, have a sensuous bath or shower, and take time to learn to do a genital self exam. Try to make friends with and be positive with all parts of yourself. Touch all areas and notice the different textures. Repeat frequently. Treat yourself to a massage by an expert and/or attend a massage workshop to learn the skill so you can trade with others.

B. Practice Kegel-type exercises to strengthen the PC muscle and increase its sensitivity and control. (Appendix B)

C. Have a general checkup and ask all the questions you have always wanted to about the health-medical aspects of your sexuality. Make a list first. A woman's list should include a Pap smear, a thorough breast and pelvic exam, and a contraceptive consultation if active with a male. A man's list should include a hernia check, testicular and prostate exam, and contraceptive consultation if active with a female. Any areas of tenderness, change, or questions about "normality" should be brought up.

D. Sit down with a close friend and describe your early and recent sexual experiences and attitudes to one another. This can be repeated with other friends and expanded to include discussion in a supportive (not a competitive) group.

E. Talk to selected family members about sexuality. Relatives such as sisters, brothers, and cousins often remember important things about family behavior. Parents, grandparents, uncles, and aunts often will talk about sexuality more readily now, and reveal things that will help you understand earlier messages.

F. Explore erotic literature, movies, art, and fantasy to expand what you like. Apply the same standards of taste and style that you usually enjoy.

G. Caress your erogenous zones carefully to discover and expand areas of sensitivity. Some people enjoy using a massage attachment, a vibrator, or a shower device for stimulation. Learn and practice self-pleasuring techniques so that they become spontaneous and comfortable.

H. If you are sexually active with a partner, communicate to him/her what you like. Avoid "spectating" (evaluating yourselves) and "performing" (setting standards to meet). The goal is pleasure, variety, intimacy, relaxation, and excitement.

I. Experience sexuality as often as you choose; feel free to initiate. According to the professional literature, the more often a person responds sexually in a comfortable way, by any method, the easier the response becomes. Emotion and sensuousness enhance the genital sexual experience for most women and men.

J. Compare your sexual beliefs and values with your actual behavior. Where they are different, develop a plan to bring them closer together and end the conflict.

For some individuals the above suggestions may not be challenging enough. Further ideas can be found in resources listed in Chapter 5, Part 5.

SAR-TYPE TRAINING

Sexuality is usually a private experience, and yet sharing insights with others is powerfully enriching. One way to do this is to attend a well conducted SAR-type course or workshop series. Information about the Sexual Attitude Restructuring format can be obtained from the National Sex Forum, 1523 Franklin St., San Francisco, CA 94109. They have provided this intense learning event for thousands of professionals. Other sexuality educators have designed variations which are offered in most areas. Therefore counselors need to know the details before enrolling. These may be called Sexual Values Reassessment and focus on a topic or point-of-view.

The usual format is to expose a group to large amounts of explicit sexual audio-visual material, followed by structured small group discussion. Some courses include movement and relaxation exercises, breathing practice, massage, guided imagery/fantasy, role playing, and other awareness creating techniques. Naturally much of the effectiveness depends on the leaders' skill in designing the experience and working with groups. As in any experiential training, the individual needs to be aware of ethical issues, of vulnerabilities, and of responsibility for himself/herself while participating.

Positive data is available on the effects of SAR training, and completion is a requirement for some training programs and certifications. The purpose is to expand awareness beyond the restrictions of individual sexual experience, so that counselors can readily understand and talk directly about the variety of human sexual expression. In feedback presented during sexuality counselor training by Haskel Coplin, Ph.D., Amherst College, the following were evaluated as factors which were highly important to members of his SAR-type training courses:

Discussing attitudes and feelings openly

Exposure to explicit sexual visual material

Being give permission by the group to "own" one's sexual feelings

A positive, comfortable setting and informal atmosphere

Receiving specific information about sexual matters

"Self actualization," experience of self as released from early negative conditioning about sexuality

"Sensory flooding," a high dosage of erotic materials not previously experienced.

The following were reported as having little or no effect:

Being able to model after others

Getting insight into the causes of one's hangups

Receiving encouragement to experiment with new forms of behavior.

Apparently the majority of participants in a well run SAR find that their attitudes and understanding are affected more than their behavior, which seems appropriate to the professional purpose of these courses.

Recognizing the potential benefits from a good SAR type workshop, then the suggestion is for a counselor to consider the following:

1. Participate in a good SAR type workshop so as to be exposed to facets of experience which cannot be duplicated by self study alone.

2. Because of the intensity of SAR type experiences, attend a low-key workshop before signing up for a high impact one.

3. Look for recognized credentials in the leader or follow recommendations from someone whose judgment can be trusted, because these experiences are powerful.

4. Ask a counselor training group of which you are or can become a member to arrange for the workshop to be made available to that group only.

5. Choose to have no SAR-type course in preference to attending a poor one.

LEARNING EXPERIENCE NO. 28

Several fill-in-the-blank sex history forms are available to organize information about a person's sexuality. A helpful procedure is to complete one, using yourself as the subject. The following *Sexual Experience Overview* is a different kind of "checklist"; however, the questions are open-ended.

A. Write your responses to the following 10 activities in a private notebook, or dictate them into a tape recorder, taking whatever time is needed to be thorough.

1. Identify when you were first aware of yourself as a sexual being. How did that come about?

2. Consider the sexuality education (planned and informal) that you received. As you look back now, what did you really learn?

3. Recall the body image you had before, during and after puberty. How does the way you look affect your sexuality and self concept?

4. List some of the most positive sexual experiences you have had in your life. Add some words or phrases that clarify what made them so good.

5. Make a list of mixed or negative sexual experiences. Take each one and try to pinpoint its effect on you. Can you put it into words? Try.

6. Consider what is left out. Do you have "screen memories" of earlier experiences or partly denied ones? Did you have

sexual encounters that just weren't conventional or "didn't fit?" What about recurrent dreams or fantasies with sexual content? Did significant sex-related experiences, which occurred to close friends and family, have an impact on you? Make note of all these things.

7. Describe your present sexual expression and behavior. If you are largely celibate, is that comfortable? If you are sexually active, do you enjoy a variety of self and other pleasuring?

8. Identify how being either male or female has affected your sexual expression at different times in your life. Now?

9. Using descriptive terms, decide whether or not you have had a sexual problem. If so, what were they (it)? Do you have a sexual concern now? How would you describe it?

10. Outline the kind of sexual experiences you expect for the future. Hope for? If you can envision a better sex life, what can you do to make more positive sexual experiences really happen?

B. Put away the tape or notebook for at least a month, and then review what you originally expressed. To your surprise, doing some mulling over of your own sex history may have led you to remember more, or come to new insights.

C. Complete the following:

I, (your name) , am a sexual being. For me this means:

_____

_____

_____

D. Discuss your summary with a trusted person, if possible, or in a supportive group. No one else can define your sexuality, but others can help you refine its meaning in your life.

COGNITIVE AND NONCOGNITIVE ATTITUDES

Many helpers find that they have the "correct" knowledge and intellectual attitudes about sexuality, but that their emotions sometimes surprise them. Also a few people with either sexual disinterest or acting out are attracted to sexuality counseling because "it doesn't bother me." If a trainee has a covert agenda that others should become more controlled,or that "anything goes," he/she may be conflicted when learning about masturbation techniques or nongenital pleasuring during training. If the difference between one's deeper reactions and what is being studied are mild, the training will help bring about integration, but a counselor educator should be consulted about greater discrepancies.

LEARNING EXPERIENCE NO. 29

A. **Recognize your own assumptions about sexuality. To do so the following is intended to help you see where some conflicts could exist by looking at comfort with various types of client issues.**

1. **With what kinds of clients do you have greatest difficulty in working: age, race, sex, economic women, children, or adolescents, rape and violence, or other?**

2. **With what kinds of client values and problems related to sexuality do you have the greatest difficulty working: the "everything goes" conflict with parental values, pregnancy termination or continuation, illness and sexuality, potency issues, exploitation of women, children, or adolescents, rape and violence, or other?**

3. **What kinds of struggles have you had between your own sexual beliefs and behaviors in the past, and how others conduct themselves? Can you identify any covert assumptions you have about sexuality?**

4. **From where did the basis for answers to No. 3 come? How is this related to conflicts you have between what you think and**

how you feel, between what you "know" and how you actually react? What is your actual belief system about how sexuality is/should be for people?

B. Record your responses to the preceding four items.

C. Rethink in three or four weeks your response to the preceding four items. Can you see ways in which your answers reflect deep attitudes which could result in your being more helpful to some clients, and less so to others? On what inner reactions do you need to work in order to become more congruent, and to give a wider range of clients an opportunity for a fair chance in counseling with you?

D. Develop a plan to become aware of personal biases and to integrate your cognitive and noncognitive responses to more sexual issues.

POSSIBLE PROBLEMS

In-depth training in any area of counseling is likely to result in some personal stress or temporary conflict. This is true when focusing on issues like suicide, substance abuse, grief work, depression, or disability. Participants in sexuality counseling training usually report some discomfort and this is understandable. Very few people have a totally positive sexuality history, and value/behavior conflicts are more the rule than the exception.

As the learning experiences are worked through and training continued, most counselors arrive at broader self acceptance and understanding. The process helps the counselor be more sympathetic concerning client's anxiety about sexuality. Professional growth is not facilitated by prolonged or deep distress. If this occurs, the counselor should seek professional help, and suspend work on sexuality training until it can proceed comfortably. Rather than judging this as a setback, the person can realize that an obstacle was there to overcome. Personal growth enhances one both as an individual and a counselor.

Each of us have had our own background of experiences which could cause us personal problems, and we may or may not be aware of them. Recognizing these and their potential interference with effective counseling is not always easy. The following are a few *warning signals* to help with introspection:

1. Memories of early sexual experiences which were partially "blocked out," especially incest or child abuse.

2. Flashbacks of any forced sexual experience (emotional as well as physical coercion).

3. Persistent doubts about life style choice which are not settled, whether celibacy, marriage, living together, homosexuality, casual sex, or other.

4. An awareness of sexual disinterest, sexual inhibition, or sexual aversion which does not diminish with training.

5. Any marked increase or new appearance of a sexual dysfunction such as premature or delayed ejaculation, impotence, vaginismus, anorgasmia, and so forth.

6. Anxiety about "performing" during sex, a marked increase in "spectating," fear of losing control, or compulsion toward unwanted sexual expression.

7. Increased concern about an important sexuality-related issue like childbirth, premarital sex, oral sex, venereal disease, sex role stereotypes, or other.

8. Impulsive sexual behavior which could be exploitive or destructive to self or others.

9. Discovering a growing tendency to feel hostile toward one's own or the other sex, or toward any other group.

10. Increasing rigidity, guilt, moralizing, intellectualization, or depression about sex.

To repeat, most people will experience some of the preceding warning signals or other conflicts in a transient way. They will wonder about their body image or how "normal" their sexual response is, and work the questions out through the learning experiences, a partner, or a friend, or training group. To seek professional counseling is wise when these routes do not lead to direct improvement or when concerns like those listed as warning signals persist. Some people take counseling training to resolve known problems on a "do it yourself" basis, when a more effective approach is to sit in the client's chair and accomplish that first.

Not many counselor reactions are problematic during training. A more common, delightful effect of sexuality counseling study is increased interest and enjoyment in sex. Perhaps it is simply learning new ideas and the investment of energy, but many people report that doing training removes blocks to sexual fulfillment which they hardly knew existed.

PERSONAL RELATIONSHIPS

Another area of concern is that increased knowledge and broadened attitudes about sexuality can put stress on the counselor's relationships, especially if there are pre-existing problems. When the counselor has usually "taken the lead" in sex, then the new learning by the counselor may cause him/her to have increased expectations which can pressure a partner. Change also can be threatening if the counselor had previously been more passive. During training some interpersonal dynamics and sexual expression will change, so consideration must be given to the counselor's intimate relationships.

Time is required for a couple to make mutually satisfying adjustments and the person learning sexuality counseling can not expect instant fulfillment. Finding fault with another's lovemaking from an "expert" point of view can lead to serious, even unreconcilable conflict. Should a sexual dysfunction or significant relationship problem exist, seeking outside help is wiser than trying to be both counselor and partner. While potential risks do exist, the great majority of people who are learning sexuality counseling report highly positive benefits for their intimate relationships.

Other significant people also may react to the counselor's interest in sexuality as if it were threatening. When others become aware that someone is becoming proficient in sexuality counseling, mixed reactions can occur. Remarks may be made at staff meetings or social occasions that are half teasing, half put-down, and half interested (that sum does not add up, but neither do these kinds of comments). This is an opportunity to demonstrate comfort in talking about sexuality by not responding to double-entendres, to jibes about "fads" in counseling, or to jabs at the counselor's motives.

Most counselors get a few remarks that are so raw or personally insulting that to react professionally is difficult:

> *"Now I know what your divorce was all about."*
> *"How can your type of person give advice about SEX?"*
> *"I always thought you had queer interests, old pal."*
> *"If you can't do it, talk about it!"*
> *"Let's go where you can show me what you put out now."*

Knowing that some people are reacting to their own feelings of competitiveness, inadequacy, and discomfort about sex helps a little. Positive confrontation is sometimes necessary, because avoidance may imply acceptance. Usually a few assertive comments about the therapeutic effects of sexuality counseling for your clients, and an admission that it is seldom boring, will generate public acceptance and distance the jokers.

Having come this far in the training program, probably some personal changes have occurred or can be expected. To gain more understanding of oneself in relation to others at this time in the training, Learning Experience No. 30 is provided.

LEARNING EXPERIENCE NO. 30

A. **Complete the following in regards to yourself as you are at this time:**

1. **Compared to people with whom you work and other acquaintances, are your attitudes and sexual behavior (circle one):**
   Conservative   Moderate   Liberal

2. Have your attitudes and sexual behavior changed in the last:

Five years	yes	no
Three years	yes	no
One year	yes	no
Half year	yes	no
Month	yes	no

3. Jot down what aspects have changed after the yes answers.

4. Compared to your family of origin, are your attitudes and sexual behavior: (circle one)

   Conservative   Moderate   Liberal

5. Compared to sex partners or intimate friends, are your attitudes and sexual behavior: (circle one)

   Conservative   Moderate   Liberal

6. In terms of being open about your sexuality, consider the following list:

   Mother, Father, Sister, Brother, Social acquaintances, Clients, Students, Clergy, Health care professionals, Supervisors, Teachers/professors, Mentor, Long time friend, Current friend of the same sex, Current friend of the other sex, Present lover or partner, Colleagues, Other.

   Then rank the top three from the list using their actual initials for each of the following:

   a. I can communicate sexual attitudes and values to __
      _____
      _____

   b. I can be most honest about my sexual behavior with
      _____
      _____

   c. I avoid discussing sexuality with _____
      _____
      _____

        d. **I actually misinform or cannot be honest about sexuality with** _____

_____

_____

        e. **I would like to begin to be more open about changes in my sexual beliefs, needs, and experiences with__**

_____

_____

B. **Put the list aside, then review it in two weeks. Is there anything you want to change? Are there people you would like to be clearer with? Do not be surprised if you differ from some valued family and friends in what you know and believe about sexuality, after studying counseling.**

C. **Allow time and good communication to bridge the gaps, especially if any marked changes have occurred for you in the last 1 to 2 years. How will you handle differences which may arise, and be positive about yourself, whether they are resolved or not? Can you accept the right to different viewpoints as you would in politics, and not personalize or get into win-lose situations?**

D. **Try to sort out what it is that makes differences about sexuality seem so intensely alienating and significant to some people.**

PROFESSIONAL RISKS

A counselor cannot practice in a vacuum and must rely on others for cooperation, referrals, and administrative support. No areas in human services are more controversial than those involving sexuality. Even so, or perhaps because of the controversy, many people simply prefer to ignore the topic. Professionals who do sexuality counseling in a college, rehabilitation facility, social agency, residential facility, or any other setting are likely to encounter both overt and subtle resistance. Self confidence is necessary to tolerate harmful attitudes from others and still accomplish good work.

Counselor education programs strongly encourage helpers to apply insights learned from their work with individuals toward improving the larger system. Most people find that the more they know about a subject, the more sure they are about the value of change, and the more urgent is their need to do something. When new awareness is growing, a helper can be overwhelmed with the need to convince others immediately. This can be problematic when sexuality is involved.

EXAMPLE: School Counselor, Urban Junior High

A young woman became frustrated doing career guidance with school dropouts and began to see life planning issues as critical. She found it easy to talk to students about sexuality and took some in-service workshops on adolescent sexual problems. Some of the experiences described by the students were very similar to the counselor's in junior high, but most of those memories had been repressed. In a short time, the counselor became enraged at the number of pregnancies, forced sex, incest, conflicted abortions, and pressure for intercourse as described by her clients. She took these concerns in anecdotal form to the parent-teacher group. As a result the counselor's contract was barely renewed after alarm about public relations.

The counselor gathered data and laid careful groundwork, while continuing to see individual students under the supervision of a sexuality counselor, with the approval of the guidance director. Two years later, the school board initiated the beginnings of a sexuality education program after a balanced, informative presentation led by the counselor. Other counselors also will find that "being right" about sexual issues is often not sufficient, and that considerable negotiation and education of others is needed to do sexuality counseling effectively.

Courage is an unexpected necessity in sexuality-related counseling and education, and comes after thoughtful knowledge of oneself. Because sexuality is still a volatile topic, even with people one knows well, restraint is also a necessary quality. Individuals who are usually supportive may question aspects of sexuality counseling, and a counselor can weather that best by anticipating it. Expanding the circle of people with whom one can really be honest will help the counselor clarify ideas and attitudes about sexuality and keep a balance between caution and courage.

CONCLUSION

Learning any specialty has its assets and drawbacks in terms of how the counselor is affected. Because talking and acting somewhat sexual is part of many social situations, it may be difficult to distinguish when a purely professional demeanor is expected. Also, many sexuality-related questions and comments arising from the media and people's personal problems may be focused on the sexuality counselor when he/she is "off duty." In time, one learns graceful ways of handling these situations and leaving one's responsibilities at work. Overall, having expertise in an area which is interesting and important to most people is generally positive.

Part of the gift a counselor gives a client is contact with a real human being who has rich experiences and individualized values. The goal is to help the client attain his/her own sexual belief/behavior system and in no way to replicate the counselor's. When a helper owns his/her sexual style as an individual, and in no way perceives those reactions as universal, the helper will not want anyone else to adopt them. In doing so, no conflict or power struggle will occur within the counselor or between the dyad. A free feeling can be achieved by owning one's integration and by believing absolutely in the client's ability to forge meaning from his/her own raw material. Counselors can model health and be capable of higher level practice by working through their own conflicts and attaining personal sexual integration.

CHAPTER

COUNSELING SKILLS
APPLIED TO SEXUAL
ISSUES

Research on the counseling process has arrived at the point where we can say:

1. No two people provide counseling in exactly the same manner;

2. Yet competent counselors offer services which are essentially similar.

How can this be? Beginning with the identification of key elements in the helping process by Carl Rogers (1942), researchers such as Carkhuff (1983), Ivey (1980), Kagan (1975), and many others have continued to delineate exactly what facilitates or impedes growth during the counseling process. Classic texts which are listed under "Resources" summarize the fund of knowledge which a trainee can combine with courses, workshops, and labs. While counseling is an art as well as a science, much has been de-mystified so that a conscientious person can develop the necessary skills.

LEARNING EXPERIENCE NO. 31

A. Tape record a 30 minute interview with a well adjusted person who is willing to discuss a sex-related subject that is usually difficult for them. Your purpose will be to draw the person out, identify the uncomfortable aspects, clarify, and summarize. Before beginning, make it clear that the goal is to evaluate your counseling skills and to help them discuss this subject more easily, not to focus on or resolve deeper problems.

B. Since most people interested in sexuality counseling have already studied general counseling, obtain a valued textbook on the helping process and review it. Refresh yourself with its vocabulary and then review the tape of your interview. Listen to your input rather than the client's, to evaluate what you were doing. What aspects do you like and not like on playback?

C. From the list provided in the Suggested Resources on General Counseling, choose two or more to enlarge your familiarity with the process. After reading them, listen again to the tape, evaluating your strengths and weaknesses in an opening interview. If possible, do this with a colleague for more objective input. Further 30 to 50 minute interviews, followed by critical review of your counseling techniques, will integrate your counseling skills with sexual issues.

RESOURCES REGARDING GENERAL COUNSELING

The following are only some of the best current sources of information on the counseling process. Varying levels of sophistication are represented, and while some are oriented toward theory, others are more applied in their approach. Many contain practice exercises or are accompanied by workbooks and useful "how to" information.

The growing field of counseling is so rich that many of these could be read with new learning rather than repetition. For further detailed instruction, counseling journals contain up-to-date articles.

Auvenshine, C., & Noffsinger, A. (1983). *Counseling, issues and procedures in the health and human services.* Baltimore, MD: Universtiy Park Press.

Baruth, L., & Huber, C. (1985). *Counseling and psychotherapy: Theoretical analysis and skills applications.* Columbus, OH: Charles E. Merrill Publishing.

Benjamin, A. (1981). *The helping interview* (3rd ed.). Boston: Houghton Mifflin.

Brammer, L. (1985). *The helping relationship: Process and skills* (3rd ed.). Englewood Cliffs, NJ: Prentice-Hall.

Carkhuff, R. (1983). *The art of helping* (5th ed.). Student workbook and trainer's guide available. Amherst, MA: Human Relations Development Press.

Carkhuff, R., & Anthony, W. (1983). *The skills of helping.* Amherst, MA: Human Resource Development Press. Videotapes and workbooks available.

Corey, G. (1982). *Theory and practice of counseling and psychotherapy.* Monterey, CA: Brooks/Cole.

Combs, A., & Avila, D. (1985). *Helping relationships: Basic concepts for the helping professions* (3rd ed.). Newton, MA: Allyn & Bacon.

Cormier, W., & Cormier, L. (1985). *Interviewing strategies for helpers.* Monterey, CA: Brooks/Cole.

Egan, G. (1982). *The skilled helper: A model for systematic helping and interpersonal relating* (2nd ed.). Monterey, CA: Brooks-Cole.

Gazda, G., Asbury, F., Balzer, F., Childers, W., & Walters, R. (1984). *Human relations skills development* (3rd ed.). Newton, MA: Allyn and Bacon.

Ivey, A. (1980). *Counseling and psychotherapy: Skills, theories and practice.* Englewood Cliffs, NJ: Prentice-Hall.

Kanfer, F., & Goldstein, A. (1985). *Helping people change: A textbook of methods* (3rd ed.). New York: Pergamon Press.

Kagan, J. (1979). Influencing human interaction: Eleven years with IPR. *Canadian Counselor, 9:2,* 2, 74-97.

Okun, B. (1982). *Effective helping.* Monterey, CA: Brooks/Cole.

Patterson, C. (1980). *Theories of counseling and psychotherapy.* (3rd ed.). NY: Harper and Row.

Perls, F. (1973). *The Gestalt approach and eye witness to therapy.* Ben Lomond, CA: Science and Behavior Books.

Pietrofesa, J., Hoffman, C., & Splete, H. (1984). *Counseling: An introduction* (2nd ed.). Boston, MA: Houghton Mifflin.

Rogers, C. (1942). *Counseling and psychotherapy.* Boston: Houghton Mifflin.

Rogers, C. (1951). *Client centered therapy.* Boston, MA: Houghton, Mifflin.

Sydnor, G., & Parkhill, N. (1973). *Systematic human relations training: A programmed manual.* Monroe, LA: Human Relations Development Training Institute.

Wicks, R., & Parsons, R. (1984). *Counseling strategies and interviewing techniques for the human services.* (2nd ed.). NY: Longman Publishers.

PART 1. THE COUNSELING PROCESS

Because sexuality counseling is practiced by individuals from many different training backgrounds, a common vocabulary is needed in order to communicate. Regardless of one's original model, the following is presented as a synthesis for use in sexuality counseling. Any approach used should stress careful evaluation of progress and flexible application to the individual case.

WHAT HAPPENS DURING COUNSELING?

Early researchers defined basic counselor attributes such as empathy, genuiness, and positive regard, and then gradually discovered the importance of specific skills such as appropriate self disclosure and therapeutic confrontation. After a while, a grumbling in the literature criticized helpers for simply forming talking relationships, so the emphasis evolved toward counseling for measurable change. This coincided with a wider use of behavioral techniques and cognitive strategies, so an importance was placed on goal setting and evaluation. At regular intervals throughout the history of research on counseling, strong, persuasive arguments have been made for the vital role of the counseling relationship itself.

Generally accepted is a flow to the helping process, from exploration and assessment, through focus and goal setting, to intervention and strategies for change. One can subscribe to a two-stage model such as Ivey's "listening" and "influencing", or Gerald Egan's (1982) four-stage, eight step elaboration, or others which emphasize any phase, but the process is essentially similar. Regardless of conceptual model, the counselor must realize that treatment is occurring in all phases from the time of the first greeting until after termination. In Figure 4 is presented a diagram of the counseling process which is the model used in this book. An eclectic model allows a practitioner to identify when counseling is or is not going well and why.

Phase Number	I	II	III
Name of Phase	Cooperation	Focus	Working Through
Activities During Counseling	Establishing Rapport	Developing Themes	Strategies for Change
	Exploring Concerns	Deeper Work	Intervention/ Homework
	Determining Tentative Direction	Mutual Assessment	Evaluation/ Modification
Product	Working Relationship	Clear Objectives	Improvement

Figure 4. A diagram of the counseling process.

During counseling, the client can be expected to cycle back and forth through the phases, both during and between sessions. Rather than one-way movement, a continous spiral would be a better image, in which assessment, focus, and improvement continue through various levels of problems and growth. For instance, a client may initially describe a sex-related trauma like rape, and yet come back for a second session needing to build the counseling relationship before going deeper into threatening material. Another client may seem to stay fixed in exploration, or else want to set goals prematurely, and then it is the professional's experience which can clarify what needs to precede or follow where the client is.

What is a frequent mistake in counseling? Most new counselors listen some, as in Phase I, the *Cooperation Phase,* and then jump to problem solving and prescribing, as in Phase III, the *Working Through Phase*. They meet with resistance or inadequate progress, go back to question and then ahead to solve, thus putting the client in the passive role. For a convincing learning experience, a counselor can try this negative model with someone who has severe menstrual cramps or a person experiencing sexual disinterest (with the person's foreknowledge of the experimental nature of the interviewing). The complete ineffectiveness of the "quick listen and prescribe" model will become apparent, and hopefully alert the counselor when falling into that pattern again.

Initially the client has a set of symptoms or concerns, and simply exploring them with the counselor is basically therapeutic. This builds the relationship and leads naturally to the second, or focus phase, which is the least understood and most often skipped. Many successes will be just luck until one develops an array of attitudes, skills, and techniques which help both counselor and client learn what the issues really are. Usually clients come to a helper because they cannot focus effectively, and significant blocks may need to be worked through. As the real issues emerge, directionality develops in the focus process; Phase II is concluded as mutually agreed upon goals are defined.

A large amount of literature is available pertaining to Phase III, the *Working Through Phase* of counseling. The bonus of a solid focus in Phase II, the *Focus Phase,* is that interventions which work are then much easier to design. By the actual treatment phase, the counselor has had an opportunity to model ways of approaching problems which makes them more manageable and helps alleviate discouragement. Arguments about the efficacy of insight/education vs. behavioral assignments abound, and clear goals help the counselor and client develop a combination to meet their needs. Sexuality counseling is especially strong in both insight and behavioral approaches, so the challenge for the counselor is to select appropriately and follow through carefully.

LEARNING SPECIFIC SKILLS

The teaching literature on counseling is almost overly explicit on the elements of Phase I, Cooperation Phase, since detailed suggestions exist on discrete aspects like non-verbal empathy (mirroring) and summary feeling statements. Assessment skills also can be learned in a step-by-step manner, because with experience the counselor can reflect on what is being presented in order to make decisions about direction. Once attained, skills in building the relationship and exploring concerns tend to be second nature, and the counselor learns to adjust for many client personalities and resistances. Some successful counselors describe their subjective experience as a kind of mildly altered state, in which all their attention is deeply focused on hearing and relating to the whole client.

Phase II, Focus, has a bewildering array of theory and techniques for focusing and goal setting, but agreement is minimal among different authors and schools. Focusing is an evolving area of mental health work which can be impactful for the client, and some methods are controversial. Usually counselors are first trained in direct verbal techniques like asking for alternatives, reframing a problem, imaging "ideal" solutions, therapeutic confrontation, centering questions ("what" rather than "why," a focus on "needs" rather than "shoulds"), and ways of formulating realistic behavioral and attitudinal goals. In addition helpers may be exposed to one or two theories with specific focusing techniques, such as Adlerian and systems theory, or an approach to problem oriented casework and behavior therapy, or psychosynthesis and pastoral counseling.

Many counselors find, with experience, that they need additional focusing approaches to add to their individual repertoire. The spectrum ranges from the powerful but gentle client-centered technique of helping the client confront self, to TA script or "game" analysis, art and movement therapy approaches, intense Gestalt methods, Bioenergetic centering, postures and pain pressure points, NLP anchoring, or rebirthing exercises. Gendlin's focusing process, the Rational-Emotive approach by Ellis, guided imagery, aspects of Glasser's Reality Therapy, and behavioral techniques like desensitization heirarchies also are widely used. Because many focusing techniques are part of a complex system, each new focusing approach must be studied with great care, without claiming expertise after a two-day workshop.

For skill in Phase III, Working Through Phase, the counselor can add therapeutic intervention strategies gleaned from reading, experience, and seminars. Some knowledge of learning theory is essential, since growth and change follow known principles of behavior. Many practitioners believe that clients have persuasive motivation not to change, and have subjective reasons for resistance and opposition. However, other trainers state that clients' resistance is not the problem, but rather uncreative counselors. Many of the resources in sexuality counseling give the practitioner suggested treatments for particular problems. Essentially the client must perceive the counselor as trustworthy and expert, so as to follow the suggested intervention toward mutually agreed upon goals.

COUNSELING VS. PSYCHOTHERAPY

Distinctions between counseling and psychotherapy come up most noticeably in Phases II and III, because listening, assessment, and relationship skills are essentially similar in both. Many theories of behavior change assume that their approaches will be used by both counselors and psychotherapists, as evidenced by conferences and textbooks which use both words in the title. Also most programs in counseling, clinical social work, and mental health nursing use the term psychotherapy for intensive or extended counseling.

One distinction which can be made for sexuality counseling is the ability of the client to be a full participant in the focusing and treatment phases. Without question, many techniques that could be utilized produce altered state of consciousness or result in change which is beyond the client's awareness. The suggestion here is that if a counselor uses a treatment technique to facilitate insight and movement with the client's full knowledge of purpose, that is counseling. When a trained person uses impactful techniques to bring about fundamental changes in the client, psychotherapy is occurring.

EXAMPLE: Differences Between Counseling and Psychotherapy

A person skilled in the use of guided imagery uses the technique to

1. Help a client get in touch with or improve attitudes toward his/her body image. This could be part of the focusing or treatment phase in counseling.

2. Change a client's perception of him/her self as feminine or masculine. This could be part of the treatment phase in psychotherapy.

Admittedly the differences are often very subtle. Distinctions cannot be made simply on the basis of techniques used or the helper's title. A continuum on the following variables can be visualized: the degree of client distress, the amount of fundamental change required, the ability of the client to fully participate, and the relationship of the presenting problem to the overall context of the client's life. Counseling shades into psychotherapy when the client needs broad or deeper change, and requires more intensive assistance in order to accomplish it. Counselors need to know their boundaries of practice and refer when appropriate.

COUNSELING SKILLS SELF ASSESSMENT

Self Assessment

A counselor needs listening and assessment skills, focusing skills, and treatment and evaluation skills. Few people have them in equal measure and room is always available for growth. The overall helping skills used in general counseling transfer smoothly to sexuality counseling and are basic to its success. Through study, counselors can adapt strategies for change developed in general counseling models to sex-related concerns, and apply some created specifically for sexual issues.

Figure 5 is provided to assist with self assessment of counseling skills. Responses to this checklist should be discussed with a more experienced counselor, who need not be a specialist in sexuality. The trainee can describe his/her specific counseling skills, being sure to dwell on the assets, giving examples from actual experience. Both can suggest a plan to strengthen those areas of counseling which need work. The usual methods are a reading program, coursework, video and audio tape analysis, workshops, joint counseling, and supervised practice. Writing an informal contract and checking with a mentor as counseling skills improve are helpful.

	High Level Skill	Moderate Skill	Need More Skill
Phase I: Cooperation			
Establishing Rapport	─────────	─────────	─────────
Exploring Concerns	─────────	─────────	─────────
Determining Tentative Direction	─────────	─────────	─────────
Phase II: Focus			
Developing Themes	─────────	─────────	─────────
Deeper Work	─────────	─────────	─────────
Mutual Assessment	─────────	─────────	─────────
Phase III: Working Through			
Strategies for Change	─────────	─────────	─────────
Intervention/ Homework	─────────	─────────	─────────
Evaluation/ Modification	─────────	─────────	─────────
Knowing where you are in the process	─────────	───────────	─────────
Knowing how to resolve lack of progress	─────────	─────────	─────────

Figure 5. General counseling skills checklist used for checking overall skills, not specific sexuality skills.

Caution

If the trainee knows very little about the counseling process, any attempt to do sexuality counseling with real people is unwise until coursework and supervision in general counseling is accomplished. The exercises in this book are intended to build upon skills and not to serve as a substitute for the necessary professional training in the basics. Naturally one's sexuality counseling can only be as good as one's general counseling skills and success in sex-related counseling will transfer positively to other counseling applications.

Encouragement

Surprisingly little exists in general counseling texts and courses about sexual issues. This integration must occur within the professional development of each individual as training in sexuality counseling proceeds. For that reason the trainee will sometimes be blazing trails, and can be creative in applying counseling approaches that work well in other areas to sexual concerns.

PART 2. PHASES

PHASE I: COOPERATION

Establishing Rapport
Exploring Concerns
Determining Tentative Direction

People who come to see a counselor often are indirect about their purpose, they may not now exactly what the trouble is, or they may be relieved to bring it right out. Whatever the timing , building a trusting, working relationship is important before one can expect much movement to take place. With some client/counselor dyads this may take ten minutes, but with others the testing continues for the duration of the counseling.

The counseling relationship often may be built with ease around sexual concerns, because the client has not shared them freely with many others. He/she can be relieved to find empathy instead of ridicule or judgement. Reflection of feelings, sensitivity to body language, and other means of attaining an *I-Thou* relationship are helpful here. Occasional brief self disclosure, willingness to use varied sexual language, and seeing things from the client's point of view are effective. Attitudes like "You're not alone, it certainly is hard to find out anything about sex," and "Your behavior was understandable in those circumstances," can be highly facilitative.

One thing to avoid in Phase I, the Cooperation Phase, is becoming too involved in the specific content of what clients report. Before the counselor has much experience, the details of how people make love or were victimized in a sex crime (or committed one) can result in ordinary conversation.

EXAMPLE: Responding to the Whole Communication

Client: *"When he wouldn't leave I knew what was going to happen."*

Counselor Error: *"Did he grab you there by the door?"*

Counselor Correct: *"You began to feel dread...as he kept drinking...(hanging around)...(toying with you)?"*

COMMENT: Counseling theory teaches that an empathy response, at an interchangeable level or deeper, facilitates exploring the problem; closed questions do not. If the error-type fact question is used, the client would talk about the rape as though the incident happened to someone else and is likely to take a recitation role while waiting for counselor questions.

Based on counseling research, the choice as to whether to use "dread" or another feeling word depends on the client's body language, and which of the content phrases to choose depends on the context. The skill is to stay with the client's experience in order to share her perception, almost as though she were reliving the incident in a safe place. The depth at which to work depends on the client's strength to handle the impact on herself, and the counselor's judgement of whether the rapport is strong enough for her to feel catharsis and support through it.

When counselors work with alcoholics they make note of what and how much is drunk, but their real interest is in more individual aspects of the problem. In the same way helpers working with people who make suicide attempts become skilled at hearing the underlying issues rather than the sensational details of attempted self destruction. Therefore sexuality counselors need to become so comfortable with sex that they are more interested in the individual than in specific sexual content.

EXAMPLE: Responding to Client Experience Rather Than Sexual Content

Counselor: *"So you liked it when your wife braided your pubic hair because of the playfulness, but it is still hard to ask her for anything? Could you say more about that? (Silence.) Is the surprise what turns you on, or do you hesitate because she might refuse?"*

COMMENT: The point is not to stay with sexual specifics during exploration but rather to understand the meaning of any sexual event. The above client could reply: *"Not exactly....I'd just feel kind of foolish..."* The counselor can help him find a way to let his wife know that he would like erotic surprises without asking for each one. The idea is to stay with his experience, not the details of sexual behavior.

Timing

How much exploration is necessary before focus and intervention begin? Counseling generally tends to stay with a client's issues rather that taking a directive, questioning approach. Sufficient listening is needed to gain perspective on what the client is concerned about and wants to accomplish. Counselors often employ a "give and take" approach, in which they listen and reflect, suggest some tentative focus, supply some education, and perhaps offer some remedial techniques. As this process continues, the counselor will see how much exploration and relationship building will be needed before major focusing and goal setting can be done.

Each professional has an individual way of putting a client at ease and facilitating the telling of their story. When the presenting problem is clearly sexual, it may be useful to do a sex history, either brief or formal. Some helpers use a printed form with a chronological outline, while many develop their own style of touching on key areas in a systematic but relaxed way. Some structured experience is recommended in order to form a basis for a flexible approach which can be modified for each client.

LEARNING EXPERIENCE NO. 32

A. **Look up sex history forms and structured interview outlines in books by Kinsey, Kaplan, Pomeroy, Hite, or Masters and Johnson; a basic sex history form is provided in the Appendix of this book. If you have the opportunity to read the book by W. Pomeroy entitled** *How to Take a Sex History,* **The Free Press, New York, or view the film by the same name, you will obtain useful insights. Phrases such as "how often..." rather than "have you ever..." are effective, as is alternating between comfortable and sensitive material.**

B. Choose one form or make a combination, and interview at least three adults using your form. You may or may not tape record; however, taking notes or filling out the form is essential. The goal is to practice history taking until you feel competent obtaining an overview of a person's sexual development, education, and experience.

Some sexual problems clearly require more historical background than others. For instance a young teenager who comes in about pressure to give oral sex in exchange for beer is likely to require less history taking than a midlife couple who says one of them never reaches climax. In any case be alert for whether or not sexual problems have existed for some time, whether the problems have a developmental history, or whether they are of fairly recent duration and a more proximate cause. Generalizations are not possible, however, so with experience the counselor will know how much time to spend exploring current concerns, and when to go into background learning through the sex history. In this matter one must be sensitive to the client as rapport is being established.

Pacing

From the very first counselor-client exchange, both relationship building and exploration of client concerns are occurring simultaneously.

> **EXAMPLE: Relationship Building, Initial Interview**
>
> **Counselor:** *"Won't you make yourself comfortable?"*
>
> **Client:** *"Sure, but I'd rather be anywhere else."*
>
> **Counselor:** *"It's hard to talk about some things?"*
>
> **Client:** *"They say you are an expert in sex, but I don't know where to start."*
>
> **Counselor:** *"I'd like to help you with whatever it is, but we don't need to rush. Why don't you describe what is important to you?"*
>
> **Client:** *"You must see a million men like me, who can't satisfy a woman sexually."*

Counselor: *"You are right, many men do worry about that, Carl. If you'll clarify what's happening for you lately in terms of sex, we'll go from there."*

COMMENTS: Often pain causes people to seek help who would not otherwise. Just because a person starts talking about a sexual problem does not mean the counselor can assume rapport, and hurry on to focus and action. The counseling relationship needs attention at all stages of the process but most especially in the beginning. Also some issues such as sexual avoidance or victimization involve problems with intimacy, so that rapport building will possibly take longer. A lack of skill in forming relationships may be partial cause or effect of the sexual difficulty itself. Taking time to build rapport is essential because the client may remain consistently guarded if the counselor moves too fast.

EXAMPLE: Opening Discussion, 1st Session

Client: *"So my lover/husband/wife is going to leave if I don't do something about my sexual problem. I can't depend on a few quick drinks to get me in the mood either."*

Counselor Error: *"So describe how you usually make love,"* or *"Is alcohol abuse a problem for you?"*

Both leads are focusing and problem-oriented which would be threatening when no evidence of empathy/rapport has yet been demonstrated by the helper.

Counselor Correct: *"You have a real feeling of threat hanging over you and old solutions aren't working...."* OR any response which illustrates understanding for the client's painful situation: alone, fearful, angry, helpless, blamed—depending on context and body language.

COMMENTS: Inexperienced helpers may think reflection is empty repetition, when in fact a necessary component of counseling is to show the client regularly that the counselor is able to understand. Then further exploration will bring inner conflicts safely out into the open for consideration, as well as the external problems and pressures.

The formula developed by G. Sydnor and N. Parkhill (1973) in their Human Relations Training series is a good fallback for even the most experienced professional: *"You feel ___X___ because of ___Y___."* If the counselor can stop action at any point and use this formula to restate the client's inner experience, then real empathy has been achieved. With time the helper needs to make only occasional deliberate empathy reflections, e.g., at ambiguous points to check accuracy, for help at stress points, to reassure the client of support, to encourage going farther into a difficult area, to respond to the client's reaction to confrontation, and to model good communication about sex.

A most important use of listening skills is to deepen the discussion and avoid going off on unproductive tangents. In sexuality counseling people can "bounce away" simply from embarassment or not knowing what to say, so the counselor must tactfully keep the exploration on track.

EXAMPLE: A Foster Parent, 1st Session

Client: *"So our own son Billy is 15 and never would have started anything, before Darren"* (temporary foster child, age 13) *"was placed with us. Billy's teachers have always said how well behaved he is, and I never have to remind him about his chores, and did I tell you about Billy's favorite...?"*

Counselor: (Gently raises one hand) *"You feel very proud of Billy, don't you...and you love him very much?"*

Client: *"Oh yes, and we can't have any more natural children, and now if he's in trouble...."*

Counselor: (Stays with her experience rather than the praise of Billy.) *"Of course. Naturally you would rather discuss how special Billy is than your worries about him and Darren."*

Client: *"But I am worried—the coach heard the other boys talking about Darren—and maybe about Billy—fooling around with those nasty girls when they got off the bus."*

Counselor: *"You sound angry and scared...at Darren, Billy, the girls, the gossip, and maybe even a little bit at yourself?"*

COMMENT: Staying with the client's experience is an empathic way to get to the real issues faster than the cleverest cross examination of content. At this point the client is the mother, and her tendency to defend her parenting skills with her natural son must be acknowledged. A potentially time consuming tangent has been redirected toward her real feelings, which will facilitate exploration of the boys' sexual behavior.

Accuracy in Listening

The counselor attempts to reflect the client's experience as completely as possible, but no one can be correct all the time. In the preceding example the mother might have denied being angry at Billy, but then gone on to say that she feels guilty for taking in foster children who are bad examples. The dialogue then would continue in an important direction. If the counselor is a little bit "off," the relationship can become stronger when the client is encouraged to correct the communication.

EXAMPLE: Somewhat Resistant 30 Year Old Teacher

Client: *"So I had a checkup like you said, and can you imagine they called it vaginismus?"*

Counselor: *"When the gynecologist was doing the pelvic exam she noticed a tightness around your vagina, and you felt surprised at the term vaginismus?"*

Client: *"Well no, that's not it at all. I was doing the exam OK, but it is funny that the doctor could notice it. Lately I've realized how much it has to do with my boyfriend."*

COMMENT: Actually the counselor seems very accurate in the reflection, but it seldom helps to argue exact words with a client. Following the client's recent awareness of variations in relationship to her boyfriend is more important. Some clients will "Yes but" and modify almost everything the counselor says, but continue to make progress as their exploration continues.

When people describe their experiences they may contradict, suppress, or change as they communicate. Rather than trying to point out passing incongruities, a better procedure is to stay with the client and reflect the journey as clearly as possible. People will often give a confused, changing, guarded picture about sexual concerns which clarifies during the process. Movement in understanding is desirable rather than trying to pin down definitive statements. The counselor will be more patient if he/she remembers that interventions will work much better at a later time when the client is clearer. The sessions spent expressing and evolving issues are worthwhile.

A matter-of-fact summary of mixed feelings can be helpful: "You have so many reactions to having sex with Jack. Sometimes you question it, at other times your voice is warm, often you praise men loving men, and yet on many occasions you seem angry about having to deal with bisexuality at all. What other attitudes do you feel?" If conflicts do not evolve over time to a more definite pattern, then it becomes clear that the ambivalence itself is part of the problem to be dealt with in later stages. In Phase I the counselor expands rather than tries to get to "bottom line" feelings rapidly, since that can lead to superficiality.

LEARNING EXPERIENCE NO. 33

A. Practice your Phase I skills and extend them into sex-related areas. Since some of this was done for Chapters 1 and 2, look for more challenge now.

B. Choose a person whom you know less well or who communicates with more difficulty than some of your earlier interviewees. Ask the person to discuss for 30 to 45 minutes what he/she thinks and feels about marriage and sexual behavior today. As rapport is built, invite the person to become more specific about aspects like monogamy, pornography, AIDS, premarital sex, and changing men's/women's roles. Don't push, but explore personal experiences if they are offered. Summarize to the person's satisfaction his/her views.

C. Repeat the activity in Item B several times, also selecting people whom you find personally appealing or intimidating (but do not have a personal relationship with). Tape one or more sessions.

D. Ask a colleague to review your tapes, checking to see whether your listening, empathy, and exploring skills, and relationship manner are as professional on sexual issues as they usually are in other mental health areas. Discuss your assessment of each interviewee's attitudes and possible problems with the aspects of sexuality which were discussed. Continue to ask for input on interview tapes until your skills in the first phase of sexuality counseling are comfortable.

PHASE II: FOCUS

Developing Themes
Deeper Work
Mutual Assessment

Seldom are dividing lines sharp in counseling. The helper will know when to begin focusing as the client repeats or goes off on tangents. Usually a theme, a relationship among variables, or a causal connection has emerged which provides the opportunity. The counselor can always go back later to explore other concerns (sexual or not), and the client may be more ready when some progress has been made.

EXAMPLE: Focusing, Developing Themes

Danny: (Middle of first session) *"So I was going to ask her out, but figured she'd rather dance with a tall guy..."*

Counselor: *"You weren't feeling confident about her response?"*

Danny: (Ten minutes later) *"When I went home I wanted to look at some pictures and fool around with myself, but that would be weak, so I watched some football."*

Counselor: (Focusing lead) *"You know Danny, you have brought up a couple of examples where you had a normal desire to date or be sexual, but kind of talked yourself out of it. Would you like to sort out what thoughts and feelings get in the way?"*

COMMENTS: Discovering the relationship among the underlying attitudes will be more productive than simple education about *"It's OK not to be tall, and masturbation is healthy."* The interchange which follows focusing marks a crucial point in counseling. Counselors have a natural tendency to want to prove and explain what they believe are helpful insights. But a better procedure in counseling is to follow a focusing lead with an empathy response, no matter what the client says. Time for the content can come later.

Danny: *"What good would it do? Knowing more won't help me get a girl."*

Counselor Error: (Follows own train of thought) *"But Danny, it's the self defeating way you are thinking about women and sex that leads you to give up...etc."*

Counselor Correct: (Follows client response) *"You seem so discouraged...as though there's no hope at all for a good social or sex life."*

COMMENTS: Continuing several exchanges like this, the counselor will be going deeper into Danny's helpless/hopeless feelings. Together they can surface Danny's irrational conviction that his height is the problem (short stature equals impotence), or that letting oneself care means losing all power in a relationship, or any of a hundred other doubts. Careful empathy and focusing will bring them out and also illustrate how Danny is creating his own failing script.

Danny: *"Sure, but it's not me that's doing the stopping."* (He goes on to give anecdotes about negative social experiences)

Counselor Error: *"But when each of these rejections happened, you put up a wall to avoid more turn downs."* (Argues in a way which puts blame on client)

Counselor Correct: *"They were so painful. Your eyes just sag and you look sick remembering the hurt. Let's talk about how anger helps you cope."*

COMMENTS: The counselor bypasses a content discussion about the client's defensive reaction and empathizes with his vulnerability as well as the anger. Gradually the counselor can focus on internal/external locus of control and Danny's tendency to project blame when hurt. "It makes sense to keep yourself away from a rebuff like that." and "Certainly we want to find ways for you to be social but not get hurt in that kind of situation," etc. It will be easier for Danny to change his fixed, social-avoidant belief system when he grasps the idea of how he has been protecting himself.

The counselor needs to recall repeatedly that most of the skill in sexuality counseling lies right here in the shared focus on issues. The client in the preceding example may have come to the counselor with the goal of wanting a girlfriend and "to get over his virginity", yet the counselor sees the self defeating atttitudes and behavior. Success will lie in the counselor's ability to arrive at a shared understanding with Danny about where the trouble is, and mutual focus on realistic goals. Having a weekly action plan to "get a girlfriend" would be hit or miss social coaching, with Danny continuing to sabotage himself and the helper pointing out mistakes. Focusing on the underlying problems will translate to a treatment plan with a higher probability of success.

Mutual goal setting is the eventual product of Phase II, but most often a series of tentative goals are explored and modified or rejected. In the preceeding example, several sessions may be set aside to discover and list self-defeating thoughts and behaviors, with Danny feeling successful as he finds them between sessions. With realistic goals at the end of Phase II, the counselor can easily help set up Phase III: a communication group, assertiveness skills, body image work, positive self talk, the martial arts (or other sports from rock climbing to flying), guided imagery, sex education, or whatever else would help. Danny's unconscious plan was to keep up his protective barriers and still achieve a satisfying sexual/intimacy life; this couldn't work, so the counselor helped him go deeper in Phase II and see the real problem before setting goals.

LEARNING EXPERIENCE NO. 34

A. Ask a cooperative colleague or acquaintance to discuss with you an area of sexuality that is puzzling or unclear to him/her. Explain that your task will be to clarify (focus) and not to problem solve. Tape the session and try to keep it to approximately 45 minutes in length.

B. Listen to the tape. Notice that you probably explored and indicated empathy (Phase I behavior) until you began to see patterns or a specific issue to follow. Write down your first focusing lead. Ask yourself:

1. Did I listen long enough to have a valid point of focus?

2. Am I sure the focusing lead was drawn from what the client was sharing and not from prior opinions of the client or from my own concerns?

3. Were my early focusing attempts phrased in a non-threatening way?

4. How did the client reply, and was my response to that one of empathy rather than pushing my point of view?

5. Do I notice how the content of the focusing improved and evolved as I worked with the client?

6. Did I find myself trying to give suggestions or to do problem solving instead of staying with the focusing?

7. Did the client indicate relief at being more clear about the issue after the interview?

C. Listen to the tape a few weeks later. Do you now hear the client expressing things you missed the first time? Can you think of a more helpful way to focus the concerns that were expressed? Write down how you would phrase some focusing leads, now that you have the benefit of hindsight.

D. Listen again to the ending. Was the client eagerly adding to the joint insight which was developing, or were you persuading a half-convinced person? If the latter, then you moved too fast, had an incorrect focus, or presented it in a threatening manner for that client. To be "right" is of no value if the client isn't with you.

E. Continue to practice this exercise again with other colleagues until you have real confidence in your ability to focus on sexual issues and arrive at mutual goals for improvement.

Accuracy in Focusing

The all-too-human counselor is bound to initiate some incorrect points of focus. However if the approach is tentative and non-judgemental, the client is moved to help find a more useful focus point. Working too hard in a grim, cognitive way is not productive; clarifying most of the deeper material requires trust and creativity. That is why each school of counseling has a variety of insight and uncovering techniques. A patient, flexible approach will allow the client to participate in arriving at valid themes on which to focus in order to set mutual goals.

More open rather than narrow focusing leads are helpful at first. For instance, "Don't you think your mother's emphasis on religion prevented you from owning your sexuality?" would not be as effective as "How do you look at the way your family's religious beliefs affected you as a sexual person?'' The client may say that their parents never agreed on anything, from religion to politics, and that the whole family took sides. At this point religion is not a useful focus for the client, but the influence of parental sexual attitudes could be approached from the direction of conflicted loyalties. Actually the best procedure is for the client to help evolve one focus point after another, rather than for the counselor to be "right" immediately each time.

In the beginning of the focus phase, counselors tend to use verbal techniques such as interpretative feeling statements, open-ended insight leads, and varieties of therapeutic confrontation. Increased directionality and counselor-client alignment emerges from this.

EXAMPLES: Helpful Counselor Responses, Early Focus Phase

"So you are feeling like a "dirty old man" when you have an erection here in the hospital and enjoy seeing all the nurses? Do you know that you looked the same ashamed way when you described the affair you had, which nearly broke up your marriage ten years ago? How do they seem alike?"

"Could it be that your teenage experience of always being on the defensive around your stepfather and uncle has led to this habitual body tension and recoil? Perhaps you're not cold at all, but just learned to be on guard against unwanted touch...and now it's a learned habit."

"On the one hand you have been insisting that you intend to sleep only with guys you really care about. Yet you laugh when you tell me that every weekend you wake up with a hangover after 'putting out' with someone you just met. What do you think is happening?"

Very often verbal techniques like those in the preceeding examples, followed by empathy and deeper exploration and insight, lead to mutual goals. Then the counselor goes into Phase III with more specific interventions which form a plan for improvement. Simple focusing techniques are the most elegant, and as long as they are sufficient for movement, they are preferable to more forceful or dramatic ones.

Deeper Work

Each school of counseling has some powerful and more elaborate focusing techniques for accelerated focusing. If direction is difficult to achieve through conventional verbal approaches alone, either because of the nature of the problem or the client's resistance, a more useful procedure can be to employ guided fantasy, role playing, a script analysis, Gendlin's focusing exercises, empty chair work, dream exploration, a data-base journal, or any recognized technique the counselor knows well. As Joseph Hollis, an experienced counselor-educator, states, some action is often necessary to integrate insights and behavior, thoughts and feelings (personal communication). The purpose is always to bring about a better understanding of the client's issues so that attainable, helpful goals can be set.

LEARNING EXPERIENCE NO. 35

A. Attend a workshop or training session where you will experience some powerful focusing techniques (Gestalt, Movement Therapy, NLP, Bioenergetics, Psychdrama, Rational-Emotive). If no group is available, contact a reputable therapist for several sessions to work through a real issue for yourself, with the understanding that some deeper focusing techniques will be used.

B. Jot down notes to yourself immediately after the experience, and then again at later intervals. Reread them to recall the compelling quality of the experiental exercises, and appreciate both the excitement and the vulnerable feelings. Do you remember the difference between exploring familiar ideas verbally, and then delving into unknown territory with a guide? What physical and emotional sensations occurred during the experience? Did you find that too much speed (or too little), or over-under interpretation by the counselor or workshop leader, interfered with your progress?

C. Summarize any awareness gained. Were new themes discovered, such as: *"A penis is an image of threat,"* *"Nobody will love me if I'm strong,"* *"My father never liked my kind of man,"* or *"Losing control, even in sex, feels impossible."* What do you know about yourself that you hadn't realized before?

D. Consider whether conventional counseling techniques could have helped you develop the same awareness. Also, can you think of other powerful techniques which could be used to arrive at the same focus, or go further? Work through your new insights to a comfortable level, and choose to volunteer for focusing technique as the opportunities arise and seem right.

One advantage to using multi-sensory or more powerful focusing techniques is to motivate the client. Through Phase I the counselor often begins to see what themes are emerging, and sometimes through traditional counseling interchanges in Phase II the client does too. However not all clients confront their issues and drop old rationalizations, projections, and habits easily.

EXAMPLE: Deeper Work, 5th Session

In order to focus below the surface, a counselor does a brief relaxation exercise with an intellectualizing client in his early 40's, and then chooses a fairly low key, modified TA exercise.

Counselor: *"Now Bill, you can picture the family kitchen in Philadelphia. I'd like you to just come out with any messages you can think of that your mother used to give you—'wash your hands, practice the trumpet, ...' what else?"* (Bill responds). *"Fine, and now what were some typical sayings from your father?"* (Bill replies). *"OK, Now would you kind of summarize them—as if they were put up on a family bulletin board?"*

Bill: *"Let's see. 'Don't make a mistake! Try hard.' Funny, that sounds all right, but I feel tight saying it...like I can't win."* (pause) *"They called me 'klutz' too."* (Red face)

Counselor: (Medium silence) *"You know, Bill, I guess those messages about possible failure were so deeply engrained that you hardly noticed...a sort of automatic caution."*

Bill: *"Yeah, for some crazy reason I just flashed back to what you said two weeks ago about my reaction to not having an erection..."*

COMMENTS: In this example the client will be more profoundly moved by his own insight than by the counselor's expertise about erection and the fear of failure. Earlier counseling exploration of family pressure, and education about negative expectations also played a part in the client's "ah ha" experience, but his own application to the sexual context will be remembered.

Some schools of counseling interpret and process the deeper focusing experiences, whereas others leave it to the client to make the associations. Certainly the counselor should *not* use uncovered feelings or insights as a way of proving a point forcefully ("I knew you loved as well as hated your brother during the painful doctor-sex games," or "You see it isn't just the abortion that led to the breakup but your fear of commitment"). Because of the many facets and the depth of an impactful focusing exercise, the counselor needs to avoid being too didactic or rushing to overinterpret. A helpful procedure is to guide the client supportively toward making applications to his/her present concerns.

EXAMPLE: Evolution of Feelings Without Premature Interpretation

A counselor asks a client to draw different family diagrams and symbols to express her relationship with an identical twin, and the diagrams clearly show a "good girl, bad girl" split. It might be wise to ask the client to leave these drawings and bring in more to illustrate the relationship with her family. This permission allows the client to become aware of potentially threatening but liberating material at her own pace. There is room for the evolution of feelings without premature interpretation, and whichever role the client assigns to herself can then be related to her sexual issue. A delicate balance must be maintained to facilitate a client's movement during focusing, but not to interfere so much that the client becomes a spectator of his/her own process.

LEARNING EXPERIENCE NO. 36

A. Listen to your best focusing tape from the previous learning experience. If you were to have further clarifying sessions with this client, what other focusing techniques might be useful? List those you have been trained to employ and others which you would like to learn.

B. If possible, request another interview with the same person and use more accelerated focusing techniques to further clarify his/her issues or find deeper concerns. Explain that the goal is to become even clearer about the client's experience, using more intensive approaches.

C. Practice this with others to expand your catalog of focusing techniques. Be sure to work with professional colleagues who understand the training nature of the experience. Practice in the focus area is potentially the most threatening to others, and therefore must be done with great care and respect.

Choice of Technique

Experience, training, and supervision help a counselor know when to go beyond traditional verbal techniques to the more powerful focusing approaches. Each client has an individual way of learning, so exercises must be individually designed. During any personal growth workshop, some people get more out of drawing or movement exercises, while others prefer word association, meditation, family sculpting, or role playing Adlerian early recollections. Trial and error is often needed, coupled with close observation, to determine which approach will be most helpful for a particular client.

Caution needs to be used when focusing. An impactful technique should not be used automatically, based on the type of problem. Not all couples with inhibited sexual desire will respond to getting their anger out with batakas (plastic bats), nor do all boys who are victims of sexual abuse need to stand on a chair and tell off a feared assailant. Specific techniques may be especially useful with a type of problem, but even then the priority must be the particular client.

Focusing techniques of any kind can alter the counseling climate, since the early rapport building and exploration feel more supportive. The client must move into unknown territory and try to integrate new thoughts and feelings. As focus evolves the client may become defensive about old habits and beliefs that aren't working, and needs to know that looking more deeply can lead to positive change.

Words of reassurance alone may not be sufficient. Sometimes an image, story, or metaphor will help. Holding onto a scarf and dropping it after asking the client to pull on the other end, makes the following exchange more meaningful. *"Do you feel effective pulling on the dropped scarf?"* (Allow time to process feelings.) *"Could that be how your boy(girl)friend feels during your withdrawal and quiet disapproval?"* (Allow time for seeing the other side.) *"What could you do to stay engaged in a negotiation, and not drop out?"* A positive image can be created together to illustrate sharing a problem in order to resolve it, such as the client and the partner carrying a canoe over a portage. Application to a sexual issue can then be made using more imagery, to achieve nondefensive understanding.

Because focusing techniques are both threatening and liberating, the emotional climate between client and counselor becomes more intense. At this point feelings are most acute, both real here and now ones and transference/countertransference. The client is most vulnerable, and at the same time the counselor is required to draw on cognitive, emotional, creative, and interpersonal resources in depth. The real encounter is most likely to happen at this point, and the counselor is urged to stay open to his/her own experience as a further avenue to understand what is happening with the client.

Carl Rogers (1951) stressed the necessity of genuineness and congruence on the part of the counselor; Perls (1973) modeled the avoidance of "chickenshit," "bullshit," and "elephantshit;" Ivey (1980) trained people in direct-mutual communication; and other schools support the importance of interpersonal warmth. During focusing no room exists for artiface or mixed messages from the counselor, and the client must feel especially safe with sexuality issues at stake.

According to most of the research, the Focus Phase (Phase II) is the place for increased genuiness about counselor feelings and reactions. For instance, a client who has episodes of a stereotyped butch or camp manner can hear a counselor's question about its intermittent timing without feeling criticized, if it seems part of an honest search for understanding. Owning the reactions as one's own ("I" rather than "you" messages), being descriptive rather than accusatory, and following with empathy are essential. Almost anything can be approached in the context of *"I've noticed...and wonder whether it can tell us anything about your problem with..., or is it something else?"*

Observations about obvious client characteristics can often be offered casually during the focus phase, to contribute to genuine openness. Counselors can say things like *"Of course I've noticed your height and athletic build and wish I had them too, but standing out might not always be comfortable I would guess,"* or *"You have shared your anger about your face breaking out, and I can feel for you because I had eczema for 7 or 8 years in my teens. It's hard to explain to anyone who has clear skin, isn't it?"* The only caveat is that the preceeding be meant honestly, not condescendingly, and with the intent of enhancing communication.

The focus phase usually continues until an area is understood and the client feels ready to begin to move ahead. In sexuality counseling an effective approach is to work on several subparts of a goal rather than exploring all possibilities. Sometimes a list or a visual diagram helps, where clients can see their spectrum of concerns and set priorities. The counselor can suggest: *"Let's focus on one or two for now and move ahead with those; that should help with the others."*

EXAMPLE: Letting the Couple Choose Direction, 4th Session

Counselor: *"So this diagram (shows Figure 6) indicates most of the concerns you have brought up in our three meetings. Can you see some connections and ideas for where to start improving things?"*

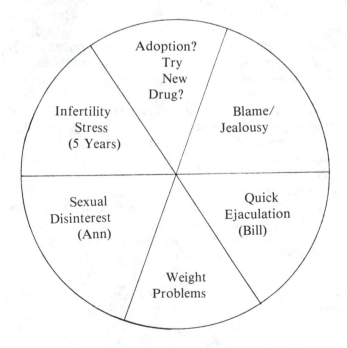

Figure 6. Diagram of concerns expressed by a couple.

Ann: *"Maybe I could stop threatening to leave if you wouldn't get mad and talk about seeing someone else."*

Bill: *"That would be a lot easier if I thought you ever wanted to have sex."*

Counselor: *"Let's find something you're each willing to do to improve the situation."*

COMMENTS: The counselor is wisely giving the couple choices about direction, so they will have an investment in making it work. From a systems point of view, many of the problems are interdependent and time will be available later to see the relationships among them. For now the counselor may be able to negotiate a 4 to 6 weeks "safety zone," where both agree to focus on the marriage and to do non-demanding sexual exercises. Other interventions and plans would be equally effective; the goal is to find some manageable points of focus and make progress.

Goal Setting

The counselor pulls together Phase II by helping the client set clear, realistic goals, based on the previous exploring and focusing. Tentative, sequential goals are more attainable than sweeping ones.

EXAMPLE: Enabling the Client to Have Input Over Time

A sixteen year old high school student learns that she is six weeks pregnant, and is shocked and confused. After a half hour:

Counselor Error: *"Well, it seems you have to decide whether to have a baby or not. An abortion is more complicated with every passing day."*

Counselor Correct: *"Naturally you are upset. You have mixed feelings and many pressures on you from your family and ex-boyfriend. Why don't we make it a goal to meet for at least a few minutes every day this week? You can cry or get mad, confide in others, get more information, and then before too long decide what is best for you?"*

COMMENTS: In the correct response, the counselor has established the girl's position as decision maker, has given permission to have mixed feelings, shown confidence in progress, and offered structure and support. An overloaded school nurse or counselor might find that 15 to 30 minutes a day with this client is less burdensome than any pressured, half-day decision session. Based on research, we know that working through a crisis causes a young person to move to a more mature developmental level, regardless of the content of that decision. Therefore goal setting which allows for as much input as possible is more important than the specific direction taken by the client.

Phrasing the goals. Training in behavioral counseling methods, and experience in writing educational objectives are helpful. Clients are confused by abstract, vague goals and need clarity.

EXAMPLE: Phrasing of Goals

Counselor Error: *"What about a goal then of regular orgasm with intercourse?"*

Counselor Correct: *"As a start, what about a goal of avoiding any experiences of painful intercourse, by substituting comfortable, mutual pleasuring? As long as sex is negative for you, no wonder you can't imagine what you would enjoy."*

The following characteristics should be incorporated into the formation of goals:

1. appropriate, individualized;

2. graduated, realistic;

3. clear and simple rather than complex;

4. measurable in some way;

5. within the client's power to attain; and

6. flexible, lend themselves to modification.

Most counseling texts have sections on goal setting, as do behavioral program guides and educational design books.

Goals must be genuinely understood and desired by the client in order to be successful. If there is ambivalence, this can be brought out and worked on but not ignored as goals are established.

EXAMPLE: Goals Differ Between Husband and Wife

Bob: *"So I want to work on having real sex rather than the substitute."*

Eileen: *"I can't seem to enjoy it — until I know how I feel about other things."*

Bob: *"Isn't that the normal thing though? How many years do we have left? Just because you had some surgery.... Well, I'm sure we just need a little push here."*

Counselor Error: *"OK. I'll outline some arousal exercises and we'll see about getting toward intercourse again as soon as possible."*

Counselor Correct: *"Let's keep working until we find a goal on which you both agree."*

Both: *"We would like to improve our sexual and personal relationship."*

Counselor: *"Good, you want the same overall goal. Now let's focus on exactly what is bothering each of you, because that is where some differences lie, I believe."*

COMMENT: More depth is clearly necessary here. If the husband finds emotional intimacy easier after sex, and the wife has now become aware of things which have bothered her for years, their ideas about a better marital life are very different. The resultant plan could include both counseling and sexual enrichment, so that each receives some of what they need and a power struggle is avoided.

As counselors work in Phase II and directionality develops, practice helps to translate themes into useful goal statements. Important counseling dialogue occurs as goals are struggled with. Even more positive outcomes occur as clients try, succeed, modify, fail, and change aspects of subgoals in their "real life" experience.

LEARNING EXPERIENCE NO. 37

A. **Recall your childhood, adolescence, and adult years and jot down some sexual concerns and problems you had. A few minor ones and some major issues will give good practice. For each one, write a general counseling goal statement and then some specific objectives for change. The following two problems with related goals and specific objectives are provided as illustrations:**

> **Problem No. 1.** *"I experienced 'funny feelings' with certain boys in high school and avoided dating them because they were the occasions of sin I had been taught about. I had hardly any social life."*

> **Goal: Looking back, a possible goal for counseling could have been the following: to learn about normal sexuality, and to examine religious teachings so I could make appropriate decisions for myself.**

> **Specific Objectives: I had a need to bring my overall sex education up to date, especially in regard to sexual arousal, to accept my sexual normalcy, to distinguish between feelings and actions, and develop trust in my ability to make ethical choices in social situations.**

> **Problem No. 2.** *"I idolized another guy in high school and even maneuvered to go to his summer camp. Then for three or four years I dated compulsively and pressured girls for sex to prove to myself I wasn't queer."*

> **Goal: Looking back the goal could have been the following: to develop an understanding of my feelings, and initiate more appropriate social/sexual interactions with girls (or people).**

Specific Objectives: My need was to learn more about arousal, role models, sexual expression, the male role, and sexual development. A clearer understanding of homosexuality would have been helpful, too. I also needed to think through what I really wanted from girls, and better ways than conquest to feel good about myself as a human being.

B. **Work on your examples, the more the better. Begin with general goals and then practice translating them into more specific objectives. Remember that this is the "what" and not the "how." A good writer of objectives could break down each of the above examples into even clearer, more concrete objectives. Ask for help from another counselor where you have difficulty finding goal statements or objectives for a particular problem.**

Pacing. Major skill in Phase II is the timing of the focusing and goal setting by the counselor. A balance is needed between following a client's every pathway, and prematurely cutting them off in order to set goals. Naturally counselors tend to see the issues first, and may expect that after considerable focusing clients will have the same awareness. Without specific goals being verbalized, however, treatment suggestions often must be over-explained and the client can lose direction.

Sometimes the only way to obtain a goal discussion is for the counselor to say *"Yes, a, b, c, and d are very important, but let's look more closely and set goals for one,"* (or work on a goal for themes underlying three of the problem areas). Clients are very quick to criticize "not getting anywhere," so the counselor can be confident encouraging work toward goals.

Human beings are not divided into compartments; therefore, the counselor and client may by necessity have to look at general personality or life issue rather than just sexual ones. When this occurs trainees are often uneasy about "getting off the subject", especially as goal setting is being accomplished. Remember that as the client comes up against deeper work or choices for change, related obstacles and problems will surface.

EXAMPLES: Relating Sexual Goals with Other Goals

A disabled client may need to look at a defeatist attitude toward a handicap, before refocusing on specific sexual goals. Or a woman might need to acknowledge the pain of her partner's past infidelity and go through some accepting and letting go, before she returns to the goal of becoming orgasmic. Fortunately, refocusing and covering related issues tend to go faster at the end of Phase II, since trust and a working relationship have been built.

Motivating. Often a useful incentive is to give clients choices about goals. A counselor might say: "You originally came to me about your delayed ejaculation and growing sexual avoidance. Now when I try to move toward sex-related goals you often change the subject to the kidney machine and dialysis, and concerns that your wife thinks the fatigue is laziness. Sometimes people put off talking about sex because they are discouraged, but other times they have more pressing issues. What do you think is happening here?"

Remember that the best goals and objectives are only useful with the client's participation. Overexplanation and urging are better avoided. When the point comes that some issues are fairly clear, a counselor must sit back and provide the opportunity for the client to make commitment to a goal.

PHASE III: WORKING THROUGH

Strategies for Change
Intervention/Homework
Evaluation/Modification

The counselor knows the time has arrived to initiate strategies for change when the client has agreed to a clear, appropriate goal in the focus phase. During Phase III, the *Working Through Phase,* the helper's expertise comes to the fore, but the counselor must maintain the client's active involvement in working through problems. Many sexual issues have well researched treatment procedures, but as recent controversies about success rates show, careful counselor judgement and client cooperation are vital.

Most sexuality counseling goals involve (1) knowledge, (2) attitudes and feelings, and (3) experience and behavior. Very often the counselor can explain the different components to clients and apply each to their concerns. The best sequence is that some knowledge eases some attitudes, resulting in some behavior change, which influences some feelings, which creates some readiness for more knowledge, and so on. Clearly another spiral. A treatment plan which involves non-threatening levels of all three gives the best results.

EXAMPLE: Post MI Client, Phase III Work, 3rd Session

Client Focus: *"So even though my sex life wasn't great before my heart attack, I desperately want to be alive and that means sexually too. My cardiologist says to resume normal relations, but I've been inactive these last six months."*

Client Goal: To make a broadened and improved sex life part of a holistic health plan.

Specific Objectives:

> To build confidence in self as a sexual person
> To regain the ability to become sexually aroused
> To improve lovemaking with partner

Counseling Suggestions:

1. Read the book by Barry and Emily McCarthy entitled *Sex and Satisfaction after Thirty* with your spouse. Discuss the first two chapters together this week. (KNOWLEDGE)

2. Note and report next week any fears, fantasies, and dreams about the hypothetical dangers of sex for people with heart disease. Jot down any you can possibly think of for discussion during next week's session. (FEELINGS)

3. Experience a half hour of non-genital caressing and pleasuring with your partner, taking turns giving and receiving, at least twice during this week. (BEHAVIOR)

The counselor might suggest the above for separate weeks, or two or three at once, depending on the client's readiness and the pressure of other issues. In subsequent sessions the counseling suggestions will be discussed and modified or increased, as circumstances indicate. Success lies not in completing rapid homework, but in lowering anxiety and having a comfortable increase in sexual pleasure.

Clarity

Written suggestions are more useful than merely verbal ones. A counselor can keep a stack of colored index cards or distinctive memo pads (or printed forms), and put each suggestion clearly in writing. The writing, however, is not done until the details have been agreed upon, or the process will seem too prescriptive and lead to client passivity. Each session which has Phase III work will contribute a new card to keep the treatment moving, and avoid giving the client "multiple choice" groups of vague suggestions.

Follow-up on counseling suggestions is extremely important, so that good case notes are efficient. Each session should begin with listening/exploration and focus, since new developments may require re-focus and modified goals. The previous week's homework is important, however, and can be brought into the ongoing discussion in a natural (not judgemental) manner.

EXAMPLE: Pregnant Woman, Avoiding Counselor Suggestion

Counselor: *"It sounds as though these last few days were very stressful. How are you feeling about what we discussed last week? The plan was to talk to your obstetrician about the effects of intercourse and orgasm, considering your cervical problems and history of miscarriage. How did it go?"*

Client: *"Yes, well...but as I was saying, my husband's binge and what you call 'abuse' took all my energy. I cancelled my clinic appointment this week...I didn't need any more pressure."*

Counselor: *"It was crucial to cope and take care of yourself* (empathy), *and maybe hard to even think about sex with him?"* (focus)

Client: *"Yes, or let anyone see the bruises. But now that he's sorry and being wonderful I can't refuse him. He would really give up on me then, don't you think? I was kind of scared two nights ago."*

Counselor: *"It must have been hard. Let's rethink our progress. You seem to have two major problems: safety for you and the baby, and improving your relationship with your husband. Which is emotionally more important to you?"* (Back to Phase II, deeper work)

COMMENT: A counselor who is disappointed because the client "didn't do her homework" has clearly lost perspective. Nothing was wrong with last week's counseling suggestion, but the situation changed. Now the counselor must re-focus with the client and help set new goals, being mindful of the risk of further abuse and possible miscarriage. Jumping ahead to action strategies such as she must see her doctor, bring husband in for counseling, contact Alanon, learn nonintercourse pleasuring techniques, join women's support group, practice saying no, and so forth are premature. New interventions will not work until the client has agreed to a goal for the coming week; sensitivity will be needed to help her choose realistic next steps.

General goals are important but are usually too global to work unless subdivided. Counseling suggestions cannot always be selected with precision, because neither the counselor nor the client can cognitively analyze all possible variables. Very often the point of the homework is to further refine objectives that are subparts of each general goal.

LEARNING EXPERIENCE NO. 38

A. For each of the client goals listed below, jot down some counseling suggestions or treatment strategies which are intended to influence (1) knowledge, (2) feelings, and (3) behavior. It is not necessary to be comprehensive.

1. A young woman has lupus, a non-contagious chronic illness, and cannot risk becoming pregnant. She decides that her goal

is to explore birth control options, learn to obtain her full share of sexual pleasure, and become confident interacting with potential partners. On what specific objectives would you work first, and why?

2. Social service workers have required a family to admit that generational boundaries around sex have become blurred. The father and uncle have foundled and sexually harassed the 10 and 12 year old girls, and alternately mocked and challenged the teenage sons to join them. The parents' goal now is to improve their own sexual relationship and to begin to remedy the damage suffered by the children. What specific objectives could be identified and what are some possible counseling interventions with which to begin?

B. Look at your list of possible specific objectives and see how they naturally lead to intervention strategies. For instance in Item A. 2, if the teenage boys are identified as potential clients, what specific objectives and types of intervention for knowledge, attitudes, and behavior come to mind?

C. Check that the more subtle attitudinal aspects are not ignored in favor of knowledge or behavioral goals. All three — knowledge, attitudes/feelings, and behavior — must be considered. Sexuality counseling has such a rich array of treatment and growth suggestions that one can simply select a good combination, rather than search for a "perfect" plan.

Modifying Homework and Counseling Interventions

Very often the best counseling suggestions are those which the client reports "didn't work". Even if the result differs from the intended plan, a new dimension has been added to the client's experience if the intervention was reasonably close.

During Phase III of sexuality counseling a couple may be asked to alter their usual patterns of lovemaking, in order to bring about improvement. To everyone's surprise, the person who is complaining the loudest about wanting more or better sex may have a difficult time making necessary changes. Common reactions which interfere with pleasure are "This isn't really my problem", or "Maybe he/she isn't doing this right". or ":What if I don't get turned on this way?" Both people will need support to see that the homework is helping by uncovering blocks which no one realized were there.

A helper needs skill sorting out where the problem is, if a client doesn't follow a suggestion or obtains an unexpected result. An attitude of "we can learn something from this" encourages progress. Clients may not discover obstacles to change through just talking in the office, and that is why action assignments of all types are so effective in sexuality counseling.

Noncompliance. On occasion a person will not follow through on their homework, or participate fully during treatment phase sessions. Usually it is necessary to go back and look again at what the client's goal really is. Often the status quo is a known discomfort, whereas change is threatening. Sometimes the client is so ambivalent and influenced by various others that they just can't move. Even if an intervention or suggestion isn't followed, it may bring important insights to the client's awareness.

EXAMPLE: Goal Forced on Client, 4th Session

A 45 year old man has an extensive library of both classical and crude pornography. His formerly tolerant wife is threatening to leave him if he does not stop using the material during their lovemaking.

Counselor: *"The goal you insisted on when you began to see me was to get rid of your library and save your marriage. But Ted, it seems hard for you to do the breathing together and other sexual enrichment exercises with your wife."*

Ted: *"Well, I just haven't been getting to bed early, and can't get interested at all."*

Counselor: *"Since you found the visual erotic material stimulating for 30 years, it seems natural to me that you would be angry and depressed when pressured to do without it."*

Ted: *"I should outgrow it, but nothing turns me on anymore."*

Counselor Error: *"Well, lets go slower on giving away the library. And have you and your wife tried the mini-vacation yet, or the vibrator?"*

Counselor Correct: *"Ted, you shouldn't be hurting like this. I suspect that you are angry and upset at being between a rock and a hard place. Let's rethink the whole thing and come up with realistic goals."*

COMMENTS: If Ted's depression is transient and largely a way of communicating to his wife that he cannot abruptly lose his major source of sexual arousal, new goals can be set and counseling proceed. However if the problem is a dissolving relationship or the client's deeper conflicts, this will become apparent as the counseling shifts back to exploring concerns and focusing. The counselor needs to remember that at times a client will insist on a goal and need to try it, before knowing where the problem really is.

Realistic Goals and Objectives. Counselors must avoid accepting counseling goals and strategies which are based on the client's "superego demands", and "parent" messages, "oughts and shoulds", guilt, RET irrational thoughts, or other people's pressure. Borrowed goals tend to break down under the experience of daily living, so that interventions based on them are unlikely to succeed. Some clients may become disabled, suicidal, psychotic, or substance abusing when they cannot force themselves to proceed in the action phase (Phase III) toward inappropriate or imposed sex-related goals. This is one of the few dangers of sexuality counseling, so the counselor needs to be aware of the impact of guilt, perceived failure, and self disparagement during the treatment phase. The way to avoid this is to monitor work toward gradual goals which are attainable and genuinely desired by the client.

Intervention Techniques

When a client and counselor have reached mutual goals, the next logical question is the process of achieving them. Some schools of counseling balk at the word "treatment" and prefer a term like "counseling plan", because considerable treatment has occurred before the client arrives at this point. The more specific the problem, however, the more likely that the helper will be asked for definite suggestions. Counselors follow a variety of philosophies about directiveness, but can expect that clients with sexuality concerns will look for an informed way to proceed.

An early mistake in sexuality counseling was taking a too literal, "cookbook" approach to treatment. It was naively assumed that if one prescribed the squeeze technique all premature ejaculation was taken care of, or a set of glass dilators cured vaginismus. In the following list are some general categories of change and improvement strategies. Obviously this is only an introductory categorization; a more extensive list could be compiled by each counselor after drawing upon a lifetime of practice. Some very effective intervention techniques are available but their success lies in appropriate choice, timing, and individual application.

1. Education About Sexuality

   Most clients have misconceptions and a lack of knowledge about sex which contribute to their current problems. The counselor also can prevent later difficulties by supplying appropriate information as each developmental stage of life approaches. The helper can instruct by

   a. verbal dialogue;

   b. using charts, models, spontaneous drawings;

   c. recommending or providing books, films or videotapes;

   d. suggesting groups, workshops, classes, clinics; and

   e. preparing handout sheets and reprints for specific concerns.

2. Values/Attitudes/Feelings Clarification

   Most clients have unexamined attitudes or conflicted values which impede the appropriate expression of sexuality. During counseling the client can be helped to clarify, confront, resolve, and make comfortable choices about these cognitive/emotional constructs.

The exploration of concerns and the sexual history in Phase I give many glimpses into sexual attitudes and values which need to be considered in the intervention phase. The focusing techniques used in Phase II can be extended to go further and work through problematic feelings and values during the final phase of counseling. These range from the traditional methods of verbal confrontation and interpretation, to the impactful techniques developed by each school of counseling.

Drawing out clients on their feelings and attitudes as they complete counseling suggestions in Phase III adds further information. Asking clients to keep a journal, to talk with friends, or to otherwise be responsible for tracking sexual values and feelings also will facilitate working them through to a comfortable place.

3. Stopping Negative Sexual Thoughts and Behavior

One of the most helpful counseling suggestions is asking a client(s) to change a sexual pattern for a time-limited period. Often this is a relief and allows more positive thoughts and behaviors to occur. Frequent interventions are

   a. stop having sex with a specific person, until the relationship improves;

   b. refrain from intercourse for_____time, while learning other sexual expression;

   c. agreement to have no intercourse without birth control;

   d. cease to masturbate to a destructive fantasy;

   e. refuse to "go through the motions", learn to say no in order to say yes; and

   f. decide not to obtain sex by pressuring/forcing others.

4. Sexual Enrichment Techniques

Many people have a limited sexual routine and need help enlarging and varying it. If the client has no partner, much can be added to self stimulation. Where a person does have a partner, they can be encouraged to find creative ways to enhance their sexual pleasuring. With experience the counselor will be able to ask an individual or a couple how they presently enjoy sex, and then help them enrich the pleasure curve in comfortable ways. Intervention techniques such as the following are often helpful:

a. some techniques like imagery and the enjoyment of erotic literature are more interior;

b. some ways appeal to many senses, like non-genital caressing, making love to music, or creative, playful approaches;

c. suggestions such as locating sensitive areas in the vagina or using a vibrator intensify sexual stimulation; and

d. some strategies broaden experience, such as new positions, locations, role playing, or erotic massage.

5. Masturbation

Self pleasuring is a frequent method-of-choice to help clients learn about their sexuality without the stress and distraction of a partner. The following are some of its advantages:

a. arousal problems can be approached by learning a variety of types of stimulation without the pressure of an observing partner,

b. timing issues can be improved as the client learns what intensifies and what prolongs sexual pleasure,

c. the ability to reach a climax can be learned through guided experimentation,

d. independence is achieved since finding a partner for sex is not the only option, and

e. self pleasuring with structured fantasy can modify existing sexual patterns.

6. Gradual Shaping

Many sexual problems are caused by "skipping steps" or rushing ahead on the pleasure curve. Suggesting that clients go only to a certain point and rehearse (practice) it well, often results in the next logical step being more spontaneous and successful. The following techniques are helpful:

a. encouragement of stimulation without penetration for vaginismus, working up gradually from little finger insertion by client or partner, to penile containment and thrusting (when desired);

b. much imagery, relaxation, building of an erotic repertiore, manual and oral stimulation, before gradual genital contact, are used for sexual inhibition and arousal difficulties;

c. start and stop arousal patterns are suggested for premature ejaculation, which focus on the sensations and feelings just before climax, and the squeeze technique can be added to extend the pleasure curve;

d. a frequently suggested pattern is for clients to re-learn aspects of the pleasure curve alone, then share with a partner without penetration, then allow a gradual approach to more intense arousal, and then finally share intercourse, and

e. adding desired new fantasies and behaviors when already aroused, and fading out destructive ones, can bring about gradual changes in response.

7. Modifying Sexual Goals

Part of a successful treatment may be helping a client learn new ways of experiencing his/her sexual potential. Either because of necessity due to disability or changed life circumstances, or by choice, a person may need to discover pleasure in one or more of the following:

    a. a different kind of stimulation;

    b. a new method of sexual arousal and release, a climax before or after a partner;

    c. accommodation to a prosthesis (ostomy, penile implant), medication, high risk pregnancy, herpes;

    d. pleasure rather than orgasm or ejaculation as the goal (non-intercourse sex);

    e. a new partner, or cope with the loss of a partner;

    f. celibacy, and

    g. change in life style, motivation for sex.

8. Confronting Trauma

The counselor can help the client bring out destructive sexual experiences, confront them, understand and resolve anger, shame, and subsequent negative experiences. Some examples are as follows:

    a. child sexual abuse victims and offenders, incest, and others;

    b. rape victims and offenders;

    c. other sexual variants and their unwilling participants (exhibitionists, voyeurs);

d. "failures" at sex, including both chronic and acute difficulties;

e. upsetting or shame producing fantasies;

f. role-inappropriate sexual behavior or feelings, as judged by the client;

g. pain and sex, degradation to self or others;

h. arousal techniques and lovemaking styles which are unacceptable to the client or their partners;

i. scripts that one is a "Don Juan", "secret whore", "damaged goods", and so forth;

j. difficult pregnancies, birth experiences, abortions, and

k. episodes of conflict, blame, punishment or humiliation connected with sex.

9. Encouraging Communication

Many sexual problems are alleviated through helping the client accomplish better communication with significant others:

a. between parents and children of all ages

b. with sexual partners regarding

1) lovemaking
2) assertion to use birth control, or voice the desire to become pregnant
3) unplanned or unwanted pregnancy
4) discussing an STD or other health condition which affects sexuality; and
5) relationship problems.

c. with various persons regarding

      1) assertion to halt harassment
      2) potential forced sex situations (such as to avoid acquaintance rape where possible)
      3) express anger and other feelings about past victimization
      4) selected sharing of any sexual preference to others; and
      5) learning to talk comfortably about sex in general.

10. Referring

Very often a counselor knows another source of help which will contribute to a client's personal/sexual growth or will help resolve a problem. Careful choice and timing are important so that the referral is a comfortable step for the client. The referral can be

a. for health and medical information and treatment, physical therapy;

b. for body image work, i.e., weight, exercise, hair removal, dance;

c. to support groups, i.e., male role, preorgasmic women, infertile couples, teenage mothers;

d. to workshops-study groups, i.e., birth classes, contraceptive information, rape prevention, religious/ethical values study;

e. for skills training, i.e., couples communication, assertiveness training, sex education skills for parents,;

f. for social services of all kinds, public and private;

g. to other mental health professionals; and/or

h. to another sexuality counselor or sex therapist who has more experience with the client's particular issue.

LEARNING EXPERIENCE NO. 39

A. Consider the preceeding ten categories of therapeutic input and add some of your own where you see the need.

B. Reread each category and picture a sexuality counseling situation in which that particular kind of counseling intervention techniques would be useful.

C. Circle the three category numbers which you are most likely to use in your work. Put check marks beside the three which you are least likely to use. Consider whether you rely too heavily on a narrow range of treatment categories or whether you recommend a diverse spectrum according to client need. Discuss your choices with an interested colleague.

D. Review your least familiar categories and find at least one practitioner who is skilled in each. Ask him/her for tutoring in the use of these intervention strategies. You may want to do some reading first.

E. While working through this training program, seek out and judiciously try new intervention strategies. Many counselors find that in addition to their usual Phase III approaches which affect knowledge, feelings, and communication, they need to employ more behavioral suggestions in sexuality counseling. Of course the technique alone is not a cure, because much depends on how the client uses it.

F. Practice explaining and writing suggestions clearly, making the process a dialogue and not a lecture.

Evaluation of Progress

As all phases of counseling proceed, informal monitoring of progress by both the counselor and client naturally occurs. The expectation is that as exploring leads to honest focus, which results in workable goals and specific objectives, the client's experience from counseling suggestions will give constant feedback. The key is to help the client with understanding and insight during the sessions (motivate, clarify, make connections, remove obstacles), and then give individualized suggestions for further work.

The pressure for achievement is a well known barrier to enjoyment of sexuality, so for best results the counselor needs to be subtle about evaluation. Monitoring progress is a professional responsibility and a vital part of Phase III, but the helper needs to be careful not to add stress.

EXAMPLE: Discussion of Homework Adds Insight

A couple with very different religious and cultural backgrounds are having difficulty adjusting to married sex, experiencing intercourse very seldom.

Counselor: *"So we missed three weeks, due to vacations and cancellations. How would you say things have been going for you?"*

Husband: *"Terrible. We had sex only twice, and once was because we had this appointment scheduled with you."*

Counselor: *"You sound frustrated about the number, but let's not measure progress only that way. Why don't we leave all the report cards aside and look at some of our earlier ideas? Remember the goals of feeling more comfortable talking about sex and enjoying general pleasuring?"*

Wife: *"Yes, I thought we were doing fine until Angi began to insist on having intercourse right away."*

Counselor: *"Let's look at what is happening on the pleasure curve and see if we can't all have the same goals for this week by the end of the session."*

COMMENTS: The counselor tries not to take sides, but knows the goal must be quality and not quantity at this point. The man had been learning to arouse his sexually-avoidant wife, and in the process was afraid he would "come outside": in his culture this was definitely not doing it right. When the wife learned that her husband's urgency was not impatience or unconcern for her, she could cooperate with him in the gradual management of arousal and ejaculation. Here again, knowledge, attitudes/emotions, and behavior were all involved. High gains in evaluation of progress were made in this session, since important blocks to mutual understanding were uncovered, even though the initial report of progress was negative.

An important procedure in evaluation is to record goals, specific objectives, setbacks, and small gains in the counseling notes. Otherwise the counselor can become defensive about complaints like: "It still takes me too long to climax," or "Sometimes I want to turn a trick again." The goal can't be automatic orgasm or no unwanted impulses, but rather progress toward desired sexual expression. The counselor is not responsible for meeting the client's goals in any case, but can only facilitate improvement in a healthy direction.

EXAMPLE: Woman, Age 38, 6th Session

Counselor: *"You've felt like turning tricks? Sort of to your surprise, you are drawn to the street?"* (empathy, not defensiveness)

Client: *"Yes, but whenever I'm talking to you I remember that it isn't sex I like, but getting the guy.... what leads up to it."*

Counselor: *"You really do know how to connect with a man, and of course it feels good. Can some of those skills be useful at a party, or meeting men in other situations, but with the immediate sexual invitation left out?"*

Client: *"Maybe...but I'm afraid that without that I don't have anything. Huh...I'm really scared about being turned down, but I hate it if sex is all there is..."*

COMMENT: By not taking responsibility for the client's progress toward the goal of avoiding prostitute-like behavior, the counselor refocuses on underlying conflicts. The client can make progress on understanding the impulses, while also working on a goal of defining what she does want from men. The counselor's evaluation process is internal, and what the client feels is support toward attainable goals.

In the majority of cases client evaluation of progress is fair, but there are times when the client shifts the goal and seems to be demanding change. At this point the counselor can clarify past issues, consider overall goals, or move toward new client directions.

EXAMPLE: High School Sophomore, Regular Meetings for Several Months

Client: *"But this counseling isn't working. My mother still won't let me stay out after midnight, even though there is nothing to worry about since I'm not pregnant anymore."*

Counselor: *"Becky, you are saying that the worst thing for you right now is some restrictions you're getting from your mother?"*

Client: *"She's afraid I'll meet Denny somewhere."*

Counselor: *"Oh, and you may want to...let's talk about that and your mom in a minute. But I thought we were working on getting through the pregnancy shock, and the abortion, and regaining confidence in school again after everyone found out. Do you feel you have accomplished most of those things?"*

Client: *"Now that you mention it, I guess I have. I got a B in my personal computer class, so my teacher is letting me use the Apple!"*

Counselor: *"Great! So let's go ahead and focus on where the pressure is now. Sounds like we need new goals."*

COMMENTS: Sometimes the client takes success for granted and then is impatient about new conflicts. The counselor must have perspective and not depend upon constant appreciation. In some situations a counselor need not automatically accept a new focus but can recommend staying with the original one to maintain gains, or refer (*"Ms. Hernandez has a great group for people who have communication problems with their parents"*).

Here again good counseling notes are important for maintaining direction and seeing progress.

LEARNING EXPERIENCE NO. 40

A. Relax in a comfortable position and follow your breathing in and out for several minutes. Focus on a time when you sought help from another person, either in formal or informal counseling. Try to recall the goal that emerged from your discussions, and write it down. Include any specific objectives.

B. Ask yourself the following questions, jotting down notes:

1. Do I remember the various steps needed to achieve the goal or specific objectives?

2. Did the other person give me any suggestions to help me move toward the goal? What were they?

3. Were the suggestions immediately helpful? Did I modify some alone, together? How did I evaluate the worth of the suggestions then?

4. Was the interaction successful in the long run? Did I meet my desired goal or find an alternative?

5. Could I judge the effectiveness of the help I received as accurately at the time as I believe I can now?

Fortunately many outcomes of sexuality counseling are visible to the client and are not too subtle. Of course at times all of us have to accept a compromise between an absolute ideal and what is realistically possible; clients can be helped to do this. The unpredictability of client progress means that the professional must make continual assessments in order to adjust the work accordingly. Counselors need to be self affirming about their work, because while some clients are extravagently grateful, others are difficult to please.

Termination

When is sexuality counseling finished? No arbitrary point exists because people continue to grow and experience as sexual beings before, during, and long after the counselor sees them. In one school of thought the suggestion is for the "least necessary intervention," so that the goal becomes getting through a negative spot and setting positive growth in motion. Other practitioners arrange contracts with specific goals and a set number of sessions, which they renegotiate depending on progress. Still others meet over a longer time span and suggest that the client stop in for "10,000 mile checks" every few months for a year. Some feminist counselors choose to convert the professional relationship to a pleasant social one after termination, and see past clients for an occasional lunch or friendly meeting. The pattern should depend entirely on the practice or agency, and fit in with one's overall counseling philosophy and client needs.

A point occurs during counseling when goals have been met or are re-evaluated. If met, then the client or clients need to be encouraged to be on their own. Abruptness in ending is not comfortable, however, even if the client is largely satisfied. Some sexuality counseling may take only thirty minutes, such as before an uncomplicated vasectomy, and other times many sessions will be needed stretching over years, as when a college counselor works with a fragile incest victim (survivor). Obviously the intensity of the client's issues and the length of time in treatment affects client attachment, so gentleness is often necessary at termination.

Suggesting that termination is approaching allows the client to negotiate the ending and not feel rejected. Sometimes clients "get worse" temporarily, or bring up important new material. Often further work is done in a fairly short time and the counselor can acknowledge that the client is now in a good place to move ahead. The philosophy that people do have resources enables the counselor to encourage clients toward independence at a reasonable rate.

How often do clients leave sexuality counseling before goals are met? "No shows" are not common when goals are realistic, especially since the stress of failure and inadequacy are being reduced. When clients stop coming, often the cause is due to complex personal factors which have a higher priority for the person. Rather than trying to retain all clients, the helper can work sincerely to be helpful, while accepting some attrition as the clients' right to autonomy. Alertness to patterns of premature termination, however, will help prevent the helper from contributing to early departures from counseling.

Because sex is a private subject, genuine praise and encouragement when ending will be warmly remembered. Recapitulation of gains made and assurance of the possibility of continued growth show that the counselor has confidence in the future. Clients are often left with a general program rather than specific counseling suggestions; the long range benefit is their responsibility through utilizing the cumulative effect of the work together.

LEARNING EXPERIENCE NO. 41

A. Look for and spend some time with a person in leavetaking; a person may be leaving, perhaps moving, from a place or position that is important to him/her. In one's life someone often is leaving, either for a brief or a long time, or forever. Be sensitive to tendencies in yourself to joke, pull away, to reminisce, make promises, or to communicate something you wished you had shared before. Notice what is going on with the other person and if possible ask them about it. By doing this with other people on other occasions, you will find that you become more sensitive to issues of separation, and yet feel more at peace with them.

B. Repeat this thoughtful separation with someone whom you feel dependent on or look up to, in order to have a better idea what a client experiences when finished counseling.

C. Use some kinds of creative material and symbolize separation, leavetaking, and termination. Forms such as poetry, diagrams, clay, writing, music, drawings, body movement, or any expressive medium are effective. Apply insights gained from this activity to your termination interviews with clients.

PART 3. ISSUES RELATED TO ALL PHASES OF COUNSELING

RECOGNIZING A CRISIS

The major consideration when the counselor encounters a possible crisis in any of the phases of counseling is to face it. Staying with the familiar, being supportive, and just giving information are ways of ignoring a developing problem. Sometimes a client is aware and asks directly for more help, but often the counselor is the one to realize that a possible critical issue needs to be confronted.

A professional cannot be excused for ducking an uncomfortable problem, whereas a client will respect a counselor who cares enough to ascertain the truth, even if it is difficult. Examples of potential crises are increasing depression, suicidal thoughts, hints of illegal or destructive acting out behavior, drug or alcohol abuse, or slipping out of touch with reality. If the client cannot contribute to counseling because he/she seems resistant, immobilized, deeply troubled, or unable to communicate, that shows the need for inquiry. Even if a serious crisis does not develop, the helper has demonstrated responsible concern for the client's welfare.

Contracts with clients are a useful tool when confronting a possible crisis. These are simply agreements which are written down, for the sake of clarity and working out the wording together. Counseling is a place where rage and despair may be expressed safely, but the client also must understand the boundaries between expression and acting on those feelings.

When the counselor reasonably believes that the client is able to make a rational choice and is able to control him/her self, an agreement which is read aloud and signed is one safeguard. Copies of a form similar to the following may be in the counselor's desk or briefcase:

I, _____(client's name)_____, agree that no matter what happens I will _____

Date _____ (Signature)_____

A frequently used phrase is "not harm myself accidently or on purpose, in any way". However something as individualized as "not be alone with X on weekends," or "will see a doctor before the end of March," underline the importance of an issue where health or safety are at stake. By watching body language as the client reads the contract aloud, and through negotiating details, the helper can gauge the person's readiness to follow through. Clients often are relieved to have the potential crisis monitored closely, and they feel a greater sense of control when specifics have been explored and agreed upon.

Even with a contract the wise counselor generally seeks supervision or consultation if a client is in crisis, especially when a threat of psychosis or harm to the client or others exists. In all cases where the counselor believes a possibility of danger exists, safety is a more important consideration than confidentiality. Also, when problem information come up in a history, or is mentioned and then denied, a good procedure is to continue to inquire in a supportive manner. If in doubt about a crisis, or if one exists and is getting worse, the counselor must refer, arrange to meet with the client and another professional, or seek a consultation to discuss how to proceed.

CLIENT-COUNSELOR RELATIONSHIP

The feelings which a client and counselor have toward one another are an important part of the helping process. Occasionally a client just doesn't like a particular counselor's characteristics, so that referral is indicated rather than a strained relationship. A counselor could seem to resemble a clergyman who molested a client, or a woman who ridiculed someone's sexual "performance." Most of the time clients can separate out any irrational transfer of hostility or dependency and form a working relationship; this becomes an important part of their growth.

EXAMPLE: Positive Support, 4th Session

Counselor: *"You have really been working to get your anger out the last few weeks, Sally. I know these things are hard to talk about."*

Sally: *"When I start to explain to you what happened, I feel so weird."*

Counselor: *"Yes, sometimes I can see you begin to get that distant, closed look, but I don't think that is what you're feeling."*

Sally: *"You know, I never thought I could talk to a man about any of this. I'm sorry if I give you a hard time."*

Counselor: *"Thanks, I know it isn't me. Let me help you express some of your anger at what happened. (client nods) Let's put two pieces of garbage paper on the floor over there called Scum 1 and Scum 2. You can tell them what you think about putting sticks in your body in the park. You couldn't do that back when you were eleven, but now you can at sixteen."*

Sally: *"They couldn't do it again (Counselor points to paper). I mean...you jerks couldn't trick me with that now. I shouldn't have...oh"* (pales) *"... I just remembered they said they had a switchblade..."*

COMMENT: At this point the client is into the treatment phase with the recovery of suppressed material. Sally is likely to return to acting distant at times, or exploring new concerns, but she is reaching her goal of not being haunted by the traumatic sexual molestation.

Unless the counselor had been able to understand and tolerate the client's negative feelings toward men without personalizing them, the counselor and client could not have reached the treatment stages together. Initially Sally might have found working with a woman counselor easier, but advantages are gained by forming a positive relationship with a male counselor.

The term "transference" is used broadly to mean those prior learnings which a client brings to the counseling situation; this can lead to expectations or reactions which the counselor did not intend to elicit. In a more classical analytic sense, the term refers to feelings from the past which are projected onto the therapeutic relationship, and are worked through as an important part of treatment. Much of this analysis of transference depends on the therapist being a neutral figure, so that indeed the client reactions are transferred rather than truly involving the helper.

Not all client feelings are due to transference, however. With today's self disclosing, interactive helper, one may have difficulty saying whether a client's reaction is to past learning or to something about the particular here-and-now counselor. Feelings of personal attraction which the client may honestly have toward the counselor can be a problem. In the early phases of counseling the helper may simply take note of apparent client reactions, correct any important misconceptions, and expect many of the feelings to settle into comfortable limits with time.

In our society an intimacy often occurs when talking about sex which can be arousing and potentially confusing to a client. Without question dialogue about sex is often an accepted part of social mating and dating rituals. The professional has the responsibility to convey interest, support, and positive regard without seductiveness or self importance. The client needs a safe place to be unselfconscious about sexuality, without fearing mixed messages or manipulation.

People have learned habits of presenting themselves which may have sexual overtones. If a client is sitting, dressing, talking, or acting in a sexy way, which could be a carry-over from their social behavior, the counselor will note it but does not respond in kind. Clients of all ages and both sexes may test any counselor without being aware of it. If the behavior continues, it can be addressed gently in a low-key manner during the later phases of work.

Counselor Feelings

Unconditional positive regard as a therapeutic condition has been extensively studied and is a worthwhile goal even if the helper cannot establish it in every instance. If the counselor's feelings of attraction toward a client go beyond this, how are they handled? It can be done by acknowledging someone's attractiveness to oneself, and accepting the situational limits. This is similar to feelings toward any appealing person who is not available as a sexual partner, such as the spouse of a friend, a relative, minors, celibate clergy, or someone who wants to stay platonic.

Any person who has difficulty with impulse gratification should not be doing sexuality counseling until that is thoroughly under control. A satisfying sexual adjustment outside of one's professional work, whatever that means for the individual counselor, helps to avoid even unconsciously looking at clients as partners.

CONCLUSION

People in human service professions carry the essential part of their work always with them. Counseling skills are portable, light, potent, flexible, and do not require machinery, a library, or lab to use. Once learned a good set lasts for a lifetime and they are infinitely expandable. Sexuality counseling skills are a further refinement which can be kept current through frequent use and continued study. A systematic body of knowledge in this specialty is constantly growing, and each counselor can attain a unique integration by drawing on general counseling skills and applying them to sexual concerns.

PROFESSIONAL ISSUES IN SEXUALITY COUNSELING

Sexuality counseling is provided in many settings, by practitioners from varying backgrounds. This is fortunate for the general public because a trained person can be found in a family practice clinic, a church, a social service agency, or a school. It does mean that professional matters cannot be completely standardized, however, and that individual differences must be accomodated.

The checklist in Figure 7 is intended to help the reader assess where further study and consultation are needed in the areas of professional responsibility which relate to sexuality counseling. Each person must consider his/her own particular situation.

TOPIC	FAMILIAR	UNFAMILIAR	UNSURE
1. Professional Organizations	_____	_____	_____
2. Certification And Licensure	_____	_____	_____
3. Codes of Professional Ethic	_____	_____	_____
4. AASECT Ethical Guidelines	_____	_____	_____
5. Crisis Intervention	_____	_____	_____
6. Case Records	_____	_____	_____
7. Process of Referral	_____	_____	_____
8. Business Planning	_____	_____	_____
9. Fees	_____	_____	_____
10. Continuing Education	_____	_____	_____

Figure 7. Checklist for self-assessment regarding professional issues.

Fill in the checklist in Figure 7 and then read through the following ten parts to this chapter. When you have completed the reading and the Learning Exercises, review your answers to the checklist. Decide whether the topics you were unsure about belong in the familiar or unfamiliar category.

Develop a plan to put all the professional issues into the "familiar" category. These topics may not seem as compelling as the client-oriented study, and yet it is vital to the success of sexuality counseling to have professional issues firmly managed.

CHAPTER 4, PART 1

PROFESSIONAL ORGANIZATIONS

The field of sexuality counseling is moving so rapidly that the only way to keep abreast is to belong to one or more professional organizations. The counselor then receives newsletters, journals, and conference notices, and is put on mailing lists for new information. In addition, participation in professional organizations is an indication of commitment when applying for a new position or further certification.

Dues can be expensive, and yet this is part of the professional investment of counselors; they usually do not need the equipment dentists require, the library a lawyer has, or the elaborate computers accountants use. During training student memberships are generally available and, when necessary, two or more people can agree to share materials. These expenses are tax deductible, and membership often brings reduced charges for training opportunities and publications.

First of all, a helping person needs to belong to the major national and regional organizations which represent her/his profession. For some, this would be the National League for Nursing, for others the American Psychological Association. Clergy, social workers, and teachers all have their own national professional organizations to uphold standards of practice and advance the needs of members. For many counselors the American Association for Counseling and Development (formerly APGA) is their primary organization, whereas others choose the American Association of Marriage and Family Therapists (AAMFT) or the Association of Women Deans and Counselors. Many people belong to more than one.

Once the counselor has achieved membership in a general professional organization, several choices are available in the sexuality field. Organizations are subject to evolution, so specific information about their membership requirements and services changes. The quality is generally high, and strong attempts are made to inform members about the field and to meet their professional and training needs.

The following list includes some of the major organizations; several focus largely on information. Notices about other groups often occur in their publications and conferences.

American Association of Sex Educators, Counselors and Therapists (AASECT), Eleven Dupont Circle, NW, Suite 220, Washington, DC 20036.

Institute for Family Research and Education, 760 Ostrum Ave., Syracuse, NY 13210.

Planned Parenthood of America, 810 Seventh Ave., New York, NY 10019.

Sex Information and Education Council of the United States, Inc., 80 Fifth Ave., New York, NY 10011.

The Society for the Scientific Study of Sex, P.O. Box 29795, Philadelphia, PA 19117.

LEARNING EXPERIENCE NO. 42

A. Write to some professional and sex-related organizations to receive the information necessary to make a choice about joining. Find the best combination for your own needs.

B. Consider additional regional and state organizations which offer meetings, even if they are oriented toward sexuality education rather than counseling, to be in touch with local people, resources, and events.

CHAPTER 4, PART 2
CERTIFICATION AND LICENSURE

Professional journals carry frequent articles informing their members of state-to-state changes in the regulation of the helping professions. Organizational and private registries and certification, as well as an increasing number of state conferred credentials, are in existence. The person practicing counseling must be active in professional organizations to stay informed.

The requirements, advantages, and terminology must be read carefully in all cases. In some instances, certification is little more than a registration of names after paying a fee, whereas in other instances, it is a rigorously monitored screening process with national recognition. Licensure is also varied, in that some statutes protect only the use of a professional title, and others describe and regulate the practice of counseling. The number of states is increasing where laws have been passed to license or certify counselors. This is encouraging to the profession, but since the system is still evolving the practitioner needs to be tolerant of change.

CREDENTIALS

Academic Credentials

Many applicants are surprised to know that few preparation programs which specialize in sexuality counseling exist. To enter the field, one must usually obtain general professional preparation first and then take additional sexuality courses and supervision. Professional status can come from degree programs such as the M.S., Ed.D., R.N., M.Ed., Ph.D., and M.S.W. Other degrees are less well known but also help the public distinguish professional competence, such as the Certificate of Advanced Study, Certified Nurse Practitioner, or Pastoral Counselor. The degrees give no indication that a person has specialized in mental health or sexuality counseling, however, and therefore other certifications are often added.

Professional Credentials

Regulation of professionals is intended to protect the consumer and not to enhance the status of providers, as any Attorney General will point out. The effect of establishing credentials does make some mental health professionals appear more competent and reliable than others, however. Proponents of de-regulation have suggested that no one be licensed, thus allowing the consumer to decide who deserves to practice in a free market. But how can a pregnant teenager distinguish the professional counselor from a "counselor" whose training consists of several workshops in "past lives aroma therapy?" Society does not allow people to designate themselves as surgeons or master electricians, and in similar ways is beginning to define who is a mental health counselor, social worker, or a family therapist.

A problem exists since the words "counselor" and "counseling" are used by many, such as camp counselor, nutrition counselor, or religious counseling. It is encouraging, but sometimes confusing, to see attempts to cope with this by using fuller and more descriptive titles such as: Professional Counselor, Clinical Mental Health Counselor, Certified Sexuality Counselor, Registered Practicing Counselor, and Clinical Mental Health Nurse. A strong movement exists both toward specifying who is qualified as a professional mental health counselor, (generic certification), and in addition who has specialty skills as a career counselor, pastoral counselor, or sexuality counselor.

The National Board for Certified Counselors (NBCC) is an organization established as a result of APGA's (now AACD's) interest in granting formal recognition to individuals who meet professional practice standards. Information on the criteria for their certification (NCC, National Certified Counselor) and its advantages may be obtained from NBCC, 5999 Stevenson Ave., Alexandria, VA 22304. Other national registries, associations, and academies offer either general or specialty certification when their standards are met.

Some states have created superboards to assess the qualifications of all applicants for certification/licensure in the various mental health professions. Charges of "elitism" can easily be brought if only a few professions are regulated and given special status. The challenge for counselors is to protect their profession and the consumer without infringing on the rights of others, as they progress in the arena of credentialing. After a decade of legitimate complaints about being discounted by older mental health groups, it would be ironic indeed if counselors joined in oppressing others as soon as they were aboard the roster of regulated providers.

Specialty Credentials

Sexuality counselors may have a greater need than general counselors for obtaining specialty recognition, since the public is likely to have heard more about fraudulent sexuality counselors and the harm they can do. In addition to obtaining professional credentials from their state and organizational regulating bodies and from academic programs, counselors can join professional organizations which offer specific certification in areas such as biofeedback, Transactional Analysis, family mediation, or Reality Therapy. Other organizations such as the National Academy of Certified Clinical Mental Health Counselors, The Commission on Rehabilitation Counselor Certification, and the American Association of Marriage and Family Therapists, are widely accepted as recognizing particular kinds of competence.

The specialty of sexuality counseling has been recognized by AASECT and their requirements for certification as a Sexuality Counselor are as follows:

AASECT REQUIREMENTS FOR SEX COUNSELOR CERTIFICATION*

I. Full, Institutional, or Life Membership in AASECT.

II. Educational/Professional Certification

The applicant shall hold a regulatory license and/or certificate, valid in the state in which he/she practices, in one of the following disciplines: counseling, medicine, nursing, social work, psychology.

  A. If such a regulatory systems is not in effect in the state in which he/she practices, the applicant shall meet one of the following criteria:

   1. Certification by the National Academy of Clinical Mental Health Counselors.

   2. Certification by the National Board for Certified Counselors.

   3. Certification by the Academy of Certified Social Workers.

4. Clinical membership in the American Association of Pastoral Counselors.

5. Clinical membership in the American Association for Marriage and Family Therapy.

B. In lieu of meeting the above stated requirements for certification, the applicant may hold an academic degree in a human services program from an accredited college or university recognized by the Council on Postsecondary Accredition and have accumulated professional experience as a counselor. Either

1. A Bachelor's degree plus four years of professional experience as a counselor (1000 hours/year = 20 hours/week x 50 weeks/year), or

2. A Master's degree plus three years of professional experience as a counselor (1000 hours/ year), or

3. A Doctorate degree plus two years of professional experience as a counselor (1000 hours/year).

III. Human Sexuality Education

The applicant shall have completed a minimum of ninety (90) clock hours of education covering knowledge in the following core areas:

A. Sexual and reproductive anatomy and physiology.

B. Developmental sexuality (from conception to old age) from a psychobiological perspective.

C. Dynamics of interpersonal relationships.

D. Gender-related issues.

E. Sociocultural factors in sexual values and behavior.

F. Marital and family dynamics.

G. Medical factors that may influence sexuality including illness, disability, drugs, pregnancy, contraception and fertility, sexually transmitted diseases.

H. Sex research.

I. Sexual abuse.

J. Personality theories.

IV. Attitude/Values Training Experience

The applicant shall have participated in a minimum of twelve (12) clock hours of structured group experience in which the major focus was on the personal attitudes and values of the individual regarding human sexuality. Such training is *not* to be construed as personal psychotherapy, on the one hand, nor, on the other hand, as an academic experience in which the primary emphasis in on cognitive information. Rather, the experience should consist of some kind of process-oriented exploration of the applicant's own feelings, attitudes, and beliefs regarding human sexuality and sexual behavior (e.g. a SAR). It is strongly recommended that this experience occur early in the applicant's training.

V. Sex Counseling Training

The applicant shall have completed a minimum of one hundred thirty-five (135) clock hours of training in how to do sex counseling. Up to forty-five (45) of these hours may be in general personal counseling (for example, an undergraduate or graduate course in counseling), but at least ninety (90) of the one hundred thirty-five hours must be in sex counseling. Sex counseling training may be obtained through credit courses, tutorials, workshops, practicum experience, etc. Such training is to include the following:

A. Theory and methods of general counseling.

B. Theory and methods of sex counseling.

C. Theory and practice of consultation, collaboration, and referral.

> **NOTE:** The difference between the requirements in III and V is that the education requirement in V is directed at clinical skills. The two overlap, but they are sufficiently different that documentation is necessary in each.

VI. Field or Work Experience

The applicant shall have completed a minimum of five hundred (500) hours of supervised group or individual counseling where the focus was on sex counseling. Sex counseling is seen here as being conducted in various settings, i.e., public or private clinics, social and educational organizations, colleges and universities, professional schools, family planning centers, community health centers, school setting, and churches.

VII. Supervision

The applicant shall have received a minimum of one hundred (100) hours of individual supervision or two hundred (200) hours of group supervision, or a prorated combination of individual and group supervision, on the treatment of the Psychosexual Disorders listed in DSM-III. This supervision shall have been received from an AASECT Certified Sex Counselor or Sex Therapist. If a Certified supervisor is unavailable or otherwise inappropriate, then another professional with comparable qualifications must be approved by the Committee on Sex Counselors. It is strongly encouraged that such approval be sought in advance.

A. The supervisory process should be conducted face-to-face, have continuity, and be a systematic learning experience.

B. Ordinarily, supervisory sessions should be scheduled on a weekly basis for a period of at least one hour per meeting. Several sessions per week and not fewer than one every other week are considered acceptable alternative arrangements. *Minimum duration of clinical supervision is six months.*

> **NOTE:** In situations where geographic necessity requires modification of published standards, special arrangements may be approved in writing by the Committee on Sex Counselors, provided that the conditions of face-to-face meetings and continuity are maintained.

C. A total of one hundred (100) hours of individual supervision is required for a candidate to be designated an AASECT Certified Sex Counselor. Credit for individual supervision may be granted when two supervisees who are co-therapists meet simultaneously with the supervisor. Two hundred (200) hours of group supervision may be substituted, provided that the group does not include more than four supervisees and that the sessions are extended to a minimum of ninety (90) minutes each.

D. In all instances, the focus of supervision should be the raw data of the supervisee's actual therapy practice, made available by means of any one or a combination of the following: anecdotal report based upon notes, direct observation, or audio or video recordings. The supervisor is encouraged to utilize direct observation or audio or video recordings.

E. The supervisory process is to be clearly distinguished from personal psychotherapy. The supervisor is expected, however, to point out the intrusion of personal material and any inappropriate behaviors surfacing during the interaction between supervisee and his/her patient/client. The goal of supervision is limited to the improvement of professionalism by emphasis upon enhancement of skills and continuing the educative process.

The following do NOT meet the supervision requirements:

A. Supervision from a family member

B. Peer supervision

C. A process which is primarily didactic, such as a workshop or seminar, wherein teaching is focused upon material other than the raw data of the supervisee's clinical practice.

D. Management and/or administrative meetings with an organizational director or executive.

The responsibilities of the supervisor include the following:

A. The supervisor may discontinue or decline starting supervision if there is reasonable doubt that a particular candidate has the potential for ultimately qualifying as an AASECT Certified Sex Counselor. In such instance, the candidate is entitled to a full and frank explanation and is not prevented from seeking supervision from another supervisor, who should, however, be informed of the situation by the supervisee.

B. The supervisor is responsible for ascertaining that the candidate has appropriate academic credentials.

C. The supervisor is expected to oversee supervisee's familiarity with pertinent literature in related fields, as well as keeping current with literature on the cause and treatment of sexual disorders.

D. All supervisory work is to be conducted in an appropriate professional setting.

E. The major goal of supervision is to enhance the knowledge and skills of the supervisee in assessment, consultation, collaboration, and referral of patients/clients. It is also expected that the supervisor will facilitate the supervisee's meeting of the requirements for certification as herein stated.

VIII. Documentation

The following documentation must be submitted in order to be eligible for review by the Committee on Sex Counselors. All supporting documents must be submitted in triplicate and will become the property of AASECT.

A. Completed formal application for AASECT Certified Sex Counselor.

B. Official transcript of program in which highest degree was earned (Item II).

C. Official transcripts, attendance certificates, syllabi, etc., documenting ninety (90) hours of education in the designated core areas of human sexuality (Item III).

D. Official documentation of participation in a structure group experience focusing on sexual attitudes and values, e.g., a SAR (Item IV).

E. Official transcripts, attendance certificates, syllabi, and other credible evidence documenting one hundred thirty-five (135) hours of training in counseling, a minimum of ninety (90) hours of which is in sexual counseling in the designated areas of focus (Item V).

F. Documentation from employer(s) and/or supervisor(s) certifying a minimum of five hundred (500) hours of group or individual counseling experience serving as the sole or primary counselor, where the focus was on sex counseling (Item VI).

G. Letter(s) from one or more clinical supervisors attesting to the applicant's having received a minimum of one hundred (100) hours of individual supervision, or two hundred (200) hours of group supervision, or a combination of hours totalling two hundred (200) hours, on a face-to-face basis, *in the practice of sex counseling*. Such letters must include the time period(s) during which the supervision was received as well as the total number of hours spend with the supervisor. If the supervisor is not an AASECT Certified Sex Counselor or Sex Therapist, he/she must submit a professional resume or curriculum vitae to demonstrate comparable qualifications (Item VII).

H. References must be received from the following persons on the appropriate forms:

    1. *A Clinical Supervisor or Trainer* involved in the applicant's training and/or supervision *in sex counseling*.

        NOTE: This letter is separate from the documentation of hours of supervision described in Item G above.

    2. *A Professional Colleague* who can comment on the applicant's professional responsibilities, professional ethics, and overall ability as a sex therapist.

    3. *A Character Reference* from outside the applicant's immediate work setting.

I. The appropriate certification fee.

IX. Miscellaneous

A. All certified members will be required to comply with the ethical standards established by AASECT as expressed in the AASECT Code of Ethics.

B. Upon approval of the Committee on Sex Counselors, the successful applicant will receive a certificate in recognition of having met the AASECT requirements for certification in the area of sex counseling. This certificate will be subject to renewal every three years.

C. Each AASECT Certified Sex Counselor will be listed in the National Register of AASECT.

D. Membership in AASECT must be maintained on an annual basis to retain the AASECT status.

---

*Reprinted with permission

The preceding guidelines are excellent to follow whether or not a counselor intends to apply for AASECT certification.

USE OF TITLES

Ordinarily, only earned degree initials in the field being practiced are placed directly after a person's name when offering services to the public. Other qualifications may be listed below the name, on stationery, business cards, or professional announcements. One of the important things to remember in listing different credentials is to indicate which state or organization granted the certification. It is also important not to combine the designations in a misleading manner.

EXAMPLES: Listing of Name and Credentials

Error:
Dana L. Damion, M.S.
Certified Clinical Sexuality Therapist

Correct:
Dana L. Damion, M.S.
AAMFT Certified Marriage and Family Therapist
AASECT Certified Sex Educator

Error: Kim Sung, D.Div., C.S.C.

Correct:
Kim Sung, D.Div.
AASECT Certified Sex Counselor

In some areas counselors have a tendency to call themselves "therapists", another term confusing to the consumer because it is used for diet and massage as well as mental health. Many counselors, social workers, and others are trained to offer both counseling and psychotherapy, and yet, need not assume the vague title of "therapist." A professional person, should use the most appropriate title for the educational background possessed and those services being offered.

OBTAINING CREDENTIALS

LEARNING EXPERIENCE NO. 43

A. Investigate your potential for certification/licensure in your own and neighboring states.

B. Write to professional organizations for their certification guidelines and application blanks.

C. Ask a colleague to help you review requirements and encourage you where necessary. Many people hesitate for years before applying for professional recognition and do so only with trepidation. The reality is that only a minority of applicants have "perfect" credentials. Take it step-by-step: sending for transcripts, asking for references, completing lengthy forms, taking courses or workshops to fill in weak areas. This may seem arduous at first, but of course the new knowledge not only makes you more certifiable but a better practitioner.

D. Keep a professional log of all workshops, conferences, in-service training sessions, staff development presentations, and all formal and informal supervision (group and individual). Include transcripts, continuing education credits, letters of recommendation, and the degrees and certifications of your professors and supervisors.

Keeping a Log

Specific information may be very helpful in the future when applying for membership or credentials. The following are illustrations of entries to make in a log:

1. Internship at the Greenlane Mental Health Center, two days per week, Jan. 15, 19 _____ to May 15, 19 _____ . Case load average 7-9/week. Emergency on-call one evening/wk. Clients: 9 women with sexual disinterest, sexual conflicts. 6 sexually abused women, depressed, ages 22-47.

   Bi-weekly case discussions with John H. Loobin, M.D. (Minn.), Board Cert. Psychiatrist. One and one half hours each, one other participant, Jan. 15, 19___ to May 15, 19___ . Discussed dynamics, assessment, clients' sexual development, treatment options, and appropriate counseling techniques.

2. "Treatment of the Young Incest Victim (Infant to Age 10)", Workshop offered by Alabama State Dept. of Health, Nov.

12-14, 19____ . 20 CE credits. Presenters: Doreen L. Brittan, R.N., Certified Mental Health Nurse (NY), author of "Assessment and Treatment of the Infant/Child Incest Victim," in *Treatment of Child Sexual Abuse* by Smith(Ed.), Published, 1985, and Jonathon L. Sperry, Ph.D., Licensed Psychologist (NJ), specialist in counseling and family systems (bibliography and workshop outline attached). Strong points were videotaped practice in simulated situations for 6 hours on the third day.

When applying for credentials, many applicants say x number of hours, or equivalent, when asked for training and experience. Such statements are insufficient because the preparation and supervision experiences must be detailed. By keeping a log as suggested in Learning Experience No. 43, Item D, everything can be documented. Very often counselors have most of what they need, or could obtain it, but are unsure about how to put it all together. When a person sees what is needed, and makes a step-by-step plan, obtaining recognized professional credentials is a manageable task.

CONCLUSION

Counseling is both a profession and a word used by many other occupations to describe a part of their work. Therefore academic degrees, certification/licensure by state government, and professional organization credentials are important to help the public identify an appropriate sexuality counselor. By knowing the possibilities, the counselor can shape training toward accepted professional standards, thus benefiting both self and clients.

CHAPTER 4, PART 3

CODES OF PROFESSIONAL PRACTICE

Many helping professionals can indicate immediately which code of ethical conduct applies directly to them. This is especially true for people trained in fields such as social work, psychology, nursing, medicine, or education. For some of these occupations, licensing, certification, or membership in professional organizations requires the acceptance of specific ethical guidelines. Other professions, such as some counselors or clergy, residential treatment facility staff, or health care counselors, may turn to the ethical guidelines of their organization or institution.

Only a short while ago, ethical guidelines were published as "rulebooks", and were studied by applying cases to specific numbered principles. More recently, the field has moved in the direction of "ethical dilemmas", where the practitioner is expected to analyze a complex set of circumstances, balance competing rights and principles, and rank alternatives. The latter is more realistic in our complex society, since no code can substitute for individual judgement. In most cases, standards of professional practice are broad outlines of responsible conduct, which must be applied carefully by the counselor.

Many ethical codes say very little about sexuality counseling directly. One must study the codes carefully however, because the counselor will encounter many issues in addition to the obvious one of prohibiting direct sexual interaction with clients. In addition, specific state laws and regulations on issues relating to the treatment of minors, sexual harassment, abortion, divorce, confidentiality, and the reporting of child sexual abuse are important to the practitioner.

LEARNING EXPERIENCE NO. 44

A. Go through the ethical guidelines which apply to your profession and try to focus them on sexuality counseling issues which could

be encountered. As an illustration use the American Psychological Association, Ethical Principles of Psychologists, 1981. Principle 6. Welfare of the consumer, (Item b) "When a psychologist agrees to provide services to a client at the request of a third party, the psychologist assumes the responsibility of clarifying the nature and the relationships of all parties concerned."

1. What if a parent asked you to counsel his/her 18 year old daughter whom you had recently seen soliciting sex in a very rough local bar? Would the situation be different if the girl were 16?

2. What if you were asked to counsel a man as a condition of probation, and suspected ongoing child molestation?

3. How is No. 2 different from No. 1?

4. What and to whom would you communicate in No. 1 and No. 2?

5. For counselors who follow another organization's set of ethical guidelines, what do No. 1 and No. 2 cause you to consider about third party communication? Talk this kind of situation over with colleagues, since questions about the limits of confidentiality are confusing and controversial.

B. After going though an ethics code with hypothetical incidents, call to mind the most recent sexuality counseling case in which you participated, or one you have heard about. Try to think of possible ethical complaints and then play the role of a representative from the State Attorney General's Office pressing charges. What would be the arguments in looking for ethical misconduct? Remember that often several parts of an ethics code apply to one case.

PREVENTION OF ETHICAL PROBLEMS

The enforcement of ethical guidelines is unpredictable. In the same county one person can seem to get away with flagrant violations whereas another will have humiliating hearings upon a lesser charge. Counselors can protect their reputations by advertising their professional title as clearly as possible, and by informing the public of their practice in a conservative way, without exaggerated claims or sensational emphasis on sexuality counseling. Many counseling agencies and practices prepare a brochure for clients which clarifies rights, responsibilities, expectations, fees, and ethical guidelines.

State and national conferences often include workshops utilizing the technique of ethical dilemmas. Counselors can take these opportunities to bring up sexuality counseling examples, and enlarge their ability to reason about complex ethical issues. Surprisingly few ethical decisions fit perfectly in any rulebook. A text like the following is helpful in gaining skill in ethical judgment:

> Corey, G., & Corey, M. (1984). *Issues and ethics in the helping professions.* (2nd ed.). Monterey, CA: Brooks Cole.

The sexuality counselor's best guideline is to be conservative. Unfortunately, clients with serious emotional problems can present sexuality problems with nearly unsolvable ethical situations and where no course of action seems correct. In the absence of a definite violation of a statute or code, ethical hearings come down to the "accepted practice of respected peers." Frequent communication with credentialed colleagues and mentors help keep within high standards of professional practice. In addition, should a case be questioned, the counselor's best interest is in showing that the difficulty has been discussed in confidence, and guidance received from a respected professional consultant.

CHAPTER 4, PART 4

AASECT ETHICAL GUIDELINES

The most complete ethical guidelines for professionals working with sexuality-related matters was adopted by the American Association of Sex Educators, Counselors, and Therapists. The chairperson of the task force was Robert Kolodny, M.D., of the Masters and Johnson Institute, and the work was first published in 1979 with input from many professionals. The sections of the code are Competence and Integrity of Sex Therapists, Counselors and Educators; Confidentiality; Welfare of the Client; and Welfare of Students, Trainees, and Research Subjects. The *AASECT Ethical Guidelines* are subject to ongoing revision and clarification by members of AASECT, and recent copies may be obtained from the address listed in Learning Experience No. 45.

Not all sexuality educators, counselors, and therapists agree with the guidelines as adopted, and vigorous debate occurred during their evolution. Some practitioners have questioned the prohibition of sexual touching between counselor and client, and others find the standards for training, advertising, and/or research too conservative. No doubt other counselors would prefer more, rather than less, rigorous standards.

The suggestion in this training program is that people learning sexuality counseling would be well advised to adhere closely to the *AASECT Ethical Guidelines* in all respects. After considerable practice and experience, if a practitioner has questions or objections, these may be written or brought up at annual meetings, or with regional ethics committees. Those person who object responsibly to the *Guidelines* do so on the basis of their own professional experience, and a counselor would seem to need extensive time in practice to justify a credible challenge.

Ethical guidelines are in everyone's best interest. Issues can quickly become complex and a practitioner does not have the time to reinvent the wheel of accepted conduct, nor the social and cultural background (acceptance) necessary to develop a separate base for professional practice. National organizations and insurance companies have stated publicly that lawsuits in mental health have increased, with large damages being awarded in sex-related cases. Guidelines are especially needed in sexuality counseling, because challenges occur unexpectedly and when they do, one is in a much better position if practice is in keeping with recognized ethical guidelines.

EXAMPLE: Using the AASECT Guidelines

"AASECT Section II. Confidentiality in Sex Therapy (refers to counseling as well). 6. A sex therapist may discuss in a professional manner information about a client or matters related to the evaluation, treatment, or follow-up of a client for purposes of consultation with professional colleagues, when there is reasonable assurance that the identity of the client will not be disclosed."

Questions:

1. Can a college counselor talk to a residence hall director about a client's allegations of sexual harassment and acquaintance rape, which are related to male attitudes on a particular floor? Would this or other sections of the *Guidelines* cover the question? Would it make a difference if the counselor believed that the client could not be adequately treated as long as she/he feared continuing harassment?

2. Can a counseling study group continue to discuss details of a sexuality counseling case without names, after one or more members mentions that they may know the person (s)?

3. Does this section cover the issue of writing up an ongoing counseling case as a project for a graduate class?

Even the AASECT Ethical Guidelines can not completely answer every situation, but they do provide a background for resolving ethical dilemmas, especially when several sections are combined. These can be integrated with the individual states' varying statutes and regulations which apply to mental health treatment. For instance, minors may

receive counseling for a number of sex-related conditions without parental notification in many areas. The recommendation is to keep well informed by looking for definite answers to questions and to obtain copies
of state statutes and regulations. To stay fully informed a counselor may
need to check with a state's attorney or private lawyer from time to time.
An in-depth knowledge of sex-related ethical guidelines and statutes
helps a counselor articulate his/her position, and stands as a shield
against uninformed complaints.

Criticism of a counselor on charges of ethical misconduct often includes a variety of issues like professional judgement, fees, competence,
inappropriate referral or follow-up. However, if any sex-related aspects
exist in a general ethical complaint, often these are seized upon by the
media. Also, while the general public may understand the goals in
treating depression or alcoholism, they may not agree with some sexuality counseling treatment modalities (contraception for teens, masturbation for sexual dysfunction, acceptance of homosexual expression, and
so forth). For these reasons a person doing sexuality counseling is more
vulnerable and needs to be especially circumspect about ethical conduct.

LEARNING EXPERIENCE NO. 45

**A. Send for the most recent *AASECT Ethical Guidelines* for sexuali-
ty counselors, and therapists, in order to have your own copy. The
material is useful whether you join the organization or not.**

      AASECT
      Eleven Dupont Circle, NW, Suite 220
      Washington, DC 20036

**B. Read the following illustration of an ethical dilemma and then
answer the questions which follow.**

**You are having lunch with a friendly colleague who seems
especially "high" and excited. Both of you are feeling comfortable sharing confidences about changes in your work situation.**

Suddenly the other counselor admits to being in a new sexual relationship and says: "But it's OK since after we got started I referred him/her to an excellent social worker I know for counseling. It's fine to talk with you about it since he/she isn't my client now."

1. Find what sections of the *AASECT Ethical Guidelines* apply to the preceding example.

2. What should you do and/or say? What is your responsibility?

3. What type of reasoning is behind your decision in Number 2?

4. Does it matter whether counselor or client are male/female?

5. What would you really do in this type of situation?

Books such as *Sexual Dilemmas for the Helping Professional,* by J. Edelwich and A. Brodsky (NY: Brunne-Mazel, 1982) and articles on specific topics like: "Ethical Considerations Concerning Adolescents Consulting for Contraceptive Services," by T. Silker, in *The Journal of Family Practice,* 15(5), 1982, pp. 909-911, are helpful in resolving ethical problems.

C. Write an ethical dilemma for each major section of the *AASECT Ethical Guidelines* and practice resolving each one. Your dilemmas may be similar in format to that found in Item B of this Learning Experience.

CONCLUSION

The counselor has to be responsive to state regulations of practice, to current court cases, and to professional codes of conduct in considering situations from an ethical perspective. The ethical guidelines developed by AASECT can assist with this task by being more specific about sex-related counseling. While nothing can be absolute, the *Guidelines* represent a thoughtful attempt by a large number of experienced sexologist-practitioners to be clear. Because simple answers seldom apply to all cases, the sexuality counselor is well advised to consider hypothetical problems in order to be prepared for weighing the real ones.

CHAPTER 4, PART 5

CRISIS INTERVENTION

One sometimes hears the phrase "sex is never an emergency" in talks to adolescents by adults, but some sexual issues are part of a crisis. The point to remember is that the counselor cannot expect to remedy everything, but can help the client prioritize and set the first steps in motion. Coordinating subsequent care is also an important role, and assuring follow-up is very helpful.

A major problem with crisis intervention is that the emergency often happens when the counselor is tired, busy, or least expecting it. For this reason alone, plans must be developed in advance for all types of possible crises. A good procedure to follow is to have personal relationships with staffs in crisis centers and emergency rooms so that last minute thumbing through phone books is avoided.

Individual situations vary, and many of them are crisis situations which not only require counseling but also assistance from persons in other professions. Recognition of these situations is the first step.

1. Health Care Emergencies

Health care emergencies often have emotional/psychological aspects but the counselor must prioritize and obtain medical assistance rapidly. Counselors may be accustomed to working in a non-directive way with feelings, but in a possible health crisis one needs to support the client while care is obtained. Resolving related issues can then occur later.

EXAMPLES: Health Care Emergencies

"I've been having these awful cramps for two days, and bleeding, and can't sit in study hall." (possible etopic pregnancy or other serious gynecological condition)

"I took this medicine my boyfriend got for me to bring on my period but I feel funny and everything looks double." (dangerous abortificant, drug, or a panic state)

"These guys beat me up behind the station. They said I'm a fag if I tell. Why can't I get my breath and I keep spitting by blood?" (possible broken ribs, internal bleeding)

"Last year I felt this lump in my breast but read that most of them go away. Now every month it hurts to sleep on that side but I can't have an examination." (terrified client, fearful of family history of cancer)

2. Issues of Forced/Coerced Sex

Believing the victim, accepting and reassuring them, obtaining legal and medical help, and then providing protection to prevent further trauma are accepted procedures in coercian. This is harder than it sounds, because the victim is part of a system and needs to be extricated, often with resistance from others. In addition, he/she will need assistance and a plan to prevent further exploitation in the future.

EXAMPLES: Issues of Forced/Coerced Sex

"And they just took off—I don't feel anything—not even these scrapes from the gravel." (rape victim)

"My father says I can't have a blanket in winter until I work for it." (nine year old incest victim in a cold climate)

"Guess I got drunk before heading for my aunt's. She always wants to fool around on the couch a long time." (15 year old boy after minor bicycle accident)

"And the worst thing about going back to that correctional camp is that I'm smaller than the other guys—I know what will happen again." (sexual assault victim, age 13)

3. Depression Masking Other Emergencies

A client may focus on the depression (how bad they feel), and seem out of touch with its cause. If the crisis has continued to the point where the client is overwhelmed, outside intervention may be needed.

EXAMPLES: Depression Masking Other Emergencies

"Well...I just don't feel like a man anymore...I've been awful down...what was I saying? uh,...funny how my hands shake." (client presenting impotence, having undiagnosed brain tumor)

"Yes, so I just don't care anymore. I seem to be too tired to get out of my room. But my husband is sure it's all my fault." (battered wife presenting with lack of interest in sex)

"My wife blames her drinking on me and maybe I haven't been the best husband. It doesn't make sense to keep struggling." (man in mid-life, suicidal)

"I can't do my homework. My father says that this weekend he'll fix it so no guy will want to fool around with me again." (adolescent girl, physical abuse)

4. Reproductive Issues

In reproductive issues, the crisis may require intensive work, referral, immediate health care or legal protection, and yet it is especially important that the emotional/psychological not be neglected as the case continues. The counselor may need to coordinate the assistance provided by other professionals, while continuing to give the emotional psychological care.

EXAMPLES: Reproductive Issues

"I didn't think you could get pregnant during menopause; our marriage can't stand starting over....we're almost separated now." (couple in their 40's)

"I was sure I was pregnant this time and now I'm spotting. Maybe I'll take a job in another city—I can't let my husband down again." (flight reaction/infertility problem)

"I go back in the Air Force on Monday. If she wants to make the baby legal before then I'll go through with it, but that's it." (19 year old man, 15 year old woman, missed second menstrual period)

"They'll stop this baby too. But they won't find me." (learning disabled woman, after two abortions, ready to run away)

5. Mental Health Emergencies

In a mental health emergency the counselor must look at the underlying deterioration rather than dealing exclusively with the sex-related content being expressed. Usually a counselor will take a person like this for another assessment and referral, protecting the client from harming self or others. The important thing is that the client receive treatment from people trained in working with major mental disorders. In the examples which follow there are sexual issues, and the counselor could be helpful working as part of a treatment team.

EXAMPLES: Mental Health Emergencies

"Someone has to help God get rid of old men who bother little girls. I'm not afraid to...they keep shuffling down the hallway at night. There's going to be a big fire—everything's ending." (victim of childhood sexual abuse, psychotic episodes, close to acting out)

"So what else can I do? The pretty ones keep looking at me on the street. But they don't know what I've got—one by one they'll stop laughing." (paranoid personality, rape fantasies, may act out)

"When I wear my boy clothes I feel some peace, but it's all a sham. I'm going to do it the way the Romans did—a warm bath." (suicidal woman, gender disturbance)

"I'm going to Hell. No matter what I do—usually I take a shower and touch all the tiles in order, and then read three passages in the Bible following the number system, but it doesn't work anymore. I keep thinking about sex...it won't stop!" (acute anxiety state, obsessive-compulsive defenses)

LEARNING EXPERIENCE NO. 46

A. Go through the examples provided for the previous five kinds of crises and for each one identify resources in your area. Do you know where to obtain an emergency psychological/psychiatric assessment for a person you believe to be out of touch with reality? Would you call a sheriff, a colleague, the campus police, or a member of a client's family if a person seemed a danger to self or others? Do you know of a shelter for battered or threatened people? Be sure to locate low cost and public resources as well as private ones.

B. Think of clients with whom you have worked or cases you have heard others discuss. Identify crisis situations and add those examples to the lists provided in the previous five categories. Would you know what to do if these situations came to you now for counseling?

CONCLUSION

As sexuality counselors, most of us think our jobs would be far more gratifying if all clients were agreeable, thoughtful, and moved quickly toward comfortable behavior. Bill Kell, Ph.D., the deeply experienced trainer differed however: "If you aren't seeing any tough ones, you aren't working with the right people. Maybe you're wasting your time" (workshop presentation). Crisis intervention skills are needed. While emergencies aren't routine, doing sexuality counseling will necessitate being prepared for surprises, to consult, to refer, and to expect the occasional challenging client. Being prepared with the knowledge and skills to handle each crisis effectively is an assumption not only by the profession and the public, but also is expected by each client with whom one counsels.

CHAPTER 4, PART 6

CASE RECORDS

Varied approaches can be taken to record keeping, although this is not one of many counselors' favorite activities. One problem may be that few people take the time to design and maintain a satisfying system. Organizations who conduct peer review or accredit counseling agencies usually require that records be consistent, clear, continuous, and complete. For a sexuality counselor to try to "keep everything in my head " would seem arrogant, because the details of treatment plans and client response are so individual. On the other hand, voluminous records waste valuable professional time. What is the happy median?

AN EFFICIENT SYSTEM

Many people in training write case notes which resemble a journal or log, and find these helpful as a learning device. In practice however, a long narrative record is inefficient and seldom consulted. The solution is to design a system of file cards, folders, or outline sheets which can be added to at the end of each counseling contact or day. Such a well used record keeping system helps provide better service to clients.

In some employment settings records are kept in a central place with information added from various personnel. Some schools and practices have a main file which contains names, dates of appointments, test data, and general demographic information. This is available to the staff, to the client, and sometimes to the parents and legal caretakers of minors. These records can be distinct from the counselor's personal notes, which are viewed as the counselor's property. Other counselors are expected to follow a one-record format which is open to clients and selected others. Without fail, be sure to review the laws and regulations which apply in a particular locality, before setting up a record-keeping system.

The most helpful records for a sexuality counselor are those which are completely confidential and uncensored. However, if the possibility exists that records are or may become open to other people, then discretion is needed about what is recorded. Even where basic agency records are kept in a central file, the counselor can keep ongoing personal notes for professional growth, and destroy these in a reasonable time after terminating with a client.

Sexuality counseling notes must always be kept in a locked file or other safe place. For instance, a briefcase needs to be locked in a car, and kept out of the view of others. Unwise practices such as leaving notes in a nursing station, on a dresser, in a graduate student desk, or simply in office drawers are to be avoided. Because almost no place is totally secure from vandals or accidental discovery, a good procedure is to omit last names of others mentioned by clients, and to be somewhat cryptic about events which could be embarrassing if known.

SUGGESTED SYSTEM

Client File

The mechanics of note keeping are changing rapidly as more offices turn to tape recorders, photocopiers, and computer use for records. Any multi-person system raises questions of confidentiality, and therefore great care must be taken in the design and maintenance of a record system. Regardless of the actual physical format, total clarity needs to exist about the purpose and type of content expected in each and all records.

For personal counseling notes, a distinct file, folder or casette tape will be needed for each client. Some of the contents to include are such things as the interview notes (long and short forms), sexuality history, any test results, communication regarding the client from other professionals, stress or health checklists, any drawings and charts made with the client, and copies of counseling suggestions. At first, complete client records may seem time-consuming, and yet as a counselor become busier and sees more people (with longer time periods between contacts), the files become invaluable resources for individualized sexuality counseling.

Long Form

   Much important information which should be recorded is covered in the first one to three counseling sessions. Therefore, each client's file usually begins with "intake notes", "data base", or "initial interview form". Remember that rapport building and exploration of the client's concerns are the goals of the early sessions, whereas information gathering is secondary to that. As the counseling proceeds, some of the categories of information which are important to elicit are as follows:

1. basic demographic information (name, address, telephone number, age, sex, marital status, children, education, occupation, health insurance, referral source),

2. client's presenting problems (listed and described, sexual and nonsexual),

3. additional content of the interview,

4. goals and needs statements (related to specific concerns),

5. procedures and plan (interventions related to goals),

6. counselor's impressions (subjective reactions, assessment),

7. ongoing progress notes in detail, and

8. revised plan (status of the process, counseling suggestions, new goals).

   The preceding list can be expanded to many pages or categories and is called a *long form,* when detailed notes are deemed necessary. In a simple case of sexuality counseling which involves mainly information or ventilation, for only one to four sessions, the counselor may choose to use the long form only once. This can be supplemented with a short form, to complete the records. However in a complex case, often a long form will be necessary for each visit or at frequent intervals. Where legal issues could be involved, a wise procedure is to write notes regarding every interview using a long form as a protective measure.

Short Form

A briefer form (*short form*) of recording is often used as an alternate to the long form. Some agencies use the short form or a modified version and require the *summary form* (described later in this chapter) after every four to six interviews. In Form 4.1 is an outline which may be used as a short form to keep a brief record of ongoing interviews. Many variations are possible, but the overall purpose of designing a short form is to find a way for busy counselors to keep interview notes current.

RECORDING CLIENT PROGRESS

Attention to the phases of counseling helps in keeping useful records. On both long and short forms space is essential to outline the exploration of client concerns (Phase I), the points of focus and clear objectives (Phase II), and program for change (Phase III). Ordinarily, the counselor can record fairly easily the content of interviews and the concrete goals and plans agreed upon with the client.

The more specific the plan is in the written record, the more likely that this clarity will be reflected in the next interview. As the counseling proceeds, the expectation is that the notes will contain less history and more about intervention, counseling suggestions, and client progress. A record which contains basic data, interview contents, and the client's progress, provides a strong basis for review and planning.

RECORDING COUNSELOR'S IMPRESSIONS

At first the counselor may have more difficulty recording subjective data than the objective information received from the client. Practice is helpful in learning to record impressions of

1. the flow of the counseling process,

2. the client's unique response,

3. the counselor's own reactions and concerns, and

4. apparent counselor-client interaction.

Form 4.1. Short form for a brief record of ongoing interviews.

CLIENT   _____

COUNSELOR   _____

Telephone   _____   Date _____

Client Concerns:	Progress:

1. _____   _____

2. _____   _____

3. _____   _____

4. _____   _____

5. _____   _____

6. _____   _____

7. _____   _____

8. _____   _____

Counselor's Process Notes:

At times a record made separately of 1, 2, 3, and 4 will be useful. The following example illustrates this point. The next example illustrates a record which interrelates the four impressions rather than recording separately. Regardless of the format used to record subjective counselor data, it is extremely important to the ongoing management of the work.

EXAMPLE: Counselor's Impressions, Separate

1. Good rapport developing. Exploration of client potency concerns slower than last week. Began to focus on obsessive worries about pleasing partner.

2. Client seemed more apathetic, depressed.

3. Found myself feeling protective, taking too much responsibility for the interview at first.

4. Client expressed discouragement that he now realizes there is no pill or medicine for his sexual problem. We were successful in turning the insight from helplessness to working together toward improved pleasure.

EXAMPLE: Recording Impressions, Integrated

In other instances the counselor may combine impressions of 1, 2, 3, and 4 which are necessarily interrelated. For example:

> *"Client appeared highly anxious and avoided discussion of the sexual abuse described in her first session last week. She became more relaxed with guilt-relieving information and support.*
>
> *Felt it was too soon to confront, but am concerned that increased anxiety symptoms are due to client's fear of change and pressure at home to deny. This client should be in control of disclosure, and needs to build a support system. When I didn't push, she confided that she is relieved that her "bad" uncle has left the state, and tentatively began to express her fears. Holding me at a distance, even when she was so terrified, showed the extent of her lack of trust in anyone."*

SUMMARY RECORD

At the end of each sexuality counseling case, one needs to review the folder; study the mix of long and short forms, index cards, possible client drawings, memos or data; and write a *summary record* which includes the final interview. Most counselors keep all these records for a few years, carefully locked, in the event that the client returns or there is a question. At some point, however, they serve no useful purpose and can be destroyed.

Counselors need to consider what is to be done with confidential sexuality counseling records in the event of their own serious disability or death. The options seem to be to leave a statement to the effect that the records should be destroyed by a trusted person, or that they be turned over to a particular colleague who would then be responsible for their use and/or disposal. Mailing them to clients does not seem a solution, because mental health records are not handled in that impersonal fashion. Again the decision depends on how personal and complete the counseling notes are. General agency records usually pose no problem. Rather than leave the disposition to chance, counselors should make arrangements for the management of notes before files of any consequence have built up.

LEARNING EXPERIENCE NO. 47

A. **Make a decision to become an expert in record keeping. If you are in a school, practice, or agency where the format is set, look carefully to determine whether or not the form is sufficient for your needs in sexuality counseling. If not, check into modifications or a supplemental system.**

B. **Should you have no established format as yet, use resources in your locale to design your own structure. As soon as possible, try to use your system with the goal of making further improvements.**

C. **Look into computerized record keeping if you have any knowledge in that area. For instance, the *Counseling Goals Systems*, published by Accelerated Development, is a computerized** case management, research, and program development tool. Experiment with that, or modify other software to accomodate sexuality counseling records.

REASONS FOR RECORD KEEPING

The best reasons for good record keeping are first to improve the counseling offered to each client and thus, second, to improve the month to month management of one's counseling work. A third important reason is for the client's benefit if case history and/or treatment data are needed for referral situations or if a client is legally involved. A fourth reason is for the protection of the counselor.

EXAMPLE: Records Used to Limit Liability

A college counselor might see a junior twice in October for mild premature ejaculation, successfully treated through information and behavioral shaping. It would be shocking to learn that the student shot himself after a family argument while at home for the midwinter holidays. In the event of an inquiry the records could show that the counselor was working within the bounds of his/her competence, and employed accepted counseling practice.

Mental health professionals cannot be expected to foresee and prevent all problems, but must be able to show evidence of responsible work. The counselor would feel better with complete notes also, even though suicidal situations are always painful, knowing that the counseling done was appropriate for what the client chose to address in October.

A fifth reason for complete records is their usefulness in enhancing professional growth. When clear notes are shared with peers or supervisors, others can see where a particular client's need remained unmet, or a theme ran through several sessions. Even experienced counselors pull out a folder once in a while, and discuss a difficult client with a colleague (consultation is an excellent means of professional growth as well as providing assurance that the client is receiving comprehensive counseling).

A sixth reason is so the counselor can keep track of which counseling interventions were the most successful with particular sex related problems. This can develop into helpful research.

Records reflect the work a counselor does, and the better one keeps records the better his/her counseling can become. Thus, developing a fine case record system and keeping it up to date are essential components of each counselor's work.

CHAPTER 4, PART 7

PROCESS OF REFERRAL

This is a challenging topic to generalize about. Almost never will the counselor see anything definitive about a particular referral situation in a textbook, because the considerations are

1. refer when you can't provide all the necessary help,

2. find the appropriate resources in your area, and

3. make the referral persuasive so the client will accept it.

Therefore, each client referral situation is unique.

Two types of referral exist: a client can be transferred entirely to other care givers, or simply referred for additional help while the sexuality counseling continues. Referring for professional services in addition to sexuality counseling can greatly increase counselor effectiveness. Sometimes an advisable procedure is to make the referral desirable, but not necessary. How strongly should referrals be made? The following example is provided to facilitate consideration of that question.

EXAMPLE: 19 Year Old Client, 60 Pounds Overweight, 6th Session

Counselor: *"Diana, we've made good progress on overcoming some of the negative consequences of the early sexual and physical abuse from your stepfather. Because you keep coming back to body image as a problem, why don't you join a weight-losing group? We'll continue with our work, of course.*

Should the referral for other help be firmer if the client has a serious alcohol problem, instead of a weight issue? Why? What if the referral was for persistent pain during intercourse? The counselor has the right to establish the limits within which he/she will work, if the client refuses referrals. No absolute guidelines are available, but the more resources a client uses for personal growth, the greater the probability of a successful outcome.

A transfer-referral presents a different kind of resistance, because the client has to deal with termination from one counselor, starting over again, and possibly a feeling of failure/discouragement. When the counselor has decided that referral-transfer is necessary, sufficient time needs to be allowed to clarify, support, and offer the best assistance possible.

EXAMPLE: Counseling Husband and Wife, Condensed from Early in the 2nd Session

Counselor: *"Probably you will want to make progress on your sexual disinterest and concern about loss of erection at a later date, Mr. S. But for now, I believe that you need an individual therapist to help modify your mood swings and depression."*

Mrs. S.: *"You don't think the only problem is sex? I don't either, but Sam keeps saying it is. I've been really worried when he can hardly get himself to work. We can't keep living like this."*

Mr. S.: *"Well, I really don't care. If it isn't one thing it's another. I just thought if I could get one part of my life together..."*

Counselor: *"And you are, Sam, but I think it will be easier when you feel better generally. An associate of mine, Dr. W., is one person I can highly recommend, and you may have heard of Dr. B. also. I will gladly speak to either of them, with your permission, or any other psychiatrist or psychologist you might suggest. Then I'd like to give you a call in two weeks, and ask you how you are doing. Now how shall we go about selecting a doctor to work with your depressed feelings?"*

COMMENT: It is wise to make as non-labeling a referral as possible. If Mr. S. had refused, the counselor could have expressed more concern about health, and encouraged a thorough physical and another assessment. Under no circumstances should a counselor work with a client who is beyond his/her expertise simply because the person would rather not go elsewhere.

MAJOR CONSIDERATIONS IN MAKING
A REFERRAL DECISION

Expertise of Counselor

Counselors can become aware of their style when working in strong specialty areas, noting confidence, flexibility, and general helpfulness to the client. This comfort level can be compared to working in an unfamiliar counseling area, with a difficult client, in order to get in touch with the difference. Responding to the inner experience of being uncomfortable with a client is important in addition to knowing one's limits intellectually. Counselors generally continue to work with those clients where they are prepared and effective, and to refer when they are not. The scope and quality of competent work can be enlarged through experience and training.

Content Areas

Various experts suggest that some sexual problems are so resistant to treatment that they should automatically be referred to specialists. Among those often mentioned are primary impotence (a man who has almost never had an erection), sexual aversion (high anxiety about most aspects of sexuality), and gender disturbance (a person who believes he/she should be the other sex). Other conditions which are often suggested for referral are people with long-term sexual dysfunction, traumatized rape and incest victims, serious drug/alcohol abusers with sexual problems, couples with very serious personality or relationship disturbances, special syndromes like anorexia nervosa or other specialized mental health problems, and health-dependent symptoms. Sometimes sexuality counseling is useful when the more serious problems and symptoms have been alleviated through other forms of treatment.

Specialties

Most counselors are trained in specific areas, and therefore have to be careful about the boundaries of practice. For instance, one school counselor could be knowledgeable about children and train easily in the direction of helping young victims of incest or child sexual abuse. Another school counselor who is skilled working with adolescent groups, could move toward counseling teens about sex, contraception, and relationships. Whereas one nurse might prefer work with women regarding infertility problems and sexuality, a nurse on a rehabilitation unit might specialize in sexuality and disability. The goal is to be competent in one's specific area of sexuality counseling, and to know when to refer other clients appropriately.

Health Issues

Almost every resource points to the important physiological substrata of sexuality. A non-medically trained person cannot rule out physical contributing causes of sexual problems, especially since some are very subtle. According to the literature, ten years ago the estimate was that only about 10% of sexual problems had a physical factor, whereas now some clinics report 30% to 40% medical/health factors. Except for the educational or moral-ethical kinds of sexuality related counseling, ("Do other people's worries about past experiences affect sexuality?" Should I stop this extra-marital affair?"), a medical checkup with direct reference to the sexual difficulty is always recommended.

Value Conflicts

As noted elsewhere in this program, when a counselor cannot empathize with the life style or significant values of a client, the individual or couple must be referred elsewhere. Because the counselor may become aware of this after the counseling has begun, one must be especially careful and considerate about this kind of referral.

Lack of Progress

Even when practicing within a familiar area of expertise, some clients will not improve as expected. Counselors vary in their degree of persistence and will often stay with a slow moving client as long as progress occurs. However, if the counselor believes the client might make better gains somewhere else, it is important to offer referral rather than remain stalled.

Danger to Self or Others

Nothing about the specialty of sexuality counseling prevents the counselor from seeing suicidal or dangerously destructive clients. Since the landmark Tarasoff case, human service workers have become sensitive to the importance of going extra lengths to protect the client and significant others. The recommendation here is that one be careful, rather than casual, in making these judgments.

EXAMPLE: Counseling a Client Who Is Potentially Dangerous to Others

No excuse would be acceptable for continuing to counsel a client about a ten year old rape incident, knowing that she has current fantasies and mentions plans to "cut up" her sister. An immediate consultation with a supervisor and an assessment by a licensed professional, are necessary. The sister must be warned, as unpleasant as it is to do, or, if she is a minor, her parents must be informed. Then if the client is diagnosed a risk to herself or her sister, the procedures for voluntary or, if necessary, involuntary treatment will be initiated. During this kind of assessment some clients "snap out of it", have tearful reconciliations during family conferences, and a treatment plan is accepted. The limit setting and modeling of priorities are therapeutic in themselves, but it will be important to continue the sexuality counseling at some point rather than just attend to the crisis. Some clients who have it impressed upon them that aggression will not be tolerated, turn the anger toward self mutilation, substance abuse, or promiscuous acting out. The treatment would only be beginning once the overall safety needs were recognized.

SUCCESSFUL REFERRALS

The counselor who knows a great many referral sources personally is likely to be highly successful in convincing people to use them. When a particular STD clinic is described as having a discreet, respectful approach, or a home for "unmanageable girls" (often those who don't meet someone's sexual standards) is compared to other facilities, the client can make the best choice. A vague, impersonal, or lukewarm referral is seldom utilized by a client.

LEARNING EXPERIENCE NO. 48

A. Consider some likely referral sources you might use and make a list of ten. Visit at least half of them and ask the following questions:

   1. *"What can I tell my clients which will encourage them to make use of your services?"*

   2. *"What percentage of the people referred to you actually receive help?"*

   3. *"What can I as a counselor do to help make the referral process successful?"*

B. Discuss with three colleagues their procedures when making referrals. What works and what doesn't? Candidly exchange referral resources and techniques. Expand this when you attend workshops and meetings in your area, by looking for specialties which you might need.

Confidentiality

When making a referral, remember that the client is the person seeking help from you and one or more other sources, and the helpers have no right to manipulate behind the scenes. In every instance when asked for information gained in counseling, the practitioner must have the client's signed statement before releasing anything. A simple form like the following can be available in a desk or briefcase:

I, _____(client's name)_____ , give permission to

_____(counselor)_____ to share with

_____(referral resource)_____ information learned

during the course of our counseling relationship.

   Limitations: (For example: "only material relating to my life at this college," or "excluding mention of abuse in my marriage".) _____

_____

_____
(date)

_____
(client's signature)

The counselor needs to keep the signed statement in a locked file indefinitely in the client's folder. The only exception to a signed statement for the release of information would be a critical health emergency, serious danger to self or others, or a prior agreement with a referral source (such as a probation officer) understood by the client.

Special problems often occur with referral when the person doing counseling has some other relationship to the client, such as teacher, hall advisor, youth group leader, or co-worker.

EXAMPLE: Confidentiality, Dependent on Staff Role

A boy in a residence hall tells a staff person in a cafeteria that some bigger boys are masturbating him and threatening him with other sexual acts. A counseling relationship may exist if the boy has been seeing the staff person as his "counselor," however, the situation would be different if the boy was reporting the problem to the staff person as an "authority." Whenever the situation does get to the counselor, he/she has the responsibility to carefully check out the boy's expectations, in order to retain his trust and that of other residents. The issue of safety and sexual abuse must be dealt with and resolved, but communicating about the limits of confidentiality in the counseling vs. staff role would be important.

Facing Failure In Referral

What happens when a counselor knows that a client is likely to benefit greatly from a referral to a couple's communication group, a gay men's support group, or a second gynecological opinion, and yet the client refuses to go? First of all, was the helper guilty of "listen a little and prescribe", or has time been taken to focus and set realistic goals? If the latter was accomplished, perhaps not enough effort was made to identify the client's objections to the referral. Finally, the counselor has to remember that a client has complete freedom to choose among resources, and the helping role is to facilitate, not dominate.

EXAMPLE: Preorgasmic Woman, Age 66, 4th Session

Counselor: *"We were talking about the importance of your body image last week. So how did you find the yoga class?"*

Client: *"Well, it was probably full, and it would have been awfully close to supper in our dining room."* (retired persons' residence)

Counselor: *"It sounds as though you lost enthusiasm for the yoga, Martha. Can you explain what got in the way?"*

Client: *"I'd feel so stiff with all those people—on the phone they said to wear loose clothes and leg warmers, and I kept thinking of those girls that dance in leotards..."*

Counselor: (does not debate exercise clothes) *"You somehow felt you wouldn't fit in....."*

Client: *"And I'd be a stick."*

Counselor: *"OK, I understand, it was too big a jump. What could you do to feel better about yourself physically?"*

Client: (describes and rejects several possibilities) *"And one of my friends is signing up for an adult education class called Stretch for Retirement. You have to be over 50, and we could go together."*

Counselor: *"Um, hmmmm..."* (friendly silence, encouraging planning)

Client: *"It's in the morning too. Do you think it will help me with the problem I came to you about?"*

Counselor: *"That sounds definitely in the right direction. Now I'd like to explain to you a special group of exercises called Kegels, which will help increase circulation in the private area of your body around your vulva. It will combine well with that exercise class."*

COMMENT: The above is condensed since the actual discussion could have taken 20 minutes; it is included to show that a client cannot be hurried to action. Most people will not assertively voice objections to counselor suggestions, especially sexuality-related ones, and yet lack of follow-up on referrals gives the counselor a deeper view of client fears and intentions.

Using Humor

Sometimes an impasse in counseling can occur around a suggested referral, and here humor may help: "Are we working on the same thing?" or "Maybe you're afraid that a scorekeeper publishes a record of everyone who goes in and out of there?" Occasionally simply asking: "Is there something more important to you than this?" or "Is there an aspect we haven't talked about?" will bring out a crucial element. The main thing to remember is that people will usually accept a reasonable referral which is made with encouragement, unless there is a reason. Discovering that, sometimes with humor, is part of counseling.

CONCLUSION

The counselor should not become invested in a particular referral, but does need to be interested in the process of overcoming obstacles and finding solutions. Negotiation with a client is a necessary skill, and each time a referral is avoided more is learned about a client's problems and resistances. In like manner when a referral is accepted as part of on-going counseling, monitoring how it is going will add helpful information.

CHAPTER 4, PART 8

BUSINESS PLANNING

Many of the issues involved in the practical management of sexuality counseling need not be covered in this book, because these are no different from other counseling. Readers are referred to books and periodicals which focus on the business side of mental health care for more specific information. Also, because this training program is intended for counselors working in a wide variety of public and private settings, by necessity the information must be somewhat general. However, a few areas require some special attention for sexuality-related counseling.

PLANNING FOR CHANGE

One of the most frequent and painful problems encountered is a practice or staff which is so successful that it grows too fast. Each practitioner may have a general idea about the appropriateness of advertising, policies, or specialty areas, but due to the pressure of growth neglects regular conferences with others. Often this weakness in communication and planning is invisible until a crisis occurs, and that is the worst possible time to set policy calmly. Because sexuality counseling can receive unusual public attention, procedures and management must be consistent and clear.

A tool which contributes to good management and orderly growth is the annual work expectation review. Current job descriptions are essential for any counselor; even the person working alone can benefit from making the effort each year to rework goals, commitments, and responsibilities. In any larger unit, the sexuality counselor must be especially clear about expected interactions with the group and the degree of autonomy expected. Clear job descriptions and policies are those which change with circumstances, cover the issues of professional discretion, and define those areas where colleagues or a supervisor must be consulted.

EXAMPLES: Types of Issues Which Should Be Clear In Advance

May the school counselor transport a sexually abused child to a medical center for evaluation without checking with someone else?

Can the nurse-counselor decide when to bill for a half hour of counseling, or are there set protocols for allowable conditions?

Who decides which trainees accepted by a group are qualified to provide sexuality counseling, and what are the standards for supervision?

What guidelines are used for the purchase of explicit sexual videotapes and books to be used in couples counseling?

Should one counselor in a group choose to meet with alcohol abusing sexuality offenders, when others in the practice see this as condoning continued exploitation of victims?

People seldom enter practice thinking of separation or divorce, any more than most married couples do. However, change is the way of the world and sexuality counselors often seem to grow in different directions from one another, and at a different pace. Arrangements need to be made for people to leave a staff, and for policies to change, without intense power struggles. An accountant's or attorney's fee is a small price to pay for the relief that comes with the structure that is there should problems arise.

WORK LOAD

While money could seem to be a large potential problem, most people believe they can negotiate salary, perhaps because of its concreteness. A frequent bone of contention, however, is how to balance the time spent on public relations, attracting clients by serving on health care and consumer service boards, speaking to PTA's or other community organizations, and attending professional meetings. Practices and staffs are often made up of people having different skills; some prefer doing more direct counseling service while others excel at outreach. Still others are efficient at administration, grant writing, or supervising interns.

The important point to remember is that many talents are needed in a successful delivery system, public or private, and that salary compensation can only begin to reflect the total amount done by each person. The goal is to arrive at a balanced load for each counselor, appropriate to training and responsibility, and to compensate everyone fairly. The following example illustrates how time spent on different functions may vary for two counselors in the same practice.

EXAMPLE: Work Variance Between Two Counselors

	Counselor A	Counselor B
Individual Counseling	30%	10%
Couples/Family	30%	10%
Group Counseling	0%	30%
Administration	20%	10%
Public Relations	5%	10%
Supervision	10%	0%
Consulting	5%	30%
TOTAL	100%	100%
Total Work Hours	44 per week	52 per week

In this example, assume that Counselor A is a senior member who employs Counselor B to do group work and to get out in the community. Their sexuality-related counseling specialities complement one another. While the actual hours worked and the income generated by each may be different, their overall input can reflect exactly what each one prefers. The concrete data also gives an objective basis for negotiation about salary and income.

LEARNING EXPERIENCE NO. 49

A. Find a place where sexuality counseling is being done; ask several people on the staff to go through random weeks in their appointment books and list their hours. Provide categories which cover everyone's major responsibilities such as individual counseling, couples counseling, family counseling, group counseling, record keeping, administration, supervision, educational groups, courses taught, health care provided, research, consulting, public relations, public service, case work, professional development, and other.

B. Give each person (who wishes to cooperate) a one-page sheet with all the categories listed, and ask each person to estimate his/her work by percentages of the total for several representative weeks. This is similar to the "Example: Work Variance Between Two Counselors" previously shown.

C. Ask individuals to indicate what proportion of their work is sexuality-related.

D. Ask if you may review each person's data in confidence, and note the range of work counselors do and the amount of time spent on business aspects.

E. In finishing this exercise and if you have permission, share the actual hours and percentages with individuals, or the whole group may discuss the results.

F. If you do not have access to a whole staff or group, interview individual counselors for the same information.

G. When you have finished examining other people's work outline, develop an ideal one for yourself.

SUPPORT STAFF

Most sexuality counselors find that regardless of the setting, before long they need some additional help. Procedures will be needed for enlarging the staff, including what the duties will be, before implementing the plan. If no expansion in staff is possible, then a process must be developed to limit clients if and when needed.

Vital support in the form of cooperation received from other staff members such as secretaries, accountants, health educators, interns, and other non-counselors is essential. They must understand the importance of confidentiality and know how to respond to people. A sexuality counselor could be excellent, and yet, if an aide or receptionist is habitually brusque or gossips, much good work will be nullified.

PROFESSIONAL INSURANCE COVERAGE

Counselors frequently receive brochures in the mail describing a bewildering number of plans for homeowner's insurance, disability insurance (coverage for income protection and office overhead), various kinds of life insurance, retirement investments, health insurance, and liability insurance. Insurance is a technical field and the counselor will need to take time to understand the many kinds which can fit into financial planning.

Without question, a person practicing sexuality counseling is well advised to obtain the best possible professional liability insurance. The premiums for mental health malpractice insurance have escalated rapidly in the 1980s and according to insurance companies this was largely because of sexuality related claims.

Any practitioner can be held responsible for an alleged malpractice, negligence, or mistake, and the claim must be defended even if it is later proved invalid. Preparing for litigation is expensive even when innocent, and in the case where the plaintiff is awarded damages an uninsured counselor could be financially devastated.

The easiest way to obtain liability insurance is through a plan offered to members of a professional group, such as AASECT, the

American Association for Counseling and Development, the National Association of Social Workers, or the American Psychological Association. The annual premiums are reasonable, but the coverage has special limitations for people doing sexuality counseling.

Some policies will provide protection against all types of malpractice suits except those alleging sexual misconduct, or will set limits for this type of case. Other policies will pay for the defense of a claim arising from alleged sexual contact with a client, but will not pay for any damages awarded if the counselor is found guilty. A policy may limit damages arising from allegations of erotic physical contact with a client, a person in the client's family or household, or any other person who has an affectionate relationship with a client or family.

Individual circumstances vary, so that a therapist who treats couples with a co-therapist might be adequately covered by some policies which would not suit the needs of a solo counselor. Since a number of organizations offer insurance plans, a reasonable procedure is to write to those professional associations for which one is eligible and to check with a private insurance agent as well. In this way a counselor can select the policy which underwrites the most complete coverage.

Sexuality counseling is especially vulnerable to allegations of malpractice, even when counselor/client sexual contact is not the issue. The following illustrates how the counselor can become involved in litigation even when his/her behavior has been professional:

> Relatives of clients may be upset about sexual material which comes out in counseling, and find fault with the counselor (adolescent sexual activity, forced sex, atypical sexual behavior, homosexuality).

> Seriously troubled clients, angry at the world, may not have their expectations met if sexual symptoms are not quickly "cured," even though the causes are deeper issues.

> Issues of divorce and child custody can involve counselors who have worked with the couple or any of the parties.

> Families in conflict over battering, rape, or child sexual abuse may sue a counselor for malpractice as part of their general denial.

No matter how expert and ethical a counselor is, it is vital to have good insurance coverage...and then hope never to need it.

EXAMPLE: Insurance Protects Counselor

A counselor in a private school worked with a shy 16 year old boy who had a low self concept, partly because of childhood instances of sexual molestation by a family friend. During the following year the boy's parents withdrew him abruptly from the school, following which the teenager became depressed and revealed how much he missed his girlfriend. The parents then instituted a lawsuit against the school specifically naming the counselor, "for having pushed the boy toward precocious sexual activity." It required two years for the process of proving the allegations false, and the suit was dropped, but it was fortunate for the counselor that the school had a comprehensive insurance policy which covered a highly competent attorney. The entire matter could have destroyed a valuable career.

Individuals who practice in agencies or institutions might consider checking into the insurance coverage there. Sometimes conditions exist in the insurance coverage which the person doing sexuality-related counseling needs to know. The counselor may join a staff committee working to improve the quality of insurance coverage for the group, and at the same time supplement the agency's insurance coverage with a policy of his/her own.

Other kinds of insurance also should be considered in any practice or agency. The premises where sessions are held and records kept should be covered against fire, theft, and personal injury (accident) claims. Even in the most carefully maintained offices a distraught client can slip, and/or important records can be vandalized.

Counselors often relish the sense of accomplishment that comes from providing a direct service, and yet income to a group or individual stops when clients cannot be seen for some reason. Therefore disability insurance and retirement plans such as a Keough and IRA are not a luxury, since they are most valuable when started early. Sensible insurance and investment coverage of all kinds will reduce stress for the sexuality counselor by providing financial and legal protection against the unexpected.

PUBLIC RELATIONS

Little needs to be said about communication with the public because professionals in human services usually have good skills in this area. The important thing to remember is that the general public is not as comfortable with sexuality as practitioners are, so misinformation can spread rapidly. Regular professional communication with community groups, other practitioners, and the public is extremely important. This not only encourages a steady flow of referrals, but also provides a support network in the event of problems with a client, staff member, or policy. Until more of society accepts sexuality as a comfortable part of human experience, sexuality counselors will need to be especially careful to attend to public relations on an ongoing basis.

CONCLUSION

Many counselors are surprised when they become aware of the large proportion of time they must allot to arranging a practice, becoming known, doing public service work, and achieving professional recognition. As counselors become efficient service providers, they also are likely to encounter more administration and supervision challenges, and the need for continued public information programs. The whole purpose of paying attention to the many business aspects of sexuality counseling is to free the counselor to work under the best possible conditions, in order to provide excellent service.

CHAPTER 4, PART 9

FEES

Compared to some goods and services, sexuality counseling is expensive because it is labor intensive. Given the present state of knowledge, treatment usually requires a number of hours by a trained professional. Although not every client pays a direct fee-for-service, the cost must be covered in some way. Naturally, fees have an influence on both the counselor and the client regardless of how direct or indirect the funding. Because of cycles in the political, economic, and social climates, the proportion of public, private, and charitable payment for services fluctuates, and the counselor needs to be aware of this very real factor.

NO DIRECT-FEE COUNSELING SERVICE

Sometimes clergy, graduate students who volunteer at a drop-in center, institutional staff, and school counselors have difficulty in thinking of money as a major consideration. Because their income covers other work and clients are not paying by the hour, many counselors can seem to ignore finances. Reflection reveals that in some way the congregation, tuition, staff salaries, or some form of funding covers all counseling done. Usually the premises and supervision are provided, even if the counselor isn't paid directly.

Clients may find that counseling, which is received as part of the general student fee or overall employee relations program, is more comfortable than a $60.00 an hour charge (where the client realizes that five dollars went by talking about the counselor's dog). The other side of the coin is that without fees a tendency can occur on both the part of the counselor and client to drift, and to expect an indefinite number of sessions. This can be a special problem in sexuality counseling where clients may avoid the anxiety of working on those problems which brought them to counseling.

One solution for counselors working in a shelter agency, a residence hall, or a situation where counseling is mixed with other duties is to be clear about when counseling is being done. If the counseling time is clearly identified, the counselor and the client can work as though they were receiving a reward of infinite worth for each counseling session. An interesting situation often occurs when grants terminate or economic cuts force a shift toward "fee for service." At that time many counselors find they can deliver high quality work more efficiently than they had previously, and also that most clients will manage to pay reasonable fees.

The experience of a counselor in a woman's center who agonized about charging $15.00 an hour, after a reduction in United Way funds, is enlightening. A grateful client agreed that she should save from her grocery allowance and pay the fee gradually. She went on to explain that in her home culture of Korea, a person acting in a counseling role was spoken to using only the highest level of formal language. She considered being able to obtain counseling a privilege. This example is included not to put counselors on a pedestal, but to emphasize that when ordinary people (all of us) train and take on the responsibility of counseling, that activity is valuable work. Whether paid directly or not, counselors need to model belief in their worth and become comfortable with fees as the type of exchange expected in our society.

FEE FOR SERVICE

Many counselors have a small private practice in addition to work elsewhere, whereas others are in full-time agency or private practice. Sexuality counseling may be the major focus of one's work or only a small part. Counselors usually have a standard hourly rate, often for a 50 minute session, and may charge a different amount per person for group or family work than for individual counseling. Establishing fees is often a balance between overhead expense and the local rate for one's level of experience.

EXAMPLE: Determining Fees On Basis of Cost of Operation

One counselor's rent, heat, office supplies, secretary, answering service, fee for supervision, insurance, custodial charges, parking garage, and other expenses cost about $25.00 an hour per client. Another high school counselor uses his wife's accounting office several evenings a week for his private practice, makes the appointments, and keeps his own books. Certainly the second counselor's overhead would be much lower than the first's, so that he could charge half the rate and make about the same amount per client hour.

When calculating income, remember that a person cannot see 8 to 10 individual clients per day, for hourly sessions, five days a week, for very long. Many agencies consider 20 clients or sessions as a full case load and assign other responsibilities for the remaining time. Most private practitioners also vary their week with consulting, groups, or teaching in order to avoid the well publicized "burn-out."

Group practice (two or more professionals working in the same setting) has many advantages over solo practice. The obvious benefits include shared overhead, clerical, legal, accounting, answering and cleaning services, and easily arranged coverage for one another. The more subtle advantages are the ability to share knowledge, peer supervision, and an understanding atmosphere for pressure times. A group practice consisting of at least one person who is trained in sexuality counseling will receive referrals from other professionals and also will attract clients to the practice who otherwise might not come. A counseling or mental health team which works well together will find that indeed the gestalt is greater than the sum of the separate individuals working alone.

NEEDY CLIENTS

Sexuality counseling is done by varied professionals in all the human service and educational settings, so that sometimes fees are set by the counselor and at other times by an agency. In any case, the counselor must be sensitive to where costs are preventing needy clients from seeking or continuing important treatment. One method is to offer a flexible fee scale whenever possible, with the session rate based on client income. The mechanics of setting standards takes time, including a way to handle exceptions, but once in place a sliding scale facilitates fee discussions.

Other options for reducing costs to the client are to offer services on a group basis (seeing two or more clients together) or as part of a funded project. Another procedure is to have the counseling setting (agency or private practice) established as a practicum or internship site for counselors in training. Good client service can be provided through carefully selected and supervised counseling trainees. Another recognized practice for mental health workers is to fit a few clients into their work week who can pay only a token amount or barter, or who cannot pay, strictly on a charitable basis.

EXAMPLE: A No-Fee-Paying Client

A counselor in a community mental health center has an agreement with the supervisor that up to 3 hours each week will be spent with low-income clients. A typical free client would be a teenager who was raped while going home after babysitting in her neighborhood. Her single-parent mother is fighting debts while she works and supports three children; they are just above the income level which would make them eligible for public assistance. The counselor decides not to take the $10.00 minimum sliding fee from the teenager because she desperately needs shoes, haircuts, and other necessities. This client brings a rather crisp loaf of homemade bread and a poem to the last interview. The $60.00 which could have been charged for the six sessions clearly meant more to the family than it would have to the agency budget.

Considering the number of people who are living below the poverty line, counselors must be creative and make arrangements to assist those in need. A counselor can collect data about free service for the needy, and approach philanthropic or civic groups to help fund counseling for high risk groups. At times counselors may have to extend their usual hours to do some *pro bono publico* work. Sexuality counselors are especially needed to assist victims of sex offenses, the disabled, those with unwanted pregnancies, or adolescents acting out, who have little or no money. Naturally the total amount of below-cost service usually has to be limited, but human service professionals demonstrate integrity when working in the spirit of Adler's "social interest."

HEALTH INSURANCE

Many clients ask about the possibility of insurance coverage for sexuality counseling. On a national level, the amount of mental health care which is being covered by insurance has been increasing. Third party payments are uneven, and vary from client to client, company to company, and state to state. Counselors in a number of states are being recognized as independent providers, and in some other areas insurance companies make their own determinations and cover particular counseling groups. Many counselors are supervised and signed for by other mental health professionals, although this practice is subject to change.

Insurance is not the only way to pay for counseling services, but counselors can become active in professional organizations which influence more favorable and fair coverage. Within recent years a shift has occurred from the concept of "medical insurance" to "health insurance," especially as research has shown that a high percentage of patients seen by the general physician have stress related symptoms. As a result, more patients are accepting referrals for counseling or thinking of it themselves.

Counselors owe it to their clients to obtain coverage wherever reasonably possible. Aspects like assessment using the **DSM-III** or other coding systems, procedures for keeping records, and communication with supervisor and insurance companies take extra time and training. Because the only adjectives for the status of third party payments for mental health work are "variable" and "changing," the counselor must work out how to be both persistent and practical.

ARRANGING FOR PAYMENT

Because sexuality counseling is challenging, the counselor needs to find a balance so that neither self or client is stressed by the fee aspect. Clients need a clear, matter of fact explanation of charges and billing procedures before they become involved in the counseling relationship. No one is served by erratic billing or avoidance of talking about money, because a debt which builds up is harder on everyone. In thinking about charging for sexuality counseling, if people can pay for treatment of a rash or toothache, a dented fender, or a case of drinks for a party, then they can pay for necessary sexuality counseling in most instances.

A particular difficulty with symptom-oriented sexuality counseling is the issue of cure. As clearly as possible, the client and any one else involved in paying for the counseling must understand that the counselor will help to improve the potency problem, or work out a resolution for an unintended pregnancy; however, the fee is on a per session basis and is not contingent on an outcome which is satisfactory to all concerned.

One final caution is the importance of considering collection of an account as part of the professional relationship. A surprising number of ethical complaints involve practitioners who become rude or otherwise unprofessional in their attempts to extract payment from former clients, their parents, or ex-spouses. No matter how abrasive the client becomes, the counselor is still bound to act within a therapeutic framework.

LEARNING EXPERIENCE NO. 50

A. **Try to identify the range of fees for counseling services, especially sexuality-related counseling in your area. Public and private agencies and individuals should be willing to explain their fee schedule when they know you are gathering information as part of a training project. Be sure to ask about the intricacies of insurance payments, service to the needy, overhead, and sliding scales.**

B. **Ask counselors who do not charge by the session how their work is funded and how it would change if they had to require payment for sessions. Try to learn more about the various ways, from grants to charitable donations to creative budgeting, that sexuality counseling expenses can be covered.**

C. Ask a number of people from different income levels what they think sexuality counseling costs, and whether they believe they could manage to pay, if needed.

D. Decide how much you could afford for sexuality counseling if you were a client now, and how you would pay for it.

E. If you are currently using a fee scale, examine it for fairness to self and others. If you are not working, or are not on a fee-for-service basis, consider what your counseling time is worth and design a balanced scale.

CONCLUSION

Most human service training teaches very little about the financial side of managing a successful private or agency practice. This is especially vital in sexuality counseling because a reputation for professionalism, respectability, and competence is critical for a continuing service. If people training in sexuality counseling plan ahead to deal with economic issues, they will be more comfortable with this "bottom line" aspect of their work.

CHAPTER 4, PART 10

CONTINUING PROFESSIONAL EDUCATION

All professional groups in human services have made continuing education an important priority. Counselors are expected not only to stay current, but to progress in skill development and add to their knowledge base. The first part of this training program, Chapters 1 through 4, is intended to help a person obtain the background for sexuality counseling. After the counselor has the necessary information about sexuality, the required counseling skills, comfortable attitudes and values, and a knowledge of professional issues, then is the time to assess what else is needed. The remainder of this book assumes the above and focuses on specific sexuality related counseling techniques.

SOURCES

Clearly no training program can encompass every facet of sexuality counseling in depth, so at this point one may find reassurance by noting that numerous supplementary sources of education are available. Organizations, newsletters, and journals already cited publish regular notices of training conferences, courses, and workshops in all areas of sexuality counseling. Nurses, special educators, social workers, school counselors, rehabilitation specialists, clergy, and other counselors often have local, regional, and national meetings where time is devoted to areas of sexuality. With the exception of continuing education which requires prior specialized knowledge such as biofeedback, hypnosis, or particular psychotherapy techniques, a person who completes this program will be prepared to participate competently in any other sexuality counseling training.

TRAVELING TO SOURCES

Until recently, less affluent counselors had difficulty moving geographically to obtain advanced training, unless they worked for a system which encouraged some kind of "sabbatical." Now however, individuals and families are arranging for many creative kinds of advanced study plans. People trade houses or jobs, they commute long distances three days a week, or make arrangements for a two week to two year leave of absence in order to gain new skills and credentials. Many individual counselors never allowed their "significant others" to know how important obtaining additional training is, and they are convinced that spouse, supervisor, or some other person would not cooperate. A first step is to view the decision about obtaining training which is located at a distance as a process, expecting compromises where necessary, and begin the dialogue.

CREATING A LOCAL GROUP

If a counselor is not free to travel at a particular time, he/she probably could attend available local workshops and possibly could help form a peer supervision group. A new group can be started, or the one begun for studying this program can be continued; as members know one another the value increases. Sometimes to encourage a friendly activity together and to save time, a group will choose to meet and have a meal (a breakfast meeting may be a possibility). One person can be the facilitator, or the task can be rotated, but an agenda for each meeting is necessary to keep focused on professional issues.

A good plan is to begin the meeting with one person presenting a summary of a particular topic, e.g., sexuality and depression, new research on AIDS, sources of assistance for sexually abused children, or counseling techniques with adolescent sex offenders. A dialogue on that topic can integrate everyone's knowledge, and then a specific amount of time can be set aside for discussion of ongoing counseling work. Such a peer supervision group in sexuality counseling will need to set goals, work out guidelines for the process, and commit to confidentiality about what is discussed. Members can then help one another stick to the plan and share expertise in ways beneficial to all.

OBTAINING SUPERVISION

An excellent way to improve one's work or to expand sexuality counseling skills is to find a mentor and receive supervision directly. Usually a contract is arranged whereby the individual supervisor is paid and assumes responsibility for regular meetings. A counselor also can volunteer time in an agency or practice and exchange direct service for supervision. Some agencies and individuals offer a training stipend in exchange for the work done, even if they cannot pay a regular salary, and may allow participation in a study or research project.

LEARNING EXPERIENCE NO. 51

A. Relax and consider how much background knowledge and skill you now have in sexuality-related counseling. Appreciate the positive.

B. Arrange several occasions over a week when you are relaxed and enjoying the outdoors or a meditative time, wherein you acknowledge your developing sexuality counseling competence.

C. Make a commitment to approach the Section II of this program looking for your strengths and simply noting areas which need more work or training. Begin to want to find what you don't know, so it can be learned without defensiveness. Enjoy what you know.

SECTION II.

SKILLS FOR SEXUALITY COUNSELING

FACILITATIVE SEXUALITY COUNSELING

    This chapter applies to working with people who are functioning fairly well, but who have an area of difficulty involving sexuality. The five sections overlap with more serious problems discussed in Chapter 6, although they have in common that the distress is part of the usual order of things. These clients may be very unhappy and uncomfortable, suffering from lack of confidence or permission to be normal, believing myths and blocked in their sexual expression, yet the counselor is working with issues which effect many people. In most instances the client is not immobilized.

Problems which fall in the following categories may be ongoing, or of a crisis nature. They may temporarily overwhelm the client or simply be part of the background stress which interferes with daily life. The counselor who provides facilitative sexuality counseling prevents more serious mental health and social problems from developing. Even though every person experiences some difficulty described in this chapter at one time or another, the pain for the client should not be minimized. The relief, which good counseling brings about, is rewarding and growth producing.

Readers are asked to assess their level of skill for each topic by using Form 5.1, both before and after studying the chapter, and to make plans to strengthen areas where more training is needed.

Form 5.1. Checklist for Self Assessment of Sexuality Counseling Skills

CATEGORY	KNOW ENOUGH	NEED MORE	UNSURE
1. Problems Caused by Lack of Information	_____	_____	_____
2. Sexual Concerns of Life Stages	_____	_____	_____
3. Sexual Health Counseling	_____	_____	_____
4. Life Style and Partner Choice	_____	_____	_____
5. Problems with Sexual Expression	_____	_____	_____

CHAPTER 5, PART 1

PROBLEMS CAUSED BY LACK OF CORRECT INFORMATION

All evidence points to the real difficulty people have obtaining good information about sexuality. Even when a reliable source is found, individuals may not absorb what applies to their particular situation. One of the strongest tools a counselor has is the ability to "hear" what a client's misconceptions are and to supply accurate, personalized information. The client may not be aware of what he/she doesn't know, so that the counselor also needs good focusing skills (Phase II) to avoid triggering defensiveness.

Almost all sexuality counseling interviews require some sex education, but certain cases are resolved completely through good information. A counselor may have to add to the background knowledge gained in Part I, in order to obtain more specialized information between sessions. An important skill is to know enough to hear what is erroneous or missing; not only are the facts significant but also the connections between ideas. Permission for clients to talk about sexuality accurately, and "own" their own sexuality is always a part of educationally oriented sexuality counseling.

TIMING

Good counseling requires listening, empathy, and rapport building before most treatment approaches are effective. Sometimes the relationship is enhanced by giving early information which is likely to reduce anxiety, but it should be brief until the client has an opportunity to be heard.

EXAMPLE: Male Client, 1st Session, after 15 Minutes

Counselor: *"You seem to have heard that every man, whose mother took DES during pregnancy, is likely to develop cancer or sexual identity problems. I'm relieved to tell you that only a small percentage of males are affected that seriously. Also, I will be recommending a good checkup before we finish today, and I believe you will feel more secure after that. Perhaps it will help you talk about your delayed ejaculation if you keep that reassurance in the back of your mind."*

Client: *"It just seemed a funny coincidence to have a sexuality problem only a little while after reading about a drug that my sister says my mother took."*

Counselor: (leaves time to discuss the DES issue as needed at this point.) *"Now would you go back to describing what else was going on when you first noticed the ejaculation problem?"*

COMMENTS: As the counselor listens to a client and begins to realize that erroneous information is a major cause of the problem, the timing issue must be considered carefully. One does not want to waste helpful information when the client is in a "yes but" frame of mind, or is not trusting enough to receive new ideas. A few pieces of specific information may create a therapeutic bond, but often the best procedure is to save the major kinds of education until after counselor and client have focused on the whole problem.

CONFRONTING CLIENTS' MISINFORMATION

Some counselors hear a client's errors and try to correct them by indirectly adding better information. This may seem tactful, but does not usually work as well as first stating that misinformation itself may be causing the problem. In the following instance, the client has focused on the need to feel better about his sexuality, even though he is still upset after a contested divorce.

EXAMPLE: Pastoral Counselor and Parishioner, 2nd Session

Counselor: *"Jack, you seem to take for granted that masturbation is weakening, and have felt guilty about it since your* *divorce. We need to talk about two things—the impact your wife's leaving had on your sense of masculinity, and the value of considering self pleasuring as an acceptable thing to do."*

COMMENTS: The point in confronting and labeling is to create readiness for new information and to discover important obstacles if they exist. Many counselors give the client a re-inforcing article, book, or handout sheet if reluctance to accepting new ideas is present. Also the "tincture of time" and repetition in varied ways, allows for gradual internalization of useful information. At the next visit, the client may have integrated some ideas, and be ready to discuss and hear a broader viewpoint.

An important strategy is to avoid a power struggle when giving information; the counselor does not want to appear to argue about what is correct. Sometimes saying: "This is not a matter of opinion—there is very solid evidence that..." or "You have a lot of company in believing that this is so, because the information is hard to find, and yet (my experience, or the research) shows that..." It is important to be honest about the degree of certainty behind the particular point of sexuality education and to offer it while not forcing the issue.

EXAMPLE: After Thorough Discussion, 1st Session

Counselor: *"Well Martha, I understand that several of your friends told you that sex during pregnancy would harm the baby, yet your doctor and I have explained in detail that an easygoing sex life is fine for you now. And here's an article about it. Let's get together next week and see if you have begun to feel better about some sexual closeness without intercourse with your husband. Would you spend a little time this week thinking about what else might be holding you back?"*

COMMENTS: When good information does not resolve an issue in a reasonable length of time, even when carefully presented, probably more is involved. Sensitivity is needed with clients like Martha because the block to accepting information may be either a sexual or non-sexual issue. For example, Martha could have vaginismus (involuntary tight muscles around the vagina), or she could be an alcoholic who is constantly fighting with her husband about not drinking during her pregnancy (and refuses to make love). A little more time is needed to build trust and sort out the isses.

TEACHING METHODS

Words, words, words—not everyone learns best through hearing, especially abstract ideas. Counselors need to use examples, images, language familiar to the client, humor, and dialogue. In addition, diagrams, pictures, and models help immensely. This can be tested by using just words to describe to someone how to use a diaphragm or condom, then explaining it with pictures, and finally including an example of the contraceptive itself. A sexuality counselor can have a blank pad and marking pencil readily at hand. Simple diagrams like the one presented in the following example, which are sketched as one talks, may help a client more than glossy wall or book charts. Some professionally printed materials may be necessary for more complicated anatomical or pleasuring explanations.

EXAMPLE: Technical College Junior Asking About Sex After Several Career Sessions

Counselor: *"So if this is the pleasure curve, you seem to be having a problem part way...would you say that you get turned on but tend to lose an erection here?"* (As the interview continues, the counselor adds to the diagram to discuss what happens.)

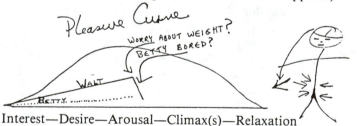

Interest—Desire—Arousal—Climax(s)—Relaxation

Walt: *"Well, it varies, but when it's gone—it's gone!"*

Counselor: *"So sometimes it's easy to stay aroused to climax, but other times the good feelings stop abruptly. Do you have any hunches of what may contribute to that?"*

Walt: *"Well, it doesn't help to think about how much weight I've gained, and that Betty works with this guy who is a fanatic runner."*

Counselor: *"Mmmm, that could be important. Can you think of other things that bother you when you are getting in the groove over here?"* (As the client concentrates on the diagram, the counselor goes on to other possible blocks, planning to respond later to doubts about body image.)

Walt: *"Well, usually when I, how do you say it...start actual sex, Betty begins to look uninterested..."*

Counselor: *"Is what you are calling actual sex, intercourse? There can be much more to sex before that. Could it be that Betty is still over here at the early arousal stage when you are building up to a climax?"*

Walt: *"I don't know. But now I just kind of fade when she gets that expression I suppose...I hadn't realized how that was getting to me."*

Counselor: *"Of course, you would react to her lack of excitement.* (Draws a stick figure next to the pleasure curve and shows how thoughts and feelings can block Walt's physical response.) *Also, let's look at the mechanics of sexual arousal in women. It is easy for a man to feel inadequate if he expects thrusting to do it all."*

Walt: *"Nobody ever talks about any of this."*

Counselor: *"I know.* (Finds chart of male and female anatomy.) *The drawings in this sexuality text are kind of small. But if this is the clitoris, the bud of tissue at the front of the vulva, and this is the anal opening, then in the center are the labia, or inner and outer lips, O.K.? In women too, the physical basis for feeling good sexually is increased circulation in this genital area. As a woman is stroked, kissed, and massaged anywhere, the increased circulation here makes touch feel better and better."*

Walt: *"How can I tell when she is ready?*

Counselor: *"The idea is not to rush to penetration, but for both to feel good longer. Let's look at the diagram again. When a woman is feeling a great deal of sexual pleasure, all these tissues become pink and puffy and engorged with blood...parallel to a* man's state of erection. When this 'sensory overload' becomes strong enough, the nerves fire and the muscles contract, resulting in the pleasurable waves of feeling called orgasm. A woman can't make that happen, but has to relax enough mentally and physically to just focus on good sensual feelings." (Counselor illustrates the mental-physical connection using the earlier stick figure.)

Walt: *"Yeah, once in a while I've seen Betty like that."*

Counselor: *"So the answer to your question about penetration is really not to focus on it. Make love longer in more ways, with your hands, mouth, body, and by talking a little, maybe laughing and playing, until Betty indicates that she wants intercourse. It can't feel good for a woman until she is already excited."*

Walt: *"Maybe I'd better talk to her about this...I think I've been feeling there's something wrong with me when it isn't that at all."*

Counselor: *"That's an excellent idea, and she is welcome to come in with you for your next appointment. In the meantime, would you practice some counseling suggestions? Try changing the goal to increased mutual pleasure, to take the pressure off what you called your potency problem."*

Walt: *"The suggestion is great. But tell me again—why do I keep losing my erections?"*

Counselor: *"Well, anxiety about your partner's lack of excitement and doubt about yourself seemed to have blocked the input of good physical feelings. So of course, circulation slowed down and you lost your erection. Emotions like anger, anxiety, competition, and resentment can ruin it for men and women. Along with doing a larger variety of lovemaking physically, it will be important to avoid negative thoughts."*

Walt: *"Is everyone pretty much that way?"*

Counselor: *"Yes, contrary to the myths. And it's healthy to have a close mind-body connection. You aren't a stone or a machine and that's good."*

COMMENTS: The counseling suggestion index card for this session might read: "Allow yourself to experience touch and feelings which increase sexual pleasure and circulation for yourself and Betty this week. Think of an erection as coming and going like the ebb and flow of the tide, with your feelings being better when they happen naturally. Take plenty of time before beginning intercourse or wait until another time."

More specific suggestions could be listed if the counselor chooses to do so. A general rule to consider is that with insightful clients who are moving ahead, less directiveness is required. However, when a client is resistant, rigid, anxious, or moving slowly, often a helpful procedure is to list out:

1. Talk with your partner about...(Specify)
2. Set aside a time twice this week to pleasure your partner without intercourse.
3. Look into two or three health clubs or exercise gyms in your area.

Any good teaching practices are helpful when helping clients learn.

EXAMPLE: Another Use of Diagrams, 1st Session

Amy: *"So at the end of my second marriage I had some of this discomfort too, but then I met Richard and it was different. It was 4 years after that when I found out I had herpes. And as I said when I came in a while ago..."*

Counselor: *"Just a second...since you have been married three times and have a mixed history of comfortable and uncomfortable sex, let's see if this helps visualize it for us more clearly."* (Picks up a colored pen and draws a line on a plain sheet of paper on the table beside them both. Hands a pen to Amy.)

Amy: *"What should I write?"*

Counselor: *"First, I'll write ages along the bottom of the line. Here you were five years old, ten, fifteen, and so on. Now you are 65; here you will be 80, 85, 90..."*

|||||||||||||||||||||||

0 5 10 15 20 25 30 35 40 45 50 55 60 65 70 75 80 85 90 95...

Amy: *"Maybe I won't live that long!"*

Counselor: *"But none of us ever know, and there is really no reason to put a limit on it. Let's just add dots at the end because you will always be a sexual being, regardless of how active you choose to be. Now would you write in your three marriages on the time line?* (Discusses briefly.) *Also would you indicate any other important sexual relationships? As we talk I'd like you to put *'s and x's on the more positive and negative sexual times so we can see the pattern."*

COMMENTS: As the counselor and client continue to explore and focus, referring to the time line and making brief notes adds clarity.

In addition to drawings of all kinds, counselors can use books, films, anatomical models, and videotapes to teach and instruct. With the age of photocopied material, the helper can draw or write educational handouts and reprint useful ones prepared by others. Remember that whatever the teaching techniques used, the client's attitudes and values are affected, as well as content/facts. Information in isolation is usually not useful; a number of sessions may be needed to personalize it.

PROBLEM AREAS

Occasionally a client seems unable to accept good information, even when carefully discussed in varied ways. In this case, the counselor needs to look for a deeper reason than the facts in question. A helpful point to consider is what the client has to gain by continuing to hold on to an error. Or, what is avoided by not accepting a more accurate piece of information? Sometimes change feels more impossible than the status quo and this needs to be explored. Many times sexual information alone may be necessary but not sufficient to resolve the problem.

EXAMPLES: More Than Information Needed

Client: *"You say I could be sexually responsive even after my hysterectomy, but I'm not sure it would make any difference to my husband."*

Client: *"Maybe I do like girls but the other guys will still call me queer."*

Client: *"I just can't take the pill if it causes cancer, and other methods don't work...I'm going to have to tell my boyfriend to take care of it."*

COMMENTS: With situations like the above, it is necessary to go into the feelings and concerns the client has rather than to hammer on the facts of sexual response after surgery, homosexuality, or the relative merits of contraceptives. When good information is not sufficient to resolve a sexuality-related concern, the counselor may uncover problems discussed later in Chapters 5 and 6 of this program. Occasionally a client's persistent refusal to deal with incoming information indicates the need for a referral to a sex therapist or mental health specialist.

A particular frustration in cases involving misinformation is that the ignorance or damaging information developed over time and is seldom corrected instantly. Repetition and presenting material in varied ways are valid for any teaching. One technique is to ask the client to catch himself/herself "thinking in the old way," as part of the counseling suggestions. The habit can then be discussed as part of their action plan for change. This shifts responsibility to the client for changing destructive ideas, once the counselor has helped put the problem of misinformed ideas in focus.

RESOURCES REGARDING SEX EDUCATION

Brilliant sex education books for all audiences are listed throughout this training program which model excellent ways to present material. Curricula and workbook materials for sex educators also contain effective approaches to good information.

Some of the newest material can be found in periodical literature. On-line bibliographic data bases will, if you give key words to a librarian, locate a wealth of journal articles on sexuality-related topics. In addition, bibliographies on special topics are published regularly and advertised in newsletters and journals. Counselors looking for material can check the following journals:

Archives of Sexual Behavior
Family Life Educator

Family Planning Perspectives
Medical Aspects of Human Sexuality
Journal of Homosexuality
Journal of Marital and Family Therapy
Journal of Sex and Marital Therapy
Journal of Sex Education and Therapy
Journal of Sex Research
Journal of Social Work and Human Sexuality
Sexuality and Disability

Consulting regular summaries also helps keep up with information:

Current Research Updates in Human Sexuality, PO Box 2577, Bellingham, WA 96227. Monthly index to current journal articles and books on human sexuality.

Emphasis Subscriber Service. Department of Education, Planned Parenthood Federation of America, Inc. 810 Seventh Avenue, New York, NY 10019. Newsletter, reference sheets, periodical and annotated bibliographies oriented toward educational uses.

Sexual Well-Being, PO Box 60332, Palo Alto, CA 94306. A monthly newsletter focused on recent research and publications, written in non-technical language.

Sexuality Today, The Professional's Newsletter on Human Sexuality, 2315 Broadway, New York, NY 10024. Weekly summaries of important articles, publications, and issues in sexuality.

SIECUS Report, Sex Information and Education Council of the U.S., 80 Fifth Avenue, New York, NY 10011. Bimonthly articles, books and media reviews, and bibliographies cover the latest in sexology.

CONCLUSION

The helping professional can count on a lively flow of information being a part of all sexuality counseling. For better or for worse, a steady barrage of ideas about sexuality is in the daily papers, magazines, and entertainment media. New books are constantly published on sex etiquette, sexual fitness, and do-it-yourself sex therapy. People often need help selecting what applies to them.

Most helping professionals have done some formal or informal teaching during their careers, and any experience in working with teen or adult learners is invaluable. Then if a counselor subscribes to periodicals in the field and is in touch with current resources, imparting knowledge will be a powerful sexuality counseling skill.

CHAPTER 5, PART 2

SEXUAL CONCERNS OF LIFE STAGES

Counselors are often consulted about sexual problems which are largely, or in part, developmental in nature. These present themselves in three ways, even though they may be part of other issues:

1. The client is having trouble in the present accomplishing appropriate sexual development tasks, or has other stage-related concerns.

2. The client did not/could not accomplish earlier sexual development tasks and therefore is slower than expected in sexual development.

3. The client is dealing with a sexual issue out of sequence, because of a particular situation, either earlier or later than usual.

Any of the above can come in disguise as "I have this rash that hurts when I shave and the dermatologist says it's mostly nerves," or "All the other girls in my dorm are sleezes and easy pickups." Actually both clients may be unsure about their own sexual development; therefore the counselor's ability (over time) to make an assessment of the real issue is important. This type of problem tends to be invisible to the client, so quick labeling is not welcome. Considerable exploration and support have to come before focusing and goal setting (Phase II).

Generalizations about sexual development are not intended to be ideal norms and they may not apply to each individual. Some experiences like puberty are common to all, but the specifics of adolescent sexual stress are dependent on culture and individual circumstance. Figure 8 contains a chronological list of sexual life span concerns. The counselor can use a knowledge of sexual concerns at various life stages to inquire into possibly relevant areas, and to help the client prepare for future experiences.

Chronological list of sexual life span concerns.

STAGE/AGE	SEXUAL CONCERNS
INFANCY (0-3 years)	Discovery and enjoyment of genitals Sensual feelings, touching Beginnings of language, sense of self Sex role identity forming Trust-mistrust and awareness of others developing
CHILDHOOD (3-10)	Experience with self pleasuring Possible sex play with others Interest in reproduction Expanded language for sex Observance of adult behavior and sex roles Experience in varied relationships Questions about sexuality raised by media and peers
PUBERTY (10-14)	Serious need to understand changing physical self Body image and self worth developing Curiosity about intercourse and masturbation Concerns about menstruation and ejaculation Peer competition and relationships intense

Chronological list of sexual life span concerns (continued).

STAGE/AGE	SEXUAL CONCERNS
ADOLESCENCE (14-18)	Formation of identity which includes sexual self Confusion about appropriate sexual behavior Sexual experience with peers, self, and others Questions about contraception Relationships very important
YOUNG ADULT (18-25)	Adequacy, skill in sexuality stressed Partner choice, intimacy explored Experimentation with sexual life styles Questioning of traditional sex roles and values Avoidance of unwanted pregnancy important
ADULT (25-40)	Values continue to develop Choices about fertility, pregnancy Integration of sexuality with adult life style Increased expectations for sexual pleasure Experimentation with wider sexual expression
MID-LIFE (40-65)	Evaluation of sexual satisfaction Questions about menopause, mid-life sexual changes Awareness of relationship between stress and sexuality Balance of self and partner(s) reconsidered Life style changes may be urgent

Chronological list of sexual life span concerns (continued).

STAGE/AGE	SEXUAL CONCERNS
RETIREMENT (65-75)	Health issues important Adequacy issues again questioned Interest in sexuality may diminish or gain new meaning Loss of partner may require adaptation
ELDERS (75-100)	Acceptance of change in frequency, sexual interest Sexuality often denied by significant others New goals for sex (non-performance oriented)

Figure 8. Chronological list of sexual life span concerns.

Few people move through all stages of psycho-sexual development with complete ease. The counselor must focus on what went well and not just on the problematic aspects of development.

The counselor can do a formal or informal sex history to determine how comfortably a client's sexual development has proceeded to the present. Usually more work will have to be done with a client whose history reveals a troubled or conflicted sexual development than with one whose course was relatively smooth. Many clients remember symptoms or crises of earlier life stages which were not resolved then. The counselor needs to keep in mind that chronological age does not always indicate where the client is in sexual development.

EXAMPLES: Sexual Development Different Than Chronological Age

A 24 year old medical student agrees that his sexual development is essentially where he left it at age 15, when he put all his efforts into academics and felt he couldn't compete socially.

A 49 year old woman comes in to discuss problems which she attributes to menopause and physical changes. The counselor discovers that the client's symptoms are related to conflicts concerning her body image and about being active in lovemaking. These were issues which she did not work through earlier. With a correct focus the action phase will be far more effective than education about menopause alone.

SPECIALIZED SKILLS

Mild sexual problems which develop at predictable points in the life span are part of normal development when they occur as a result of maturation or widespread cultural press. The counselor can expect to find anxiety, frustration, or inadequacy feelings at particular stages, and help clients through information and support. Beyond this, a person who experiences more interruption of normal sexual development may need an individualized plan. Methods will be outlined later in Chapters 5 and 6 to help remedy even more serious disruption of sexual development.

ASSESSMENT

When a client seems to be dealing with a sexual issue usually resolved at an earlier age, the counselor can be helpful by assisting the client in clarifying what happened. As a rule, the rapport-building phase in developmental problems is easy. Because some history taking and exploration of the problem are necessary, the client becomes comfortable with the counselor and receives support as the obstacles to development are uncovered.

EXAMPLE: An Unresolved Childhood Sexual Issue

A boy learned that he had been placed for adoption at age two because of sexually irresponsible parents. After finding out, an unconscious decision was made to keep sexuality under strict control. He joined a religious group at age 19 and left when he was 27 and then at age 32 he consults a counselor. The client's inability to develop an intimate relationship with anyone had led to serious depression, and in some ways he seems like a repressed 18 year old. The counselor makes an assessment of where the client really is psycho-sexually, and then helps develop a program of attitudes and experiences appropriate for the transition to adult sexuality.

Assessment of sexual development is complex because a person may be facing issues which are either behind or ahead of where they are expected to be. A 27 year old woman who has just had a hysterectomy may need to have sexuality counseling regarding issues which usually do not present themselves until menopause. Her peers may be able to offer her little in the way of knowledgeable support. The counselor's task is to assess where each client is in relation to expected development, and help him/her attain a comfortable degree of sexual adjustment.

Sexual development does not exist in a vacuum but is dependent on other aspects of a person's growth, and this presents an assessment challenge. The diagram in Figure 9 briefly illustrates some related developmental aspects, and while a counselor is not likely to do a formal assessment of each one, problems with sexual development are often accompanied/caused by uneven maturation in these areas.

GROWTH	PHYSICAL	PSYCHOLOGICAL	COGNITIVE	ETHICAL	SOCIAL
IMMATURITY ↓	Birth ↓ Adult ↓ Death	Undifferentiated ↓ (Erikson stages) ↓ Integrated	Simple ↓ (Piaget stages) ↓ Complex	Primitive ↓ (Kohlberg/ Gilligan) ↓ Advanced	Me ↓ Us
MATURITY					

Figure 9. Developmental areas.

Thousands of developmental studies have been conducted by gifted individuals but there are too many to be acknowledged even by "schools of thought." Most counselors have studied human development, however, and know the importance of assessing the degree to which any of the areas of individual differences identified in Figure 9 affect a person's sexual self.

EXAMPLES: Variations In Development Stages Among Areas

If a client's cognitive development and learning style are within the usual expectations for chronological age, the counselor has an easier task. But the sexual development of a learning disabled, mentally retarded, or gifted client is likely to be affected by these aspects of development. Here again stereotypes need to be avoided.

A ten year old girl may be socially, physically, and verbally precocious but emotionally and cognitively young for her age. Because she gives the impression of far greater maturity than she possesses, she may be exposed to sexual issues beyond her ability to cope.

A couple can be in very different developmental stages in several areas which affect their sexual compatibility. The counselor may have to help one or both with social, psychological, or ethical development, to create a readiness for greater sexual maturity.

The task for the counselor is to be aware that other aspects of human development may affect sexual development, and to look closely for clues in related areas.

Confrontation and Labeling

No one likes to hear that they are retarded in an area of development, or haven't accomplished age-related tasks, especially in a sensitive area like sexuality. Therefore confrontation is delicate in the focus phase of sexual problems which are related to developmental issues. Simple clarification and information should be utilized wherever possible. Confrontation may be necessary at times, however, because people take where they are as "given" and are unaware of their power to change.

EXAMPLE: 17 Year Old Girl, 1st Session

Nancy: *"But maybe I could be pregnant if the test is wrong."*

Counselor: *"I understand how worried you are. Remember that the test and pelvic exam both say you're not pregnant. We've done five tests for you in six months and you report that irregular periods are pretty common for you?"*

Nancy: *"The nurse practitioner said I'm underweight and run too much, and that affects my cycle. But I can't be fat."*

Counselor: *"What is really important to you, Nancy?"*

Nancy: *"Well...I guess how my friends say I look, and what my boyfriend thinks...and keeping my parents happy—proud of me."*

Counselor: *"Nancy, I admire your coming here on your own and I'm interested in all your accomplishments. But there is one thing which I think you need to work on."*

Nancy: *"Like what?"*

Counselor: *"Your own sense of who you are—your identity apart from others. And I believe it would be good to think how health and sex, especially intercourse, fit into that."*

Nancy: *"You mean I shouldn't have sex?"*

Counselor: *"Sex can be wonderful. But I don't believe that you have taken time to sort out who Nancy is and what you really want. It is normal in your teens to react to guys and friends and parents, but I'm concerned that you maybe leave yourself out. (Pause, no response.) It isn't selfish to put your own health and welfare first—I doubt that you really enjoy intercourse from what you've said."*

Nancy: *"Won't more birth control fix that?"*

Counselor: *"It will help avoid worry. But I'm concerned about your finding the perfect place for sex in your life and not just fearing pregnancy."*

Nancy: *"I'd like to think about that and maybe talk to you again."*

Counselor: *"I hope you understand that I'm not against sex, but want to see you in charge of your own life."*

Nancy: *"Usually I think I am. But I do try to figure out how other people see me...and I really don't like sex much."*

The counselor in the previous example may seem confrontive and is so because of a belief that helping an adolescent client focus on a normal developmental conflict about choice and sexuality is growth producing. When a human service professional has seen dozens of young women through abortions and divorces before taking charge of their sexual selves, the professional's experience can lead to a belief in early intervention. The point to remember is that the counselor can raise developmental questions directly, may bring up possible consequences of behavior, but must not try to make decisions for the client.

Counseling Techniques

1. Assess when and where obstacles to comfortable sexuality occurred.

2. Facilitate reality-based self worth, rather than idealized body images, hypersex, or stereotypes.

3. Pinpoint cultural, sexist, religious, ethnic, or other social pressure which lead to feelings of failure, guilt, or inadequacy and thus difficulties with sexual development.

4. Assist the client to verbalize real motives and fears about his/her changing body or some new aspect of sexuality.

5. Help the client develop perspective and own the pressures which interfere (now or in the past) with comfortable sexual development.

6. Recognize that reasons for developmental sexual problems are important to acknowledge, but are not excuses for discouragement. The counselor can help the client understand the obstacles and then obtain needed information and experiences.

7. In the action phase, develop a clear plan to remedy past developmental lag and deal with present attitudes and behavior.

EXAMPLE: 28 Year Old Woman, 3rd Session

Counselor: *"So your lover continues to be possessive and demanding of your time. Yet you still want to make a commitment to her?"*

Laurie: *"She is just so suspicious and can't stand to see me flirt with anyone."*

Counselor: *"Are you aware of any need on your part to be free, to experiment, to check out who's interested in you?"*

Laurie: *"Well, I never had a chance to do much before..."*

Counselor: *"Are you suggesting that maybe it's fun, now that you have come out and can approach other women openly?"*

Laurie: *"Really it is. I don't always mean anything by it, but sometimes—well—"*

Counselor: *"Perhaps you are just in a different place than Lisa is. You may want a relationship but an open social life too, until you have experienced more."*

Laurie: *"I guess that's my conflict—whether to match Lisa's idea of a relationship or find my own. But I can't hurt her."*

Counselor: *"Why don't we meet again to sort out a balance of your needs and hers and try to be creative in working this out?"*

COMMENTS: The counselor is trying to help the client see where she is developmentally, without criticism or pressure. Real life is usually more complicated than expressed in this brief excerpt, and yet one of the issues frequently presented is that of couples being in different places in their sexual/personal development. When this is clear, often compromises can be worked out or ways can be found for individual needs to be met, either within the relationship or outside it. Should a couple decide to separate based on different developmental needs, at least a clear reason would be known rather than one sided rejection.

Potential Problem Area

The major pitfall when a counselor looks at a client from a sexual development viewpoint is the possibility of jumping to unwarranted conclusions. For instance, not all women and men at mid-life will be dismayed by gradual changes in sexual performance. One can think of the needs and concerns usually associated with various life stages as a broad stencil, and use this knowledge to illuminate possible reasons for a client's sexual problems.

RESOURCES REGARDING SEXUAL DEVELOPMENT

Chilman, C. (1983). *Adolescent sexuality in a changing American society: Social and psychological perspectives for the human services professions.* 2nd ed. New York: John Wiley and Sons.

Goldman, R., & Goldman, J. (1982). *Children's sexual thinking.* Boston, MA: Routledge and Kegan Paul.

Golub, S. (Ed.). (1983). *Menarche.* Lexington, MA: Lexington Books.

Kirkpatrick, M. (Ed.). (1980). *Women's sexual development: Explorations of inner space.* New York: Plenum.

Olds, S. (1985). *The eternal garden: Seasons of our sexuality.* New York: Times Books.

Russo, R. (1983). *Sexual development and disorders in childhood and adolescence.* New Hyde Park, NY: Medical Examination Publishing Company.

Sarrell, L., & Sarrell, P. (1984). *Sexual turning points: The seven stages of adult sexuality.* New York: Macmillan.

Weg, R. (Ed.). (1983). *Sexuality in the later years: Roles and behavior.* Orlando, FL: Academic Press.

CONCLUSION

As people live their lives they are considered healthy or self-actualizing in Maslow's terms, if they are largely centered in the present rather than in the past or future. The counselor can work to keep a focus on the present, while recognizing the influence of the past and the importance of the client's expectations for the future. In most cases, a client's sexual problems will be better understood if the counselor has a developmental perspective, even while focusing on current issues.

CHAPTER 5, PART 3

SEXUAL HEALTH COUNSELING

Counselors generally have more training in the psychological, interpersonal, and behavioral aspects of sexuality than in the physiological ones. Because sexuality is clearly rooted in biology, a counselor needs to learn enough about sexual health to see potential problems. Sexual activity sometimes results in a health problem (gonorrhea, ectopic pregnancy), while at other times health affects sexuality (irregular menstrual periods and fear of pregnancy leading to a lack of arousal). Both directions are common, and an informed counselor can focus appropriately on possible cause and effect.

The following three sections cover health related aspects of sexuality, some of which almost everyone has experienced at one time or another. Making a medical referral is usually necessary, but follow-up counseling can encourage attending to the health problem and working out any personal aspects. The areas of sexuality and health, contraception, and sexually transmitted diseases cover mild to serious problems; good counseling is valuable to supplement treatment.

SEXUALITY AND HEALTH

People often ask counselors questions about health and sexuality which offer an opportunity to explore more complicated sexual concerns. These questions generally can be grouped under eight areas which are presented and discussed in this part.

Pre-Menstrual Syndrome (PMS)

A client may say: "There are times when I can't bear to be touched," or "I'm oversexed before my period and just can't trust myself." A counselor's response which suggests that hormonal rhythms can influence the intensity of feelings, and guidance toward information about PMS are helpful. An important point is not to make assumptions that women with PMS experience the same kinds of symptoms, since the variance is so great. Allowing time to describe the individual differences allows trust to build.

When the relationship is established, the counselor can communicate that the client's experiences may not be totally created by PMS. These interpersonal and sexual feelings can be intensifications of issues which also exist at other times of the month, but are more noticeable just before menstruation. These themes can be explored productively in counseling, with the goal of discovering how much the woman is truly bothered by them and how much is an uncomfortable awareness before the menses. Only the client can arrive at a balance concerning how many of the feelings are actually important (even though often suppressed), and which are transient symptoms.

EXAMPLE: College Student, 2nd Session

Kim: *"My roommate said that I was better after talking to you last week. Probably I wouldn't do it, but I did feel like killing myself. It was awful then...and now I'm fine."*

Counselor: *"I'm really glad you're better this week. And have you read the booklet on PMS? I know your being upset was not all premenstrual, but you did describe monthly swings."*

Kim: *"I never wanted to admit it because my brothers always gave me a hard time about being a bitch, and now so does my boyfriend. And then when I feel OK it seems silly to worry about how I was before."*

Counselor: *"That is understandable, Kim, and you end up not taking yourself seriously either. The five 'no's' should help with the physical side* (salt, sugar, alcohol, caffeine, smoking), *and a checkup with our nurse practitioner who is knowledgeable about PMS."*

Kim: *"Will that make it go away for good? Mel and I can't get engaged until we stop fighting about sex every few weeks."*

Counselor: *"Certainly you can learn what your sensitive points are, and sort out the sexual issues which lead to conflict. Why don't we meet regularly for a while, no matter where you are in your cycle, and come to understand what leads to such anger and despair?"*

Kim: *"I know that when I'm down no one can ever stand me."*

Counselor: *"Like no one is there for you?"*

Kim: *"Once in a while if I'm not in a good mood...I just blow..."*

COMMENTS: At this point the counselor begins to explore Kim's "script" of never admitting she needs anything, and feeling acceptable only as long as she is cheerful. While away at school Kim had been keeping up the family pretense that "everything is fine," but became angry/depressed just before her period. Those are the times that Kim cannot defer to her boyfriend sexually nor does she confide in him.

This counseling will not improve the family problems, but will help Kim integrate her real feelings, be more honest with her boyfriend, and take good care of herself when she is most vulnerable. An important learning will occur when the counselor helps Kim catch herself before covering up feelings in the here and now, so she can learn to be appropriately "real." Counseling what appears to be only a PMS issue can encourage Kim to deal directly with things rather than only pleasing others.

Menstrual Health

Far more than reproductive and "cramps" issues are involved when the topic of menstruation comes up. Counselors can help women deal with issues like painful periods without resenting their sexuality. Painful and heavy or irregular menstruation is a real health problem; it is the most common reason for school absenteeism for adolescent girls. With two-thirds of teen women experiencing distress, many could benefit from a referral for possible treatment with newer medications which can provide significant relief. Older women also find discussing problem periods helpful, and an easy way to initiate a sexuality-related discussion.

Silence and vague shame about menstruation mean that even discussing tampons and toxic shock syndrome can be a positive learning experience. Girls who are comfortable with their femaleness and are relaxed about their natural processes, are more likely to be responsible for their sexuality. Many behaviors do have risks and benefits, especially those involving sex, so that women can learn to take good care of themselves but not be ruled by fear. In addition, questions about menstruation can lead naturally into broader discussion of women's sexuality with both sexes.

Menopause

Later in life, similar discussions about menopause can help a woman have a positive attitude toward her health and sexuality. Only a minority have unpleasant symptoms with menopause, but these women deserve attention since their quality of life is seriously affected. Other women without physical symptoms at mid-life also can have important concerns. Questions about attractiveness, bodily changes, and femininity easily shade into direct sexual concerns; many women have no reliable person to ask. Because changing hormone levels influence vascular supply and endometrial tissue, sexuality is often directly affected. The counselor can be helpful by cooperating with a gynecologist who keeps up with the latest research in the use of estrogen and other hormone therapies.

Menopause is indistinct in its beginning and ending, may last for 10 years, and women live an average of 25 years after it is completed. Little good information is popularly known about "the change of life," and yet it occurs when other changes may be happening which are easily attributed to it. A familiar tragedy is the woman who succumbs to the life stress of this period by becoming seriously disturbed, and then is written off as "menopausal." Just as with PMS, menopause can bring to light existing suppressed problems which took years to build up. Change may not be pleasing to others, because as the woman realizes her dissatisfaction, the family/couple or work system may need to change. The counselor will find this client challenging.

Self Exams

Counselors who leave literature around on sexual self examination, or mention it in classes and interviews, can expect people to use this as an opening to sexual discussions. Testicular self exam leaflets can help boys talk about their anatomy, and then go on to other sexual concerns. Since 40% to 50% of boys experience some breast enlargement during puberty, this subject lends itself well to reassuring discussion. Recent articles have pointed out that we don't even have language for when a boy becomes fertile, and the terms "spermatification" and "spermarche" have been suggested. People of all ages may wish to discuss male self exams, ask about circumcision or vasectomy, and demystify issues about the male genitals.

Breast and cervical self exams have the same potential for helping girls and women understand and integrate all parts of their body. A woman who is shown how to check her cervix at home learns to be comfortable with her vagina, and feels more of a sense of ownership. For both sexes, taking responsibility for genital health provides a good opportunity to alleviate anxiety about sexuality.

Minor Physical Concerns

Since some people find it difficult to ask about sexuality directly, they may bring up the subject by asking whether they need vitamins or some advertised aphrodisiac. Others mention tender breasts or scrotum, a possible urinary tract/vaginal infection, or a localized rash. Of course, any of these could indicate a health problem, so that STD pamphlets and medical referrals are important. Hygiene issues concerning vaginal deodorants, douches, and reactions to lubricants or other personal supplies also come up. Taking the health inquiry seriously and going beyond it will encourage a person to explore the sexual aspects.

Men may ask whether or not such a thing as "male menopause" exists, and mention several health problems and changes which occur at mid-life. They may benefit from a referral to an internist or urologist, but also need a place to express their sexual concerns. A man may want to talk about patterns of sexual activity, either from a values point of view or needing to inquire about a sexual problem. Usually one or more interviews are needed to reduce the anxiety; some reading about men's sexual health is often useful. An attitude of "listen to your body" often leads to important learnings when minor physical complaints are mentioned.

Alcohol/Drugs and Sexuality

Questions may come up regarding loss of self control, pressured sex, compulsive sex, or decreased ability to reach/maintain arousal and climax. The counselor needs to make sure he/she is non-judgmental when alcohol or drugs are mentioned, and to build a working relationship in order to uncover the real issues. The counselor will encounter statements like the following and can avoid focusing on the substance abuse at first:

> *"I shouldn't let myself drink vodka unless I know what I'm doing, but I'd never have sex if I didn't."*

> *"When I'm wasted I can grass off the girls who say no, but what would happen if one said yes?"*

> *"I can't stand for him to touch me unless I've had something to drink or smoke."*

> *"It helps so much to party with a woman first, but lately I seem to stay soft if I've had more than two beers."*

All too often the problem is sheer substance abuse, but many people will continue to have sexual problems even if they abstain. Both conditions require attention. Individuals may be willing to appear to be discussing "problem" questions around alcohol and drugs, when they actually need to ask about sex. Often these clients have not thought through what is bothering them, and need help articulating it. Because alcohol and drugs may affect sexuality in complex physiological, psychological, and social ways, a counselor would be wise to become informed about their interaction.

Aging, Health, and Sexuality

Older people are likely to experience a wide range of health problems which influence sexuality: urinary incontinence, hernias, vaginal dryness, a congested prostate, pelvic relaxation, arthritis, cystocele/rectocyle (tissue bulging into the vagina), and others which require sexual adjustment. Many older people report that they stopped having sex after a corrective operation, a minor heart attack, having their teeth pulled, or convalescence from a fall. Also, because the ways of having sex which "worked" when younger might not be comfortable later in life, many people just give up.

While all data show sexual activity declining with age, ability and interest can certainly be present. Often no one is available whom the senior citizen trusts to answer questions, the person feels "too old and awkward," so avoidance becomes the norm. However, continued sexual expression is usually very positive for both health and well-being. Discussing general health conditions is expected by most older people, so this provides an avenue to inquire about sexuality and for the counselor to assist with information and encouragement.

RESOURCES FOR SEXUALITY AND HEALTH

Boston Women's Health Book Collective (1984). *The new our bodies ourselves.* New York: Simon and Schuster.

Budoff, P. (1983). *No more hot flashes and other good news.* New York: G.P. Putnam's Sons.

Brecher, E., & Consumer Reports Books Editors. (1983). *Sex & aging.* Boston: Little, Brown.

Forrest, G. (1983). *Alcoholism and human sexuality.* Springfield, IL: Charles C. Thomas.

Golub, S. (Ed.) (1983). *Lifting the curse of menstruation: A feminist appraisal of the influence of menstruation on women's lives.* New York: Haworth Press.

Green, R. (1979). *Human sexuality: A health practitioners text.* 2nd ed. Baltimore: Williams and Wilkins.

Greenwood, S. (1984). *Menopause, naturally: Preparing for the second half of life.* San Francisco, CA: The Volcano Press.

Harrison, M. (1982). *Self-help for premenstrual syndrome.* Cambridge, MA: The Matrix Press.

Higgins, L., & Hawkins, J. (1984). *Human sexuality across the life span: Implications for nursing practice.* Monterey, CA: Wadsworth.

Lumiere, R., & Cook, S. (1983). *Healthy sex and keeping it that way.* New York: Simon and Schuster.

Mental Health Materials Center (Eds.). (1983). *Education for health: The selective guide to audiovisuals and publications for health promotion, family life, and mental health.* New York: National Center for Health Education, 30 E. 29th Street.

Powell, D. (Ed.). (1984). *Alcoholism and sexual dysfunction: Issues in clinical management.* New York: The Haworth Press.

Stewart, F., Guest, F., Stewart, G., & Hatcher, R. (1981). *My body, my health. The concerned woman's book of gynecology.* New York: John Wiley and Sons.

Swanson, J., & Forrest, K. (Eds.). (1984). *Men's reproductive health.* New York: Springer Publishing.

Wallerstein, E. (1980). *Circumcision: An American health fallacy.* New York: Springer Publishing.

CONTROLLING FERTILITY

Ever since pioneers like Margaret Sanger ventured to insist that pregnancy need not be left to chance, a quiet army of people (professionals and volunteers) have been active in teaching others how to use contraception. The effects have been measurable in terms of population control, size of families, a lower maternal death rate, and the proportion of sexually active teens having unprotected intercourse. Although more information is circulating, not everyone has access to birth control and so counselors often find themselves providing information.

Clients who try to absorb their contraceptive education from the media are a special challenge, because they may have no perspective on the overall picture. They may have read that a researcher found a side effect of vasectomy in monkeys, or that someone is studying the pill and jogging, and be resistant to several methods based on hearsay. The counselor will have to clarify that all methods have their disadvantages and try to discover what the client's real needs are. Skepticism about available methods is certainly valid, and the counselor can help clients find the least objectionable choice rather than risk unwanted pregnancy.

Non-Contracepters

Counselors who are comfortable talking about sexuality are in a good position to learn of unprotected sexual activity, and are able to anticipate the possible consequences with clients. A helper learns with experience to differentiate the uninformed person from the client who is conflicted about birth control and sexuality.

The counselor in the following two examples needs to distinguish counseling about birth control from those situations where misuse of contraception indicates other problems. Focusing becomes the most important stage of counseling in these instances, because the client has to see the problem before it can be addressed.

EXAMPLE: High School Sophomore, Cooperative

Client: *"I know that I should get something, but keep thinking that I'll break up with my boyfriend. OK, I'll go to the Under 21 Clinic, yes—even if I stop seeing him. You're right, I could use a checkup anyway, and I might need what they teach in their groups some other time."*

COMMENTS: This high school student will probably respond to support and help clarifying her needs. If her sexual activity is satisfying then it is no one else's business, but if it seems a source of distress, then she can be offered help deciding what she really wants.

EXAMPLE: Woman, Age 19, Confused

Marianne: *"It just doesn't seem to work out, so I've been pregnant three times. My cousin is keeping the first baby, and I didn't have the other two. No, the birth control stuff seems to just stay in my drawer, and I'm never home when someone wants to have sex. A couple of guys use a rubber."*

COMMENTS: What this client wants isn't clear. With this limited information, the counselor is unable to determine if she is passive about life generally, is self destructive, is otherwise OK but not in charge of her relationships with men, has experienced sexual abuse, or just never accepted a birth control method. Counseling with this woman will require skill.

Counselor: *"Marianne, what if we look at it this way? Maybe you want a relationship so much that you let yourself be sexual with most guys who try? Yet you feel bad about that and tend to ignore birth control. Or is something else happening?"*

Marianne: *"Every single time I go out I promise myself I won't do it—have sex—but I'm never able to stick to it."*

Counselor: *"Let's talk about what happens then, because you're not happy this way."*

COMMENTS: The counselor can assume that when a sexually active client knows a sufficient amount about birth control and doesn't use it, there is more to explore. Taking an informal sex history, doing some sexuality education, and inquiring carefully about recent sexual experiences (and suppressed ones), can show where the blocks are.

An interesting point to remember is that when the motivation for sex is comfortable (intimacy in a relationship, or pleasure), there are few non-contraceptors. However, when men and women are having sex to meet a stereotype, please someone else, for power, popularity, revenge, or to get something, the mixed motivation often results in ineffective birth control.

The counselor who sees non-users of birth control as stupid people is going to be of little use to anyone. This is especially true with the adolescent, where a no-win power struggle can quickly develop, or between a counselor and a client with different value systems. A question and answer debate style is best avoided, so that the client does not keep coming up with objections which the counselor frantically tries to answer.

EXAMPLE: Bypassing Resistance

Client: *"I'd seem weird if I stopped right there in the car and had to find a bathroom to put something in."*

Counselor: *"Can you think of some creative way which other girls may have found to deal with that?"* or
"Is suddenness the problem, or what the guy thinks? Let's sort out what you need to be prepared."

COMMENTS: Giving clients as much input to the solution as possible is a good way to model the importance of their gaining control over their own fertility. Also, they are much more likely to comply with a plan which they help make.

The less sense the client's non-use of birth control makes, the more likely that the psychological causes are outside the client's awareness. Health educators report that their greatest frustration is with flippant

teens who invest so much in "feelin' free" that they won't look at consequences, and with women who lose all sense of themselves around a
potential male partner. Another kind of difficult client for a helper who
feels strongly about responsibility is the sexually active man who seems
unconcerned about his fertility. A flexible counselor can see where a
client is, uncover underlying issues, and help him/her achieve acceptable
birth control within the limitations of available technology.

Specific Problems Using Contraception

Very often a counselor will have a client who understand the importance of birth control and has tried several kinds, but has objections
which make use sporadic. When the question is simply one of method,
referral to an expert family planning clinic or practitioner is advisable.
Since the contraceptive field moves so fast, specialists have to keep their
training up to date. Unless the counselor works in a clinic, referral to
other providers is necessary. The counselor would make a serious error
to advise based on outdated methods, or just recommend drugstore birth
control.

What the counselor can contribute is helping the client put his/her
needs into words: "Well I suppose I could remember to take the pill
every day, if all those cancer reports were about older women who
smoke," or "We have to be able to have oral sex or I won't use a
method—it would spoil our lovemaking." Considerable counseling skill
may be required to bring out unverbalized fears, sexual practices, and
values, and help the client resolve conflicts about birth control.

Motivating clients to find and use a contraceptive may be complicated by the fact that people ask whether their sexual problems are the
direct result of a particular birth control method. No absolute answer
can be provided as to whether the pill can result in some loss of interest in
sex, or if a condom can contribute to potency problems. Certainly if pain
results from an IUD or diaphragm, or a reaction occurs to foam, sponge,
cream, or jelly, these should be discontinued and a substitute found at
once. If a contraceptive could be the problem, counselors often suggest
that clients try another method while they explore related issues during
the sessions.

Another issue which the counselor may pick up indirectly is a
client's fear of becoming/causing a pregnancy which verges on the
obsessive. While contraceptive failure is a real and present problem,

some people are so insecure about it that they sabotage their sexuality and hurt their relationships. Sometimes the client does not admit this directly, or else the partner has the problem and doesn't talk about it. Most clients have to balance both the security and the interference-with-pleasure aspects of birth control, but the overly worried person may require special understanding.

Comments for which to listen:

About men:

"He always makes me rush to douche, so I never get to come."

"He often doesn't complete the act—I don't know—he hears a noise or goes to the bathroom."

About women:

"She avoids and avoids, and then when she has to, she does it to me so fast that I never get inside."

"She says it hurts—is so tight, but loosens up and enjoys it if I promise to withdraw."

These clients may find their difficulties solved by more agreement about birth control, but could require further help.

Sometimes seeing both members of a couple together is the only way to sort out what originally seemed like a birth control block. "He made me have two abortions when he was in graduate school..." or "She'd have eight kids like her mother and I'm never going to live like that," may need to come out. The counselor can help a couple see that they are expressing important issues in a struggle about birth control, and that interpersonal questions are better dealt with directly.

Another contraceptive problem is presented by the person who wishes to use "natural family planning" for religious, health, or other reasons. Counselors may be skeptical because they have encountered many unwanted pregnancies from calendar rhythm, temperature, or withdrawal methods. Significant advances have been made in fertility awareness, however, so that referral to an informed source is possible. The counselor can focus on the necessity for good communication with partners, protected or non-intercourse lovemaking during fertile periods, and planning for an accidental pregnancy should it occur.

Sterilization

Because vasectomy and tubal ligation are the most common methods of birth control in the world, the counselor will find that clients often need to discuss them. Of the 33.5 million American women using some form of contraception, 11.6 million rely on sterilization (their own or their partners'). In a single year (1983), The Association of Voluntary Sterilization gathered statistics showing that over 455,000 vasectomies and 622,000 tubal ligations were performed in the United States.

Books and pamphlets are available to answer common questions, and again the counselor should focus on each client's concerns and not be invested in the contraceptive method chosen. A suggestion such as "It helps to talk to friends who have used this method" clarifies that the information gathering is the client's responsibility. More importantly, questions about sterilization often reveal subtle concerns about potency, femininity, lovemaking, family size and relationships which the counselor can bring out and help explore.

EXAMPLE: Father of Four Children, 1st Session

Alan: *"Vasectomy sounds good, and Carol is pushing it. She had her IUD taken out after all those scare stories."*

Counselor: *"But you frown about being pushed...pressured?"*

Alan: *"Well, I've been wondering how it will affect my stamina, but I can't talk about that with Carol."*

Counselor: *"Your stamina? Staying power during sex?"*

Alan: *"Actually I tend to have good sex when I'm on the road—I travel about 40 percent of the time for my work. Since I usually stay in the same places, I have semi-regular arrangements with women who like to go out and have a good time."*

Counselor: *"And you're concerned that a vasectomy could interfere with your usual sex life?"*

Alan: *"Most likely when I'm at home. It's been sort of an effort with Carol for the last couple of years."*

Counselor: *"It hasn't been too comfortable, and anything like a vasectomy could tip the balance?"*

Alan: *"As we talk about it, I see that I just don't want anything to change. It's OK and I can't start questioning anything with Carol."*

Counselor: *"We all choose the level of intimacy we want at a particular time, and certainly not everyone is monogomous...and this is where you are now?"*

Alan: *"Yeah, it's sort of OK with Carol. She kids about my travel and may have a relationship too. I think...am pretty sure she does."*

Counselor: *"It sounds like a kind of understanding. But could it change suddenly? What do you need to take care of yourself?"*

Alan: *"Actually, a vasectomy might be good. It would show Carol that I care...she's taken the risk for 18 years...and I'd feel better about my other partners too."*

Counselor: *"That's an interesting connection and you have several concerns. Why don't you think about it for a week and let's talk again? Maybe we can be thoughtful and prevent some problems by scoping them out before they happen."*

Alan: *"I'd really like that, because I know I'm sensitive about my double life sometimes; it's one way I've always rebelled. But I don't want to lose my family, and I could."*

COMMENTS: Many other issues come up around sterilization, probably because of the need to decide about the surgical step and the relative permanence of the procedure. This results in some good opportunities for facilitative counseling.

Birth control is a comfortable way for the average person to get into a personal discussion about sex with a counselor. The question of "Should I use birth control, when, what kind, how reliable?" can evolve into "Why am I being sexual?" and "How can it be better?" Whether the counselor works in a school, a special program for women, with couples or teens, the subject provides a helpful way to get into important sexual questions.

RESOURCES REGARDING CONTRACEPTION

The following books are some of the classics in the field:

Goldstein, M., & Feldberg, M. (1982). *The vasectomy book: A complete guide to decision making.* Boston, MA: Houghton Mifflin.

Hafez, E. (Ed.). (1980). *Human reproduction: Conception and contraception.* Philadephia, PA: Lippincott.

Hatcher, R., Guest, F., Stewart, F., Stewart, G., Trussell, J., Cenel, S., & Cates, W. (1986). *Contraceptive technology 1986-87, 13th Edition.* New York: Irvington Publishers.

Holmes, H., Hoskins, B., & Gross, M. (Eds.) (1980). *Birth control and controlling birth.* Clifton, NJ: The Humana Press.

Norbach, J. (Ed.). (1983). *Sourcebook of sex therapy counselng and family planning.* New York, NY: Van Nostrand Reinhold.

Regular articles appear in professional journals on all aspects of birth control and counseling. Periodicals like *Family Planning Perspectives,* New York: The Alan Gutmacher Institute, monthly, provide current information.

Audiovisual materials like movies, slides, and tapes are available in most localities and from health and family life catalogues. Often group instruction and locally prepared educational materials and information on birth control can be obtained at low cost. Considerable grant money has gone into finding innovative ways to reach high risk and special groups.

Chapters found in a wide range of current books on women's and men's health are helpful to both counselor and client. New books are regularly available. Before recommending a book, the counselor must verify the author's professional credentials and references.

SEXUALLY TRANSMITTED DISEASES (STD)

The category of illness which directly affects the physiological, psychological, and interpersonal aspects of sexuality has been called "venereal" disease. The newer term, abbreviated to STD, is more descriptive and refers to a growing list of health problems. However, even though one out of 20 Americans has a sexually transmitted disease each year, there is more fear than enlightenment about them.

The sexuality counselor is well advised to keep up with the changing literature on STD's, through articles, manuals, and concise pamphlets available from local health departments and clinics. One of the most dangerous characteristics of STD's is that the symptoms may disappear for a time, or never be apparent to the person, while the disease progresses and is carried to others. The long term effects of STD's can range from pain, to sterility, to death, and while the diagnosis and treatment are complex, most can be cured.

A listing of STD's and their characteristics becomes outdated quickly. As soon as an agency states that gonorrhea is the number 1 public health problem, another researcher presents evidence to show that chlamydia is more prevalent. Counselors need to be familiar with the following so they can be alert to their manifestations:

GONORRHEA	SYPHILIS	GENITAL HERPES
VENEREAL WARTS	PUBIC LICE	GIARDIASIS
MOLLOSCUM CONTAGIOSUM	AIDS	CHANCROIDS
	YEAST (MONILIA)	TRICHOMONIASIS
LYMPHOGRANULOMA VENEREUM	CHLAMYDIA	HEPATITIS
	GRANULOMA INGUINALE	

Broader terms like NGU (nonspecific urethritis), vaginitis, PID (pelvic inflammatory disease), and urinary tract infections, refer to symptoms which can be caused by one of the above or by another organism.

No doubt other parasites and diseases can be spread by sexual contact and a few of the above can be contracted in non-sexual ways. Rather than knowing all the details of incidence, symptoms, and treatment, the role of the sexuality counselor is to point out whenever an STD could be present, refer for medical treatment, and follow up with the person.

Counselors find that clients who have concerns about STD often bring up many questions regarding their sexuality and relationships, especially if they have any doubts.

AIDS and the Fear of Aids

Acquired Immune Deficiency Syndrome (AIDS) is thought to be caused by a virus (called human T-cell leukemia or HTLV-III). Many people have a positive screening test which shows that they have been exposed to the virus, but only a small number of them will actually develop AIDS. The high risk groups are male homosexuals and intravenous drug users and the virus is known to be transmitted through the body fluids semen and blood.

The frightening aspects of AIDS is that those people who do develop it die of infections or cancers which take advantage of the body's lowered immune system. Also no cure or preventative vaccine is on the immediate horizon. Because research has not clarified all the means of transmission, unfounded fears can occur, such as about eating in restaurants, kissing a cousin, or having a haircut.

The counselor needs to become informed enough to reassure clients that AIDS is not transmitted by casual contract. Three groups of people may need counseling:

1. those with unfounded FAIDS (fear of AIDS),

2. those who are healthy but have had a positive test and may be carriers, and

3. people diagnosed as having AIDS.

Clients in the first group may have obsessive fears or sexual issues on which they need to work, those in the second group will require support for the ambiguity and sexual decision making, while the third group will need the kind of help any terminally ill person does. Client reactions of panic, homophobia, anger, guilt, fear, grief, and terrible uncertainty will require strength on the part of the counselor.

EXAMPLE: Sexual Disinterest Related to Fear of AIDS

Counselor: *"You say you've found yourself avoiding sex with Shirley?"*

Mac: *"She got the flu and then I did, and I just can't seem to get turned on at all..."*

Counselor: *"Because...?"*

Mac: (Uneasy, agitated) *"Well, her old boyfriend I never could stand. And she used to do mushrooms with him—they were both kind of flaky five years ago. Now he's been seen in gay bars!"*

Counselor: *"So you thought...?"*

Mac: *"Sure. She hasn't seen him in four years but maybe he gave her AIDS back then. I'm exposed to it now. On a TV program they said it could be ten years before anyone would know."*

Counselor: *"And how were things with Shirley before the flu and all?"*

Mac: *"Fine. We've been together four years and were almost engaged. Maybe I should stay with her anyway; if it's too late, I couldn't sleep with anyone else now, could I?"*

Counselor: *"Mac, you said Shirley hasn't seen the guy for four years. AIDS is a new disease in the U.S. and we know that heterosexual transmission here is rare. Your chances of even being exposed to the virus is remote, from what you describe. You can get a screening test, but when it comes back OK will that take care of everything?"*

Mac: *"Well, what does it say about me that Shirley's old boyfriend is queer? And now I can't even perform myself!"*

Counselor: (Dialogues and educates about male sexual arousal, masculinity, and bisexuality) *"And Mac, you were probably having some variation in sexual response, due to normal emotions about a four year serious relationship, and the fear of AIDS blew it out of proportion for you."*

Mac: *"So what should I do?"*

Counselor: *"Think about getting the screening test to set your mind at ease. Also, this may be the time for you to move forward with Shirley or to separate, but you want to decide that on*

solid grounds. You can meet with me to sort out what is bother-
ing you about the relationship, or you and Shirley could do
couples counseling for better communication and sexual
enrichment.''

Mac: *"OK. I feel better already. I think I really just hate that*
guy. I'll talk to Shirley and we'll be in next week.''

COMMENT: Giving Mac an AIDS booklet or showing an informative videotape would help keep him from slipping back into
projecting all his anxiety on AIDS. Mac is not likely to even get
the screening test, however, but may need to look at his anxiety
about sex and marriage. The counselor can help the couple explore their compatibility, any blocks either has about commitment, and assist with working out sexual problems.

Many clients will ask about preventing AIDS and can be encouraged
to know their sexual partners, to always use condoms and avoid anal intercourse if there is any question of exposure, and to remain in as good
health as possible. The important point is not to exchange body fluids
with a person who could have done so with a person exposed to the virus.
AIDS and herpes have already resulted in many people becoming more
conservative about their sexual expression.

STD Counseling Leads to Important Issues

In addition to raising concerns about current relationships, sexually
transmitted diseases bring up conflicts about past sexuality. A person
may have had a suspicious symptom, and then because of fear or shame
hoped it would go away. Something like herpes or hepatitis could have
been transmitted during an abusive or painful relationship which the
client had considered finished, and the STD seems like one more long-
term reminder. At the other end of the spectrum are persons who feel
anxious about sexuality, and believe they have every STD reported in the
media. The counselor needs patience and sensitivity to help a client work
through ambivalence about seeking help for possible STD.

Once a sexually transmitted disease is diagnosed, the client may have
a number of issues. One rule of public health is to inquire about and inform sexual partners concerning the possibility of infection, so that all
may receive treatment. Naturally this can be difficult for people to do,

since they must acknowledge sexual activity and question partners' sexual behavior. Sometimes a client will agree to write a note or have someone else make a telephone call, if he/she cannot discuss it in person. At times the discovery of an STD threatens a long standing relationship, and yet also shows that something needs to be improved. Where realistic, the counselor can help a client see the STD as an incentive to make positive changes in his/her life.

A counselor can provide therapeutic support, if for instance, the client has a resistant strain of gonorrhea and is frustrated by repeated cultures, has partner conflicts about recurring vaginitis, is worried about STD and a pregnancy, or desperate about the risk of possible complications such as cervical cancer with herpes. Fortunately some good films, phamphlets, and groups are available for STD sufferers, on curing, coping, and prevention. It is extremely important that the counselor not take a punitive approach, and that the client see the disease as caused by a virus, bacteria, or parasite. When this is accomplished, other meanings can be explored.

EXAMPLE: Young Married Woman, 1st Session

Sally: *"It had been bothering me before, but these things usually clear up."*

Counselor: *"You didn't expect it to be anything?"*

Sally: *"One of the people in the clinic gave me a hard time for waiting so long...I may even be sterile. I just don't know!"*

Counselor: *"It's hard to be blamed when you're hurting—and you know that PID is like any other infection. But you though it would go away?"*

Sally: *"I've had cystitis and yeast things before that flared up and disappeared. This came and went with intercourse mostly."*

Counselor: *"The pain did? How did you interpret that?"*

Sally: *"Well my husband is kind of large, and he has a bend in his penis. Oh—I don't know...Then I thought maybe I wasn't relaxed enough. At the clinic they said that the first signs of infection might not be much, but that the pain of thrusting in* intercourse is typical of PID. I'm pretty sure I never had gonor-rhea...well...the questions they asked me were incredible."

Counselor: *"A health problem like this forces you to deal with sex all at once. And you seem to keep thinking of things and getting more upset. What is it?"*

Sally: *"Everyone wants to know where I got it. There are some things I can't tell anyone about—not even you."*

Counselor: *"Well you hardly know me since we've been together only a half hour, but it may help to realize that I cannot repeat anything you say to anyone. The only exception would be if you were going to harm yourself or a specific other person, oh—and child abuse...we have to report that, but nothing else."*

Sally: (Tears.) *"I may never have children, but I'd certainly take good care of them!"*

Counselor: *"I'm sure you would, and I'm sorry about all this, Sally. But why don't you put the fertility question on hold? When the PID is better you can have tests done to see how your reproductive system is. Is that your main worry?"*

Sally: *"Not really. Right now it's—well—I'm going to have to face what I've been doing because of what my husband has been doing..."*

Counselor: *"You really look upset when you mention what your husband has been doing."*

Sally: *"Once in a while he goes to gay bars with other guys. I knew it when I married him...he and his brother used to go when we were in DC. But lately I feel different about it, and he gets mad if I bring it up. So I kind of went back to an old boyfriend."*

Counselor: *"No wonder this is tough for you...so much is involved. Why don't we take some sessions to sort out where you want to be sexually and in relationships?"*

Sally: *"But what will I tell them?"*

Counselor: *"Let's talk about that during these last few minutes today. Remember, you can be in charge of what you want to share."*

Sally: *"Maybe I'll just tell both of them that I have a 'female complaint' and can't have sex for a while. Or make it more specific so they will get checked too."*

Counselor: *"Fine. They need to be treated for chlamydia since any of you could have gotten it first and you don't want it back or passed on. And if either presses you for other information...?"*

Sally: *"I'll say I don't feel well and just can't talk about it yet."*

COMMENTS: The counselor is doing more than helping the client problem solve. Working through issues associated with the STD can be a step to greater maturity for Sally, toward improving her relationships, and taking better care of herself.

RESOURCES FOR SEXUALLY TRANSMITTED DISEASES

Self help reading for clients is available in magazines, women's health manuals, and books such as the following:

> Gordon, S. (1983). *Facts about STD.* Syracuse, NY: Ed-U-Press. Clear, easy reading.

> Langston, D. (1983). *Winning with herpes: A comprehensive guide to the causes, symptoms, and treatment of herpes viral illnesses.* Garden City, NJ: Doubleday.

> Neumann, H., & Simmons, R. (1983). *Dr. Neumann's guide to the new sexually transmitted diseases.* Washington, DC: Acropolis Books.

Current information for counselors is found in journal articles, health department publications, and in sexual health texts. The 13th edition of Hatcher et al., *Contraceptive Technology, 1986-87,* listed earlier in this chapter, contains an excellent summary of information on STD's for professionals.

CONCLUSION

Although many people doing sexual health counseling will work in clinic settings, all counselors need to have some familiarity with these common problems. Fortunately people are becoming aware of wellness issues, and are often more comfortable bringing up sexuality in this context than by itself. Also, worry about contraception, sexual health problems, and sexually transmitted diseases tends to overcome people's reticence or shyness. These topics offer excellent opportunities for counseling which can prevent or resolve sexual/mental health problems.

CHAPTER 5, PART 4

SEXUAL LIFE STYLE COUNSELING

The assumption that everyone's sexuality is confined to a lifelong exclusive commitment to a person of the other sex is clearly false for the majority of people in our society. Yet the myth remains, and many clients measure themselves or others against this standard and feel guilty or hostile. Counselors will encounter varied sexual life styles and are likely to hear about them through indirect reference. By being sensitive to subtleties, the counselor can help a person express troubling sexual style issues; when a client can talk about them easily, counseling has accomplished one important goal.

EXAMPLE: Client Expression of Changed Life Style

Less likely: *"Now that I'm a widow, I think I'll try women partners."*

More likely: *"I feel so lonely—and strange with men sometimes."*

Less likely: *"Since my wife divorced me I've been propositioning young women at work."*

More likely: *"After my divorce, I just began to—well—it was never like me to be so impulsive with women before."*

Counselor: *"It seems that the way you are feeling has changed, and perhaps you are a little surprised? Why don't we talk about different life styles?"*

COMMENT: People often appear "fuzzy" when they consider their sexual behavior or needs, especially if expectations and social rules are challenged. This is even more true because significant relationships and the opinions of others are heavily involved. It is usually a relief to explore the situation with a non-judgmental counselor.

People differ so significantly in what they judge as a suitable sexual life style that counselors must be able to hear, accept, and counsel without making a value judgment. While youngsters in one community are not even allowed to attend dances, in other areas the assumption may be that teenagers are sexually active at "the shore." However, even within these groups, great individual differences exist in the sexual styles individuals have. Social commentators point out that the 1960s and 70s were times of sexual experimentation, and although the pace of change is slower the effects continue. Counselors cannot share every possible sexual life style, but they can assist clients in finding what is best for them.

IMPORTANT VARIABLES

The following issues are present in any sexual life style choice and yet most people don't consciously stop and consider all of them. Calling these "value choices" is a little superficial, because many are deeply rooted in the identity and history of the client. Helping a person become comfortable with his/her sexual expression will go a long way toward alleviating anxiety, depression, and physical symptoms of distress.

1. *Life Stage.* Where is the client? Has he/she considered not being sexually active at this time? If a sexual experience is desired, which of the following would it be? Premarital: recreational sex, or a caring relationship? Cohabitation? Engaged? Multiple partners? Marital: with spouse, sexually open or closed? Extramarital: "affair," many partners, group sex, search for new husband/wife? Post-marital: divorce, widowed, second/third marriages. The never married. Relationships in mature years.

2. *Type of Sexual Activity.* If being sexually active is desired, what degree and kind fits his/her expectations? Is he/she aware of the range of sexual expression? Do they know how to communicate their preference for genital, non-genital, and other intimate activity?

3. *Partner Choice.* **P**ossible significant differences: age of the partner (especially if more than 5 to 10 years), the sex of the partner (especially if the same sex), racial, ethnic, religious, social characteristics, marital status of the partner.

4. *Commitment.* **H**ow interested/ready/similar are the client and a significant other in terms of sharing money, living quarters, exclusiveness (either sexual or emotional), possible children, and plans for the future? Or is the client wanting commitment but is fearful, isolated, or blocked?

5. *Gender Role.* **H**ow active or passive, traditionally masculine or feminine does the client choose to be? Is this compatible with conventions of and for their biological sex? What about expectations of and for partner(s)?

6. *Quality of Relationship.* **A** continuum from abusive to ideal is possible. How much will the client risk to attain the degree of quality desired? What will they settle for as a minimum in their sexual life style?

Any conflicts people have about sexual style choices usually involve some of the preceding issues. The counselor can help sort out whether the questions come from important others ("You can't come home if you marry into/out of an Hispanic family"), or are more internal ("I'm not sure I should live openly with another guy, but this is the best I've ever felt"). When the conflicts seem to involve mostly the self, the client can be helped to clarify them and find what he/she really wants. Clashes with significant others over sexual style can be resolved through communication practice, clarification of rights and needs, assertiveness training, and confidence building.

The following inquiries will help people who are struggling with sexual choices, in the focus phase of counseling. Does their present sexual style (or a contemplated one)

> fit their own values?
> meet their needs?
> seem not to harm others?
> appear to meet others' reasonable needs?
> result in generally positive outcomes?
> avoid emotional or legal problems?
> look appropriate for the future? For how long?

If not, what can the client do? Counseling is uniquely suited for sexual life style problems because the real issue is conflicting priorities. Asking the client to go deeper clarifies the confusion and shows how it is being expressed sexually. Usually at that point the counselor and/or the client see options or resolutions which the client has not been able to see before.

COMMITMENT AND SEXUAL LIFE STYLE

An important concern for many people is the degree of investment which they wish to make in a particular relationship. For some the issue is the greater one of whether they want (or can achieve) intimacy and commitment at all. Others find themselves so dependent on a relationship that they allow themselves to remain in an abusive situation. For both men and women the balance of self and others is becoming a more conscious choice, but this can result in conflict about options and alternatives. Many time sexuality-related counseling helps to clarify the underlying life style issues.

The counselor's skill is in helping the client explore past, present, and/or future relationships in order to discover what sexual life style he/she really wants. Rather than making abrupt changes, clients often decide to move gradually. A person may express an intention of working toward: "expressing my bisexuality, treating my partner better, getting a divorce and being celibate for a while, seeing people my own age, or clinging less and having more friends." Counselors find that feelings about relationships evolve, and situations change, so that thoughtfulness rather than trial and error is a better way for a client to sort out sexual life style and commitment.

CHANGING MARRIAGE PATTERNS

Sexual life stye choices often involve the decision to marry or divorce, live together, re-marry, or re-divorce. A show of hands in a college class may indicate that over half of their parents are divorced, and many recall this as the worst period of their lives. As a result, some young people are saying they will wait until they are older to marry, but this leaves them with the decade between 18 to 28 years of age to plan for relationships and sexual expression. Often they find very few, if any, comfortable role models. Each generation reacts to the experience of the people before it and is faced with new problems of commitment and life style.

The counselor who sees individuals and couples is inevitably going to hear conflicts about commitment, and whether a change in marital status will help solve sexual problems. This question can have many facets.

EXAMPLES: Typical Questions Regarding Changing Marriage Patterns

A person who was molested as a child may assume that marriage will take care of his/her sexual avoidance. A lingering trust issue is activated because the partner would rather live together without marriage for an indefinite period. Should he/she press for marriage?

A twice divorced man or woman doesn't want to marry their current lover because they were always "unlucky" with sex after marriage. They ask the counselor for a recommendation.

A young woman has been the "other woman" with several semi-married men, and experienced painful intercourse as each relationship deteriorated. She wants help "dealing with this."

A person has broken three engagements and comes to a counselor saying that maintaining arousal is the problem. He/she has assumed it meant that the other person wasn't "right" for him/her.

A young man took responsibility for his mother after her wrenching divorce. He experiences premature ejaculation with women and reports that they accuse him of "using" them, but he can't seem to find the right person.

Without training in sexuality counseling, the helping professional might focus only on qualities of the relationship and the client's family history, even when the presenting problem was stated as involving sex and commitment. If the counselor tries it the other way around, and encourages a sensitive discussion of sexuality, underlying goals concerning relationships may emerge quickly. People often say one thing to themselves while they actually do another, but can see the contradictions when their sexual inhibition or potency problems reveal deeper conflicts.

EXAMPLE: Widow and Divorced Man Considering Marriage

Counselor: *"Last week you both talked about sex in somewhat different ways. Could we clarify that?"*

Doug: *"Well, it's great. There's absolutely no problem."* (Repeats at some length.)

Counselor: *"So this is the best sexual relationship you've had, Doug, and..."*

Doug: (Interrupts.) *"And the best she's had..."* (goes on.)

Counselor: *"OK, but Cindy, I'd like to hear from you. It isn't always the same for both people."*

Cindy: *"What's the use?"*

Counselor: *"In expressing yourself?"*

Cindy: *"Umm, mmm, mmm."* (Shrugs.)

Counselor: *"Here?"* (Keeps eye contact with Cindy and puts out a hand to silence Doug.)

Cindy: (Silence.) *"Well, I must have said a dozen times what I don't like and it never sinks in."*

Doug: *"But it only has to do with your drinking. I can't listen to you with that mouthwash smell over bourbon."* (Goes on dogmatically.)

Counselor: *"Let's leave the alcohol issue out of it, for now. What is a good sexual experience for you, Cindy?"*

Cindy: *"Well...when we're laid back and relaxed, and Doug responds to what I want too. (She describes a vacation with good* lovemaking). *The problem isn't just my drinking, but...I tend to speak up and tell him off when I've had a few."*

Counselor: *"Doug, you obviously have a habit to break, too. It is clear that often you don't listen to Cindy. Do you enjoy sex when you are being responsive to Cindy's verbal and non-verbal signals?"*

Doug: *"Sure, and that's what I usually do..."*

Cindy: *"But lots of times you do what you think I should want."*

Doug: *"Well, I have to. You're changeable. I need to decide for both of us. Especially if you drink at all."*

Counselor: *"Wait a minute. This is very positive. I think we have uncovered the key to your largest problem. You know that you've tried to break up 5 or 6 times and can't, because you care too much. Right?"*

Both: (Nod, agree.)

Counselor: *"Cindy, you clearly feel steamrolled by Doug sometimes, and use alcohol instead of dealing with it. Possibly you choose to drink to tolerate it or tell him off. Doug you feel out of control when Cindy drinks, and become even more dominant and critical. Can you both see that transaction and agree it is a problem without pointing blame?"*

Doug: *"It's hard, but in some part of me I know you're right."*

Cindy: (After a long silence.) *"It won't work. He'll never keep listening."*

Counselor: *"I hear your discouragement, Cindy, and agree that Doug can get overbearing. But did you hear what he admitted? Wouldn't it be a reversal if you have to practice listening to Doug when he is really communicating, after you have worked so hard against being overpowered?"*

Cindy: *"I wish we could do it. I'd like to be married to Doug."*

Counselor: *"Sometimes starting with sex is the best place, because the pleasure is so much greater for both people when the control is equally shared in the here and now. I'd like to ask you not to have intercourse this week, but to enjoy some communication and intimacy exercises which I'll describe, and write on a counseling suggestion card for reference."*

COMMENTS: As compared to most issues, listening and responding to one another during sex is immediately rewarding (or an obvious problem). If Cindy can be empowered during sexual activities, to speak up rather than make a passive-aggressive withdrawal to alcohol, this couple may well decide to marry. For his part Doug can learn to be more respectful of Cindy's input first in sex and then more generally. It will be important for him to withdraw from a power struggle over alcohol and for her to be responsible for treatment. If this couple can work out a good sexual relationship in spite of both of their problems, they will be clearer about the kind of life style which they can achieve.

This dialogue and the five examples entitled "Typical Questions Regarding Changing Marriage Patterns" illustrate how varied the presenting problems can be. By focusing on the sexual aspects, often the counselor can help the client determine when a sexual problem would be present regardless of whom the partner was, and when sex is reflecting a commitment/life style issue.

Resources listed elsewhere in this training prgram are applicable to commitment and changing marital life style counseling. In addition, numerous texts on couples' counseling are available. Self help books cover every life style and commitment issue, from letting go of negative relationships to blended families. The counselor can find many books to apply to particular client situations.

SAME-SEX PARTNERS

Although counseling people whose affectional/sexual preference is toward their own biological sex is like most counseling, a sensitive counselor may find some differences. By being open to the possibility of either sex partner with any client, a counselor will hear of homosexual experiences when taking sexuality histories. What cannot be predicted is the client's reaction to them. Same-sex experiences may be rare or continuous for a client, but attitudes toward it can vary from self condemnation to celebration. The tendency to be critical varies with circumstances, but based upon research data approximately a quarter of most homosexual samples have serious reservations about their orientation at some point in time. With these clients the first concern is not a sexual one; they need to deal with questions about their own identity and self worth.

Issues arise about changing a person's preference for the sex of a partner. An interesting distinction is made in the literature between sexual orientation and sexual behavior. Many contend that the basic sexual orientation toward male/female partners is established very young (and no one has yet proven the factors involved), but that sexual behavior is more flexible and can be modified. Therefore, clinics can publish studies which show success in helping homosexual clients who want to change their sexual behavior, but no one knows if the basic orientation is altered. Also, since many people can relate sexually to either sex, it is possible for them to encourage their sexual fantasy, skills, and behavior toward one sex, rather than the other. The major task is for the counselor not to become embroiled in academic debates on unsettled issues, and instead to help each client find the sexual expression most comfortable for him/her.

Individualization

Although an obvious point, the counselor must be careful not to make generalizations about one gay client from other homosexual clients or friends, or one's own experience. A socially established married man who has a long standing relationship with a male lover will have very different counseling needs from the college junior whose whole identity is absorbed into gay pride activism. Two feminine women who are discreet lovers may be disturbed beyond belief by the shocking (to them) behavior of some gay men, who dress as nuns or dancers and create public scenes to make a valid point (for them). People who are sexually relating to their own sex are as diverse as can be found in any random sample of society.

The counselor may be celibate, bisexual, heterosexual, or homosexual, but needs to be careful not to make judgments about independence/dependence, monogomy/varied partners, desirability of political activism, types of sexual activity, and sex role style. Both the diversity of individuals with same-sex experience and the widespread homophobia in our culture make it challenging even for gay or lesbian counselors to work with homosexual issues. Language itself is limited, so that if any counselor uses words like "preference," orientation," "homosexual," "gay," or terms for sexual activity, some clients may be offended. This need not keep counselors from being helpful, however.

EXAMPLE: Student In Veterinary Medicine, 4th Session

Counselor: *"Larry, I know this isn't an easy subject. Last Tuesday it took courage to bring up your hitchhiking. Did I understand that you really don't think about it much, but just kind of go cruising when the tension builds up?"*

Larry: *"Yes, but I'm getting worried because I know all the stuff I could catch. I've gotten less selective...and been roughed up some. It doesn't make sense to get sex that way, but I can't stop."*

Counselor: *"Let's not try to change anything until you understand what you need, then you'll be able to make safer, more satisfying decisions..."*

Larry: (Really upset, flushed) *"...There you...g... go...calling it a...a...choice!"*

Counselor: (Pauses, waits until Larry looks back.) *"I'm sorry. I didn't mean that your experiences with men are casual choices. Honestly, I wasn't weighing my words. What I meant was for you to take it easy before trying to stop something so compelling."*

Larry: *"It's hard for me...to...talk about."*

Counselor: *"Sure. Also, I was trying to bring up tactfully something I noticed last week. When you described the time that you came out to your parents, I noticed that your tendency to stammer increased. You were picturing your father's icy detachment."*

Larry: *"Crazy. I get mad at you for saying 'decision,' because my...father...th...thinks..."* (Can't speak.)

Counselor: (Shakes Larry's elbow.) *"I know—I know it hurts. But why is his reaction so important? Do you need his permission for an adult sex life? Shall we talk first about any reservations you have concerning sex with men, or about how you resent Dad's rejection?"*

COMMENTS: Larry was saying a great deal with his body language and speech hesitation. If the counselor had been intimidated by accidentally using a painful word, they would have both been stuck. Larry will need to deal with both his hurt and anger about his Dad, *and* his own negative feelings which lead him to express his same-sex preference in anonymous, risky situations. Also, this meeting was only the fourth, so much more can emerge and be worked out.

Timing

The point in time when a client brings a same-sex issue to a counselor is significant. Occasionally a person has had little or no homosexual experience, but is attracted to people of his/her own sex and is confused or conflicted. This can occur at any age, but the counselor needs to be especially concerned about the child or adolescent who may have no way of sorting this out and establishing a support network. A delicate balance is needed to convey that many people have same-sex experiences who later enjoy a heterosexual life style, without sounding as though that is preferable. Giving a young client accurate information that homosexuality is not necessarily a crime, sin, or illness is important, but also helpful is to explore the negative attitudes and restrictions surrounding this life style. Some young people need to talk only once, while others need years of help, but all benefit from a trustworthy counselor.

Other clients have had some or considerable same-sex sexual contact (some of it may be blocked or denied), and need support, information, and clarification. Clients may describe years of drug or alcohol abuse or other self damaging behavior because of being threatened by their homosexual feelings/behavior. Fortunately this is becoming less common, now that activist gay movements have shown that theirs is a large minority, and organizations like *Parents and Friends of Gays* and *Integrity* are being heard. In many places, women's groups which are matter-of-fact about a diversity of life styles are positively influencing public opinion. A good counselor can be immensely helpful to the individual who has had some same-sex experience and needs to come to terms with it.

Coming Out

The question of being openly gay or "in the closet" is another misunderstood one. Most mental health theories would recommend that any person be open within himself/herself and integrate his/her sexual orientation and behavior with the self concept in a positive way. How open to be with others is another consideration altogether. Naive helpers may believe that the more self disclosing a person is, the healthier.

Research does not support the necessity of wide disclosure in regard to individuals sharing their sexual orientation. While the research data appear to support that self acceptance of homosexual identity is related to higher overall mental health, these data do not show a positive relationship between mental health and telling parents, employers, and friends. Many find that simply to avoid living a lie they tell others about their preference for same-sex partners. The counselor can help each client be selective and find a mature balance between disclosure and privacy.

EXAMPLE: Being Discreet About Same-Sex Preference

A moment's reflection will clarify why a teacher who prefers his/her own sex and lives in a conservative community, shows excellent reality testing by being private about sexual orientation. If he/she comes out publicly and is interested in becoming a principal, guidance director, or even keeping a teaching job, the decision may not be based on the person's qualifications. Many school boards and community groups do not question myths about sexual life style, and those who do may be subject to smear campaigns. The counselor can help the client when stereotyping, unfair practices, violence toward gay men (one third experience this), and other forms of homophobia are a possibility. Being a support person and assisting in problem solving around the issue of coming out can be done without assuming that "more is better."

Same-Sex Lovemaking

All the familiar issues of performance instead of pleasure, questions of attraction, arousal, climax, timing, and partner communication will come up with gay men and lesbian women. Asking a client how they are currently enjoying or not liking sex, about their best sexual experiences, and about fantasy, will help the counselor focus with a particular client. Exploring any negative sexual experiences and trauma in a homosexual client's history is also helpful in clarifying where any conflicts originated.

Counselors need to read materials about the joy of gay sex, just as they read heterosexual manuals, to gain better awareness of sexual practices beyond their own limited experience. The counselor must know far more about same-sex lovemaking than the dangers of intercourse with the fist or blowing air into the vagina, or cautions about STD's. As always, the counselor is expected to demonstrate genuine, non-judgmental interest consistently. As with any client, real concerns about adequacy, lovemaking, and sexuality may be critically important to the person, but hard to express.

EXAMPLE: Lesbian Woman, Age 34, Recent Suicide Attempt

Counselor: *"So how have you been doing since vacation? You and Gail were getting close as I recall."*

Wendy: *"We did start living together—once we got my dependency tendencies straightened out. But I have a terrible time with jealousy."*

Counselor: *"It bothers you to see Gail paying attention to...dancing with...other women?"*

Wendy: *"Well, she doesn't want to imitate traditional marriage and I understand that. But I'm having trouble sleeping again."*

Counselor: *"I remember that when you felt short-changed back when you were married, you've told me you hardly slept."*

Wendy: *"Even with sleeping pills sometimes...and usually I went for days on coffee. By now I know it means I'm upset, and it doesn't seem to be about my former husband."*

Counselor: *"Perhaps angry...about Gail? What's really happening?"*

Wendy: *"Well, we've worked out a semi-open relationship, but she won't—really make love—well, it's probably me."*

Counselor: *"You look as though you'd like something different sexually?"*

Wendy: *"Gail should know about sex...she's been an active lesbian since high school. But I like—deeper feelings—well, maybe because I was married."*

Counselor: *"Perhaps you feel good within the vagina as well as with clitoral stimulation, is that it? Lots of women do, both gay and straight."*

Wendy: *"I don't know if being lesbian is a state of mind or a kind of politics or sex, but I long for deeper sexual feelings with Gail."*

Counselor: *"That could certainly be worked out, with her fingers, a vibrator, or safe kind of dildo. But more important is your being able to respect your womanly sexual feelings and stand up for them."*

Wendy: *"Let's talk about that. I back down so easily."*

COMMENTS: The counselor can suggest self stimulation with penetration, to help Wendy "own" her own style of sexual feelings and stop attributing them only to heterosexual experience. The next step might be to role play good humored, decisive communication with her partner. The counselor can remind Wendy that a strong stand and challenge to Gail could improve their lovemaking more than insomnia would. Any couple could find they are not sexually compatible, but most differences can be accomodated to enhance their sexuality, if the relationship is strong in other ways.

Some counselors have the misconception that they need extensive knowledge of local gay groups or that they must be homosexual to do sexuality counseling with clients who have same-sex experiences. What is far more important is being sensitive, open, and honest when doing sexual life style counseling, and the helper can expect some intense emotion. However, people are people, and the sexuality of one's partner or the politics of sexual orientation are only aspects of the person.

For the counselor without same-gender sexual experience, a bridge can be found by extending expertise the counselor already has. A large minority of any group such as youth, the elderly, the disabled, families, college students, or women at mid-life are homosexual, and the counselor may already be familiar with the overall group. Within this familiar population the counselor not only can be helpful by working with individuals, but also can intervene on a systems level to work for policies which are respectful of the right to choose same sex partners.

RESOURCES FOR COUNSELING ABOUT HOMOSEXUALITY

Gonsiorek, J. (1985). *A guide to psychotherapy with gay and lesbian clients.* Binghamton, NY: Harrington Park Press.

Hetrick, E., & Stein, T. (Eds.). (1984). *Innovations in psychotherapy with homosexuals.* Washington, DC: American Psychiatric Association.

Hidalgo, H., Peterson, T., & Woodman, N. (Eds.). (1985). *Lesbian and gay issues: A resource manual for social workers.* Silver Springs, MD: National Association of Social Workers.

Loulan, J. (1984). *Lesbian sex.* San Francisco: Spinsters Inc.

Moses, A., & Hawkins, R. (1982). *Counseling lesbian women and gay men: A life issues approach.* St. Louis: The C.V. Mosby Co.

Woodman, N., & Lenna, H. (1980). *Four resources for counseling gay men and women.* San Francisco: Jossey-Bass.

Clinical presentations and research reports are planned for the American Psychological Association's new Division 44, The Society for Psychological Study of Lesbian and Gay Concerns. The American Association for Counseling and Development can be contacted regarding the Caucus of Gay and Lesbian Counselors. Other professional and human service organizations have similar groups which are especially good for training.

UNCERTAINTY ABOUT PARTNER PREFERENCE

For every client like Wendy or Larry who is quite definite about preferring their own sex, the counselor will see several people who really don't know. Some individuals may have little sexual life experience while others' is extensive. They may be comfortable or conflicted about being sexually attracted to individuals of either sex, and it can be lifelong, recent, continuous, or variable depending on circumstances. These clients may be single, divorced, married, have children, be highly educated or impoverished, and of any age.

The counselor can be helpful by broadening the issue from "What really am I sexually?" to "Who am I and in what ways can sexuality be comfortable and positive for me?" The client may need to do a brief relaxation exercise at the beginning and end of each session, and learn ways to be self affirming. Going over the sex history carefully allows important ventilation and will bring up self doubts and sources of conflict. An important goal is to help the client see many alternatives and develop ways of trying out the more promising ones.

EXAMPLE: Couple Living Together 3 Years, 5th Session

Ariel: *"We've been doing the pleasuring sessions and I think it's great. I don't care if we never do anything else. All my old feelings of being uptight and clumsy are gone."*

Mike: *"Sure, we can make each other come just fine, but I still don't know if I'll always have a good erection."*

Counselor: *"Let's not worry about 'always,' OK, Mike? But is something about this bothering you?"*

Mike: (Non-verbal irritation and restlessness.)

Ariel: *"We don't have to hurry. I especially like your suggestion of lying together like spoons and breathing to our favorite music.* (Teasing) *I know you do too, Mike. Men can't hide it when they like it."*

Mike: *"I really do...it's almost too good.* (Turns to counselor.) *I...maybe I have to talk to you alone and work out some things."*

Counselor: *"As I said in the beginning, sometimes a separate session is a good way to make progress. Is that all right with you, Ariel?"*

Ariel: *"Sure, I think Mike has to sort out some things by himself."*

COMMENTS: The above dialogue suggests that this couple's growing attachment and the resolution of Ariel's mild sexual inhibition, resulted in Mike's worrying about possible problems with erection. Progress in their relationship brought this couple closer, so that Mike could no longer not "see" his avoidance of marriage.

With the counselor, Mike explored feeling comfortable having an occasional sexual experience with a man, as long as he was not married. Having both had been no problem for him, until living with Ariel brought up some "flight" responses. Fortunately Mike could see the patterns, work through his traumatic family history of inconsistent adopted-step parents, and explore all the alternatives. Numerous healthy outcomes could occur, but the point is that what looked like regression in counseling was necessary movement.

Alternatives

The **COUNSELOR** could:

work individually with Mike.

refer Mike to another competent counselor/therapist.

continue with Ariel and Mike to concentrate on couples' work.

refer Mike to individuals, groups, and reading material to learn more about bisexual options/lifestyle.

MIKE could:

choose to express himself heterosexually for a while, with or without marriage as a goal.

decide to enlarge his experience with men, in order to assess how important this area of expression is for him.

decide that bisexuality is natural for him, and work out what that means.

choose to share none, any, or all of his dilemma with Ariel.

direct fantasy and self stimulation toward his choice, in order to strengthen it.

develop a strong, competent, positive sense of himself, which includes a realistic plan for sexual expression.

ARIEL could:

benefit from supportive counseling herself or continued couples work, while Mike is working out his sexual and emotional issues.

find a short term support group or woman's group helpful.

leave the relationship and explore other possibilities for herself, if Mike cannot resolve his issues or takes too long for her.

try to communicate with Mike about his issues, and then work out how that affects her.

COMMENTS: While exploring his painful family history, Mike may come to realize he has difficulty in feeling safe when being emotionally close to only one person. The counselor must not jump to the conclusion that this is the cause of his sexual experiences with men; obviously Mike could relate to several women at once if the fear of dependency were the only issue. A destructive interpretation for a counselor would be to attribute life style choices which differ from the published "norm" to present or past pathology. However, working on issues around intimacy may make a difference between Mike and Ariel.

Often a counselor will work with a couple where life style choices are in flux, and will have to focus more on one person than the other. Usually the best procedure is to acknowledge this in an open way, without any indication of fault. The obvious need is to keep concern for both people active and not become invested in helping only one or in finding a particular outcome.

CONCLUSION

Basically the counselor can use a knowledge of sexuality counseling in two ways to help commitment and life style choices; each is critical to clients' self worth and adjustment to society:

1. Helping clients improve the sexuality in existing or contemplated relationships (whether or not these conform to accepted stereotypes), strengthens their self esteem and security.

2. Assisting clients to look at the specifically sexual part of life style choices helps them see what is occurring in current/past relationships, and to decide what is their own healthiest life style.

The deepest roots of personal identity, individuation, taking risks, and finding a balance of self and others are involved in life style choices; it is a privilege for a counselor to be able to facilitate this process in a respectful way.

CHAPTER 5, PART 5

PROBLEMS WITH SEXUAL EXPRESSION

Many people in our society can talk about sexuality, but few describe their actual sexual behavior. When individuals are asked, "Do you have a sexual dysfunction?" the majority say they don't; however, if interviewed about their sex life, a large proportion reveal "diagnosable" sexual problems. Is counseling always needed? Not necessarily, because some people choose to maintain the status quo. Also many lovemaking and response difficulties are resolved through self-help reading, coaching from the media, and experience with partners. Certainly many people find increasing sexual satisfaction with maturity.

Counselors often learn indirectly about difficulties clients are having with the experience of sexuality, while they are discussing something else. Or clients may reply to a counselor's question by admitting that they do not enjoy sex, or just volunteer that they have a problem. No matter how the subject of sexual difficulty arises, the counselor needs to ask whether the person wishes to explore the sexual issue, and allow time for them to accept/reject that focus. The counselor expects to model relaxed attitudes about working on sensitive sexual behavior, but must be sure that clients are not led in an unwelcome direction.

EXAMPLE: Client Inadvertently Discloses Sexuality Problem

Counselor: *"We've been talking about marital problems and fatigue, Eileen, and you just referred to restless sleep because of nasty dreams. I believe it will help to spend some time talking about the sexual part of your life. Would you be willing to describe some of what wakes you up?"*

COMMENTS: The client is being asked to become involved before focusing on sexual details. The counselor will probably need to spend time reassuring Eileen that dreams often contain sex which seems unacceptable, and that most marriages have some sexual problems. Counseling to encourage a client to explore sexual behavior often requires more skill than actually working on the sexual problem.

FOCUS PHASE

Probably the most critical point when working with unsatisfying sexual experience is sorting out what the trouble is. Several interviews may be needed to build rapport, explore concerns, and begin to focus. Clients need time to discover deeper issues and for related memories to surface. Many sexual satisfaction problems which come to light overlap with issues covered elsewhere in this training program, and all need to be referred for a medical checkup. No one can succeed by simply counseling a man with a low sex drive due to high circulating levels of prolactin. The condition is easily treated medically but the man may want counseling to regain confidence. Multiple determinants of sexual expression problems can be expected in most cases.

Assessment begins immediately; it must be broad and ongoing. After the relationship is established and the clients' issues are explored, the counselor will have some idea where the problems in sexual expression might be. Through dialogue with the client(s) and counseling suggestions, the counselor assists with focus as the opportunities arise, and continues with assessment until all likely avenues are explored. A mistake could be made easily by jumping to conclusions too soon, because then the suggested remedy will be inadequate. Because of the many possible contributing factors, the counselor must keep careful records, and seek supervision when working with unusual difficulties of sexual expression.

Problems with experiencing sexual pleasure have so many potential causes that the counselor needs a frame of reference to proceed. Sex therapists such as Masters and Johnson and Helen Singer Kaplan have defined categories of sexual dysfunction, and provide guidelines for differential diagnosis and treatment. Other eminent clinicians focus on a particular problem such as anorgasmia (no climax), or premature ejaculation, and publish their assessment and treatment programs. As these formulations are established, they often are challenged by others, and then evolve and change. Counselors can refer to this rich literature for detailed help, but need to begin with sexual expression clients by locating the difficulties.

FRAMEWORK FOR ASSESSMENT/FOCUSING

Clients can be asked to be descriptive so that a global picture is developed, rather than trying to narrow to a specific diagnosis too soon. Past and present sexual experience can be discussed in terms of:

1. THE PLEASURE CURVE. What points are generally successful/comfortable, and where does the difficulty occur?

Interest—Desire—Arousal—Climax(s)—Relaxation

2. What contributing factors are ATTITUDINAL (more internal)?

3. What contributing factors are SITUATIONAL (more external)?

4. Which sexual problems are rooted in relationship issues?

Using the Concept of the Pleasure Curve

Clients usually cannot label their sexual expression difficulties accurately before counseling, so the descriptive approach is best. Useful inquiries include:

> *"Describe how you make love these days."*
> *"When it's good?"*
> *"How is it when it's not good?"*
> *"What is sex like by yourself?"*
> *"With any other partners?"*
> *"What was sex like in the past...?"*

A variety of client sexual experience can then be related to the diagram of the pleasure curve.

A client who says, "My problem is that I can't come," may later say, "Now I realize that it's hard to let myself get into sex enough in the early part." In a similar way, someone may say he/she is "cold," and yet after using the pleasure curve diagram to describe sexual experiences with self and others, realizes: "Yes I do get very excited but can't let go with a partner, so maybe that's why I've been avoiding sex altogether." Part of this use of the pleasure curve diagram is for the counselor's assessment needs, but the process also serves to give the client perspective on sexual experience.

Fixed ideas about how sex "should" be are also easily clarified using the pleasure curve concept. Clients may not realize they are measuring themselves against idealized goals, or an impression of the partners' expectations. Typical comments reflect "We should both be at the peak of excitement right away (automatically), every move will be sensational, and then we would have intense intercourse culminating in thunderous, mutual climaxes." Of course people don't actually say this, but when the counselor asks what they do behaviorally to get from interest to desire to arousal to climax, clients "don't know" and their impossible expectations come out. The counselor can use a light touch with some clients about unrealistic expectations, and then look at how real people become sexually interested/aroused/released, after a busy day's work.

Using a diagram of the curve, tentative formulations can be checked out with the client in a non-critical but explicit way. Looking for causes is to be avoided until the patterns of sexual difficulty are clear to both client and counselor.

EXAMPLES: Comments By Counselor While Utilizing the Pleasure Curve Diagram

"It seems that you'd like to enjoy being over here on the curve with a firm erection, and yet you come before you expect to?"

"Are you saying that once you are lubricating it is fine to begin penis-in-vagina thrusting, but that you would be interested in receiving oral sex at this earlier point, instead of always giving it?"

"You and your partner fight because he sometimes likes the 'back passage' (anal penetration). *It's pleasurable for you if you are really turned on...over here on the curve...but painful before that? What helps you get excited in this desire/arousal part?"*

The client tends to feel less of a failure when he/she views the pleasure curve as a natural response process, and becomes interested in where the "hitch" is. When partners are involved, they can be non-judgmental about their individual patterns and discuss how they can be integrated. Not only timing issues but specific sexual preferences and behaviors can be described in a non-threatening way, and compared to masturbation or other experiences/fantasies.

EXAMPLE: Couple In Their Thirties, Marriage Fine, Sex Isn't

Counselor: *"So when you are daydreaming or self pleasuring, what do you find exciting to picture at the beginning of the pleasure curve?"*

Jack: *"Nothing too different, just some women with amazing bodies, stroking, and licking me until I can't stand it. I have to beg them to stop but they won't until I come."*

Janet: *"A great looking guy—sometimes partly like Jack—is making me feel good all over. Only he can touch me and his hands are strong but gentle, for a long time. He goes in and out of me everywhere and pushes through my hesitation."*

Counselor: *"So both of you find that the image of receiving lots of attention and stimulation builds sexual excitement?"*

Jack: *"No wonder we're having trouble. We each expect the other to get us in the mood first."*

Janet: (Shows facial expression of agreement.)

COMMENTS: The counselor can connect this description to the couple's avoidance pattern, and encourage private exploration of solutions.

Counselor: *"Now that you both see the importance of helping the other become aroused with mutual touching, why don't you* *enjoy that this week? I don't need to know the specifics, but this counseling suggestion card says: 'Share with each other three arousing ways of touch, and experiment with them at least twice during the week,' OK?''*

COMMENTS: Later in counseling, the pleasure curve provides an easy reference point for ongoing discussion about sexual experience. The couple could work out approaches to their sexual arousal problem, and then focus on concerns about orgasm. The counselor must become clear about exactly what is happening, and balance communication issues with sexual technique suggestions.

Same Couple, Later Session

Janet: *"Can a person feel quite aroused, like about here on the curve, have a little climax...and then get wound up again?''*

Jack: *"She seems not to know when she's finished, and wants a long relaxation part. How do I know when I've taken care of her?''*

Counselor: *"It isn't up to you to orchestrate sex, remember Jack?''*(Describes variations in women's orgasm, perhaps sketching inflow and outflow of circulation and waves of feeling.) *So a woman's climaxes can vary—little, large, many, none, warm feelings or intense...there is not one event to reach every time. Janet, do you know when you want release of sexual tension, or more holding, relaxation...?''*

Janet: *"It isn't always the same...''*

Jack: *"But how am I supposed to know? You make a fool of me sometimes!''*

Counselor: (Focuses on Jack's projection of blame and feelings of responsibility for Janet's pleasure.) *"Demanding won't work, Jack. Can you let her know your experience and then ask for hers?''*

Jack: *"Sorry, old habit of blaming. We have talked about that a lot.''* (Looks at Janet.) *"I feel stupid that I can't satisfy you.''*

Janet: *"Here we go to all this counseling for me to get interested in sex, and now you're worried about satisfying me!"*

Counselor: (Laughs.) *"You have a point that it's a good sign, Janet. And what's the goal, Jack?"*

Jack: (Sighs.) *"Enjoying the sex curve, pleasure. I know, and we do have lots more of that."*

Counselor: *"You aren't responsible for making things happen magically for Janet. Let's work out some nonverbal signals, since both of you find that talking during sex jars you out of the sensual mood. Janet, you need to think about where to put Jack's hand, or any part of him, to show whether you want to cuddle or become more excited or whatever...can you do that?"*

Janet: *"Sure, I never thought of it. It's kind of fun that it's not always the same. I'm still just shy about it."*

Jack: *"I need to remember that, and not try to plan it like a project."*

Counselor: *"Perfect, Jack. Just refer back to the idea of the pleasure curve once in a while. Whether either or both of you has a climax isn't important. Sex is successful when there has been a pleasant buildup and relaxation of sexual pleasure."*

Janet: *"I can't believe the things we used to let stop us."*

Jack: (Nods agreement.)

It is impossible to list the hundreds of patterns which emerge as people describe sexual experience in terms of the flow of behavior. The pleasure curve is simply a vehicle which facilitates the frank discussion of sexuality for individuals, couples, either sex partner, and any kind of sexual technique or variant. It helps place apparently separate acts and sexual feelings in a coherent perspective. The counselor needs to use techniques satisfactory to his/her style of counseling that facilitate direct communication about private sexual behavior without embarrassing the client.

Contributing Factors: Attitudinal

Once the lovemaking/sexual experience problem behavior has been described and mapped on the pleasure curve, it may be treated with information or counseling suggestions. During the focusing, however, the counselor may hear damaging internal attitudes which cause or maintain the sexual problem. Inhibiting sexual attitudes can have a thousand variations and some major categories are covered in the following two categories. Others are described in sections on health, lifestyle, or development. The counselor's task is to listen for and help the client understand the relevance of particular attitudinal blocks.

Attitudinal Problems Rooted in the Self Concept. The importance of self-concept and self-esteem has wide acceptance and most counselors routinely check to see whether a client's overall sense of himself/herself is essentially positive. Very often a client who has a low self image in general will feel inadequate, unlovable, and unappealing sexually. When this occurs, the counselor cannot focus only on sexuality, because usually the overall negative sense of self needs to be addressed.

Many clients have general low self worth which is directly related to damage done to their sexual self. In these instances, the counselor will find specific trauma to the sexual self, either through child sexual abuse, forced sex, severely inhibiting family beliefs, sexism, or some other unhealthy circumstance. The counselor can help people see the connection between the painful or condemned sexual experience and their low self concept. The client is often convinced that he/she is worthless or ruined because of something sexual, so that compassion, patience, and sometimes referral are needed to lift both the sexual and overall sense of self.

For some people other aspects of the self concept are generally okay, but the sexual self is low. Then the focus again belongs on sexuality and the counseling tends to be less complex.

EXAMPLES: Low Sexual Self Comments

Popular Hospital Employee:

"I love parties and doing things in groups. But I'm too heavy...and just try to get sex over with. Anyway, I don't get turned on except with magazines."

Successful Businessman:

"Why drag it out like she's always pressuring me to? I'm not romantic, and if I try it she'll just expect more. Besides, what are you supposed to do?"

Otherwise Confident Person:

"He/she would think I'm really odd if I expected more from sex. It's probably my fault any way."

The preceding comments could be buried in 15 minutes of general discussion about personal/social problems. The skill of the counselor is to pull them out, and to focus on the low sexual self-concept as an attitudinal obstacle. Once the client understands that the sexual problem is related to a negative sexual self-concept, the counselor can work during the sessions to explore its roots and suggest ways to improve it.

Whether the overall sense of self is low or only the sexual self-concept, numerous techniques are available for changing negative to positive self perceptions (in an ordinary or relaxed state of consciousness). Behavioral tasks which the counselor can suggest, such as positive self-talk assignments, and gradual self and other pleasuring exercises have a high probability of success. Many other interventions during the counseling session, and for homework outside, can be creatively used to alter negative impressions of the general and sexual self. People with any kind of low self-concept tend to accept it as a "given," and need help to see that they can control negative self thoughts and defeating behavior. However, the counselor needs to keep a clear focus, and make the client responsible for eventually improving his/her sexual self-concept.

Attitudinal Problems Rooted in Guilt. People who believe that some aspect of their sexual self is bad are different from those who simply feel inadequate or unskilled. Most clients take their sexual attitudes for granted, either assuming they are immutable or that most people feel that way. Some believe that no one could possibly accept their sexual fantasies or experiences; often this is true even when the sexual aspects are quite usual. Counselors can find many ways to treat internalized criticism, self-condemnation, and guilt about sexuality, but first they have to "hear" it and label it so the client can see it.

Clients may have difficulty challenging a fixed belief that some aspect of their sexuality is negative, because they have felt too guilty to really face it. While this is true for past events, it is especially keen for present guilty feelings.

EXAMPLES: Clients' Expressions of Guilt

Young Woman:

"Not being able to climax is only one of my worries. If my parents knew that I let my boyfriend stay over, they would never visit me again. My father would wonder how I can do it with my mother's heart condition."

Young Man:

"I keep having these dreams—even in the daytime—of this girl I used to date a little. Lately I can't get an erection unless I think of her. My wife would never sleep with me if she knew...she barely agrees to now."

COMMENTS: In these two examples, the clients carry guilt as an attitudinal contributing factor which is a barrier to good sex. Other problems are likely to exist as well. Guilt is sometimes close to anger or fear, and may express unresolved anxieties which are suppressed. Turning feelings inward on the self, to anguish and self contempt, may seem easier than being assertive and working out what the real situation is. Supportive confrontation and encouragement are especially important here.

Many times a person's sex life may proceed well, even with conflicts, until a particular fear, anger, or stress tips the guilt balance.

EXAMPLES: Guilt Triggered By Recent Events

Young Man:

"I'm so afraid of herpes, or even worse, AIDS, that I just haven't been able to do anything lately. Maybe I should have tried harder to stay straight years ago. Anyway, I'm getting really depressed and afraid I'll lose him—my regular partner."

Young Female Employee:

"Everything was fine until just lately when I had a delayed period. I thought about the abortions I've had and all the stuff I did in high school. I can't seem to concentrate and keep my mind on anything at work. I hate to have my boyfriend touch me."

COMMENTS: In any guilt/fear/anger/anxiety about sex issue, the counselor must avoid rushing to interpret. Empty reassurance and simple facts are usually not sufficient. The client has been blaming himself/herself heavily for a purpose, so that further and deeper exploration will be necessary. Support, encouragement to confront the issues, and alternative understandings are needed.

EXAMPLE: Battered Wife, Presenting With "Fainting Spells"

Counselor: *"It was really hard to make him leave, because he could be so nice when he wanted to?"*

Wilda: *"And I put up with a lot because of my five children. No one in town could know, I thought."*

Counselor: *"And you remembered promising 'for better or worse,' you said last week."*

Wilda: *"But when he cut me down there, I knew it was never going to get any better. Before that I could usually...well...not agree with him, but..."*

Counselor: *"It took something brutal for you not to blame yourself or the kids. And you have been through so much stress since the court order, getting your husband to leave and pay child support...it's no wonder that you feel faint sometimes."*

Wilda: *"Yes, but if I weren't so...perverted...it would be OK. It happened again yesterday."*

Counselor: *"You had some sudden sexual feelings?"*

Wilda: *"I'm afraid someone will notice in the cafeteria where I work...I almost fainted yesterday."*

Counselor: *"So you continue to believe that masturbation is okay for everyone else but you, and spend hours fighting the heavy, throbbing feelings you describe? Sexual arousal is normal and healthy for a woman you know."*

Wilda: *"But it can't be normal this often..."*

Counselor: *"Remember we talked about it last week? By not helping yourself reach a climax you stay in a state of being turned on, and then feel terrified that someone will notice. The more scared you are, the more likely you are to feel faint and hold your breath and all. It must be so hard!"*

Wilda: *"And now that I have a court order to keep my husband out...the last thing I can do is be bad in sex. What would happen to my kids? I used to see women like that!"*

Counselor: *"It seems to be one of the bitter teachings which your grandmother tried to drum into you. She connected all sex to being a loose woman. What did she call you when you wore makeup in high school...a slut? Ugly word!"*

Wilda: *"But if I did it to myself, I might get to like it...and be...just awful..."*

Counselor: *"Now I really understand why you feel so scared about your own healthy sexual feelings...in fact you may feel strong when you fight them. Let's just sit quietly a minute and consider what you have said."*

COMMENTS: The counselor can allow time for the client to realize that her guilt at sex and self pleasuring is connected to earlier emotional abuse from her grandmother, and to self doubts about controlling her sexuality now that she is on her own. Other impulsive or coerced sexual experiences may emerge of which she is ashamed. The counselor can help Wilda confront her fear and work toward a goal of confidence and mastery of her sexuality. Preoccupation with guilt and sex can keep a person feeling too low to allow them to improve the present (often punishing) situation.

Many other internal values, beliefs, stereotypes, myths, attitudes, fears, and "scripts" can be major obstacles to sexual expression. They are usually a mix of ideas (cognitions) and feelings gathered from both remembered and forgotten sources, which now affect sexuality-related behavior. The counselor's task is to bring out the important attitudes and show their relevance. Unless the client accepts the goal of modifying detrimental attitudes, real behavior change is unlikely. A power struggle must be avoided, as counseling information and suggestions run into attitudinal blocks. Time often helps the client accept new ways of perceiving guilt and sex, especially when a real desire to reach a better sexual adjustment is present.

Contributing Factors: Situational

Reality based factors do exist which affect sexual expression and counselors must not assume that enrichment of sexual techniques or attitudes ("It's all in your head") provide the total answer. Some situational factors which must be acknowledged and dealt with are discussed in the sections on life stages, health/illness/reproductive issues, life style, and sexual trauma. Examples of these factors would be alcoholism, sexual assault, endometriosis, miscarriage, age, and so forth. Clients bring up other situational concerns such as sexual problems due to working different shifts, having a child sleep in their bed, or issues around a recent divorce. Questions related to time management, privacy, and lack of a partner can be brought out and put in perspective.

Situational factors may be valid explanations for sexual problems in themselves, or used as rationalizations, but they must be taken seriously. Discussing external factors in a problem solving manner often leads to deeper issues involving sexual behavior or attitudes. In any event, there can be suggestions for many situational blocks (a lock on the bedroom door, a change of medication, agreement to spend two hours a weekend of intimate time), which facilitate sexual improvement.

Sexual Problems Rooted in Relationship Issues

Couples' problems present the broadest area of sexuality counseling and one which requires highly varied skills and experience. The most important thing for the counselor to remember about this situational variable is to listen carefully and not jump to conclusions. Asking "How is your relationship?" whether speaking to one client or to a couple, brings in important information. All the sexual enhancement suggestions in the world will not help if a major obstacle exists in a particular relationship. The counselor who is trying to help an individual or a couple with sexuality has the task of assessing what role the relationship situation plays in their difficulty.

Very often people's sexual selves express emotional feelings which are not being expressed in other ways.

EXAMPLES: Emotional Feelings Expressed Sexually

Wife: *"My husband complains that I'm frigid and maybe I have become that way. I know that I don't feel a thing for him when he is home on leave for just a few weeks. He promised me that he wouldn't sign up for another hitch before we were married three years ago, but he did."*

Student: *"My girlfriend complains that I'm unromantic, and I worry about not keeping erections (also has stress-related back pain). She has this old boyfriend back home and won't promise never to see him again."*

Wife: *"So I wish he'd just hug me sometimes, but even if I'm working at the sink he's got to grab a feel...as if I'm only good for one thing."*

These previous three examples are fairly simple, and the counselor knows that an infinite variety of couples' interactions could hinder good sexual expression. In addition to the couples' issues, very often sexual technique factors and individual attitudes contribute to the problem, but in these examples a major need is for communication within the couple. Sometimes counseling can be done well by working with one person, helping him/her to be clearer and more assertive in a non-threatening way. Usually, however, the more effective procedure is for the couple to come for counseling together.

The issues in a relationship which are interfering with sexual response may be deeper and more disguised than in the previous three examples. The client may be genuinely unaware of how pressured he/she feels by responsibilities, or bullied-discounted by a partner. Sometimes the "underdog" in a relationship will go along with the status quo for a time (may be decades), and then begin to change; sexual difficulties are likely to be one of the most noticeable signs. Here the counselor will be dealing with defensiveness, anger, sex role stereotypes, projection, denial, and blame, so that good counseling skills are needed. Sometimes a referral to a couples group or family therapist is useful, and at other times one person does both the couples and the sexuality counseling.

Summary of Assessment

Most clients who see a counselor for problems with sexual expression will have sexual behavior, attitudinal and situational contributing factors, and/or sexual problems rooted in relationship issues. Sometimes only one is involved, but a combination is more likely. The counselor has the option of beginning to focus and treat one of the simpler factors (perhaps with information or suggestions) so as to encourage the client and build the therapeutic relationship. At other times, the counselor must begin to work with the most important, because it is urgent, painful, or necessary before anything else can be done.

When the relationship is a major problem, it may be useful to focus on the sexual aspects from time to time as reflecting the larger issue, but not let sex seem to be the cause in itself. However, if specific sexual difficulties are causing predictable friction in an otherwise sound relationship, working on sexuality is a good focus. Good assessment and honesty with clients allows them to participate in the goals and treatment planning.

TREATMENT, PLANS FOR CHANGE

Much improvement in sexuality counseling comes about as a result of the process of exploration and focus, as the client becomes clearer and assumes responsibility for his/her own growth. In addition, the sexuality counselor is expected to be a specialist in ways of remedying specific sexual difficulties and will find well-timed suggestions helpful.

Corrective Suggestions
Related to the Pleasure Curve

Sharp distinctions are not made for male and female sexual problems in the suggestions that follow. Simple anatomical and sex role differences are accomodated as needed. For instance, what some therapists call "retarded ejaculation" can be treated by the sexuality counselor as a difficulty within the arousal-climax phases of the pleasure curve (after physiological problems are checked out). Improvement can be expected as attitudinal and situational blocks are explored, sexual enhancement suggestions given, and some specific suggestions assigned to remove anxiety about "coming." Rather than oversimplifying, this approach can be sophisticated.

No definitive set of counseling suggestions should be used in a rote manner with a particular sexual complaint. Part of the counselor's diagnostic information will come from client feedback about the effectiveness of specific suggestions. This enables the helper to pinpoint more carefully where the trouble might be, and then to modify the specific recommendations in a more promising direction. Perhaps the most important skill at this stage is enlisting the client's support in finding the best approach and helping make the suggestions work.

EXAMPLE: Involving the Client in Finding Solutions

Counselor Negative:

"Practice self stimulation with your partner watching, so both of you will know how you like to reach a climax."

Counselor Positive:

"Since you can have a climax with self pleasuring, can you think of a way to gradually include Richard? Perhaps he could simply be in the next room at first, and then eventually hold you in the dark? Or how do you think that can be worked out?" (Dialogue follows.)

Many counselors have such a diversity of clients that they never specialize in particular types of sexual problems. They are likely to find that the overall approach presented in this training program is adequate for most people with a concern about sexual satisfaction. Clients who need even more intensive work can be referred to a sex therapist. Helpers who work in depth with a particular client population, however, can expect to develop expertise with a specific range of sexual concerns. For instance, when working with patients in a spinal cord injury clinic, or with adult incest survivors, counselors will find more specialized treatment suggestions in sex therapy texts.

SPECIFIC PHASE SUGGESTIONS

Interest Phase

The client with problems in this area reports disinterest in sexuality which can range from hesitation/avoidance to aversion or a phobic reaction. The disinterest may be longstanding or recent, situational or consistent, and the motivation to change absent or strong. For these clients the suggestions are as follows:

Explore the duration, breadth, and depth of the disinterest.

Trace the roots of the disinterest/avoidance, and explore situational aspects. Look for pressured sex, realizing the client may have blocked it out.

Educate about sexuality, clarifying any myths. Spend time helping the client become comfortable talking about sexuality.

Help the client remove the pressure of performance, pleasing others, and meeting expectations.

Help the client practice comfortable assertiveness.

Explore motivation for change. Explain the necessity for tolerating some measure of anxiety while working on replacing a negative set with a positive one.

Encourage the client to practice relaxation, breathing, becoming positive about all parts of his/her body, and tuning in on feelings.

Encourage non-threatening, gradual, positive, low-key sexual thoughts, fantasies, and experiences, moving ahead in very small steps.

Refer the clients who have extreme reactions and those clients who do not improve.

Desire Phase

Clients with problems in this area want to be sexual, but report that it is difficult to initiate or respond. They have concerns about adequacy/normalcy, and may have doubts about body image and masculinity/femininity. Again, the difficulty may be recent or longstanding, situational, or consistent, and here the fear of failing to become sexually involved may be weak or very strong. Suggestions for the counselor include the following:

Help the client learn to attain and maintain an erotic frame of mind. Expanded fantasy is one powerful way.

Suggest that the client locate new sensual/erotic stimuli and focus on them.

Recommend that the client try massage and a form of dance, exercise, or body building.

Introduce a client with a tight vaginal opening, spasms, or constrictions (vaginismus) to the concept of her own and partners' fingers (graduated sizes) being inserted as part of comfortable sex play. For most clients the recommended procedure is to refrain from attempting intercourse until quiet penetration is neutral or stimulating rather than painful.

Introduce those clients with performance anxiety (adequacy fears) to the concept of pleasure for its own sake, and the expansion of non-demand stimulation.

Refer those clients who after a reasonable period of time, make no gain in sexual comfort or beginning of sexual arousal.

Arousal Phase

Clients with problems in this area have difficulty increasing sexual feelings, often reflected in the lack of adequate lubrication or erection. Again the situation may be longstanding or recent, situational or persistent, and the frustration/anxiety level varies with the person. The suggestions for the counselor are as follows:

Be creative and encourage the client to be.

Give recommendations for expanding arousal techniques, from exploring erotic literature to imagery and new sensual experiences.

Provide well discussed, gradual assignments for genital pleasuring rather than intercourse.

Provide specific suggestions to counter self defeating thoughts and old behavior patterns.

Encourage partner communication about finding a wide variety of sexually arousing kinds of stimuli.

Help clients develop partner signals to increase/decrease/change stimulation.

Help the client who climaxes too soon (premature ejaculation), to focus on pleasure and early signals of approaching ejaculation. Discuss ways to stop or decrease stimulation to reduce erection, and then regain it ("stop and start").

Suggest new positions, different settings, shower massage attachments, vibrators, and what is referred to as "sexual toys."

Refer those clients who have persistent failure to become sexually aroused and maintain sexual pleasure.

Climax Phase

Clients with problems in this area report becoming aroused but not reaching levels sufficient for climax, or else find they remain at a particular level of stimulation without release. Again the problem may be occasional or longstanding, situational or consistent, cause great distress, or be considered less important.

Facilitate establishing realistic goals for orgasm.

Provide information about the involuntary aspects of "sensory overload," in order to counter trying too hard.

Encourage development of imagery to enjoy increasing levels of arousal without worry about climax.

Discuss learning how to attain orgasm during self pleasuring and recommend self-help reading.

Encourage those clients to transfer orgasm triggers from self stimulation to partner sex, if desired.

Work with clients having fears and blocks about pregnancy, injury, and/or commitment.

Address issues of "losing control," and becoming more abandoned.

Describe self-help sex manuals written by reputable authors and encourage specific enrichment exercises.

Encourage clients to experiment with a variety of stimuli, positions, and lovemaking patterns.

Refer those clients who have consistent inability to reach climax after considerable practice.

Relaxation Phase

Clients with problems in this area are often unaware of it, but may report frequent misunderstandings with partners, chronic dissatisfaction, routine sex, or complaints from one partner. An important distinction is whether the emotion (anger/tears/depression) after sex is related specifically to the sexual interaction, or more broadly to the relationship or other factors. Again the problem may be specific or general, and impede sexual pleasure to varying degrees. Suggestions for the counselor are as follows:

Discuss in counseling any specific post-sexual behavior which interferes.

Ask clients to focus on post-sex thoughts and feelings and write them down to explore in counseling.

Help clients explore the time, place, and importance of physical closeness and communication in their life.

Encourage clients to express mostly positive rather than negative things to partners after sexual activities.

Help clients find ways to express more of what they would like in lovemaking—a time for creative risk taking.

Recommend that clients not bring up threatening topics or try to do conflict resolution right after sex.

Refer those clients who have persistent inability to relax and be comfortable after sex.

RESOURCES FOR TREATMENT

A rich collection of books is available which focus on the treatment of all aspects of sexual expression:

Annon, J. (1976). *The behavioral treatment of sexual problems, revised edition, Vol 1: Brief therapy.* New York: Harper and Row. The PLISSIT model.

Barbach, L. (1980). *Women discover orgasm: A therapist's guide to a new treatment approach.* Riverside, NJ: Free Press.

Barbach, L. (1982). *For each other: Sharing sexual intimacy.* Garden City, NY: Anchor Press.

Hartman, W., & Fithian, M. (1984). *Any man can: The multiple orgasm technique for every loving man.* New York: St. Martin's Press.

Kaplan, H. (1974). *The new sex therapy.* New York: Brunner/Mazel.

Kaplan, H. (1979). *Disorders of sexual desire and other new concepts and techniques in sex therapy.* New York: Simon and Schuster.

Kaplan, H. (1983). *The evaluation of sexual disorders: Psychological and medical aspects.* New York: Brunner/Mazel Publishers.

Kennedy, E. (1977). *Sexual counseling: A practical guide for non-professional counselors.* New York: The Continuum Press.

Leiblum, S., & Pervin, L. (Eds.). (1980). *Principles and practices of sex therapy.* New York: Guilford Press.

LoPiccolo, J., & LoPiccolo, L. (1978). *Handbook of sex therapy*. New York: Plenum Press.

Masters, W., & Johnson, V. (1970). *Human sexual inadequacy*. Boston: Little, Brown.

Masters, W., & Johnson, V. (1974). *The pleasure bond*. Boston: Little, Brown.

McCarthy, B., & McCarthy, E. (1984). *Sexual awareness, enhancing sexual pleasure*. New York: Carroll and Graf Publishers.

Nadelson, C., & Marcotte, W. (1984). *Treatment interventions in human sexuality*. New York: Plenum.

Silverstein, J. (1980). Photographs by Jackson. *Sexual enhancement for women*. Cambridge, MA: Black and White Publishing.

Stahmann, R., & Hiebert, W. (1984). *Counseling in marital and sexual problems: A clinician's handbook, (3rd ed.)*. Lexington, MA: Lexington Books.

Detailed treatment plans and outcome studies are published monthly in journal articles in the periodicals listed under the resources for Chapter 5, Part 1.

Audiovisual materials such as movies or videotapes on communication, women's sexuality, pleasuring techniques, and potency issues are available for use with clients.

EVALUATING PROGRESS

The treatment phase may be fairly condensed if a specific problem is located, clarified, and new behavior shaped which leads to increased pleasure. Straight-line progress actually does occur often, and accounts for the rapid acceptance of sexuality counseling/therapy as a health field. When many related issues are present, progress obviously must be slower, because behavioral, attitudinal or situational contributing factors, and/or sexual problems rooted in relationship issues can require time to modify.

Setbacks and slow progress can be used to gather more understanding of the problem, uncover important blocks, and refine a better treatment program. The counselor may need to stand back regularly and ask himself/herself: "Is this person (couple) more confident than they were, and have they experienced less discomfort or more pleasure? If not, are we closer to knowing why?" Because of the nature of human learning, obstacles must first be overcome before the reinforcement of success can occur. Pleasure is a positive reward that acts to maintain the improvement once it occurs.

CONCLUSION

Sexual expression can become a problem in so many possible ways that no index or laundry list of symptoms and cures is adequate. The general counselor can develop a deep understanding of lovemaking, listen to individuals and couples, and help them remedy many sexual difficulties. Increased pleasure and awareness of improvement often allow the clients to continue to work out sexual problems on their own after counseling is completed.

Occasionally problems of sexual expression occur which are so deeply rooted in a client's history or self that even the famous clinics and specialists cannot effect a cure. The general counselor needs humility to accept failure or partial improvement on occasion, and to have effective procedures for referral. The prospects are generally very favorable for problems of sexual expression, however, even though much still needs to be discovered.

CHAPTER

REMEDIAL SEXUALITY COUNSELING

This chapter covers work with clients who have a significant area of sex-related difficulty. Although the degree of distress varies, situations covered in this chapter are generally experienced as very painful by the client. These sexual trauma can interfere significantly with other areas of life.

Sexuality counseling alone may not be sufficient to remedy the difficulty, so referral to other resources is often necessary. Sometimes counseling is a first step, to clarify what additional kinds of help are needed. At other times, sexuality counseling is recommended by another professional, and is provided during or after other services are rendered.

Problems are treated here as separate categories for teaching purposes. In real life, issues covered in these five sections may overlap with one another and with sexual problems discussed elsewhere in this training program. Frequently the counselor will find that a client is dealing with more than one.

Readers are asked to assess their level of counseling skill on each topic using Form 6.1, both before and after studying the chapter. An individualized plan can be made for improving areas where more training is needed.

CATEGORY	KNOW ENOUGH	NEED MORE	UNSURE
1. Problems with Pregnancy	_____	_____	_____
2. Illness and Disability	_____	_____	_____
3. Atypical Sexual Behavior	_____	_____	_____
4. Child Sexual Abuse	_____	_____	_____
5. Sexual Assault/Rape	_____	_____	_____

Form 6.1. Checklist for Self Assessment for Remedial Sexuality Counseling.

CHAPTER 6, PART 1

PROBLEMS WITH PREGNANCY

Sex is for pleasure, yes, but some kinds of sexual activity also result in conception. In fact, many people think only of heterosexual intercourse when they refer to sex, and make it their major source of sexual expression. Effective contraception may or may not be used. The high incidence of unwanted pregnancy in the U.S. is partially reflected in the more than one and one-half million legal abortions performed each year, which represent one quarter of all pregnancies. Because no form of birth control is absolutely safe and reliable for everyone, many other problematic pregnancies are carried to term. The counselor will frequently encounter the issue of unintended pregnancy, either currently or as part of a client's history.

At the same time, one out of six couples of childbearing age cannot conceive a child, so that infertility counseling is needed. Other people keep trying to start or add to their family, and have ectopic pregnancies or miscarriages. In addition, high-risk pregnancies may benefit from supportive assistance and sexuality counseling. Because so many issues related to pregnancy affect sexuality, a counselor needs to be able to help in a variety of situations. Even one-half hour spent exploring this subject with any woman or couple may uncover conscious and unconscious impressions which hinder sexuality:

EXAMPLES: Statements Related to Pregnancy Made by Clients

"When I was in high school my sister acted out her childbirth and I may have turned off right then. All I worry about with my boyfriend is what time of the month it is."

"He doesn't care if I get pregnant again, but tramping up to the third floor with two kids, varicose veins, and groceries after work, is more than I can do now. Maybe that's why he says I'm frigid."

"We had to get married when she got pregnant after a party, and the romance never got back into sex after that. I've always wondered if I was the only one, or if she'd have married me otherwise." (Similar statements are made by both men and women at all social levels.)

"You know, after talking to you lately I realize that ever since the two abortions in high school, I've settled for less. Like I didn't deserve a good college, or a husband who treated me well? I felt such a failure back then...that's what did it."

DECISION MAKING, PREGNANCY, AND SEXUALITY

The best time to consider problems with reproduction is well before the question of pregnancy arises. The general counselor is in an excellent position to raise the question of "Is there a chance of becoming pregnant?" or "What would it be like for you if your girlfriend got pregnant and you had to quit school?" Decisions about pregnancy are complicated by such things as changing sexual expectations for women and men, reports of negative side effects of birth control, the necessity for two incomes, and the greater frequency of divorce and single parenting as a choice.

Anticipating or confirming a pregnancy may result in mixed emotional reactions, even for people who generally want children. While pregnancy is no longer treated as a disease or passive period, it is labeled a "transition" by social scientists. In any case, the event marks a significant change in people's lives, and the counselor can help with the decision, with unexpected timing, with adjustment during the pregnancy or abortion, with post partum issues, and with disappointments.

Sexuality counseling related to a pregnancy decision often uncovers differences within a couple about whether to marry or not, to stop work, to join a church or synagogue, to move, to continue a particular pregnancy, to use contraceptives, or to go back to school. Clients may present what seems to be a sexual problem, when in fact the reproductive issue is the hidden agenda. Conflicts about having a (or another) baby can result in lack of interest in sex, persistent problems with arousal, or ejaculation difficulties. Having clients establish communication, make at least a temporary agreement about pregnancy, and then re-introduce sex in an unpressured, more erotic way usually clarifies the sexual part of these difficulties.

AMBIVALENCE

Some clients have such mixed feelings about a pregnancy that they deny it to various degrees, for a time or right through delivery. A woman may smoke or drink heavily, gain a great deal of weight, or show in other ways that she is having trouble coping with a pregnancy. Other pregnant women put themselves into a state of bland well-being, even though they may have serious problems with health, money, rejection, or a place to stay. Whether the counselor is consulted immediately or explores the subject as part of a client's history, strongly negative reactions to pregnancy can carry over to sexuality generally.

When a girl or woman is unable to express real feelings about being pregnant, the counselor can suspect a possible history of sexual abuse, some other mental health problem, or sex-related guilt. Pregnancy can activate old, unresolved issues, or create new threats to a woman's (or couple's) stability, so that careful treatment is needed. For those few women who become out of touch with reality during pregnancy, referral to a specialist is needed. Most questions about pregnancy decisions and denial can be handled by the counselor, however, with assistance from social service agencies and other health care practitioners.

Another problem with reality testing is false pregnancy, when a woman who is often very "sensible" believes she is genuinely pregnant. She may show physiological changes such as cessation of menstruation and an increase in abdominal size, or simply be convinced. Gaining the client's confidence and staying with her in a supportive way as the false pregnancy proceeds, generally leads to trust, honesty with self, and integration. The counselor should never seem to agree that a baby will be born, if medical checks substantiate no pregnancy, but can help the client gradually come to terms with her wishes, guilt, or other concerns. Heavy confrontation is not advisable in these instances of denial, but a consistent, supportive counselor can help the client become more reality oriented.

Difficulty with decisions about pregnancy are to be expected, because few other choices involve as much responsibility. Attitudes toward becoming or being pregnant vary widely and may change rapidly for a person. Ideas and feelings about it may be so complex that a client really needs help even expressing them. The counselor must make an effort to go beyond his/her own experience and deeply enter the other person's world, when helping to clarify this question.

RESOURCES FOR ASSISTANCE
REGARDING CLIENT'S AMBIVALENCE

Applebaum, E., & Firestein, S. (1983). *A genetic counseling casebook.* New York: The Free Press.

Fox, G. (Ed.). (1982). *The childbirth decision, fertility attitudes and behavior.* Beverly Hills, CA: Sage Publications.

Gerson, M., Alper, J., & Richardson, M. (1984). Mothering: The view for psychological research. *Signs, 9*(3), 434-453.

Guttmacher, A. (1984). *Pregnancy, birth, and family planning.* New York: New American Library.

SEXUALITY COUNSELING WHEN
FERTILITY IS IN QUESTION

No one can fully understand the deep pain and loss felt by a person or couple who wants to have a child and has difficulty conceiving, unless they have experienced it. The counselor will meet some of the most rewarding people to know while doing counseling where fertility is in question, and also some of the most anxious and angry. Frustration of the deeply felt need to bear children, the monthly cycles of dashed hopes, and the often painful, lengthy, and inconclusive medical testing will pressure the most stable couple.

The prevalence of fertility problems is increasing, and people are planning children later in life, so any counselor is likely to have clients for whom sexuality and fertility are problems. The overall management of infertility counseling, usually done in conjunction with medical testing and treatment, is a specialty area. An infertility counselor is familiar with the sophisticated testing done, which ranges from endometrial biopsy to endocrine evaluation, and laparoscopy. He/she also must be informed about options such as artificial insemination, in vitro fertilization, surrogate mothering, types of adoption, and evolving issues such as embryo transfer.

A general counselor who is skilled in sexuality counseling would need training and supervision to become a competent infertility counselor; resources listed later in this section are good places to begin learning. Knowing fertility specialists in the region will enable a counselor to make appropriate referrals if a couple has tried to conceive for over a year without success. In any case, the general counselor who is knowledgeable about sex can be very helpful as part of a health care team.

Problems Presented by Individuals

One person, usually the wife, may come to counseling alone when a couple is having trouble conceiving. The client may report a sexual problem, but that is seldom the cause of infertility unless ejaculation or intercourse are being interfered with. In addition to all the many reasons for sexual difficulties, the client who cannot achieve a successful pregnancy has particular stresses. Some counselors follow a grief and loss model to help clients struggling with fertility problems, and while this is helpful more can be done.

Susan Donnis (1984) has developed a comprehensive model, showing that the following themes are often presented in sequence by a client. She presents counseling interventions and examples for each theme, and suggests that healing must take place in its own time before genuine resolution can occur.

Theme 1, Part 1: "Am I Going Crazy?"
Theme 1, Part 2: "The Pain Will Drive Me Crazy"
Theme 2: "Punishment and Guilt"
Theme 3: "I Am All Alone"
Theme 4: "I Can't Nurture Myself Unless I Have a Child"
Theme 5: "With this Pain I Can't Allow Myself Pleasure"
Theme 6: "Accepting Defeat vs. Achieving Resolution"

The author of these themes points out that more than one million people in the U.S. are involuntarily childless, and that they face the most profound issues of life, death, relationships, and sexuality. The general counselor may not be an infertility specialist, but can become sensitive to the conflicts experienced by this client and be very helpful in the relationship, sexuality, and self esteem areas.

Problems Presented by Couples

Many infertile couples who consult a counselor will express the above themes and also will discuss lovemaking problems. Specific treatments for infertility make the time of sexual intercourse important, such as when either partner is finishing a limited course of medication to cause ovulation or elevate the sperm count, or to take advantage of recent surgery before its benefits diminish. A predominant problem when couples are facing difficulty having a child is that sex becomes primarily an instrument of procreation, rather than an expression of closeness and pleasure.

A focus on narrow aspects of the reproductive cycle can lead to the attitude that only a few days in the month "really count," and sex the rest of the time is empty. The husband can begin to feel like a sexual instrument that is failing, or the wife may feel feminine and attractive only when the thermometer shows mid-cycle ovulation. Out of discouragement and in an effort to maximize efficiency, either member of a couple may limit most of their sexual interest to the fertile period.

Sexual intercourse which is associated with disappointment may become mechanical and ejaculation oriented, causing difficulty with either or both partners. This is especially true when post-coital exams, supplying semen samples for sperm analysis, and other tests seem to invade the spontaneity and privacy of the sexual relationship. The counselor's task is to help the couple comply with the necessary requirements of timing and testing, while being creative and erotic in their own way all during the cycle.

EXAMPLE: Infertility of 4 Years Duration, 2nd Session

Counselor: *"Last week we were just beginning to talk about how discouraged you are getting, Mike."*

Mike: *"Yeah, well we don't have to worry about wondering this month."*

Brenda: *"I'm not a machine either, and I'd like to go to the information workshop they are having on adoption."*

Mike: (Seems really upset.) *"You know how I feel about that...somebody's kid they didn't want would never be the same as ours. Just look at Bill and Cris."* (His brother's delightful, biological children.)

Counselor: *"Before we explore differences about adoption, it seems as though there was a lot of strain around 'worrying this month,' and 'not being a machine.' You both sound miserable. What do you suppose is happening?"*

Mike: *"You're pretty sharp...we can usually avoid topics by rehashing arguments about other things. I don't know if I can talk about this. Maybe I should wait outside."*

Brenda: *"Well, I know how you feel Mike, and you know I don't blame you or talk about trying harder."*

Counselor: *"Mike, what are you worried about? Are you concerned about getting upset, or are you afraid of hurting Brenda...?"*

Mike: *"It's just...well..she knows that I figure if it isn't meant to be, then it just isn't. But she acts like I'm killing her when I say that. So Brenda pretends that every time her period comes it's OK, and goes through all those tests, and tries to drag me to talks on transplants or implants. Don't ask how she got me here!"*

Counselor: *"You care about Brenda, but this baby business just seems too much at times..."*

Mike: *"Well, it's all she cares about, really."*

Brenda: *"No it isn't...and I know you really want kids too, but don't have much hope in all this hassle. I want to keep on trying."*

Mike: *"Look, I've checked out OK and they can't find anything wrong with you. So some experts say 20 percent of infertile couples are in that boat...what good does it do us? It was a lot* *less pressured this time when we had those arguments and didn't go through the motions of trying."*

Brenda: (Can't talk. Starts to become hysterical.) *"You did it on purpose?"*

Mike: *"No, as a matter of fact you started the arguments because you are always tense when you think you might conceive. This time I just didn't let it go like I usually do."*

Counselor: *"OK, we see what happens. I'm sorry Brenda, to have to encourage Mike to bring out these painful feelings in both of you. You feel so alone, don't you? You would do anything to have a baby?"*

Brenda: (A different kind of crying, more sad, less angry.)

Mike: (Also shows real sadness, with less defensiveness.)

Counselor: *"You see, both of you feel the same way and want the same thing, but handle the problem differently. Mike, you try to just face your losses and move ahead. Brenda, you can't give up without trying everything. Both of you have a right to your reactions, but it's pulling you apart."*

COMMENTS: To reestablish honest couples' communication, the counselor could continue by exploring with Mike his feelings of failure and isolation at seeing his wife's frantic efforts. This had resulted in Mike's being unwilling to listen to Brenda's concerns or even the latest information on her medical situation. Brenda had responded by being superficially cheerful but not really intimate or sensual with Mike. An appreciation of their separate misunderstandings can bring them together, so that they are closer than if there were no problem in their life. They would then be ready for sexual enrichment counseling.

Counseling helps couples in infertility situations regain some perspective with one another, and focuses on building the relationship instead of a preoccupation with getting pregnant. Reminding a couple that going through the crisis together can make them closer, and that they can help one another, also helps them in the direction of positive resolution. This is especially important for younger couples, and for those who have not had good role models for coping with deep disappointments.

The counselor will have an indication that the work is proceeding well if he/she empathizes with first one and then the other. The couple can be helped to realize that no one coping strategy or outcome is "right," and that each needs to respect the other person's. Information which counters myths such as "you have to have a particular position and female orgasm," or "saving it for midcycle is more potent," will take pressure off. Finally, resources like books and pamphlets, the RESOLVE organization, support groups, and infertility specialists will introduce the couple to resolution which ranges from a childfree life style, to new medical treatments, to the varied types of adoption.

RESOURCES FOR FERTILITY CONCERNS

Books for the professional and client:

Andrews, L. (1984). *New conceptions: A consumer's guide to the newest fertility treatments.* New York: St. Martin's Press.

Corson, S. (1982). *Conquering infertility.* East Norwalk, CT: Appleton-Century-Crofts.

Mazor, M. (Ed.). (1984). *Infertility: Medical, emotional, and social considerations.* New York: The Human Sciences Press.

Menning, B. (1977). *Infertility: A guide for the childless couple.* Englewood Cliffs, NJ: Prentice-Hall.

Journal articles are especially useful:

Bresnick, E. (1981). A holistic approach to the treatment of infertility. *Journal of Marital and Family Therapy, 7*(2), 181-188.

Donnis, S. (1984). Common themes of infertility: A counseling model. *Journal of Sex Education and Therapy, 10*(1), 10-15.

Golden, G. (1983). Psychosexual problems in infertility: A preventive model. *Journal of Sex Education and Therapy, 9*(1), 19-22.

Seibel, M., & Taymor, M. (1982). Emotional aspects of infertility. *Fertility and Sterility, 37*(2), 137-145.

National Organization. RESOLVE, Inc., P.O. Box 474, Belmont, MA 02178. This non-profit organization sponsors counseling, referral and support groups, training resources for professionals, a newsletter, bibliographies, and a *Directory of Infertility Resources.*

Film: "Trying Times: Crisis in Infertility," 1980, Fanlight Productions, 47 Halifax Street, Jamaica Plain, MA 02130. Purchase or rental.

SEXUALITY DURING PREGNANCY

Once a conception occurs, the counselor will find that a different set of issues is presented. One of the overall problems is that in spite of the principle of cause and effect, society seldom equates erotic sexuality with maternity. Great individual differences and changes in sexual feelings are common in pregnancy, due to both physiological and psychological factors. Because some problems are temporary, an elaborate program of sexuality counseling or a referral for sex therapy is frequently not needed. For instance, nausea may result in lack of desire, or fear of miscarriage may affect erection or orgasm, but these can be transient. The important point is to reassure clients, to assist with suggestions for low-key sexual expression, and to encourage follow up.

Couples should be referred to their obstetrician or midwife for individualized suggestions and restrictions on sex in pregnancy. In particular, the counselor can help clients find balanced information to replace vague fears about injury to the fetus through intercourse or orgasm. Encouraging a woman to express her discomfort about changing body shape, and finding ways to receive reassurance from her partner is often helpful. The counselor can give suggestions to the couple about broadening their sexual expression, toward a pleasure rather than a performance orientation. Asking how they make love, and then adding ideas such as breathing together while fondling, and using different positions and kinds of stimulation, can give the couple permission to enrich rather than restrict their sexual expression.

Many couples with pre-existing sexual difficulties are less active during a pregnancy, or sexual interaction is avoided altogether. If they become preoccupied with separate worlds after the delivery, or if either seeks other partners, the unresolved sexual problems can seem a real reason for not staying together. During the pregnancy, a better course is to improve sexual compatibility, so that a couple's intimacy develops rather than worsens. Working with a couple in the important post-delivery period is similar to any sexuality counseling except that unresolved issues about the pregnancy and delivery, post-partum changes, and the stress of new baby/new roles may be present.

RESOURCES FOR SEX DURING PREGNANCY CONCERNS

Bing, E., & Colman, L. (1982). *Making love during pregnancy.* New York: Bantam Books.

Jones, R. (1984). *Human reproduction and sexual behavior.* Englewood Cliffs, NJ: Prentice Hall.

Lauersen, N. (1983). *Childbirth with love: A complete guide to fertility, pregnancy, and childbirth for caring couples.* New York: G. P. Putnam's Sons.

Videotape: *Sex and Pregnancy.* (1984). Glendon Associates, 2049 Century Park East, Suite 3000, Los Angeles, CA 90067. Purchase or rental.

UNSUCCESSFUL PREGNANCY

A person/couple may be either ambivalent or joyful about a pregnancy, yet few realize that one in five ends in miscarriage (spontaneous abortion). This almost always comes as a shock, and society is usually brief in its support and condolences. When a counselor is taking a client's history and learns of "four pregnancies, two births," it is important to consider the impact of the two not carried to term.

Those pregnancies which miscarry often cannot be explained, so that the client retains feelings of inadequacy and failure. Often guilt and blame become prominent. Many painful self and partner criticisms are possible such as those in the following examples.

EXAMPLES: Statements by Clients After a Miscarriage

"We shouldn't have had exciting sex that month."
"Why did I/we try so hard to move, finish that degree?"

"If I had only really wanted this baby at first, maybe..."
"Probably we shouldn't have waited until we were 34?"
"My mother said I shouldn't jog, play in the tournament..."

A death has occurred, and post partum hormonal changes in the woman can be stressful, so that sadness and depressed feelings are normal reactions. When people are unsure about the reason for a pregnancy loss, or even if a medical cause is given, they can become anxious about many things connected with it. Both this depression and anxiety may result in avoidance of sexual intercourse, problems with arousal, or inability to become involved enough to reach climax. Of course this can make pre-existing sexual problems worse and create new ones, if the couple does not realize the reactive component and address sexuality with time and compassion for one another.

Very often both husband and wife put pressure on themselves to "get over it," and "back to normal." When people speak of "doing well" after a miscarriage, they usually mean showing few effects. Couples may try to go through the motions of sexual intercourse with increased feelings of loneliness, inadequacy, and lack of erotic feelings. Some deflect their anger onto the partner or sex, while others become obsessive or almost superstitious/ritualistic about lovemaking. As with infertility, members of a couple may cope with the loss in different ways and profoundly misunderstand one another.

EXAMPLE: Six Months after Miscarriage, 2nd Session

Wife: *"All he cares about is his computer work...he's gone from 8 A.M. to 7 P.M. Then he wants sex."*

Husband: (To counselor.) *"Last week you helped me realize that since my mother died when I was eight, I can't stand hospitals. It helps to keep busy...but she wants to talk about that awful intensive care nursery where our preemie never had a chance. And then she's cold to me."*

COMMENTS: The above is condensed, but it is true that people often do not connect losses in their lives and go back to grieve for the earlier ones. The counselor's main function will be to help the couple work out their separate mourning, express mixed feelings, understand coping mechanisms, and reintroduce pleasurable, intimate sexuality for its own sake.

RESOURCES FOR UNSUCCESSFUL PREGNANCY CONCERNS

Baker, H., & Palinski, C. (1983). Women's reactions to reproductive problems. *Psychological Reports, 53*(1), 159-166.

Pizer, H., & Palinski, C. (1983). *Coping with miscarriage.* St. Louis, MO: C.V. Mosby.

Seibel, M., & Graves, W. (1980). Psychological implications of spontaneous abortions. *Journal of Reproductive Medicine, 25*(4), 161-165.

UNINTENDED PREGNANCY

Unwanted pregnancy is reported in all the literature and tradition of recorded history. Conception often occurs without intent, and people sometimes can make room for a baby or arrange for others to raise it. However, when the pregnancy is seen as unacceptable and a decision is difficult to make, a person may consult a counselor. The helper does not have to be specifically trained in "options counseling" to assist with a problematic pregnancy, and can provide a supportive place for the woman or couple to consider the situation and work through all the alternatives.

Hundreds of studies exists in the literature which focus on different aspects of unwanted pregnancy. Some explore the pregnant woman's current circumstances, and demonstrate the importance of marital status, age, economic situation, relationships, education, and employment. Other studies look at the woman's self concept, locus of control, feelings of guilt, stage of personal development, skills in problem solving, or assertiveness. They agree that an unintended pregnancy creates a crisis, and requires decisions for which a person may not be prepared.

Pregnant Teenager

Pregnant teenagers are of great concern to society, because both they and their potential babies are vulnerable to health, mental health, educational, social, and economic hardship. The U.S. leads the developed world in the growing number of immature pregnant women, and the implications for society cause professionals to invest great energy in trying to prevent the problem. Since 40% of the 12 million sexually active teens become pregnant each year, the sheer numbers are shocking.

At present, no solution exists. All teenagers, but especially black or disadvantaged young women, are at high risk for unmarried early pregnancy. To really deal with the whole social problem, efforts must be extended toward boys (half of teenage fathers have begun sexual intercourse by age 13), as well as toward intervening with potential teenage mothers. Counseling can not prevent the entire problem but can assist individuals in making the best of a difficult situation, while helping to prevent future unintended pregnancies.

The actual counseling of a newly pregnant teenager is extremely important, not only to help her arrive at a decision but to assist with her future development and practical problems. Of those teenagers who bear a child, 25% will become pregnant again within a year. Also, 80% of pregnant women under 18 never finish high school, and teenage marriages are two or three times more likely to break up than are those begun in the early 20s. Repeated abortions are also common when no help or counseling is received. These and the many other statistics about low birth weight, poverty, repeated cycles of deprivation, and child abuse are not meant to encourage the counselor to recommend abortion. The counselor must be aware of the obstacles in order to assist the teenager who decides to continue with an unintended pregnancy, in coping with the monumental difficulties.

Developmental tasks such as establishing independence, evolving one's identity, achieving skill in relationships, and becoming oriented toward economic stability are best worked out before pregnancy. A young person has difficulty in progressing in these areas in any case, and even more so when overwhelmed by a crisis. A young pregnant client who hasn't had time to know who she is and what she wants is likely to find it hard to talk about herself and her situation. Because she is often very concerned about exposure or significant others, excellent counseling skills are needed to establish communication. However, while women aged 12 to 19 have special needs, these are more a matter of degree than of kind. The counselor's concern is with the person and his/her development, rather than seeing an individual fit specific statistical data.

RESOURCES FOR TEENAGE PREGNANCY CONCERNS

Byrne, D., & Fisher, W. (Eds.). (1983). *Adolescents, sex, and contraception.* Hillsdale, NJ: Lawrence Erlbaum.

Furstenberg, F., Lincoln, R., & Menken, J. (Eds.). (1981). *Teenage sexuality, pregnancy, and childbearing.* Philadelphia, PA: University of Pennsylvania Press.

Ooms, T. (Ed.). (1981). *Teenage pregnancy in a family context, implications for policy.* Philadelphia, PA: Temple University Press.

Stuart, I., & Wells, C. (Eds.). (1982). *Pregnancy in adolescence: Needs, problems and management.* New York: Van Nostrand Reinhold.

Films: So many films on teenage pregnancy exist that the school counselor who is interested in education/prevention can rent 4 to 8 excellent ones. They can be shown on a rotating basis for 2-3 days in a school library or resource room, asking students to use rating sheets to critique them.

MAKING A DECISION

When an unintended pregnancy is confirmed, the person may need help sorting through his/her reactions. Then either the client or counselor may initiate a discussion of available alternatives (usually abortion, adoption, or parenting), and seek information needed on any aspect. All models of problem solving and decision making stress the importance of understanding the range of possibilities before trying to prioritize or choose one. When the expression of feelings becomes repetitive, the counselor can begin to focus by encouraging tentative discussion of likely alternatives. A "What if...?" or "How could you work out..." style of inquiry encourages positive solutions, and at the same times suggests an internal locus of control rather than an external one.

Exploring Alternatives

In 1973 the landmark Supreme Court decision, Roe vs. Wade, recognized the right to legal abortion and every citizen should have full access to this alternative. The political struggle continues while the ethical and social dimensions are debated, but in the meantime a substantial knowledge base and effective treatment system have been built. Availability of health care varies greatly by region, so that helpers need to be aware of local practice; because the great majority of nonmetropolitan counties have no pregnancy termination facilities, general counselors may have to do considerable information counseling.

More than intellectual awareness is involved as the client searches through her(their) reactions, weighs having a baby with other alternatives, and may feel negative about all the options. The counselor has an important role in helping her (them) accept mixed feelings as normal in a complex situation, where competing rights are involved. The counselor's role cannot be to remove the uncomfortable feelings or find a simple solution, but is to help the client(s) work toward what is best for her (them).

Factors to Consider

The most important factor during the decision is how the woman feels about herself and her place in the world, and the most important outcome is the impact which the pregnancy is going to have on her and her life. If the woman involves her husband or lover in counseling, then these same concerns can be considered with him. The counselor must make sure that at the time of decision making the client is not sent out to collect opinions from others (although consulting trusted people for support is fine), but is focusing on her/their own judgment. In this way she/they can be helped to move up in the developmental scale, toward a respectful balance of self and others, rather than back toward a primitive survival or role-bound level.

Researchers have found that when a woman is forced or pressured toward a solution which is not her preference, the negative effects may be felt all her life, and the probability of other "unintended" pregnancies is higher. Surprisingly enough it doesn't matter whether a family coerces a daughter to keep a pregnancy, or pressures her to have an abortion to save face. Nor does it matter if a husband insists on having the child for his reasons, or aborting for practical ones. If the action taken is against the pregnant woman's inclinations, that is when depression, anxiety, and other problems with mental and physical health and life adjustment appear.

A woman's relationship to the father of her child is an important factor in an unintended pregnancy. Friedlander et al. (1984) showed that a strong relationship with a partner tends to increase the likelihood of using contraception, but makes an abortion decision more difficult. Women with no regular partner, or a poor/dissolving relationship, reach a decision about abortion more quickly. Friedlander et al. also found that a strong work-career commitment was related to a shorter and less complicated decision making process in favor of abortion. Once any decision about an unwanted pregnancy is reached, the people in a woman's support system are important in helping her make a positive adjustment.

Women having unwanted pregnancies are a diverse group, and while some confer with partners and significant others, many do not. A counselor may believe in the participation of the father of a fetus, but legally the mother is the one who may decide what to do about the pregnancy. Therefore, while exploring the partner situation and inquiring about the man's preferences may be helpful, his degree of involvement will depend on his relationship to the pregnant woman and her willingness to include him. The same is true for other family members.

Abortion Counseling

When a pregnant woman is considering the option of abortion, the information aspect of counseling is important. Although especially trained counselors are present in most hospitals, clinics, and health centers, many women will have made up their minds before they enter. Therefore, the general counselor is likely to talk to women in earlier stages and will need to deal with broader issues, leaving specific information about the procedure to the specialists.

After fertilization the embryo develops rapidly, so counselors should know what the time frame is for treatment in their area (i.e., 11 or 14 weeks after the last menstrual period may be maximum for a vacuum aspiration). Generally, the earlier the process is done the easier it is, so that a woman's need for time to decide must be balanced against the physical realities of the surgical procedure. Some clients express concern about safety, and the counselor can assure them that early abortion is a safe form of minor surgery and has a far lower complication and mortality rate than carrying to term and delivery.

One of the outstanding trainers in options counseling, Terry Beresford (1982), has developed a three stage model to help counselors respond to a client appropriately. She suggests that the client who says *"I want..."* differs from *"I want...but,"* and both of these need less intensive work than the woman who says: *"I don't know."* Most clients with an unwanted pregnancy are likely to have some feelings of *fear* (parents, relationships, sterility, pain, blame, discovery, damnation, isolation, making a mistake, risk), *ambivalence* (toward the pregnancy, sex, her family, partners, abortion, adoption, parenting, the future), and *guilt* (about sex, her family, partners, pregnancy, or the options, coming from herself or significant others). Ms. Beresford has found that when negativism is expressed toward abortion, much of it is actually anger about the unwanted pregnancy and the circumstances surrounding it.

What Should I Do?

Recent research (Luker, 1984) has shown that women who are strongly anti or pro abortion for unwanted pregnancies, have extremely different backgrounds and life styles. Counselors develop skill in helping a woman sort out tangled relationships and tendencies to give power to assorted others, more easily than they become expert at meaning-of-life counseling. The latter is profound, it should come up in conflicted pregnancy counseling, and a helper can always become wiser, kinder, and more sensitive in working with clients' moral-ethical issues.

The word "guilt" covers so much in English that the counselor probably will need to help the client translate it to a kind of grieving, a need to punish the self, stress at non-conforming, inadequacy dealing with alternatives, or anger that no option totally meets their needs. Counselors can be encouraged by the findings that those clients who have the greatest struggle and stress around the decision, also make some of the greatest gains in development; the process need not be easy to be valuable.

The older way of discussing the ethics of abortion was based on what Carol Gilligan (1982) called the male model of reasoning, and focused on competing rights, ideas of abstract justice, and definitions of personhood and viability. Working with women who had unwanted pregnancies led Belenky and Gilligan to realize that the actual decisions centered on relationships, what is fair and what is selfish, the nature of caring, and avoiding hurt. They concluded that the content of the pregnancy outcome could not be used to measure health or maturity. The process of finding one's own voice, accepting the responsibility for choice, and making the decision, were what was critical to the woman's development as measured later.

Decisions and Follow Through

As the options counseling proceeds, the counselor needs to stay in touch with his/her own reactions, and not become invested in the client making a particular choice. At times the counselor may have difficulty being supportive of the client's ability to choose: with multiple abortion patients, with a minor who has been chronically sexually abused, or with a woman who is already overwhelmed by a large number of children. The counselor can be prepared to expect that as the client starts to commit to one course of action, different feeling will arise which pull her another way. Even after a decision seems to be made, the client(s) may go home and make exactly opposite plans the next day. Counselors need to feel they have done a good job when they have assisted the client in a difficult process, not when some "preferred" solution is accomplished.

The client's high stress during any resolution of unwanted pregnancy means that the counselor needs to be helpful by continuing to follow through, if possible. Before an abortion is performed, the counselor can be sure that the client has received help from the provider to know

1. basically, what the abortion is (informed consent);

2. that they are not being coerced, but making a choice; and

3. that they are able to cope with the procedure.

Afterwards, the counselor can encourage health care follow-up, and do useful counseling with other issues which the unintended pregnancy brought to light. Also, recent studies reveal that about 10% of patients have negative emotional reactions to the pregnancy termination, and these women often need to deal with issues which were not resolved before the abortion.

Special concern is required for the many unwanted pregnancies which are carried to term; appropriate social service agencies may be contacted to arrange for financial assistance, medical care, or child care. Although a high proportion of women with conflicts about pregnancy keep their babies, each is entitled to know of all the available services and assistance with adoption (agency and private). The counselor also may hear of new programs for women to re-enter the work force, receive job training, finish a course of study, or flexible day-care arrangements. While helping with all the practical adjustments after an unintended pregnancy, the counselor also has a special role to remind the woman of her inner worth, and help her with self esteem, sexuality, and relationships.

RESOURCES: DECISION-MAKING REGARDING ABORTION AND ADOPTION

Helpful books:

Arms, S. (1983). *To have and let go.* New York: Alfred A. Knopf. (adoption)

Benderly, B. (1984). *Thinking about abortion.* New York: Doubleday.

Beresford, J., & Garrity, J. (1982). *Short term counseling of sexual concerns: A self instructional manual.* Baltimore, MD: Planned Parenthood of Maryland.

Gilligan, C. (1982). *In a different voice: Psychological theory and women's development.* Cambridge, MA: Harvard University Press.

Luker, K. (1984). *Abortion and the politics of motherhood.* Berkeley, CA: University of California Press.

Articles keep the counselor current in an evolving field:

Friedlander, M., Kaul, T., & Stimel, C. (1984). Abortion: Predicting the complexity of the decision-making process. *Women and Health, 9*(1), 43-54.

Organizations publish materials which encourage responsible decision making:

The Religious Coalition for Abortion Rights, 100 Maryland Ave., Washington, DC.

Groups such as: Catholics for Free Choice, American Jewish Congress, Episcopal Woman's Caucus, the Unitarian Universalist Association, the Young Women's Christian Association, and annual assemblies of major Protestant denominations, all publish materials on various aspects of responsible choice.

Other groups such as Birthright (for carrying to term) and NARAL (National Abortion Rights Action League, working for political protection of pro-choice), also publish material strongly supportive of their points of view.

CONCLUSION

For centuries the assumption was that bearing children was a woman's special burden, carrying with it the threat of barrenness, frequent pregnancy, dependency on others for survival, decades of responsibility for others, unbearable delivery experiences, out-of-wedlock disgrace, and often death in childbirth. Of course, privileges were associated with motherhood too, so that a certain resignation and stoicism developed about the difficulties. Alleviating some of the problems has become possible in very recent times, but to think they have disappeared is a myth. Over the course of a lifetime most women and many men will experience stressful events related to some aspect of pregnancy.

Counselors may be somewhat unaware of the impact of pregnancy-related issues on a woman's self concept and attitudes. Sometimes clients shrug off problems with pregnancy in their history, but awaken to its influence during careful exploration. Every counselor can benefit from taking a fresh look at how this important aspect of people's lives affects their self concept and ongoing sexuality.

CHAPTER 6, PART 2

SEXUALITY COUNSELING DURING ILLNESS AND DISABILITY

Sexuality is an experience of the entire person, and therefore any factor which affects health is likely to have an impact on the way sexuality is perceived and expressed. Greatly varied individual differences in sexual activity following spinal cord injury, heart attacks, and hysterectomy have led to the realization that changes in sexual expression are often due to psychological/misinformation problems. This is true for any type of disease or disability, and while a counselor should never deny the importance of an actual impairment, in most cases patients can be helped to obtain more sexual satisfaction.

An advantage is gained by putting the client in the role of resource person in regard to his/her illness or disability. The counselor who draws a human figure outline and asks the client to shade parts that have sensual feeling, is doing more that the expert who "knows" that a disease results in predictable numbness patterns. The client is being required to attend to and communicate personal experience. In a similar manner, when information is needed about whether a medication can be causing a problem with vaginal lubrication or with ejaculation, a good procedure is for clients to seek the information from their physicians and bring it back to the counselor. The goal is for people to be active in coordinating their own health care, and then work with the counselor to improve their individual sexual situation.

ILLNESS

Occasionally a person may consult a counselor, mention a sexual difficulty, and have no idea that health problems could be involved. The counselor is then in a good position to indicate that the dizziness, rash, or dysparunia (painful intercourse) needs to be reported to a physician, and can encourage the ambivalent client who may not want a pelvic/rectal exam or blood test. Having a contract with this client to come back to the counselor in order to use the information from the medical checkup to improve sexual functioning, is often an incentive to get the exam done.

In the past, people with lovemaking/response difficulties were often told that they weren't "indulging" in enough "foreplay" for lubrication, were too tense, or working too hard. Now however, each issue of a sexuality journal seems to have a new physiological explanation for sexual difficulties. The counselor need not know all the specialty areas, but can recognize when sexual discomfort is outside the norm and make a referral for a checkup.

EXAMPLES: Clients' Comments Which Could Indicate Illness

"It's sore on one side of the entrance when he comes inside, so I try to ask for oral sex first. But no matter how good I feel, it hurts anyway."

"I get all turned on, we have a great time, everything is fine until I have to ejaculate...then I can't and feel this heavy pressure. The woman I'm living with thinks that maybe I'm in a mid-life crisis."

In relation to these examples, the counselor is well advised to read articles on pain due to the occlusion of the Bartholin gland (greater vestibular) duct, and research on the prostate, but an M.D. referral is needed to diagnose and treat those conditions. Sexuality counseling may continue to be needed, both in the event that no physical cause is found (ask for a second opinion if in doubt), and to help with sexual issues if they are still present. With problems which sound as though they could have a health base, the counselor needs to know professionals who will accept referrals: gynecologists, urologists, surgeons, neurologists, pediatricians, and internists who are interested in sexual health. Sexuality counseling should not proceed until a sound referral is accepted by the client.

An illness has often been diagnosed before the client comes to a counselor, and may be in an acute, chronic, or remission phase. In these instances, the counselor can avoid concentrating solely on the symptoms of ill health, and develop a larger picture of the client as a human being. The counselor, who forms good rapport with a new client and takes an informal sex history, can then begin to focus. Statements such as the following may be appropriate and can begin to put the problem in perspective: "We might work on some general feelings of sexual modesty which held you back even before your mastectomy," or "It seems that a factor blocking lovemaking after your surgery is dealing with your wife's fear of catching cancer."

A knowledge of the time frame surrounding an illness is useful. An adjustment period may be needed if the client is experiencing an acute phase, or a new set of symptoms, and reactions like depression and anxiety may depress libido. Such clients need to know that they can adjust/get better, and may benefit from learning ways to put themselves into an erotic or sensual frame of mind. This is especially necessary for people who are used to just feeling turned on, and who need to learn how to create those feelings. If the client says the equivalent of "I can't," the counselor can confront tactfully and suggest that sex has been equated only with feeling fine. With many illnesses from arthritis to colitis, comfortable sex will help the client feel better; however, an attitudinal shift and new approaches may be needed.

A person who has had an illness for some time may be in a place to expand the sexual area of living. Sexual function is probably better if it is never allowed to fall into disuse, but the adjustment to a diagnosis, medications, hospitalizations, surgery, and other treatments can take total energy for a time. Once a person has accepted the reality of an illness, and perhaps become knowledgeable about it, he/she may be especially ready to enrich the sexual part of life.

The counselor is not expected to know all about the medical aspects of Parkinson's disease, CVA's (cardio-vascular accidents), endometriosis, the technical aspects of dialysis, or types of ostomy surgery. The patient who wishes to explore and expand sexual expression can be helped by the same kinds of techniques and suggestions that any person receives in sexuality counseling. The difference is that creativity is required to accomodate for the effects of a particular health problem, and the counselor will want to give exquisite care to deeply understanding the client's experience.

Medications

The counselor who is not in a health care setting needs to make a special effort to be aware of the importance of chemicals and sexual functioning. Surveys show that people take an amazing amount of patent medicine and prescription medication, and use or abuse alcohol and other drugs heavily. Clients frequently discount the effects of their beta blocker, antihistimine, marijuana use, or daily laxative habit on sexual health. In addition, they may selectively remember newspaper fragments or third hand information to reassure themselves about what they are taking. The counselor will need to obtain the client's cooperation in order to list all the substances which are ingested on a regular basis.

Once the counselor and client have a descriptive drug picture, the counselor is not expected nor is he/she responsible for research into their effects. The counselor is not the person to check in a PDR (Physicians' Desk Reference book) and judge that some substance has no effect on sexual symptoms. Although the counselor can have medical consultants who give general information about side effects, and while tables of the sexual effects of drugs can be found, the field is specialized and changes so rapidly that the client needs to consult a personal physician.

When a client does inquire about the sexual effects of drugs, sometimes the answer received is: "No one is certain, but there is a possibility that this substance could be a contributing factor." In these cases, a substitute medication may be tried, or the interaction effects of drugs considered, or the patient advised to stop some self-medicating. If the problem drug is alcohol, an illegal substance such as cocaine, or the overuse of medications like barbituates, amphetimines, or tranquilizers, a major withdrawal and management program may be needed. While this planning and treatment is begun, the counselor can continue to explore the client's sexual problem, giving information and beginning to focus on areas of possible improvement.

Pain and Discomfort

Most able bodied counselors have experienced pain or severe discomfort at some time, but may have no concept of the debilitating effects of acute, chronic, unpredictable, or progressive pain. Because a condition for sexual arousal is awareness of pleasure, the presence of pain is definitely an obstacle. Motor problems, weakness, nausea, and many other severely uncomfortable conditions will interfere. The counselor can be familiar with references on illness and sexuality, in order to listen carefully and help the client clearly describe how, when, and where pain interferes with sex.

The client can work with the physician and the sexuality counselor to be sure that all possibilities for physical improvement are checked out, and any unresolved pain managed as effectively as possible. Careful thought will result in cooperative suggestions around the timing of sexual activities to take advantage of more pain-free periods and to utilize the maximum effectiveness of medication. Home care nurses and physical therapists can be consulted about a more comfortable life style. The counselor can contribute ideas about varieties of sensual arousal, self pleasuring, less stressful positions, and aids to sexual pleasure. In addition, the counselor can work with the client's self image and sexual attitudes, and help facilitate communication with family or partners.

QUESTION: Does a professional have to be an expert in cerebral palsy, hepatitis, alcohol abuse, emphysema, prostatitis, or any of thousands of health/illness problems in order to do sexuality counseling?

ANSWER: *"The more one knows—the better"* is true of all health related counseling. However, the sexuality counselor who is a generalist can be very helpful by working as part of a health care group.

Summary

Sexuality counseling during or after illness is a vital component of health care. Whether due to disease, accident, surgery, or inherited condition, illness very often has an effect on sexuality. The current emphasis on the health of the whole person can facilitate the sexuality counselor becoming part of the health care team, and encourage medical professionals to learn sexuality counseling. As with any counseling, the helper's emphasis on enriching the whole person is important, to insure the maintenance of satisfaction after the original sexual and/or health problem is improved.

RESOURCES RELATED TO ILLNESS

The counselor should have an overall view of how a particular health problem affects sex, not to diagnose or treat, but to see beyond limitations accepted by the client. General references like the following can be consulted both for a broader scope and detailed information.

Texts provide careful coverage of a wide range of health issues:

Abel, E. (1983). *Drugs and sex: A bibliography.* Westport, CT: Greenwood Press. (Includes alcohol.)

Kolodny, R., Masters, W., Johnson, V., & Briggs, M. (1979). *Textbook of human sexuality for nurses.* Boston, MA: Little, Brown.

Kolodny, R., Masters, W., & Johnson, V., (1979). *Textbook of sexual medicine.* Boston, MA: Little, Brown.

Lief, H. (Ed.). (1981). *Sexual problems in medical practice.* Chicago, IL: American Medical Association.

Munjack, D., & Oziel, J. (1980). *Sexual medicine and counseling in office practice.* Boston, MA: Little Brown.

Woods, N. (1984). *Human sexuality in health and illness* (3rd ed.). St. Louis, MO: C.V. Mosby.

Sections of journals in medicine, allied health, mental health, and rehabilitation are often devoted to particular areas of sexuality. Many include counseling insights, such as:

Listor, L., & Shore, D. (Eds.). (1983). Human sexuality in medical social work. *Journal of Social Work and Human Sexuality, Vol. 2*(1). Articles include: "Assessing Sexual Concerns of Clients with Health Problems," "Sexuality and Chronic Illness," and "Social Work with Challenged Women: Sexism, Sexuality, and the Female Cancer Experience."

Kelly, G. (Ed.). Sexuality and illness. (1983). *Journal of Sex Education and Therapy, Vol. 9*(2). Articles include "Assessing Sexual Implications of Functional Impairments Associated with Chronic Illness," and "Sexual Response in Diabetic Women."

Clinics and groups with expertise in a particular area publish specific resources. While these are intended largely for patients, they can be very helpful when the general counselor shares them with a client. Examples include.

Barrett, M. (1982). *Sexuality and multiple sclerosis.* New York: National Multiple Sclerosis Society.

Clark, M., & Magrina, J. (1983). *Sexual adjustment to cancer surgery in the vaginal area*. Kansas City, KA: University of Kansas Medical Center, Student Union Book Store.

Hossler, C., & Cole, S. (1983). *Intimacy and chronic lung disease*. Ann Arbor, MI: The University of Michigan Hospitals.

Strodtman, L., & Knopf, R. (1983). *Sexual health and diabetes*. Ann Arbor, MI: Publications Distributions Service.

DISABILITY

Language evolves with social awareness and while the term "handicapped" is still used to mark parking places, many people find it demeaning. Dictionaries generally define handicap as "to place at a disadvantage," and the popular interpretation can mean "different, strange, inferior." The term "disabled" has come into use to indicate an impairment in some function, but without the assumption that the person is at a disadvantage in other respects. The sexuality counselor needs to address the total person and not the disability, and yet be open and frank with the disabled client about limitations which affect sex. In the same way, the counselor will engage in a dialogue about psychological and social/interpersonal effects of a disability, being sure that their subjective nature is explored.

The term "disabled" applies to such a wide group of clients that it is useful to subdivide for the sake of discussion. Three groups could be considered:

1. those who are disabled in a manner which directly affects their sexual performance or satisfaction (radiation therapy for breast cancer, AIDS patients),

2. those people whose disability is not directly sexual but impacts on sexuality in a significant way (removal of the larynx, paralysis of a limb), and

3. individuals who have an impairment which does not necessarily involve their sexuality (stomach ulcers, migraine headaches).

People in groups 1 and 2 are likely to need sexual disability counseling, while those in group 3 need to be assessed individually to ascertain their needs. Obviously this is a continuum, and the counselor can help the client express what the sexual implications of a disability are, and explore the physiological, psychological, and social components.

Health care workers have found that a purely medical-technical approach is limited in rehabilitation counseling, and therefore include the psychosocial and interpersonal perspectives. The following are some areas to consider with disabled clients, in addition to areas explored with any client:

1. What is the history of the disability? During what phase of sexual development did it begin: congenital, pre-pubertal, adolescence, young adult, parenting stage, midlife, older? Was the onset sudden, as in an accident, or gradual? Predictable course or uncertain? Life threatening?

2. What was the type and amount of sexuality education at age of onset, and the person's current level of knowledge?

3. How has the sexual experience of the client been affected by the disability? What is their sexual history and current experience?

4. What is the client's assessment of the actual functioning of his/her sex organs, and what ability exists to experience the sexual response cycle? What about motor and sensory capacities which are important in sexual activity?

5. Is fertility impaired? How does the client feel about marriage and family?

6. What medications are used?

7. What treatments are in process or planned?

8. How is the client's body image and sense of being masculine/feminine affected by the disability?

9. Does the disability affect communication? Will this interfere with sexual expression with partners?

10. How noticeable is the disability? How do myths and realities about it affect interpersonal relationships?

11. Does the client consider himself/herself celibate, homosexual, heterosexual, or bisexual? Does comfort exist with preferred orientation?

12. What social/sexual skills does the client possess which facilitate sexual satisfaction? What social/sexual deficits?

13. Has the client experienced sexual trauma, such as child molestation, incest, rape, or other type of exploitation? What about rejection?

14. What is the apparent level of the client's current sexual interest?

15. Has the client reached a level of acceptance of his/her disability in aspects other than the sexual? Does he/she feel differently about the sexual aspects, either more positive or negative?

After looking at this list, a person could decide that sexuality counseling with the disabled is too specialized to attempt. However a counselor is very likely to be asked for help by a partially paralyzed man who had a motorcycle accident five years ago, by a woman client who has epilepsy, or by a learning disabled teenager who is pregnant. The counselor who is knowledgeable about sexuality can be very helpful to a disabled person, again as part of a health care team, and can always go on and become more of a specialist if need requires.

EXAMPLE: A 52 Year Old Man Who Had a Stroke Last Year, 2nd Session

Ernesto: *"So I felt better after last week when I had a chance to tell you about my whole sex life. It's easy to forget, after months when half of me felt numb."*

Counselor: *"That's a good perspective! There's no question that a stroke is a setback. You must have been discouraged when the medication for hypertension added to the erection problem, before your doctor changed it."*

Ernesto: *"That's why she sent me here—when she could see how upset I was that even the new medicine didn't really improve sex much. Last week you told me not to try intercourse, and I felt less pressure."*

Counselor: *"Good. Did you discuss it with your wife?"*

Ernesto: *"I had to tell Janet, so she wouldn't think I wasn't interested."*

Counselor: *"You want Janet to know you're still a whole man..."*

Ernesto: *"But I'm not! I mean, not really. I've had to change to an easier side of my business, and still limp...can't shake hands as well or use tools like I used to."*

Counselor: *"You've mentioned important things, and I know you are adjusting to them and still improving. You have fine determination."* (Pauses, smiles at client.) *"But what do you think means the most to Janet...as far as you are concerned?"*

Ernesto: *"Well, I suppose still being here, and paying attention, and she likes me to hold her."*

Counselor: *"Can you do those things OK, or maybe even better than before?"*

Ernesto: *"Sure, I'm not in and out of the trucks all the time, and away so much...and since I've been home more we have a lot to talk about. When I hold her I get all excited, but the problem is I usually turn soft and then can't come."*

Counselor: *"What comes to mind about excitement and climax?"*

Ernesto: *"Yeah, I know, and I think Janet is even more scared of me getting too excited and straining myself. Maybe no erection is better than another stroke."*

Counselor: *"Sure. That's where we need to focus then, isn't it? You can get information from your doctor about the actual risk* *of sexual climax causing another stroke. If she says it's OK, you can learn ways to enjoy intercourse—feeling it's a healthy outlet for tension. Do you want to do that?'*

Ernesto: *"Want to?"* (Pauses, clears his throat.) *"It would make all the difference."*

COMMENTS: The preceding process is condensed, but the point is to help this client recognize the importance of his internal fears about sexual strain. In many instances, a client is more resistant, and just wants to blame his/her body. However, even if longer time is needed, a person will often see the relevance of buried attitudes to sexual behavior.

Once a medical green light is given, a good suggestion may be a gradual approach to ejaculation with hand or mouth stimulation by his partner. Using imagery first, Ernesto could "see" himself climax, feeling secure and strong, visualizing it as encouraging healthy circulation. When the client can feel positive in fantasy, and through manual/oral stimulation, he will probably be very ready for intercourse.

An emphasis on being aroused by exciting Janet also could minimize the client's tendency to judge his erection. Continued inquiries and suggestions about his wife's pleasure in later interviews (clitoral massage, vaginal sensitivity, having her do Kegel exercises against his finger), will help Ernesto feel like and become a better lover. Janet could be invited in to participate, or the counselor might continue to work with the client alone. Couples work has been show to be very effective in health-related sexuality counseling, and yet having the husband be the bearer of good news about sex helps him regain his adult masculine role. Either method would be effective.

RESOURCES RELATING TO DISABILITY

General references:

Ayrault, E. (1981). *Sex, love and the physically handicapped.* New York: Continuum.

Bullard, D., & Knight, S. (Eds.). *Sexuality and physical disability: Personal perspectives*. St. Louis, MO: C.V. Mosby.

Comfort, A. (1978). *Sexual consequences of disability*. Philadelphia, PA: Stickley.

Cornelius, D., Chipouras, S., Makas, E., & Daniels, S. (Eds.). (1982). *Who cares? A handbook on sex education and counseling services for disabled people (2nd ed.)*. Baltimore, MD: University Park Press.

Johnson, W., & Kempton, W. (1981). *Sex education and counseling of special groups* (2nd ed.). Springfield, IL: Charles C. Thomas.

Robinault, I. (1978). *Sex, society, and the disabled: A developmental inquiry into roles, reactions, and responsibilities*. New York: Harper and Row.

Sexuality and Disability, a quarterly journal, Human Sciences Press. Other medical and health journals have occasional articles on specific types of illness (i.e., heart disease) and sexuality. An index to periodicals or a computerized search using the illness and sexuality as key words will generate the most recent citations.

Films, video-tapes, and slide programs for both clients and counselor provide easily understood encouragement.

Choices in Sexuality with Physical Disability, (1983), distributed by Mercury Productions, 17 West 45th St., New York, NY 10036.

Multi-Focus, Inc., 333 West 52nd St., New York, NY 10019. Their catalogue lists six pages of films on aspects of disability and sexuality. For sale or rental.

Reputable authors and groups have published specific resources:

Doughten, R., Minkin, M., & Rosen, I. *Signs for sexuality: A resource manual.* Seattle, WA: Planned Parenthood. Photographs illustrating sign words and phrases associated with sexuality, for use with the hearing impaired.

Ebon research systems. (1980). *Family planning services for disabled people: A manual for service providers*. Washington, DC: U.S. Government Printing Office.

Eschen, A., & Hallingby, L. (1984). *Sexuality and disability: A bibliography of resources available for purchase* (Rev. ed.) New York: SIECUS, 80 Fifth Ave., New York, NY 10011.

Sha'ked, A. (1981). *Human sexuality and rehabilitation medicine: Sexual functioning following spinal cord injury*. Baltimore, MD: Williams and Wilkins.

Stehle, B. (1985). *Incurably romantic*. Philadelphia, PA: Temple University Press. Wonderful photographs and interviews portray disabled people enjoying love and sexuality.

Vaeth, J., Blomberg, R., & Adler, L. (Eds.). (1980). Body image, self-esteem, and sexuality in cancer patients. New York: S. Karger.

DISABILITIES WHICH AFFECT LEARNING

A number of particular terms are used for disabilities which hinder learning, such as mental retardation, mental handicap, developmental disability, learning disability, mental illness, or emotional disturbance. Professionals report that they have to combat more stereotypes, prejudice, and rejection toward clients who have these diagnoses, than toward physical, motor, sensory, or communication disabled clients. Again, the general sexuality counselor would need special experience to work independently with people in these groups, but can be very effective as part of a health care group. Families and friends may also consult the counselor and have issues about the sexuality of a person whose ability to learn differs from the average.

A common myth is that if the learning impaired person is necessarily dependent on others, he/she is therefore child-like and not sexual. Of course a persons' sexuality may be fully adolescent or adult, while their knowledge, social skills, and ability to make judgments are at a less mature level, and in these instances they may be misjudged as "oversexed." People in this group are often isolated or blocked ("protected") from the informal sources of sex education and experience in our culture. At the same time, people with learning difficulties are highly vulnerable to sexual abuse and exploitation, may be limited in assertiveness or impulse control, and unable to obtain help.

Recognition of these problems has led to some dedicated work in sexuality education and counseling for the mentally retarded, and more recently for the learning disabled and emotionally disturbed. The counselor can participate in individual and group education and counseling, and in education/training workshops for parents and professionals. An important contribution is to encourage policies in programs and institutions which allow sexual expression for all, arrange the right to privacy, provide sexuality education, counseling and reproductive health services, respect personal choice of marital status and childbearing, and accept a variety of sexual life styles.

While people with learning problems are entitled to sexual expression, they may need to be protected from sexual abuse and exploitation. Clearly problems will occur in providing all the above to every resident in a group, program, or institution for the learning impaired. Yet very often practical difficulties are used to mask a belief that "these people" shouldn't be allowed to be sexual. A counselor is often a good person to negotiate and mediate between the legitimate needs of the caretakers and those of the client in regard to sexual expression.

RESOURCES FOR DISABILITIES WHICH AFFECT LEARNING

Some of the resources already listed have sections on developmental disabilities/retardation; a few have material on working with sexuality and the emotionally disturbed. Those in the following list often refer to "education," but include material essential to counseling with this group of clients.

Craft, A., & Craft, M. (1983). *Sex education and counseling for mentally handicapped people*. Baltimore, MD: University Park Press.

Kempton, W., Bass, L., & Gordon, S. (1984). *Love, sex and birth control for the mentally retarded*. Philadelphia, PA: Planned Parenthood, SE Pennsylvania.

Monat, R. (1982). *Sexuality and the mentally retarded, clinical and therapeutic guidebook*. San Diego, CA: College-Hill Trust.

Audio-Visual Material:

Kempton, W. *Sexuality and the mentally handicapped*. Santa Monica, CA: Stanfield Film Associates. A comprehensive slide series.

Blum, G. *Feeling good about yourself*. Evanston, IL: Perennial Education. A film demonstrating interactive methods of socialization learning.

Teaching human sexuality to the mentally handicapped. Owings Mill, MD: Educational Division. A kit containing slides, audio-cassette, guide and teaching cards.

Gender dolls, anatomically correct, especially useful for those with developmental disabilities. Cambridge, MA: Jim Jackson, 33 Richdale Ave.

CONCLUSION

Counselors can demystify sexuality for the disabled by encouraging clients to call on strengths which they have used successfully to compensate for loss in other areas of functioning. Exceptions to the usual way of doing things are often required, so the counselor may have to counter rigid sexual rules imposed on the sick or handicapped by others. One of the hardest things is knowing that the disabled have a far higher rate of sexual victimization, and finding ways to communicate that without scaring or over protecting the client. Finally, continuous work needs to be done with the ill/disabled client's self image. As the counselor becomes familiar with the client, the disability can be accepted easily and the unfounded assumption made that the client is confident about himself/herself, too.

As counselors become more comfortable working with clients and exploring sexual histories, a fact becomes apparent: the majority of people have had an illness or disability which impinged on their sexual experience for a time. Mature counselors are able to recall how their own cystitis, acne, whiplash injuries, surgery, asthma, or perhaps angina have affected their sexuality. Perfect health over a lifetime is clearly a minority condition, if it even exists, so the line between being disabled and able-bodied is an indistinct one. Certainly some illnesses and disabilities are trivial while others are indescribably burdensome and life-threatening, but the counselor will be more comfortable working with all people if similarities are stressed rather than differences.

CHAPTER 6, PART 3

ATYPICAL SEXUAL BEHAVIOR

A counselor who is tolerant of a wide range of sexual behavior can certainly be helpful to more people than one whose view of "normal" sexuality is limited. However as counselors gain skill in sexuality counseling, they may be surprised by the amount of bizarre, scarey, unconventional, and just plain peculiar sexual preferences many people have. When is shock and distaste on the helper's part genuine and a cue to ask clients about the appropriateness of their behavior? Certainly no current Krafft-Ebing list of "perversions" would be accepted by everyone, and indeed labeling any kind of sexuality as not okay is highly subjective.

This section will not describe the legality of sexual behavior, because culture lag in sex-related law is such that the last statute forbidding physicians to prescribe contraceptives was struck down as late as 1966. Also, differences from region to region are so great that when legality becomes a client issue, both local law and its enforcement must be consulted. The counselor's main concern is the mental health aspect of atypical sexual expression, and the goal is to help each client find what is pleasurable and safe.

If counselors cannot be guided by academic definitions, by the law, or their own reactions, how can questions of atypical sexual preference be addressed? One possibility is to use the client's experience to define what is "normal," for him/her. Certainly this is a significant aspect, but the client's judgment may not totally answer the question because:

1. some clients judge themselves very harshly, such as the woman who says, *"I'm no better than a prostitute when I get turned on by acting dirty for my husband;"* and

2. other clients distort their judgment to match their behavior such as the man who says, *"My nephew (age 16) likes it to hurt when I mess with him—then he feels okay about the sex."*

Another reason for not depending entirely on the client's perception, is that they are often troubled about a sexual variant, and ask the counselor's help in deciding what is normal. While their views are important, they are asking for more than a mere reflection of what they already know. The counselor is being asked to help the client find perspective on a "nonconforming" way of expressing sexuality.

THE CONTINUUM CONCEPT

A particular sexual behavior alone does not determine whether it is "healthy," but the extent, motivation, and consequences of the sexual variation. A socially defined continuum exists from minor to extreme degrees of non-conforming sexual behavior, and people tend to view the extremes more negatively. A parallel continuum also exists in regard to whether the sexual variation is a small part of a person's sexual expression (more acceptable), or most of it. The client who wants to change an alternative sexual expression, after thoroughly considering it with a counselor, may work toward a milder form or have it occupy less of his/her life.

EXAMPLES: Sexual Behaviors

Sex for sale ranges from any kind of prostitution (child, male, female, homosexual, heterosexual, all sexual practices) to the various commercial "live sex shows," sex shop X-rated goods, and voluminous media/mail order material. People tend to allow themselves more atypical sex when they pay for it, than they usually experience with ongoing partners.

Voyeurism, being sexually aroused by watching others, is more acceptable at parties, sports events, and resorts, but is threatening when someone drifts through apartment complexes looking in windows. In addition, the impulse to touch or rub against strangers in sexual ways is sometimes grouped with this behavior.

Sado-masochistic (S-M) behavior, associating sexual pleasure with giving or receiving pain/fear/humiliation, can range from a show of strength to carefully scripted role playing with whips and bondage. Men and women can play dominant or submissive parts, and report that the physical/emotional intensity adds to their pleasure. Certainly there is potential for S-M behavior to vary from the playful to the abusive, or to be non-consenting.

Necrophilia, sex with dead bodies, is universally considered "sick." Yet if a person watches a horror movie and feels aroused by an erotic looking corpse, that doesn't necessarily motivate them to search in cemeteries. It could upset someone if they become preoccupied with sex and death, or had a continuing fascination.

Zoophilia (bestiality), sex with animals, is another widely condemned practice which evokes disgust in many people. However, a person could be aroused by a friend's dog who licks him/her at the beach, and encourage it to continue for sexual pleasure. Would it be different if that was the only way they could enjoy sex?

Fetishism is sexual excitement from involvement with specific objects. A fetish tends to be private, since arousal by an object or a part of the body is not very visible. When a person gets "turned on" touching a curly red beard it may be amusing, but a client who can only enjoy oral sex with someone wearing dentures is more limited. A surprising amount of shame may be felt by a person having a fetish, and it seems to be related to the lack of control and feeling different or restricted.

Exhibitionism, the showing of genitals in public, has received an unusual amount of recent attention. This may be because some sex offenders have revealed this variant as part of their sexual history. Other researchers have described the passive, socially inadequate "flasher" who frequently gets arrested as an exhibitionist. The counselor will see many patterns of attention getting, inferiority compensation, and passive-aggressive power in behaviors which range from obscene phone calls to forcing others to watch masturbation.

Hypersexuality, a condition of being sexually active to the point of recklessness, is seen in both men and women, but the double standard still prevails. A woman may be called a "nympho" if she bar hops and expresses a strong interest in sex, whereas a young man might be keeping to the norm for his group. Counselor and client need to look at all the sexual behavior in context, to sort out what the client chooses to modify.

This list of examples could be expanded to illustrate the most objectionable and the most compulsive poles of the continuum behaviors. Whether slight or extreme, under control or not, the counselor needs to realize that they are not all rigid, homogeneous categories. At one time, professionals tried to design research which would show that: "transvestites are not homosexual," or "voyeurs are harmless, developmentally arrested men." However, generalities do not hold throughout these groups, and the theories often missed as many people as they labeled.

NORMALIZING FACTORS

Recently an awareness has developed that sexual behavior is complex, people often have more than one atypical sexual behavior, and a great many people have always expressed themselves sexually in ways which some consider "abnormal." Society appears to apply the following guidelines in determining when a sexual variation is "kinky but acceptable," and when it shades over to "sick." Few people will agree totally, but they are likely to consider the following aspects in viewing alternative sexual behavior.

1. Rare or occasional is more acceptable than frequent.
   "My husband wants me to act like a strict teacher and punish him every few months; I can get off on it once in a while."

2. Accidental is more acceptable than planned.
   "This couple had sex after skinny dipping, so I made myself come while I watched."

3. Fantasy more acceptable than doing it.
   "To get turned on, I picture stripping slowly and showing myself to a group of men at work who think I'm very proper."

4. Observing may be viewed as more okay than participating.
   "Guys in drag can really fool you. This show gives quite a bang."

5. Commercial sex for adults more okay than if regular partners were doing the same things.
   "So these prostitutes let us tie them up and do anything we wanted—they'd take it any way. Well, they're paid enough."

6. Apparent cooperation by another makes it more acceptable.
   "Those young guys wait by the edge of the park and hop in your car like lightening—and not just for the money. I'd never turn a new kid or take someone really young."

7. Control of behavior is more acceptable than a compulsion.
   "Well, I get the hots—especially before my period—if I haven't been with a guy for a week or so. But I can resist and date, and usually find a man I know."

8. An element of role-playing and concern for safety makes it more okay.
   "We work out the 'master-slave' script pretty carefully first, and never get the leather out with someone just off the street."

The counselor may not agree that all the "extenuating circumstances" listed above render a sexual behavior harmless. Sexual behavior which involves minors, results in physical/emotional damage, or occurs without completely informed consent is not acceptable through any rationalization. In addition, the individual counselor may have other values which make some sexual variations seem repulsive. The point is to see the client's sexuality in context. Then the counselor can help the person accept, modify, or expand unusual sexual preferences to make a comfortable life style.

PROBLEMS WITH SEXUAL VARIATIONS

Clients inquiring about sexual variations are likely to ask whether their behavior means they are sick, and if so will they get worse. On exploring this concern, the counselor is likely to find that the client is worried about being attracted to more risky behaviors, or finds the variant too limiting. When an atypical sexual expression becomes compulsive, or other ways of having sex do not work, a client may force himself/herself to seek help. The counselor can feel good about being trusted and help the client assess his/her experience with the sexual variant, taking into consideration a continuum of activities and mitigating factors.

The counselor has an ethical responsibility to do something about child sexual abuse, and a duty to warn if serious harm is threatened toward the client or another person. Otherwise even if a behavior such as male/female prostitution is illegal, the counselor's ethics require the maintenance of confidentiality and avoidance of judgment. Therefore, when may a counselor question whether an atypical sexual behavior could be harmful to the client or others? The answer is that raising the question of consequences can always be done in a concerned way, so that the counselor's reservations are expressed as looking out for the client's welfare.

A common situation is when a client alludes to an unusual sexual practice and then changes the subject. The counselor can address the question of indirect approval: "It seems as if you want me to know about this, Lynn, sort of for my acceptance rather than seeing how it fits in your life. Isn't it more important to explore how you feel about it...(sex and excrement, or a compulsion to have sex with men with tatoos, or whatever); does it seem comfortable to you?" The counselor and client can then do reality testing together through a supportive dialogue.

What is appropriate pleasurable sexual behavior for one person may be repellent to many others. As a result, people who share an atypical kind of sexual expression form informal groups, finding reassurance that other real people share their secret. A variety of magazines and newsletters can be obtained in adult bookstores, sex shops, and large newsstands, which meet the needs of varied subcultures. In spite of the sexual revolution, atypical sexuality is seldom met with understanding, so the counselor can assist a number of people who feel bitterly alone and conflicted.

When a client with a nonconforming sexual preference is worried about discovery, rejection, illness, or moral judgment, the counselor can help in the same way as with any other sexual question. Some alternative sexual behavior is accompanied by guilt and feelings of inadequacy, so that information and enrichment techniques explored through counseling are effective. Assistance in expanding to a wider range of sexual expression, and encouraging fantasy and self pleasuring which is not limited to the sexual variant, are ways to encourage a balance of sexual outlets. The counselor can suggest that a client explore his/her atypical sexual preferences and

1. keep it exactly as it is,
2. increase /expand it,
3. stop it altogether,
4. modify it, and/or
5. add new forms of sexual expression.

RESOURCES FOR ATYPICAL SEXUAL BEHAVIOR

Books such as the following:

Carnes, P. (1985). *Out of the shadows: Understanding sexual addiction.* Minneapolis, MN: CompCare Publications. (Concepts parallel to Alcholics Anonymous).

Comfort, A. (1975). *More joy: A lovemaking companion to the joy of sex.* New York: Simon and Schuster. (Describes some less conventional sex.)

Langevin, R. (1983). *Sexual strands, understanding, and treating sexual anomalies in men.* Hillsdale, NJ: Lawrence Erlbaum.

Meyer, J., Schmidt, C., & Wise, T. (Eds.). (1983). *Clinical management of sexual disorders,* 2nd ed. Lexington, MA: Williams Wilkins.

PRIDE. (1984). *People reaching out in a determined effort to affect change in prostitution.* Minneapolis, MN: PRIDE Family and Children's Services. Covers group help and the stages of leaving prostitution.

Schlesinger, L., & Revitch, E. (Eds.). (1983). *Sexual dynamics of antisocial behavior.* Springfield, IL: Charles C. Thomas.

Schur, E. (1984). *Labeling women deviant: Gender, stigma and social control.* Philadelphia, PA: Temple University Press.

Journal articles are an excellent source of specific information; the following are examples of kinds for which to look:

Lowry, T., & Williams, G. (1983). Brachioproctic eroticism. *Journal of Sex Education and Therapy, 9*(1)., 50-52.

Robinson, S., & Krussman, H. (1983). Sex for money: Profile of a John. *Journal of Sex Education and Therapy, 9*(1), 27-31.

Schwartz, M., & Masters, W. (1983). Conceptual factors in the treatment of paraphilias: A preliminary report. *Journal of Sex & Marital Therapy, 9*(1), 3-18.

ALTERNATIVE GENDER LIFESTYLES

Statistics are difficult to gather on the "invisible minority," as the transvestite/transsexual community has been called. In the past, many individuals believed they were alone in being dissatisfied with living exclusively as their birth gender, and with their assigned sex role. Recently the different subgroups of the paraculture have recognized the need for mutual support, which brings more collective representation to all.

The following definitions are taken from a brochure published by The Human Outreach and Achievement Institute:

Crossdresser—A person who wears articles of clothing of the opposite gender. (Includes Transvestite, Female/Male Impersonator, etc.)

Androgyne—A person who can comfortably express either alternative gender role in a variety of socially acceptable environments. (Includes Bigenderist)

Transgenderist—A person who has decided to transit from one gender role to a preferred alternative gender role permanently. (Includes Pre-Op Transsexual)

Transsexual—A person who desires anatomical congruence with the preferred, alternative gender role preference. (Includes persons wanting sex reassignment surgery)

New Women/New Men—A person who now lives in the preferred alternative gender role and who has completed the surgery needed to achieve anatomical congruence. (Includes people who have had reassignment surgery)

CD/TS/AN Community—People whose general behavior pattern includes gender-related issues, androgyny, and crossdressing.

As with other kinds of atypical sexual behavior, a continuum exists between milder and more extensive forms of other-gender expression, and in the proportion of a client's life which is involved in the paraculture. While most counselors will not meet fully committed pre- or post-operative transsexuals very often, they can expect to have a number of clients bring up wishes and behavior characteristic of gender dissatisfaction. Rigid male-female categories simply don't hold for all individuals over their lifespan, so attempts to label what a client "really" is seem futile.

Crossdressing for personal satisfaction or sexual excitement may be a minor element in the life of a person who creates opportunities at Halloween or masquerade parties. The term *transvestite* is used when a person buys/takes/wears a wardrobe of the other sex's clothing, underwear, or makeup. Yet even within apparently similar groups, a counselor cannot generalize but must find the individual meaning.

EXAMPLE: Man, Age 50, 6th Session

Norman: *"So I wasn't sure you'd want to hear about Norma; I've kept that part of me secret so long."*

Counselor: *"I began to understand the importance of your cross dressing after you brought it up a few weeks ago. You seem more relaxed now that you have described the Norma part of you."*

Norman: *"When I'm on my way home to dinner with my wife and teenage kids wearing my banker's suit, I still wonder what people would think if they knew."*

Counselor: *"Since your wife knows, and you spend a couple of hours every week as Norma, I'd like to meet you that way sometime. I guess that's my way of answering your question about what people would think. You have to choose who to include, I expect, and be selective."*

Norman: *"Right. I know a couple of fellows who do this, too. But to tell you the truth, I'm not sure I want to go out of the house and be more convincing as a woman. I keep it small, and wouldn't want you to think I'm a homosexual or schizophrenic. Lots of people have been like me, all through history."*

Counselor: *"Norm, I'm not judging you, nor am I trying to increase your cross dressing. But I don't want you to put on a front with me, or just be intellectual about something so important. How can I help you feel confident with whatever part cross dressing plays in your life?"*

COMMENTS: The counselor can express acceptance and trust in the client by being willing to explore all aspects. The client's concern about being considered crazy or unacceptable is both a real social problem, and a painful psychological issue. The goal would be to help Norm with integration, self acceptance, and the maintenance of relationships which are important to him. The cross dressing might increase or decrease, but his degree of personal comfort and sense of integrity can certainly improve.

Counseling and Gender Issue

A common opinion is that individuals who have questions about male-femaleness must consult a specialist in sex therapy. However, many people with some concerns about gender and role choose to see a counselor but no one else. For instance, a woman who has had dreams and done art work on the theme of being a man may resolve it in the direction of modifying the kind of woman she is, without surgery or a major life style change. Or a man might select an occupation where he can frequently disappear in a big city and live as a woman on weekends, and elect only a moderate amount of consultation for hormone therapy. Counselors can be support people, referral sources, and direct care givers, especially for clients who want to explore these issues within their present life style.

The most important keyword for a counselor to remember when a client brings up other gender questions is to be DESCRIPTIVE. The biggest mistake is to try to categorize, as in "Well, if you are a woman who is interested in dressing and living as a man, does that mean you are homosexual, or do you want surgery, or are you a transvestite who is aroused by men's clothes?" The preferred course is to encourage the client to DESCRIBE how it is now/usually/sometimes, how sex roles and partner preferences seemed to develop, what present experience and fantasy are involved, and where he/she might like to be someday. An evolving sense of self is characteristic as the client describes, explores, feels, and tries out, rather than labels a fixed identity. Time and support are needed for that.

Over time the client comes to realize what is genuine, and gains a sense of the aspects which cause stress and can be modified. Further assistance for the other gender exploring client is available in most large population centers. Support groups, voice therapy, coaching in dress and behavior, medical specialists in endocrinology and surgery, and informational reading may be obtained. Motivated clients will travel hundreds of miles if necessary, to seek out specific resources. Specialists in psychiatry and psychology will meet regularly with a client who is choosing a trial period of living as the other sex, in order to make a recommendation for possible surgery. Often a counselor serves as a support person and contact, while the client searches out services or information and comes to decisions.

RESOURCES REGARDING ALTERNATIVE GENDER LIFESTYLES

Books or sections of them are helpful; texts which have "sex therapy" in the title often have chapters regarding alternative gender life styles. A variety of attitudes toward the client will be encountered in them and in the following:

Feinbloom, D. (1976). *Transvestites and transsexuals: Mixed views*. New York: Delta.

Koranyi, E. (1980). *Transsexuality in the male: The spectrum of gender dysphoria*. Springfield, IL: Charles C. Thomas.

Howells, K. (Ed.). (1984). *The psychology of sexual diversity*. NY: Basil Blackwell.

Wise, T. Evaluation and treatment of gender disorders. In J. Meyer, C. Schmidt, & T. Wise, (1983), *Clinical Management of Sexual Disorders* (2nd ed.). Baltimore, MD: Williams and Wilkins.

Journal articles can sometimes be found in medical, counseling, allied health and social work periodicals. This provides access to the most current information in a controversial and rapidly changing field. The other forum for new insight is the conference/meeting where new papers are presented.

Standards of Care apply to surgical sex change and are published by the Harry Benjamin International Gender Dysphoria Association, Inc., 1952 Union Street, San Francisco, CA 94123.

The Human Outreach and Achievement Institute, Kenmore Station, Box 368, Boston, MA 02215 provides the following services:

OPERN, a nationwide Professional Evaluation and Referral Network, for qualified professionals in medicine, law, education, the clergy, social sciences, and human services.

Seminars and Workshops presented on topics such as "Coming to Grips with Gender Role Issues in Adolescence," and "Understanding and Coping Strategies for Spouses and Families of Crossdressers."

Outreach Newsletter, Quarterly, current information on the paraculture.

Fantasia Fair, a living/learning growth experience for the TV/CD/AN Community, on Cape Cod in October.

CD/TS/AN Directory, for information and services and programs throughout North America.

Book and Publication Service, a catalogue of books and reprints, many of which are difficult to obtain elsewhere.

MODIFYING ATYPICAL SEXUAL BEHAVIOR

Who the person is in terms of sense of self is clearly more important than exactly how he/she expresses genital sexuality or conforms to role stereotypes. This is especially true with any sexual minority, since they have reason to suspect that others will judge, categorize, and criticize. Historical and cross-cultural studies show the diversity of people's views of "usual and customary" sexual behavior. Therefore, a counselor needs to be comfortable with explicit descriptions of sexual behavior, but must not appear too curious or fixed on the details of sexual behavior alone.

Sexual Variants as a Subproblem

Very often atypical sexual expression is only a small part of a client's concerns and the counselor needs to keep it in perspective.

EXAMPLES: Focus on the Person Instead of the Symptom

A school principal first talks to a staff counselor about chronic headaches and stress, and then tentatively mentions a foot fixation while exploring the question of masculinity, leadership, and body image. Certainly this man will need to be seen as a whole person and not have his limited arousal pattern be the only focus. The counselor might not even use the term "fetish," but help the principal become more personally confident and then less obsessed with only a single type of arousal. The informal talks can become regular meetings for a while, to work with the stress-headache patterns and with the sexual variant as appropriate.

A woman who has a history of overcoming serious physical health problems hesitantly confides in her social worker that she was dressed as a boy when visiting her grandparents every summer. This client may be embarrassed to admit that lately she feels sexually aroused when cross dressing or imaging some of those good summers, and that this happens spontaneously when she is lonely. At present, she is living alone with her children, in fear of losing custody to her ex-husband. The helper can model compassion and encourage ventilation of sexual issues. As the woman recalls her other emotions in recounting events, she will be able to expand her arousal and/or accept cross dressing rather than being ashamed.

In both of the preceding examples, the client has an atypical sexual response issue, but the counselor is likely to spend more time on general self worth or family adjustment after divorce. Helping the client with the sexual variant will be very important however to the person's whole mental health. At other times, the only presenting problem may be a sexual variant, such as when a person wants to stop providing or using prostitution, and then much of the focus will be on that.

STEPS TO WORKING WITH ALL SEXUAL VARIATIONS

The following six steps can be used in working with clients who have sexual variations. These steps are to be integrated with the usual phases of counseling.

1. The client is helped to explore and describe the atypical sexual behavior in the context of who he/she is and how his/her sexuality developed.

2. The client's help is enlisted in clarifying and accepting those sexual variations which come to seem correct and right.

3. The client is helped to focus on the aspects which seem to cause problems/pain/stress, and what the difficulty is.

4. Using sexual enrichment techniques which are helpful with anyone, the client is given counseling suggestions designed to build on existing arousal patterns and fantasy, and broaden in the desired direction.

5. Evaluation of progress becomes support for trying new things rather than staying stuck. The counselor encourages being creative and having a sense of humor and developing more of a feeling of ownership about sexual behavior.

6. Referrals are made as appropriate.

In the action phase of counseling, the emphasis can be on changing the cognitive part ("Only X will turn me on"), or on the behavioral part (try new sexual expression, change the reward system, learn new skills or fantasy). General agreement exists in the literature that altering cognitive distortions which maintain atypical behavior helps the client who wants to change, and success is also reported when the client works on the behavior first and then the attitudes. Often both are used in sophisticated treatment programs.

Of course the counselor is accustomed to working on internal self-talk along with behavior for other types of problems. For instance, "What goes on for you when you are planning to skip school?" and "Let's make a contract not to skip for a set time that you decide on," are familiar approaches. Referring to unwanted sexual variations as a habit like gambling, drinking, or overeating helps normalize the "taboo" sexual behavior and gives a model for dealing with change which is difficult. The counselor needs to realize that atypical sexual behavior is learned, maintained and modified just like any human behavior. Making comparisons with other kinds of habits helps a client realize that commitment, effort, and taking it a step at a time are needed for change.

EXAMPLES: Modifications Desired by Clients, with Good Results

"So I still fall back into following a great tush for a block or two, but know I'll use the image to enjoy my own partner. I just don't let myself get mad when I can't squeeze every juicy one I see. My sex life is better than most people's."

"There's still nothing quite as good for me as a full-fledged group scene with masks and medical implements, but if it's twice a year that's okay. And the rest of time sex is good, too."

"When I look back at how I used to get people to jam things into me I can't believe it. Now I'm a deep massage freak!"

The counselor should be aware that pornography is an eight billion dollar industry in the U.S., much of it portraying sexual variants. This can exist only because a great many consumers have atypical sexual preferences. Some of the behaviors and the sex industry which reflects them may be harmless, while others are criminal. The counselor is asked to help each client find what is appropriate and safe.

REFERRAL

Assessment is important in order to avoid working with deeply troubled clients, beyond the reach of a counselor's experience. A person who is functioning well in many areas, but has an unusual sexual preference, has health to build on. And the counselor can work with the strengths of people who have overcome other problems such as alcoholism, and are motivatd to work on atypical sexual behavior. However, when a really disturbed person presents an atypical sexual problem or is likely to cause distress to others (without sufficient resources for self control), a referral to a specialist is necessary.

EXAMPLES: Behavior Necessitating Referral

A 34 year old man habitually exposes his genitals to school children, and has that as his only sexual fantasy or behavior.

A young man seems out of touch with reality; he crossdresses in garish ways and keeps being beaten because he cannot differentiate between what is acceptable for main street rather than a night club act.

A heterosexual or lesbian woman finds sexual activities impossible unless she sees/tastes blood, can't keep a job, and concentrates poorly in the interview.

A woman who dresses as a man is focused on finding others to control, manipulates teens into bathrooms, requires degrading rituals, and lies about arrests.

In these examples the "unacceptableness" of the sexual variation is not what suggests referral, but rather the compulsive quality combined with risk, and the lack of broader sexuality or mental health on which to build.

CONCLUSION

A final note about working with atypical sexual behavior is to call attention to its stubborn nature. The counselor often senses a passive-aggressive power struggle, especially when the variant is stated as unwanted but the client claims he/she cannot change. If the counselor suggests that perhaps the client should not change, the person may shift to accepting more responsibility. What seems to be reflected in the counseling sessions is the obsessive quality of many of these behaviors, and the fact that they developed in opposition to what society approves. Ambivalence is to be expected, manipulation and pressure are contraindicated, and the client needs honest encouragement to move in a freely chosen direction.

The counselor can suggest reasonable goals ("Let's explore the alternatives to having sex only with young women who dress like children"), rather than being drawn into a goal the client may unconsciously resent ("...find a better outlet"). Change requires time when atypical sexual behavior is involved, and patience which reflects belief in the client. Often, no reason exists to struggle against a particular atypical sexual behavior. A mature, calm counselor who helps a client see a sexual variation in perspective will contribute immensely to the person's mental health.

CHAPTER 6, PART 4

CHILD SEXUAL ABUSE/INCEST

Some things just aren't talked about:

> 38% of all females in the U.S. will experience some form of sexual abuse (from family sexual contact to stranger rape) before they are 18.

> Half the victims of reported rape in the U.S. are under 18, and one quarter are under the age of 12.

> 50 to 80% of children in shelters, juvenile homes, or under the care of social agencies have been sexually abused.

> 1.2 million children are annually exploited in child prostitution and child pornography.

> 80% of all prostitutes were sexually abused in childhood.

This information is based on recent research and was compiled by Florence Rush, of Women Against Pornography. Varying statistics exist, due to the methodological and sampling difficulties inherent in this type of research; for instance, the subcategory of women incest victims is currently estimated at 14 to 28% of the population. Regardless of ambiguity about exact numbers, the extent of the problem of child sexual abuse is being recognized and receiving national attention.

The documentation is good enough to conclude that one out of three girls are victims of some form of sexual abuse. The number of boys is lower but significant; although statistics vary with the research methods, 5 to 20% of reported victims of child sexual abuse are boys. Retrospective research with adults shows that only 6 to 10% of those people who were sexually abused as children disclosed it to any authority. Therefore, while the full extent of the ongoing problem for male children and adolescents is not yet known, without question a widespread problem exists.

Terminology is difficult. When do you refer to sexual contact with a minor as pedophilia (preference for sex with children), and when does it become sexual assault? Do you consider it homosexual child abuse if a usually heterosexual adult male victimizes boys, and does this change if some of his victims are girls? How do you make the distinction about whether an adolescent perpetrator is a juvenile sex offender or "just a kid experimenting?" Girls from 13 to 18 years of age are a highly vulnerable group; where does child sexual abuse shade into seduction, exploitation, and statuatory rape? Is the label incest or child sexual abuse if the offender is mother's long term, live-in partner? Fortunately counselors do not have to make the distinctions that State Attorneys do, and can listen to the client in order to discover the meaning of the sexual events for that victim, offender, or family.

Denial is pervasive about all aspects of incest and child sexual abuse. Children are victimized at all social and educational levels, but it may be more hidden at the middle and upper end of the economic scale. A wise procedure is for a counselor to check for negative child/adolescent sexual experiences more than once, during any kind of sexuality-related counseling. Words such as "incest," "offender," and "sexual abuse" are best avoided in favor of simple questions like, "Did anyone touch you sexually when you were younger?" or, "Is anyone acting in a sexy way...?"

As a counselor becomes more skilled in exploring sexual issues with clients, he/she can be shocked by the amount of pressured sexual activities which are reported as ongoing, recent, or part of a client's history. Sigmund Freud had the same experience and resolved it by deciding that his women client's reports were fantasy after all. Unfortunately, the counselor will find that current data about the sexual exploitation and abuse of children and adolescents are grim fact.

Perhaps the most confusing aspect for both counselor and client is the amount of secrecy, denial (conscious and unconscious), shame, and distortion which surround incest and sexual child abuse. Where families have "secrets" (such as a sexually abusive or alcoholic parent), often the script is "Don't Feel, Don't Trust, Don't Talk," described so well in the book by Claudia Black, *It Will Never Happen to Me*. Even when recognizing the need for help, people from these situations have great difficulty being open about the circumstances, and tend to feel terrible discussing the abuse.

Counselor usually find that time and a considerable amount of listening are needed for a clear picture of what is really happening (or happened) to emerge. The need for empathy and support in order to understand the situation, can conflict with the need for crisis intervention when ongoing abuse is suspected. The counselor needs to keep the child victim's welfare in the forefront, before legal, practical, or bureaucratic needs. Experience and growing skill help the counselor decide when and how to work in each situation.

DEFINITIONS

Textbook descriptions and first person accounts of incest vary, although the central concept of sexual contact between an adult and a minor in a family-type relationship is constant. Child-adolescent/adult sexual contact beyond the family circle is covered under child sexual abuse statutes, which also vary in their details. Counselors must know the law in order to cooperate with prosecutors and courts. Yet the emotional impact on the victim does not necessarily parallel how their legislature defined the crimes of pedophilia, incest, statuatory rape, lewd and lascivious behavior, sexual misconduct, or child sexual abuse.

The factors which help the counselor assess the impact on each victim must be carefully listened for and focused on in the individual case. The following exercise will help trainees begin to think about what assumptions they presently have.

DEFINING CHILD SEXUAL ABUSE

Legal definitions of incest and child sexual abuse vary from state to state. The counselor must be aware of the legal definiton and the laws within the state where he/she is counseling. Equally important, however, is for the counselor to focus on mental health issues. The following activity is a means for a counselor to judge what he/she considers important as he/she works with a client.

1. Circle the five items which you believe to be most abusive from the following list of 10 sexual encounters which involve children. Most people find them unpleasant to contemplate, and yet specific details are necessary to clarify the issues involved.

   a. A father frequently "feels up" his 11 year old daughter and jokes with her brothers about how she is developing physically, and "will be ready pretty soon."

   b. A teacher claims that a 10 year old girl "talks like a soap opera" about her mother's boyfriends. The girl says: "I'm lucky because I can't get knocked up yet" (the only term she knows for pregnancy).

   c. A father often masturbates to fantasies of having sex with his 13 year old daughter (what if she were 6 or 16?).

   d. A 12 year old boy performs oral sex on his 18 year old brother and several of his brother's friends; he is paid $20.00. (Would it make a difference if he were a girl and intercourse was involved?)

   e. A couple with children 3 and 8 leave their bedroom door open while having intercourse. The children begin to fight, so the father breaks it up by obliging one of them to sit in the corner of the bedroom while the parents continue having sex.

   f. A mother frequently enters the bathroom when her 11 year old son is in the shower. She often gives him an enema for no reason (and the warm water is arousing to him).

   g. Parents cannot understand why the children in a family avoid one grandfather. A boy is overheard telling his cousin to "Watch out—he doesn't stop at finger fucking either."

   h. A disabled child comes home from summer day camp with a variety of little gifts. He/she has red marks on his/her neck, seems to be sore and swollen in the genital area, and suddenly is secretive and withdrawn.

   i. A twelve year old boy is found in a tent having intercourse with his nine year old adopted sister. She seems rigid, detached, and afraid of disclosure.

   j. A daughter tries to avoid being fondled by her mother, but the mother tells her that no one ever died from a little doodling.

2. Reread the other five (ones not circled) and consider whether you find them harmful or potentially so.

3. Put into words your own criteria for deciding whether sexual abuse exists in particular situations.

4. Please do not read further until Items 1, 2, and 3 are completed; reread directions which precede the list of items and make your own judgments.

5. Now notice which factors you judged as most important: age differences? gender? presence or absence of physical force? type of sexual activity? other? All ten situations are or have a potential for incest/child sexual abuse. The important learning for you as a counselor is to become aware of what you judge as most important.

ASSESSING SEXUAL ABUSE

In real life the counselor is wise to avoid making any deterministic assumptions about the effects of specific kinds of child sexual abuse. A helper who assumes that father-daughter incest is the most traumatizing might not "hear" a client who expected little from her divorced father, but was devastated by sexual contact with a respected clergyman or teacher. In a similar way, a counselor who has decided that seduction by a trusted figure is the worst, may not be prepared for the client who has a startle reflex to casual touch ten years after sexual assault by a feared, hired man. The important sensitivity for the counselor to attain is to know what some of the painful variables are, in order to individualize for each client.

Terminology is always important and the counselor may elect to refer to clients with a history of child sexual abuse as "victims" or as "survivors." Both terms are used in this training program, however no single word adequately captures the impact of this experience.

Factors to Consider

When making an assessment of sexual abuse, the following list of factors needs to be considered:

> **Relationship.** Family, friend, trusted person, authority figure, new-old relationship, expectations?
>
> **Age.** Victim? Offender? Degree of difference seen from the victim's perspective. Developmental issues at the time of victimization.
>
> **Sex.** Same? Other? Meaning to the victim?
>
> **Force.** Physical, emotional-seductive, pressure, "secret," emotional blackmail, anxiety?
>
> **Guilt.** What form? Victim blames self? Blamed by offender?
>
> **Fear.** Psychological, religious, physical, social?
>
> **Sexual Activities.** "Showing," fondling, arousal, oral sex, "games," anal penetration, intercourse, other?
>
> **Degradation, Humiliation.** "Talking dirty," excrement, pain, pictures?
>
> **Deprivation.** Was there also a lack of love, security, emotional support?
>
> **Duration.** Age begun? Ended? How often? Predictable or erratic?
>
> **Incentives.** Given a punishment, enticement, deception, threats?

Multiple. How many offenders? Other victims? Same time or separate instances?

Recall. Remembered or repressed? Flashbacks? Aspects come back with counseling?

Perspective. Incidental or a dominant aspect of growing up? Degree of cover-up which occurred?

Disclosure. Ever occur? To whom? Reactions of significant others?

Consequences. Any familial, health, educational, or legal treatment, or attention?

Residuals. What areas of the person's life seem to be affected? Self esteem, mood (depression, anxiety), substance abuse, sexuality, relationships?

TREATING VICTIMS

One cannot generalize about the effects of child sexual abuse; the counselor's strongest asset is to listen supportively and draw out the client. During the exploration phase, reactions of the client and the description of what happened are likely to change and evolve. The purpose of this dialogue is far more than just ventilation or information gathering. Much of a child sexual abuse victim's recollections are fragmented, distorted, and deeply felt, so the process of working through feelings and events with a supportive person results in necessary integration.

As the victim talks about what happened, he/she also becomes aware of long-held negative assumptions about the self and others which are damaging. The impact of the incest or sexual abuse becomes clearer as it is explored. Insight alone is not a cure, but the harmful results of the abuse can be a focus in the second phase of counseling. Then a remedial/corrective program can be planned for the action phase of counseling. The counselor's purpose is to help the client face what happened, allow the client's maturing-self to help the victim-self deal with the experience, and then to come to some resolution or remedial plan.

The counselor must be sure to allow time for feelings and reactions to evolve before trying to conclude anything about the persistent effects. Earlier questionnaires showed that whereas some respondent felt their lives were ruined by sexual abuse, others claimed that the effects were minimal or even somewhat positive. In more recent studies, such as those described in *Child Sexual Abuse: New Therapy and Research* (1984), by David Finkelhor, are outlined the characteristics of high-risk children and perpetrators, and the long term effects of childhood sexual abuse. Just as in grief counseling, the client may experience denial, anger, guilt, and depression very strongly at different points in the process of working through.

Child Victim

A counselor cannot be sure how a particular client will eventually feel about being sexually used by an older person when he/she was a child. However, having some idea about the impact on many victims is helpful in order to respond more adequately. A helping person who meets with an 8 year old in the emergency room of a hospital will have a different task than one who talks to the same patient about the incident at age 16 or 36. Knowing older victims helps with present ones.

EXAMPLE: Office Interview with Parents of a 4 Year Old

Mother: *"This whole year Carrie acted different—hyper—ever since last fall. It's hard to believe that Ginny's husband* (day care operator) *has been doing these things to Carrie. Ginny's so wonderful with children."* (Nearly incoherent.)

Father: *"What difference does that make after what he did? You'd better believe it. Carrie's probably messed up for good. She'll never be the same again."* (Bitter expression.)

Counselor: *"We need to talk about your pain and worries, and I'd like to help you pull together as a couple on this. But first, I really have to ask about Carrie. All I have is the brief ER report on your four year old. Where is she now?"*

Mother: *"At my mother's. She's playing with her cousins today."*

Counselor: *"That sounds good. Can you understand why Carrie needs security and positive attention, especially now?"*

Father: *"Well—the guy's arrested. But of course he's out waiting for trial. He knows I'll kill him if I see him around our place—I don't think he'll risk it."*

Counselor: *"Certainly, you want to protect Carrie's physical safety. I hope the law takes care of the offender quickly and I'll do anything I can to help. But there are other important things we can do for Carrie now. It is important for you to let Carrie know that..."*

COMMENTS: At this point the counselor covers the following points:

Carrie must be protected from recurrence.

The adult was wrong; his behavior is not usual or okay.

The legal system has the responsibility to deal with the offender.

Carrie is not naughty or at fault.

She can talk about the offender, about dreams, and draw pictures or point out what happened on dolls. Meetings will be arranged with the counselor to "talk about this and other things."

She will be asked what she wants to happen, what she needs.

She is old enough to be included in the new day care plans (visiting possible ones), consulted on how the counseling is going, and informed about the legal consequences to the offender (not necessarily in detail).

She will be loved and supported with special care during this time.

The counselor may have a list such as the preceding, or make one, and dialogue with the parents explaining each point. Then the counselor continues.

Counselor: *"I want to stress that while Carrie will need some careful sex education, she is still the same little girl."*

Mother: *"Maybe we shouldn't mention it to Carrie, or bring it up so much. She's young and may forget."*

Counselor: *"It's hard for you to face, I know. But according to the ER report the sexual misuse went on for a year and a lot happened. When child molesting is buried or ignored, the results are likely to cause trouble later. Now is the time to help Carrie really get over it."*

Father: *"There is no use pretending. But what can you do for a little kid? It seems some kind of punishment might help her remember and never get into anything like that again."*

Counselor: *"All of us want it never to happen again, but punishment would increase the damage. She needs uncomplicated love. A meeting soon of the three of you and me will be a good place to begin, and then some sessions with Carrie, and perhaps also one family meeting with your other children."*

Mother: *"I just wish we could go back to this time last year. Carrie was such a calm, happy 3 year old..."* (Cries.)

Counselor: *"It is not your fault that Carrie was the victim of a crime. I'd like to spend the rest of the time today, and maybe more next week, helping you see Carrie as the innocent 4 year old she is. She certainly can be happy, and it is important that you all pull together. Carrie needs her family to be solid, especially now."*

COMMENTS: The parents will need help to respond positively to Carrie and to learn about providing appropriate on-going sex education. A counselor is not always needed for child sexual abuse, when something like brief fondling by a stranger or exhibitionism occurs. Trusted, supportive family members are often able to help the child and provide education about sexual safety which is not oppressive. However when the perpetrator is a family member or trusted acquaintance, when the abuse is of longer duration or consists of threatening sexual contact, or when the family is punitive or denying, counseling is important.

Disclosure

When a counselor learns of or suspects on-going incest or child sexual abuse, reporting the crime is necessary. This is required by law to insure the greatest likelihood of a halt to the sexual exploitation, and a possibility of child protection. A counselor who promises "not to tell," and agrees to treat a victim or offender for an occasional hour, is colluding with the crime. Once the responsible human service agencies are contacted, the counselor can help the victim and family face the problem, cooperate with the authorities, and become healthier.

If the disclosure comes about as a result of the child "telling," the counselor needs to help the child know that he/she did the right thing, and that people should be upset at the offender and not at them. Sometimes an apology from the offender and promise not to ever repeat is in order, if that is possible. Apology, promises, entreaties or not, the offense must be reported and a plan made.

Should the child have positive feelings for the offender (which can well happen), a supportive procedure is to admit the offender's good qualities, "but he/she shouldn't have touched you privately. Grownups are supposed to know better than that." If the offender is a father or mother or other close adult relative, the child needs to know the offender is receiving treatment, or is being removed from the home until he/she "gets better." State laws must be followed for reporting the offense, and while an open atmosphere is important, the impact on the child of the legal procedures should be handled carefully.

Intervention and treatment programs for victims, offenders, and families vary with the resources available. A team approach with an overall treatment program and plan is best. While this practice is growing, it is not available for all and many times the counselor will be alone with difficult decisions in child abuse and incest cases. Helpers are urged to attend local training workshops, join child protection teams, and work to expand sexual abuse treatment options in their community.

Adolescent Victims

The teenager who was victimized recently, or as a child, needs to know that the following often occur:

> Self blame and guilt are common. Even if he/she liked the offender and cooperated, he/she was not responsible. (Some find

it helpful to be reminded that people are used to doing what older persons tell them, of meeting expectations and fearing rejection, and trust that the adult knows what is okay.)

A sense of separation of self from sexual feelings and behavior often occurs. They may still find it hard to say "no" to sexual overtures, and have a tendency to "just go through the motions." Or sexuality may be completely avoided.

Often a lack of trust exists in one's own judgment, leading to an apparent dependency on others or lack of caring for oneself.

Where incest exists, a child, girl or boy, may find himself/herself in a parental role at home, expected to do for others and fill in for mother/father.

Cynicism may exist that others "want only one thing," resulting in a persistent distrust of others' motives, and a decision to "play the game." The world may feel hostile; complying sexually or avoiding sex may seem the safest accomodation.

Generalized, low-level depression, low self esteem, and poor body image are frequently associated with sexual abuse.

Suicide, self harm, or running away may be fantasized or tried. Drug and alcohol dependency are common.

Real confusion about relationships and boundaries may be present if the perpetrator was a family member or trusted person.

More current fear about disclosure and change may be present than of the sexual interaction.

If the victim is a boy, he may be vulnerable to aggressive behavior in response to being a victim when young, serious alcohol/drug abuse, a tendency to separate sex from relationships, doubts about his masculinity (especially if the offender was male), underachievement, and problems with intimacy.

Not all adolescents who were or are being sexually abused develop the above, and many teens who are not victims certainly have some of these problems. However the counselor can ask any youth: "Has anyone who is older than you ever contacted you sexually?" and help work it through if it occurred. The hardest group to communicate with are those defiant, cynical adolescents who have been termed "throwaway children," and who have become delinquent or drug/alcohol dependent. Sexual abuse more often than not is in the early lives of runaways, teen prostitutes (male and female), and youth in all types of correctional facilities. Youngsters in this group do not respond well to one hour a week of counseling, but really need to become part of a rehabilitation program if possible.

Teenage victims will have some of the child's and some of an adult's concerns and symptoms. Usually the counseling will be easier if the incest or molestation was in the past and the perpetrator is no longer present. However, even in active cases, if practical safety can be arranged and a stable environment provided, teenage discovery can be positive. The adolescent is closer in time to the abuse and has had less time to develop the negative reactions, and yet has more maturity than the child to deal with it. He/she can feel the appropriate anger at the offender and/or at others who were not there for them, and then cooperate in a program to repair the resultant damage.

Adult Victims of Incest/Child Sexual Abuse

Experienced clinicians attest to the persistent negative effects of childhood sexual experiences, and the frequency of disguised requests for help. In recent literature this kind of client's diagnosis may be described as *stress trauma syndrome* or *delayed stress disorder*. However such clients are frequently misdiagnosed as borderline personality, depressives, bipolar affective disorders, agoraphobic, sexually dysfunctional, alcoholic, hysteric, bulimia, character disordered, or schizoid. While symptoms ascribed to any of these terms may certainly exist, the basic history of child sexual abuse is often ignored, both because the provider doesn't look thoroughly and the client is trying to suppress it.

Child sexual abuse, especially incest, often occurs in the context of a disordered family, a rigid family, or a family with distortions of trust and appropriate roles. The adult survivor is likely to have experienced damage in addition to the sexual misuse. Sometimes as an adult the victim can recall some sexual trauma but does not seem to "deal" with it, saying, in effect, that "so much else was going on and sex was just part of it." This distancing is used by women but especially by men. The counselor may have to focus supportively on how the child sexual abuse could be contributing to current problems with sexuality, self esteem, or relationships.

In other instances the early material can be repressed for a time, but emerges when a current "trigger" like adult sexual activity, a television show, independence from family, pregnancy, marital problems, or any other event reminds the person of the earlier trauma. Alternating repression and intrusion of sexual memories may occur countless times over a number of years, and the counselor can meet with the client at any point on this exhausting roller coaster. If the experiences have never been integrated, the original emotions of fear, confusion, sexual feelings, and guilt may be vivid; the counselor is well advised to be supportive and not push too fast.

Adults who were victimized as children need to know that the following often occur:

> The panic or regression they feel does not mean they are "crazy" but rather dealing with painful, old material. Their adult self can gradually cope with it and see the original experiences more comfortably.
>
> Although the incidents may seem long ago and insignificant, they can have considerable influence on one's life and development. Sometimes recovering the past is disillusioning in the extreme, as events are reconstructed and seen in a clearer light.
>
> Mixed feelings about self, perpetrator, and significant others may have to be worked through.
>
> Regret may be present about self defeating behavior and missed opportunities which occurred in adolescence or young adulthood as a result of the sexual misuse.
>
> Chronic low self worth, poor body image, and distrust of self and others may be partially or significantly related to the abuse.
>
> Anger at self for "not stopping it sooner," "avoiding it," or "preventing it," is common. Then anger at the mother or other family members may occur. Finally, the ambivalence or rage at the perpetrator which is often unleashed may be shattering for a while.

Current relationship problems may be related to child sexual abuse. Incest especially may lead to intergenerational patterns of distorted sexual activity.

Alarming symptoms of confusion, flashbacks, and numbing are not weaknesses, but indicate that material is present which needs to be faced, worked through, and resolved.

Awareness of what seem "inappropriate" sexual reactions in the present, related to earlier experience, increase the sense of original guilt and result in self distrust. New sexual associations in the present are needed.

A much higher incidence of all kinds of sexual dysfunction is a frequent result, but it can be treated and overcome. This can range from sexual aversion to repetitive sexual acting out.

An individualized plan is usually developed as the period of "working through" progresses. Group work such as sexual enhancement for couples, assertiveness training workshops, an incest survivors group, or perhaps a weight loss or communication skills program are especially helpful. When the client has gained a more stable feeling of integration and empowerment, he/she can increase confidence by moving beyond the shelter of the counseling relationship. The gradual reduction of counseling support and discussion of possible resources for future personal growth are advisable. When the victim sees himself/herself as a survivor and has relegated the sexual abuse to a background role in life, termination of counseling can proceed.

RESOURCES RELATING TO SURVIVORS
OF CHILD SEXUAL ABUSE

These texts provide extensive information for the counselor:

Blackman, A. (Ed.). (1984). Special child sexual abuse issue. *SIECUS Report*. New York: SIECUS.

Conte, J., & Shore, D. (Eds.). (1982). *Social work and child sexual abuse*. New York: Haworth Press.

Finkelhor, D. (1984). *Child sexual abuse: New theory and research.* New York: The Free Press.

Mrazek, P. (Ed.). (1983). *Child sexual abuse.* New York: Pergamon Press.

Renshaw, T. (1982). *Incest, understanding and treatment.* Boston, MA: Little, Brown.

Rush, F. (1980). *The best kept secret: Sexual abuse of children.* Englewood Cliffs, NJ: Prentice Hall.

Sgroi, S. (1982). *Handbook of clinical intervention in child sexual abuse.* Lexington, MA: Lexington Books.

Walker, C., Bonner, B., & Kaufman, K. (1986). *The physically and sexual abused child.* Maxwell House, NJ: Pergamon.

Weisberg, D. (1984). *Children of the night.* Lexington, MA: D. C. Heath.

Excellent self-help books for adult survivors and the families of younger victims are found in most libraries. The counselor will find them a helpful introduction:

Bass, E., & Thornton, L. (Eds.). (1983). *I never told anyone: Writings by women survivors of child sexual abuse.* New York: Harper and Row. (Helps one come as close to the experience as possible.)

Black, C. (1982). *It will never happen to me.* Denver, CO: MAC Print.

Gordon, S., & Gordon, J. (1984). *A better safe than sorry book: A family guide for sexual assault prevention.* Fayetteville, NY: Ed-U Press.

Herman, J. (1982). *Father-daughter incest.* Cambridge, MA: Harvard University Press.

Hyde, M. (1984). *Sexual abuse: Let's talk about it.* Philadelphia, PA: Westminster Press. (National resource and treatment list included.)

Loontjens, L. (1984). *Talking to children/talking to parents about sexual assault.* Network Publications, 1700 Mission Street, Santa Cruz, CA: Network Publications. Includes a copy of *He Told Me Not to Tell,* the popular booklet for children.

Sanford, L. (1980). *The silent children: A parents' guide to the prevention of child sexual abuse.* New York: Doubleday.

Materials such as the following are written for children generally, and can be useful as part of preventative education in the treatment of an abused child:

Freeman, L. (1982). *It's my body: A book to teach young children how to resist uncomfortable touch.* Planned Parenthood of Snohomish County, 2722 Colby, Suite 515, Everett, WA 98201.

Hindman, J. (1983). *A very touching book...for little people and for big people.* Durkee, OR: McClure-Hindman books.

Wachter, O. (1983). *No more secrets for me.* Boston, MA: Little Brown.

Williams, J. (1983). *Red flag green flag people.* Rape and Abuse Crisis Center, PO Box 1655, Fargo, ND 58107.

Journals. Since about 1980 an ever-increasing number of regular articles have been published on the treatment of child sexual abuse. Any index or computerized search will find hundreds of recent references. An excellent example is:

Gelinas, D. (1983). The Persisting Negative Effects of Incest," *Psychiatry, 46*(4), 312-332.

Regional resource centers offer training programs, curricula, speakers, and consultants on all aspects of child sexual abuse. Excellent new audio-visual materials are available for rental. Local health departments, human service agencies, and colleges of education have names and addresses of contact people.

Specific resources are available such as

Groth, N. (1984). *Anatomical drawings for use in the investigation and intervention of child sexual abuse.* Newton Center, MA: Forensic Mental Health Associates, 3 Ireland Road.

Sweet, P. (1981). *Something happened to me.* Racine, WI: Mother Courage Press. A workbook designed to be used by a professional with child victims.

All the preceding resources were developed in a few years because of the real concern in society about child sexual abuse. The problem has not gone away however, and the resources are waiting to be used by helping professionals.

TREATING THE OFFENDER

Counselors working in the community seldom realize that they meet child sexual abusers professionally and socially on a regular basis. Exact numbers are not yet available, but since 100,000 to 500,000 children are sexually abused each year, the offenders exist in large numbers also. The ratio is difficult to calculate since convicted child molesters often admit to 25 to 100 victims, but an incest offender is likely to have 1 to 3 contacts within the family and few outside it. Therefore, all practitioners are in a position in their agency, school, church, or private practice to meet hidden offenders.

The stereotypes are false which label the perpetrators as "dirty old men" (only 10% of offenders are over 50 years old), or drifters, alcoholics, retarded, illiterate, or deranged. Most offenders are indeed male (over 90%), a large number have suffered physical, emotional, or sexual abuse in childhood, but other generalizations cannot be made. For instance, convicted child molesters have a high rate of alcohol abuse, but no more than a similar group of prisoners incarcerated for non-sexual offenses. The minority are in jail. The counselor will be shocked to realize that men and some women who are well educated, hold responsible positions, and are law abiding in other ways will persist in having sex with children, either their own or someone else's.

Credentials

Given the magnitude of the problem, an expectation for any helping professional is to be prepared to work with adults who abuse children sexually. Many actively avoid it because they are not specialists; therefore much of the problem is never confronted. A counselor can distinguish between active and inactive offenders and report anyone who is sexually active with a child to the appropriate social service agency, and then volunteer to help with the offender as part of a team. The counselor is not to apologize to the offender for "telling," but can take the attitude that reporting was the first step toward the offender getting control of his/her life. Working as part of the process is a good way to obtain consultation, supervision, and training in working with sex offenders.

Counselors may discover that a person has a history of sex with children or teens, but is currently inactive and wants help (or is ambivalent). This offender may refuse to go elsewhere for treatment; the counselor can provide a safe place to lower the sexual tension around the secret, to strengthen the resolve not to act, and to give education and encouragement toward a positive, adult adjustment. Again, the counselor can obtain consultation and supervision and must be alert to indicators that the inactive offender is moving toward action in order to confront and prevent it. The treatment of sex offenders is a developing field and few "experts" may live in an area; therefore concerned counselors can perform a valuable service by becoming professionally involved when possible.

Types of Offenders

One of the major differences to keep in mind when working with offenders is the distinction between regressed and fixated (arrested development) individuals. A. Nicholas Groth (1979) has conducted extensive research and training to acquaint professionals with ways to assess and treat the differences. Counselors working with child sexual abuse/incest offenders can make a helpful distinction based on the question of whether the perpetrator has ever had a satisfactory, age appropriate, adult sexual adjustment. If so, then sexual offenses against children may be due to regression to an earlier stage due to present stresses (loss of a job, marital breakup, or accident).

The regressed client may benefit from counseling to find ways to reduce the stressor (re-employment, health care, couples counseling), and also from sexuality counseling focused on regaining an adult sexual orientation. As with other sex offenders, this client does best when some legal constraints or other consequences keep him in treatment. A worthwhile approach is to take time to uncover possible sexual or physical abuse in the perpetrator's own history, because this can be worked through. The more adequate and successful the offender's previous adult sexual adjustment was, the more likely he/she is to be able to regain it. Without minimizing the difficulty of this kind of counseling, the counselor and client can work with the legal, societal, and family reinforcements for maintaining an adult sexual preference.

A different situation is presented by an offender whose sexual development was fixated at an earlier age, and who never progressed beyond an immature stage of sexual development. Counseling is best provided as part of a larger treatment program, working within legal restraints on the offender.

EXAMPLE: Arrested Sexual Development

Bart, a 17 year old boy from a prominent family, was discovered sexually molesting 9 to 11 year old girls. He was allowed to join the military as soon as possible, rather than making the offenses public and pressing charges. Bart stayed in the armed forces, married a responsible, sexually inhibited woman at age 26; they had several children. He secretly continued to hire child prostitutes, to pressure sex from very young babysitters, and eventually forced his daughters, at ages 5 to 10, into sexual service to him.

Since Bart had never attained a really adult pattern of sexual expression, he required an extensive treatment program with careful follow-through.

COMMENTS: With this kind of case, the counselor can be a key person in discovering and disclosing the offense, and in acting as a support and liason person for the offender and family during the disposition of the case. Counselors with adequate training can contribute greatly to individual and group treatment of offenders like Bart.

Bart, at age 40, still has impulses toward young girls but sees this as a weakness which he can control, and he has slowly developed a better relationship with his wife. Bart avoids the overuse of alcohol, situations which are provocative for him, and chooses never to fantasize or read about sex with children. Bart continues to see a counselor every month on a contract basis (he agrees to aversive consequences if he avoids appointments), and since the children are older, an incest supportive climate is no longer present. The goal continues to be improving Bart's adult sexual/marital/personal adjustment and avoiding even the possibility of sex with anyone's children. As time goes on, the former occupies most of the counseling, and it is no longer acceptable to Bart himself to go back to his earlier criminal behavior.

Subgroups of Offenders

Other types of child sexual abuse offenders who are often treated separately in the literature include the following:

Juvenile Sex Offender. Since their early acts may be "borderline" in terms of force or appropriateness, and their behavior is not yet chronic, considerable research, programs, and public funds are being focused on the under-18 offender. Since most adult abusers report beginning as minors, this is a highly significant group.

Antisocial Offender. A person whose sexual misuse of children (relatives or not) is part of a larger pattern of lawbreaking. These individuals steal a car when they want transportation, or at a different social level rig the books at work in their favor. Treatment oriented toward the sexual issue alone is inadequate.

Sadistic Offender. Accounts of torture, sexual abuse, and murder of children and teens generate counter-rage in almost everyone, and while uncommon are all too frequent. These assailants are severely distorted toward pathology in their overall personality development.

Pedophile. Some individuals profess to love children and to be powerfully attracted to them. They want to form "boy-love" societies or adore girls, treating them in sexual role playing fashion. Seeing through their rationalizations is not difficult, but helping the pedophile develop an adult orientation may be.

Incest Offender. Many studies have delineated types of incest family systems. Some may be domestic tyrants whose families keep the fearful secret, but numerous other patterns exist. Feelings of ownership and "entitlement," with the ability to believe distorted rationalizations is common.

Stepfamily Incest Offender. One of the most common sex crimes against children, which is increasing with the number of blended families or live-in unmarried partners, is stepfamily incest. Boundaries are blurred and the offender justifies his/her actions by the lack of a biological relationship, or blames the younger person.

Rationalized Incest/Child Molester. The perpetrator justifies his/her behavior as "good" for the child or young person in some way. He/she may have a rigid, intricate thought system aimed at somehow continuing the activities. Paranoid-type distortions are common.

As with other kinds of forced sexual behavior, the counselor does not have to spend exhaustive time categorizing the offender-client. Becoming familiar with predictable patterns, however, allows the helper to intervene earlier.

Counseling Approaches

The practitioner may be more disgusted with the incest/child molester than even with the rapist, but can realize that an adult who is attracted to children is highly insecure, usually seeking a less demanding partner. Reprehensible as the behavior is, a direction toward building confidence relating to adult partners is possible.

The counselor has several tasks including the following:

1. To explore the criminal sexual behavior and impulses and to help the client see them as dangerous and "not worth it," or "not for me." Constant no-nonsense reality testing is necessary here. Individual and group work often help to internalize the difference between impulses and entitlement to act on them.

2. To treat the client as a person at an immature stage of development who is working toward an acceptable adult sexual adjustment. Good sex education is absolutely necessary. Exercises such as self stimulation with pictures of adult partners (of the preferred sex), non-pressured pleasuring with adult partners, and other sexual enrichment homework can be assigned.

3. To work on other stress areas of the client's life, current and past, in order to prevent regression. Special care needs to be given to uncovering instances of earlier victimization, deprivation, and relieving present pressures.

4. To obtain legal incentives, when appropriate, to keep a sex offender in counseling. Alternate possibilities are to arrange to contact an important relative if appointments are missed, or for a letter to be mailed to an employer if the person tries to drop out of treatment. The client will agree to these ahead of time, and may need consequences when it becomes clear that the sexual behavior really has to stop.

Working with sex offenders is not easy or comfortable, but the counselor will find that empathy usually develops for the person with a problem, and a real satisfaction comes from helping him/her reach a better adjustment. A team approach is preferable, even if the adjuncts to counseling are more general such as communications or assertiveness groups, probation and parole officers, AA, battering prevention, decision making, or parenting groups. Many universities and corrections departments also have specialized programs which use sophisticated behavioral treatments (films or slides paired with shock or nauseous smells, self-administration of ammonia sniffs during inappropriate arousal, covert reinforcement), drug therapy, or multi-family therapy. Whenever possible, the counselor should arrange to work in conjunction with experienced people and use all resources possible.

Sexual behavior toward children can be a matter of degree and is easily denied by the perpetrator who has never been convicted or arrested. With any client the counselor can listen for sexual interest and tentative behavior toward children and teens, such as intrusive touching, following peeping, fantasy, or child pornography. Such clients can be acquainted with the possibility of regression under stress, and the tragic consequences for them if they allow their sexuality to focus there. Careful empathy may uncover strong arousal to children and this can then become the focus of treatment, whether or not the client has been discovered or thinks that "will power" will prevent overt acts.

RESOURCES REGARDING TREATING OFFENDERS

Helpful texts includes the following:

Burgess, A., & Clark, M. (Eds.). (1984). *Child pornography and sex rings.* Lexington, MA: Lexington Books.

Greer, J., & Stuart, I. (Eds.). (1983). *The sexual aggressor: Current perspectives on treatment.* New York: Van Nostrand Reinhold.

Groth, A. (1979). *Men who rape.* New York: Plenum. (Part of the book is focused on offenses against children.)

Knopp, F. (1982). *Remedial intervention in adolescent sex offenses: Nine program descriptions.* Syracuse, NY: Safer Society Press.

Knopp, F. (1984). *Retraining adult sex offenders: Methods and models.* Syracuse, NY: Safer Society Press.

Longo, R., & Groth, A. (1983). Juvenile sexual offenses in the histories of adult rapists and child molesters. *International Journal of Offender Therapy and Comparative Criminology, 27*(2), 150-155.

As with other rapidly evolving topics, one of the best sources of new information is the latest journal article. In addition, papers and treatment programs are presented at conferences and regional meetings of the helping professions.

CONCLUSION

Once a counselor has begun to understand the impact of child sexual abuse on the victim, the offender, the family, and on the next generation(s), it can never be forgotten. When a local or national case of child rape/molestation/incest/sexual abuse occurs, there is widespread publicity and indignation, but no one wants to think about it for very long. However, the helping professional who becomes knowledgeable about forced sex and children-adolescents is likely to have increasing numbers of individuals and families referred to him/her for counseling.

In addition to seeing victims (survivors) and offenders, the counselor is likely to be in a good position to work with wives, husbands, or siblings when child sexual abuse has occurred. One incident in a neighborhood, school, or camp may trigger a number of people to talk to helping professionals about similar things happening to them. The counselor needs to take measures to protect herself/himself from useless rage and frustration about the problem without becoming hardened. All the familiar suggestions which are helpful against burnout are important: a reasonable work load, varied duties, a support network, peer or other supervision, personal wellness and stress reduction techniques.

An additional step toward maintaining morale is to focus part of one's personal and professional energy on dealing with the problem itself. Whether through offering education and training, or working with the legal or political system, shelters for runaways, programs for offenders or services for families, the person seeing victims needs to contribute to the prevention of sex toward children. Because of the nature of the problem, the counselor is going to be asked to give and give and give, and needs to stay centered to work in the child sexual abuse field.

CHAPTER 6, PART 5

SEXUAL ASSAULT COUNSELING

Does sexual assault/rape differ from child sexual abuse in ways significant for the counselor? Some clients are unfortunately the victims of both, and some offenders are not particular about the age of the victim.

The question is important. Both are the result of an offender feeling entitled to use someone else sexually. The similarities are probably greater than the differences in terms of overall counseling. However, knowledge of the known distinctions will help provide better individual care.

One clear difference between child sexual abuse and sexual assault is the age of the victim. A minor is unable, legally, to give consent to any sexual act with an adult, and therefore by the codes of our society all forms of imposed sexual behavior (whether seduction or brute force) are illegal. The adult crime of rape turns primarily on the issue of consent, and therefore while seduction is legal over the age of 18, coercian, pressure, and forced sexual acts (varies by state) are felonies. Guilt and the assumption of victim cooperation may unfortunately be present in either child abuse or rape, but the developmental levels of the victim and offender differ enough to affect the counseling.

The counselor is well advised not to try too hard to make artificial distinctions among types of offenders and acts, their assumed causes, and the predicted effects on the victim. The following reasons help one know why the counselor needs not spend effort labeling:

1. A jumble of terms and definitions refer to statuatory rape, forcible rape, lewd and lascivious conduct, sodomy, indecent behavior, child sexual abuse, spousal rape, aggravated sexual assault, and related crimes. Going a few feet over a state line

can completely alter the legal picture, but not the impact on the victim.

2. A steady series of research studies attempt to differentiate acquaintance rape from stranger rape, power rapists from rage rapists, or among different types of coercian. The research is important, but still in its early stages.

3. Generalizations from studies done on narrow categories of convicted offenders or on victims of prosecuted rape cases cannot be applied broadly, because most offenses are undiscovered.

The helper needs to know local law and be familiar with research reports, but the important point when doing counseling is to consider that particular situation.

PREVALENCE

A trained helper can talk to hundreds of people over a period of years and never realize that a significant number were victims or offenders of sexual assault. Because the mental health damage is largely invisible and often repressed or denied, the counselor will be genuinely shocked when his/her sexuality counseling skills begin to uncover the magnitude of the problem.

Recent researchers (Koss, 1983) using interviews, surveys, or telephone contact with random samples of thousands of women showed surprising similarity. From 37% to 45% of all women report a history of being a victim of some form of sexual assault or victimization. To corroborate the assault component, 15% or more college men admit having raped women, and over 50% say they would (depending on the sample), if they could be sure of not getting caught. Many victims do not realize they have been raped until they have described an act of forced sex and are informed of the law. The estimate is that less than 10% of victims report a sexual assault for complex reasons, and only a small number seek help.

SOCIAL FACTORS

The fact that our culture has a "rape supportive belief system" is unpleasant to acknowledge. Under the disguise of sophistication or harmless earthy fun, we are surrounded by ads, TV, popular fiction, music, films, and overt/covert attitudes that support forced sex. While checking research for this chapter in a pleasant university library, the following were found scrawled on one study carrel wall: "Smegma Rules," "Eat Pink Steel," "Pussy Wants It," "Fuck your Mother" (who says American family traditions are dying out?), and "Snatch Women." A quick check of neighboring study areas revealed the same thing; highly varied handwriting reflected coercive sexual behavior toward women.

Crude, ugly terms are not expected in textbooks, but can easily be found by anyone who looks in public places. Polite people may choose to ignore clues to sexual violence in the environment, but the daily news records the actual reality. No one is immune; recent studies show that exposure to sexually violent films desensitizes "normal" (average) men to images of rape in a short time. Repeatedly researchers have shown that only a few coercive sex offenders are "mentally ill" in the broader sense; most resemble a random sample of average men.

RATIONALIZATIONS

1. *"Well, a lot of car accidents happen too, and people quickly get over the emotional shock and drive again. So what's the big deal?"*

> **REALITY.** Society prepares and helps people to deal with more predictable losses and tragedies. The long term effects of sexual assault are just being documented.

An analysis of many research studies reported in *Trauma and Its Wake* (Figley, 1985), revealed that the most consistently devastating and long lasting trauma has been experienced by Viet Nam veterans and sexual assault victims. One study (Kilpatrick et al., 1981) showed that 17 to 25% of untreated rape victims were symptom free at the end of one year, but that over three-fourths had continuing serious symptoms a year after the assault. Other studies show similar symptoms of past traumatic stress disorder after five years. As with child abuse, all comparisons of adult sexual abuse victims show high incidence of fear and anxiety, depression, and sexual dysfunction. The large number of women and significant number of men, who are victims of some form of sexual assault, experience trauma which is not readily overcome even with counseling.

2. *"People can avoid sexual assaults if they really try. The fact that so few are reported shows that women realize it's just as much their fault."*

   REALITY. Police records, social and rehabilitative services, and all other sources of data show that the offender is more often a family member, friend, or acquaintance of the victim than a stranger. Also, the perpetrator has the advantage of surprise and determination and has usually planned the act. In any case, victims (women and men) are seldom in a position to fight, and report being in shock or trying to survive and get away.

   Shame and guilt are cultural attitudes which many irrationally feel. One example is the sleeping victim who wonders whether she could have unknowingly smiled at a man on the street, some time before a total stranger broke into her locked apartment and raped her. Women assaulted in office buildings, in a parking lot after a party, or a young man who is raped while drinking after work, can be so shocked and ashamed that they just try to forget it. Also centuries of ignorance have blamed the victim for being "the arousing factor," so that even friendliness is assumed to be a kind of contributory negligence.

   Rape combines the explosive mixture of violence, sexuality, male and female stereotypes, trust and guilt in a toxic way. The anxiety, shame, and fear felt by victims are predictable as part of the aftermath of this crime. Early helpers are important in stopping a downward spiral, in helping the victim cope with shock and decisions, and for beginning the process of recovery. However, months or years after a rape, the victim may need to talk to a counselor, especially if the trauma was suppressed at the time because of this particular myth of victim responsibility.

3. *"They call everything rape these days."*

> **REALITY.** Counselor will hear variations of this from a client's family members, personnel at emergency facilities, and many others who should certainly know better. For those individuals who think that "real" rape occurs only in situations like "the widowed grandmother who is hit on the head and forced to have intercourse by an armed stranger," the law comes as a solid correction. One of the best antidotes for this is simply to quote the definition of sexual assault from the Model Penal Code, or from one's own state statute if it is similarly broad.

The public needs to hear the simple, legal definition of consent, and the many kinds of forced non-consensual genital and sexual contact which are criminal. Ignorant people show concern only for aggravated rape, where the genitals are slashed with glass or the victim's face smashed. This probably reflects the difficulty people have grasping the sexual aspects of rape, as compared to the more familiar condemnation of violence.

4. *"It wouldn't have happened if..."*

> **REALITY.** Many family members and helping professionals seem unusually analytical about sexual assault. They make attempts to locate the so-called mistake: "You never should have gone jogging after 5 o'clock," or "Didn't you know he had a fast reputation—why did you stay alone with him after work to clean up?" This is analogous to accusing a holdup victim of "asking for robbery," if he is well dressed or has ever given away money.

A chilling experience is to witness a sexual assault victim's reactions and experience ignored, while others give advice and ask fact questions. Even though helpers and family may be both repelled and curious about the sexual details, they are often unwilling to really listen to the victim's experience. The "correctors" reduce their own anxiety by analysis, which comes out as anger, skepticism, and blame toward the victim. Counselors can counter this type of continuing victimization.

5. *"You can't tell if it's really rape. It's one person's word against another's."*

> **REALITY.** Whereas many major crimes have a false report rate of over 25%, repeated studies have shown that sexual assault complaints are false in only 2% to 4% of the cases. Until recently, the victim's sexual history was on trial because of this myth of false accusation, but in spite of statutes which now exclude it, the victim's circumstances may covertly influence the outcome. The frightening result of this belief is that even with witnesses, medical reports, and physical evidence, offenders may not be convicted or may plea bargain for light sentences.

COUNSELING THE VICTIM

Close to the Time of the Crime

A counselor may be contacted fifteen minutes after a sexual assault has occurred or several weeks later. Within this span of time any or all of the following symptoms of rape trauma syndrome may be present:

> shock, denial, fear, confusion, anxiety, generalized distress, disruption of usual activity, regression to earlier ways of coping,

nightmares, waking flashbacks, avoidance of being alone, suicidal thoughts or attempts, uncontrolled weeping, deflected anger, sexual aversion, disturbed sleep, an increase in habitual defenses (drinking, hyperactivity, withdrawal, depression...), decreased concentration, somatic symptoms such as gastro-intestinal problems, rashes, eating disorders, and headaches.

The helper must begin to restore the victim's sense of worth and personal effectiveness because of the major trauma associated with fear, loss of control, shock, degradation, pain, and helplessness. However, the client may be preoccupied with any of the previously listed stress symptoms, can be trying to repress what happened, or may focus on relationships and pending decisions. The counselor needs to build a therapeutic relationship and explore before trying to focus and move toward any action. An unqualified amount of support may be needed during this crisis time.

A complication is the client's need for medical/legal help when he/she may not have the clarity to make decisions. A delicate balance must be maintained between strong support which facilitates movement towards medical and police assistance, and that which results in the victim continuing to feel manipulated, exposed, invaded, and helpless. The counselor's task is to encourage and clarify regarding the need for other services, without taking over in the zeal to act.

For some time after a trauma a person may not "make sense" about it in the usual way. The verbal report may be confused and inconsistent. The counselor or a support person needs to stay with a client during the time of disclosure about the sexual assault. Medical attention is available at emergency rooms, women's health centers, and crisis clinics. Health care is needed for possible injuries (many cannot be easily detected), prevention and treatment of sexually transmitted diseases, possible pregnancy, and the collection of evidence.

The client needs to know that evidence must be obtained with his/her consent at the time of the first medical exam (as soon after the offense as possible), but that the decision about whether to prosecute can be made later. If the client is able to hear it, the counselor may make the point that the state (district attorney) prosecutes the criminal offense—it is a public responsibility—and that the victim is simply a witness to what occurred. The counselor can encourage the collection of evidence, and protect the client from immediate pressure to decide about prosecution by family, legal, and health personnel. If the victim is adamantly negative about reporting, that must be respected. However, an anonymous report is sometimes made to the police with as much information about the assailant as possible, for the purpose of protecting the public from repeated attempts.

If the victim is a woman, questions regarding treatment for possible pregnancy cannot be postponed as easily as the decision about future legal action. The nurse practitioner or physician who does the history taking and pelvic exam can determine the probability of pregnancy. If the counselor is present, he/she can help the patient decide about options. Treatment protocols vary by locale, but the patient needs to know her risk of pregnancy from the forced sex and what can be done about it.

After determining that no pre-existing pregnancy existed at the time of the rape, the victim has some options regarding possible pregnancy resulting from the sexual assault:

1. Wait for several weeks to learn whether she is pregnant, at which time she can decide to carry to term or have an early abortion.

2. Immediately take one of the medications used to avoid pregnancy (the so-called "morning after" pill), to prevent implantation of an embryo. This is an unpleasant course of therapy, at a time when a person least needs to feel sick, and the powerful drugs may have serious side effects.

3. Other treatments to prevent or stop pregnancy may be available, depending on the facility.

Careful counseling and medical advice are absolutely necessary at this point. It is important to remember that all women have a legal right to information and treatment to avoid pregnancy, regardless of the beliefs of the particular hospital or caregivers.

After a trauma is an extremely difficult time to make any decisions. Yet following a sexual assault, a pelvic exam is usually done, blood is drawn, saliva is collected, pubic hair clippings and fingernail scrapings taken, other invasive procedures completed, injections made, sexual history taken, description taken and recorded of the assailant, discussion held to obtain description of sexual acts, and family or friends are notified. These are clearly threatening in themselves, and after a rape they can be traumatic; there also may be police interviews immediately following. A counselor is most helpful by being consistent, clear in simple explanations, encouraging of the patient's active participation where possible (i.e., putting her own clothing in labeled bags, clipping her own pubic hairs), and supportive of the client's needs and preferences.

The time taken to obtain informed consent from the patient on all matters helps him/her to regain mastery over the world, and signals the end of helplessness and loss of control. Many hospitals have put together a rape treatment protocol which is complete for physical medicine and forensic use. However, procedures are usually inadequate for treatment of the mental health aspects which researchers have indicated are the most severe and long lasting results of sexual assault. Health care providers must consider mental health needs as an important part of the problem checklist and treatment program for sexual assault.

The counselor also can expect to encounter some of the following in the intermediate period after an assault. It is not unusual for the victim to try to get over the event, and to count on tranquilizers and sleeping pills (often borrowed from friends) to pull together a superficial, outward adjustment. The person may go over and over whether they were "really" raped, and be angry with themselves for any of the stress trauma symptoms listed so far.

The onset, severity, and duration of a person's response to rape fits no predictable pattern. One victim may be distant and composed in the ER and begin to experience "unexplained" anxiety attacks later. Another person may be depressed, shaken, want to quit their job and be fearful of going out for months. Much depends on the type of sexual assault, the kinds of assistance at the time, the person's history of pressured sex, their coping resources, and the presence of other ongoing stress.

Later Counseling

Counselors are often not consulted until weeks or months after a sexual assault has occurred. At that time, the client may need to work through significant feelings about what happened, both during the assault itself and any medical/legal proceedings after. Some will have had no medical or police assistance (and can benefit from encouragement to report for public safety purposes and to get a necessary checkup), some will have had generally positive post-assault care, and others will have had negative experiences which worsened the effects of the crime.

The counselor needs to accept the client where he/she is, establish a relationship, help focus as the situation evolves, set goals as they become appropriate, and refer for various services as necessary. The professional may be consulted as the result of one rape, or after a series of negative sexual experiences, but can expect the following to have occurred:

External Support System. A person's external support system failed at the time of the forced sex; family, friends, police, college, co-workers, lover, society—no one prevented it or rescued them. School, job, relationships, and activity patterns may now become issues. Aspects that were going well before the crime may be difficult, and areas that had been problems may become overwhelming.

Internal Support System. A person's internal support system is in question. Victims often do not trust themselves or their own judgement, may develop irrational fears, experience self doubt, and over criticize themselves. These self concept issues are tied to their pre-trauma trust levels, assertiveness skills, ideas of masculinity-femininity, sense of identity, and dependence-independence balance.

The important point to remember as a counselor is that the counseling goals are not really those of disclosure (if and to whom), treatment and reporting, or even reduction of stress symptoms alone, but rather the building of a positive sense of self in a reality-oriented world.

Fear is a real obstacle to self confidence so that any measures taken to increase the client's sense of personal safety are helpful. Through conditioning, cues associated with the rape can be immobilizing, such as darkness, a knife, a type of music, a penis or beard, smells, a mode of transportation, or walking alone. The victim may develop elaborate avoidance behaviors; for instance, a large proportion of people move abruptly after an assault, and others completely change their way of dressing to a neutral drab. Such a person needs to address this fear, add locks, find secure patterns of travel, possibly stay with others, and arrange a support network of frequent meetings and telephone calls to friends. Often relaxation practice, yoga and breathing exercise, behavior modification approaches to fears, martial arts and fitness training, and participation in support groups increase a sense of personal power.

Another frequent consequence is that forced sex may precipitate life crises out of sequence. If an issue was building up for a client, such as marriage or divorce, important financial decisions or job change, going to school versus dropping out, or the meaning of life versus suicide, the trauma may accelerate the decision when the client has few resources to meet it. Because feelings are always evolving after an assault, the counselor is usually wise to encourage the client to postpone or take time with significant decisions.

Disturbed relationships with persons of the other sex, friends, and family are another frequent consequence of sexual assault for both female and male victims. Often small group counseling with others in the victim's setting (dormitory, employment, class) is needed when one member is raped, and in other instances, couples or family counseling may be required. Of course a trauma to one member can bring out pre-existing problems in relationships, a living situation, or family. Positive contacts with supportive persons of both sexes are important, but exploitive, oppressive, or harrassing relationships may extend the experience of victimization. The client is likely to re-assess relationships with significant others in his/her life, as a result of interactions subsequent to the rape.

Extended Follow-Up Counseling

No single timetable exists, but if a counselor is consulted a year or more after a sexual assault, the client will usually present some of the previously listed issues mixed with other aspects of life. For instance a client could meet with a counselor about career change, excessive use of diet pills, depression, disinterest in sex, or difficulty stopping smoking. If one or more instances of forced sex come up, in general the advisable procedure is to spend some time on them before returning to the presenting problem. After that the counselor is expected to integrate the pressured sex topic as needed.

Professionals will find it helpful to look at where the client was in his/her development at the time of the rape, in order to anticipate particular damage. For instance an inexperienced young woman who had humiliating sex forced on her by her friend's boss, would be expected to have different issues from an elderly woman who suffered a concussion during a burglary rape. Very often clients do not see the relevance of an incident or pattern of forced sex to their current situation. The longer the time since the sexual assault the more important are the counselor's listening skills, in order to help the client untangle the result.

EXAMPLE: Newly Married Woman, Age 29, Depressed, 4th Session

Hilary: *"Oh I've already mentioned how my high school boy friend scared me at that party in the cabin by the lake."*

Counselor: *"And it seems you still avoid some kinds of parties?"*

Hilary: *"Well, it's stupid—I should have gotten over it by now...I'm married, own my own business..."*

Counselor: *"And you want to re-learn how to enjoy sex. Didn't you say that you felt fine about sex before your senior year?"*

Hilary: *"Sure, well I was young...and liked being popular and never let petting go too far."*

Counselor: *"So intercourse wasn't your idea at all...?"*

Hilary: *"Never. Joe was already drinking when I got there. He began to tease me and then locked me in a room. Right away he began to paw me and tear my clothes...and no one helped."*

Counselor: *"It was if no one else cared..."*

Hilary: (Pale, staring, remembering.) *"I wondered what was wrong all of a sudden, that he was acting like that to me. He'd go out and say it would happen when he came back, and if I pounded on the door he'd yell that I was asking for it. Every time he came back I was so scared, and it got worse and worse."*

Counselor: *"You were afraid of rape for hours..."*

Hilary: *"Yes, but maybe nothing too bad happened? Maybe I was lucky that he was drinking too much to do the whole act?*

Finally I got out on the porch roof from the window and managed to walk home hours later. I hadn't ever hitch hiked and was kind of spaced...didn't dare to knock on any strange doors."

Counselor: *"He really hurt you and said ugly things? Look how you feel? Can you remember what did take place?"*

Hilary: (Looks sick and choked up; counselor leans forward to hear.) *"...and jammed my face down on his dirty crotch and bragged about it outside to the others. And then he'd come back and make me do more things and pulled off my clothes. For the rest of the year..."* (Catches her breath.) *"...about my reputation in school...I was so ashamed."* (Ragged sobs and tears, fear, changing to shock.) *"I don't know, I just don't know..."*

Counselor: *"It felt like being trashed—treated like a cheap kickball..."*

Hilary: *"Like it wasn't me! What did I do that was different?"*

Counselor: *"Go ahead as if you were talking to him."* (Looks to empty chair.) *"Why did you do that to me? Turn against me?"*

Hilary: *"Yes, I sewed him that down vest in home ec class, and..."* (Turns to empty chair as counselor gestures.) *"and...and I gave your mother a birthday present! I never cheated, but I gave you the algebra answers..."* (Bursts out.) *"How could you do that to me?"*

Counselor: (Puts arm around Hilary's shoulders.) *"You gave so much, and yet he did a criminal act to you. You need to feel justified in your shock reaction, and not just glad you finally got away."*

Later in the Same Session

Counselor: *"Can you understand now that your experience was very serious emotionally? What happened was sexual assault and you were dazed. Hours of fear about sex changed it for you."*

Hilary: *"I kept telling myself I over-reacted. It was important to keep my head up and act like it never happened. I couldn't wait for high school to be over after that."*

Counselor: *"You would have been confused after all the negative stuff your mother gave you about men and sex, and then the trauma at the camp. Did you enjoy sex after that?"*

Hilary: *"Oh yes—but I can't be like that..."* (Begins to cry again.) *"...Oh...I know what you've been trying to tell me! It's those sexual feelings I shut off from when I see them in someone else."*

Counselor: *"You had always tried so hard to be in the right group and not make mistakes, and when that betrayal happened it really changed you for a while."*

COMMENT: The counselor realizes that this client has been rigidly cognitive about the sexual assault at age 17, and felt guilty for scorning her mother's cautions. In order to unlock her fear of sex, Hilary needed to re-experience some of the incident. The counselor facilitated this by responding to feelings not content, by using imagery, and with some leading. This broke through the client's tendency to minimize as a way of coping. Staying with the incident facilitated role playing confrontation of the offender, rather than focusing on the client's self doubt ("What did I do?") or denial.

Next Session

Counselor: *"I'm sorry it was so uncomfortable for you to get into that hurtful incident, but I believe the pain of it and distrust of yourself and sex has been there ever since."*

Hilary: *"It's OK...I know...I felt relieved afterwards. And very sad. I know I should have picked up some clues about Joe and sex but I didn't know what they meant."*

Counselor: *"Can you picture the part of you that was a teenager back then...image how you looked...hug her...accept yourself trying to be independent?"*

Hilary: (Nods, can't talk.) *"...Now...well...it's OK that I was so scared and shook up. I wasn't asking for it. Afterwards I acted sexy and felt nothing for years, and now I act cool and want to feel sexy. I'm more mixed up than I thought."*

Counselor: *"I think you are getting unmixed up."* (Stays with the image of the client accepting her younger self, understanding her defensive sexual experiences, and repairing her personal self concept.)

COMMENTS: At this point the counselor can help the client with a gradual program of building sexual competence and confidence. Probably the counselor will need to go slowly to replace avoidance with sexual interest, and uncover erotic arousal. Many counselors stress "getting the anger out" to the exclusion of other feelings. The real internal experience of the client needs to be accepted and helped to evolve, rather than the counselor imposing "appropriate" feelings. However, emphasizing the client's having compassion toward themselves is almost always necessary.

Sexual Dysfunction Following Victimization Counseling

For a period of time after a sexual assault, many victims feel disinterested in sex, or even aversive. The avoidance may persist for a time; a counselor can help with suggestions for sexual rebuilding as the client is ready. Some adjustment reaction after a trauma should be expected.

If sex is still a problem when the victim has attained his/her prior adjustment in other ways, then sexuality counseling may be needed. General sexual inhibition and avoidance, even to the point of a phobic reaction, are the most usual problems after a rape. Since post trauma depression may be present as well, the victim is likely to experience desire phase disorder. At times the husband or partner of an assault victim may develop emotional, communication, and sexual problems and also need help.

Numerous treatment recommendations are reported in the literature for rebuilding sexual comfort after sexual abuse. Some are suggested for individual treatment and other structured sessions are presented in groups, but they usually include

1. client support, attribution of responsibility to the offender;
2. education about sexuality and the effects of trauma;
3. assertion training/self defense, role playing, problem solving;
4. cognitive restructuring and correcting negative self concept;
5. relaxation and stress reduction techniques; and
6. a program for the recovery of positive sexual pleasure.

Many counselors combine elements and design their own program for helping victims regain their sexual and self confidence.

Timing of sexuality counseling is important, since the client needs to have already worked through some of the impact of the crime. Thinking and talking about sexual relationships must become somewhat comfortable before activity is begun. Once satisfying sexual fantasy is attained, self stimulation or very gentle, non-pressured lovemaking with a trusted partner may be suggested. If particular acts were especially offensive as part of the assault, they can be avoided. Eventually new associations can be made and sexual expression will once again be experienced with safety and pleasure.

Counseling to Prevent Revictimization

A sensitive aura surrounds the question of whether some women are more vulnerable to sexual assault than others. Possibly some are, without "blaming the victim" for being raped. Studies are beginning to show that women are most likely to be victimized if they have low self esteem, are subassertive, and express an external locus of control. The hypothesis is that women who signal more "learned helplessness" may be selected by offenders as being more vulnerable. Also some people report that when they aren't feeling confident, they are less likely to take care of themselves sexually.

Part of rehabilitation after rape is to help the client assess whether particular habits or attitudes render him/her more vulnerable. This must be accomplished without in any way inducing guilt for what happened. Self disclosure by the counselor can help transfer general safety measures (locking car, ways to avoid burglary, mugging) to the prevention of further sexual assault.

Those clients who have deeply repressed negative sexual experiences, who have a complex history of sexual exploitation, or who report abusive events but deny their importance, are more difficult to work with than even the ugliest single event. When a well functioning person becomes a victim it is tragic, but the client has more to work with toward wellness. The really hard ones are assault clients whose personal and sexual development were damaged together over time by forced or early sexual victimization. Supportive, informative, skillful sexuality counseling can help with all the above, but some people may have to be referred to specialists due to serious mental health problems.

RESOURCES REGARDING COUNSELING THE VICTIM

The following works are particularly helpful:

Bart, P., & O'Brien, P. (1985). *Stopping Rape*. Elmsford, NY: Pergamon.

Benedict, H. (1985). *Recovery, how to survive sexual assault*. New York: Doubleday.

Burgess, A., & Holmstrom, L. (1979). *Rape: Crisis and recovery*. Bowie, MD: J. Robert Brady.

Burgess, A., Groth, A., Halstrom, L., & Sgroi, S. (1978). *Sexual assault of children and adolescents*. Lexington, MA: Lexington Books.

Calhoun, K., & Atkinson, B. (1986). *Treatment of victims of sexual assault*. Maxwell House, NJ: The Pergamon Press.

Caplan, P. (1984). The myth of women's masochism. *American Psychologist, 39*(2), 130-139.

Figley, C. (Ed.). (1985). *Trauma and its wake*. Springfield, IL: Brunner/Mazel.

Fortune, M. (1983). *Sexual violence: The unmentionable sin. An ethical and pastoral perspective*. New York: The Pilgrim Press.

Katz, S., & Mazur, M. (1979). *Understanding the rape victim: A synthesis of research findings*. New York: Wiley.

Kilpatrick, D., Resnick, P., & Veronen, L. (1981). Effects of a rape experience: A longitundinal study. *Journal of Social Series, 37*(4) 105-122.

Koss, M. (1983). The scope of rape: Implications for clinical treatment of victims. *The Clinical Psychologist, 3*(4), 88-91.

McCombie, S. (Ed.). (1980). *The rape crisis intervention handbook: A guide for victim care.* New York: Plenum.

Rowland, J. (1985). *The ultimate violation.* New York: Doubleday.

Russell, D. (1982). *Rape in marriage.* New York: MacMillan.

Stuart, I., & Greer, J. (Eds.). (1984). *Victims of sexual aggression: Treatment of children, men, and women.* New York: Van Nostrand Reinhold.

Wooden, W., & Parker, J. (1982). *Men behind bars: Sexual exploration in prison.* New York: Plenum.

An unusual number of films, curricula, and videotapes are available to train counselors and others in the care and treatment of the sexually abused client. Local rape crisis centers and educational institutions have catalogues and materials.

COUNSELING THE SEXUAL AGGRESSOR

Counselors are more likely to be asked to treat victims of sexual assault, and yet because offenders usually force sex on others repeatedly, the counselor can do more ultimate good by working with offenders. Many helping professionals are able to treat rapists and other sex offenders by realizing that these individuals have usually been victims too, and that their problems are the result of trauma. Research does show that most people who victimize others were sexually (and/or emotionally-physically) abused as children. While this does not excuse the behavior, it may help the counselor develop empathy for a working relationship.

EXAMPLE: 22 Year Old Accused Rapist of Several Young Women

Warren: *"So I'd watch the steam in the sink to see how hot the water was."*

Counselor: *"Your father would scald you with the water?"*

Warren: *"No...uh...if I didn't...you know..."* (Pause) *"...go along...give into his sticking it to me behind, he'd hold my face under. I'd want to see how hot it was going to be."* (Twisted face, low curses.)

Counselor: *"No young boy should ever have to go through anything like that...or even have to think about it."*

Warren: (Unable to speak. Is thinking about it.)

Counselor: (Grips client's fist firmly, nonverbally encourages him to stay with it.)

Warren: *"...hold my breath."*

Counselor: *"You did what you could. Everyone has to breathe...choking...it hurts to breathe water...its terrible, terrifying."*

Warren: *"Can't think about it. Makes me feel..."* (Seems disoriented.)

Counselor: *"Crazy. And maybe a little violent..."* (Cue from body indicators) *"...but never wanting to be in that rotten place again?"*

Warren: *"Like a woman, or a punk...not me. I make myself think of being in charge."*

Counselor: *"Your father did so much damage to you and your ideas about sex. Do you want to keep on reacting to his mistakes?"*

COMMENTS: In the above case, the client later revealed that as a teenager he was concerned about "not having erections when I wanted to," "being unpopular," and that "getting tough turned me on." The insights alone were not sufficient to redirect his arousal pattern, but helped him and the counselor understand where the rough sex which he forced on younger women originated. They then worked together on a sex education and retraining program.

Identifying variations of the "coercive male" sex role will help the counselor understand how a particular client came to commit sex crimes. Studies of acquaintance rape show that many perpetrators seem honestly surprised at the seriousness of their offense. The most common strategies reported by college men in "date rapes" are lying, threats to end the relationship, pressure by argument, and force. Men rated intercourse against a woman's will (often called against her "wishes"), as significantly more justifiable when the woman initiated the date, when the couple were in the man's apartment, and when the man paid the expenses. Men in some subcultures may believe that a woman in a bar is "free game," and eventually extend this through cognitive distortion to any woman who is jogging, hitch hiking, or walking home from work.

Women who are sex offenders, usually against children, teens, or dependent adults, also justify their actions as "doing no real harm," "teaching about life," or "they wanted it." More research needs to be done to determine whether women who commit exploitive sex offenses also were exposed to sexual victimization as children. Counselors would be well advised to ask women clients as well as men whether they have forced sexual acts on others. Both sexes can be offenders or victims, even though a great disparity exists in comparative numbers. The damage to victims is well understood, but the destructiveness of an aggressive or predatory sexual life style on the perpetrator is just beginning to be studied.

Insights About Offenders

Rape is not an inevitable aspect of human nature because in some cultures this behavior is almost unknown. Studies have shown that the amount and type of sexual assault in a society depends on the values which govern the relationships between the sexes, the status of women, and the attitudes absorbed by boys. Sex offenders in the U.S. do not differ in their psychological profiles from the average, "normal" man, except in the behavior of acting on distortions of the injunction: GO FOR IT.

Counselors realize that rationalizations, believing self-serving excuses and projection of blame outside the self are common defenses. However, sex offenders of all kinds utilize cognitive distortions to an extreme degree, sometimes employing alcohol or high activity/anger levels to maintain the fiction. Rapists are not different from many incest offenders/child abusers in this respect.

EXAMPLE: Distortion (Incest Offender)

Counselor: *"So what did your granddaughter do which led you to think she wanted to stimulate you sexually and then be whipped for it?"*

Grandfather: *"Well, she jumped on my lap and rubbed herself all over me."*

COMMENT: The child was 6 years old.

EXAMPLE: Distortion (Rapist of a Pregnant Woman)

Counselor: *"How did it happen that you nearly choked that woman, especially since she was along in pregnancy?"*

Client: *"Well, she was dancing her butt off in front of everyone, and who knows if she was really pregnant? It was her fault she fought like that."*

COMMENT: The victim had been into "total fitness" and was dancing at an employee picnic as a normal activity. She delivered a premature baby four days after the violent rape.

EXAMPLE: Distortion (Gang Rape)

Counselor: *"You three guys finally make it to the national collegiate semi-finals, and then you blow the tournament by having sex with drive-in waiters?"*

Team Member: *"No way am I queer. Everyone knows my usual style. It shouldn't have anything to do with playing ball."*

Counselor: *"It's not your sex style that's important, but one car hop has a broken pelvis, and the others have dislocations, broken ribs, and a wired jaw."*

Another Member: *"Those punks are queens and do it for pay. They just got more than they bargained for."*

COMMENT: In many incidents of multi-rape, the group posture of dominance and contempt counters the guilt of the perpetrators.

Specialists describe different types/degrees of sexual assault and find them helpful in working with offenders. No one classification system is appropriate for all offenders and of course a person can commit more than one type. One model is as follows, with the classification on a continuum of severity:

Consenting sex
　　　Con/trick/seduce/pressured sex
　　　Sexual harrassment
　　　Spouse rape/date rape
　　　Acquaintance rape
　　　Power rape
　　　Rage rape
　　　Sadistic sexual assault
　　　Rape/murder

The list may lead some to categorize sexual assault in terms of degrees of violence, and yet the sexual aspects of the preceding have more similarities than differences. All the pressured sex is the result of a kind of social attitude which we have not yet been able to correct.

Sex offenders of all sorts experience a compulsive kind of pull toward their gratification. Sexual arousal is felt as a justification for action and therefore leads to the thought distortion which the perpetrator tries to believe. In many cases very little or no conscious guilt is present because the offender accepts his own myths in order to rationalize what he has done and to be able to continue. The counselor may be familiar with intense denial from working with alcoholics, binge eaters, or those who gamble or batter, but will notice a particular type in the sex offender.

The rapist will tend to be "just one of the boys," blaming the victim to a great degree, while appearing to have a vacancy where some body of positive experience, thought, and feelings about sex usually exist. Counselors can suggest any behavior which makes sex more conscious and helps make sexual acting out less likely, such as arranging for verbal or written apologies, forms of restitution to victims, contacts by telephone when tempted, and analysis of habitual rationalizations.

Any person may want satisfaction of sexual drives, and yet what leads some people to take it by trickery or force, especially when most offenders have sexual partners available? The professional can expect to find large areas of sexual ignorance with offenders, and also ambivalence about their victim category (women, girls, boys, young men) and themselves. This often amounts to well-concealed paranoid thoughts, with buried fears and inadequacy feelings which fuel urges to dominate.

EXAMPLE: Convicted Multi-rapist, 4th Session

Counselor: *"You've been real open about your life and how you got here. I think it will help if you describe what happened a day or two before one of these incidents."*

Leroy: *"Yeah...it's a couple days usually. I try to throw it off some..."*

Counselor: *"Must be hard...tense feelings, ideas, like...?"*

Leroy: *"Yeah, and I start picturing some other things I've done...with sex. Maybe a girl I know really begging for it. You know, scared, but wanting it."*

Counselor: *"Your face is red. Does talking about it turn you on?"*

Leroy: *"Well, it's been three weeks."*

Counselor: *"You can always get relief with the jacking off to good fantasy we talked about last time. And in the future you can find cooperating partners, after you do more time."*

Leroy: *"Ah, Lisa's holding out. Says she's going to move, but I'll find her."*

Counselor: *"Maybe you have to face the fact that Lisa won't ever be living with you again, since all the violent stuff came out at the trial. Also, I wouldn't be surprised if you had forced her sometimes too."*

Leroy: (Mutters, shifts in chair, flexes shoulders.) *"Sometime I'm going to make her admit she enjoys it."*

Counselor: *"You look real intense and turned on. What are you thinking about? Do you feel powerful right now?"*

Leroy: *"You could say so. Yeah, guess so. Better this way than depressed. It's a good thing for her that she's out there and not in here."*

Counselor: *"Which is why you may spend your life locked up, in here. So what if you get a surge and quick erection? Maybe you've learned to feel good when you're picturing a woman scared and impressed! There must be a better way."*

Leroy: *"I can't help it...it just builds up."*

Counselor: *"Bullshit. You've just learned to be turned on that way. And if you keep practicing it over and over in your head, you never will be safe to let out. And you'll be the loser!"*

Leroy: (Silent, head down, hands flexing.)

Counselor: (Stands up, walks to door, takes a deep breath and sits down again.) *"Sorry, I get mad when I hear you believing the same old thing. I know it feels automatic to you, but it doesn't have to stay that way. Let's look at what happens."*

COMMENTS: Again, insight alone won't cure the problem. However the client has opened up a great deal to work on. The younger or more motivated he is, the more likely that he can learn arousal non-violently, and find strength and adequacy other ways.

A helpful distinction which the counselor can make about offenders is the general idea of a criminal life style as different from the law abiding citizen whose major problem is forcing sex. A person whose habitual behavior involves stealing a motorcycle on impulse, or holding up a store for money, may commit sexual offenses if a victim is available. Forced sex is simply an occasional expression of general anti-social behavior. Counseling him might include setting the conviction that ripping off women or adolescents for sex is weak, the consequences aren't worth it, and providing sex education or social skills training toward satisfactory sex with willing partners.

An offender who shows appropriate social adjustment in other areas of life will need more specific counseling in the sex role and sexual area. He may have a history of violent fantasy associated with sex, and have arousal problems with consenting intercourse. The cognitive distortions mentioned earlier may be so obviously unconvincing that the offender will refer to them only indirectly.

EXAMPLE: 28 Year Old Man, Acquaintance Rape Charge

Alan: *"Well, as I told you I was upset about my divorce. But you know how it is, it's hard to tell with a woman. Marilyn seemed to like compliments and little squeezes. And her husband was so business-like around her."*

Counselor: *"You made yourself believe you could do better than he, and decided to push her on it?"*

Alan: (Avoids.) *"Other times I wrote to women I met from a post office box and it worked out better. If they answer one of those, you know they pretend they just want a date...but they can't complain too much. If they've been married I like to show them..."*

Counselor: *"This is a pattern then...forcing sex with women if you think they aren't sexually satisfied?"*

Alan: *"It's a rush but...well it doesn't matter now about Marilyn. I've just got to get my head straight for the hearing."*

Counselor: *"Maybe you'd like to forget about the pressured sex where you got caught, and just find a safer way to do the same thing? I'd like to help you find solid ways to enjoy sex that won't ruin your life. It's up to you."*

COMMENT: The counselor sounds blunt but has a limited time for court-ordered counseling with this client. Reflecting the client's rationalizations won't work; therefore the counselor is trying to penetrate them through confrontation. The counselor will need to reward any tentative movement the client makes with real encouragement.

Getting out the offender's distorted rationale is important, but once exposed the counselor will not gain by ridiculing the fallacies. The client can see the themes and will be less able to believe the errors with clear help. This can proceed while a positive fantasy life and sexual style is being built.

The treatment literature has focused on two approaches to behavioral change for sex offenders:

1. diminishing sexual response to inappropriate stimuli (using electric shock, nauseating drugs, bad smells, fantasied humiliation, education, peer pressure); and

2. rewarding positive sexual response to fantasy and slides (with masturbation), and teaching sex education and enhancement skills.

A counselor can encourage a client to participate in any available, well conducted program, particularly those utilizing small group counseling, anger management, and long-term follow up. Most try to combine some of 1 and 2. In a few places, drugs are being used on an experimental basis to reduce sex drive and control acting out; a client deserves to be completely informed before participating in these programs. Sexual victimization is a social tragedy of such proportions that considerable effort has finally been directed toward rehabilitation of offenders.

Working With The Judicial Process

Human service professionals realize that far more sex offenders are invisible in the general population than are identified by the criminal justice system. However, the number of arrests is increasing and counselors have greater access to accused or convicted assailants. The location where the counselor contacts the client and under what conditions is an important aspect of treatment.

The process of the prosecution of a sex crime is lengthy. With local variations, the following can be expected to occur: the initial reporting of an alleged offense, an investigation, criminal charges being filed if warranted, arraignment, release on bail (only a small fraction are held in custody), pre-trial motions, pre-trial discovery, plea bargaining, and possible settlement. Also a trial can be held (with jury drawing, conviction or acquittal), sentencing, parole, prison, or other penalty, appeal, review, and possible re-trial. The counselor cannot wait for the ideal atmosphere and motivation when working with people accused of sex offenses, and needs to have realistic ideas about what can be accomplished while the client is in the system.

Many helping professionals are optimistic about working with the juvenile justice system or family courts. Young people may have committed serious offenses but have had less time for behaviors to become deeply ingrained and chronic. A number of innovative programs, schools, and camps are being developed to treat young sex offenders. Counselors also can work with any young anti-social population, and with any group of adolescents, and find a great need for sex education and counseling which will help prevent later sex offenses.

RESOURCES REGARDING WORK WITH SEXUAL AGGRESSORS

The following texts are useful for greater understanding:

Greer, J., & Stuart, I. (Eds.). (1983). *The sexual aggressor: Current perspectives on treatment.* New York: Van Nostrand Reinhold.

Groth, A. (1979). *Men who rape, the psychology of the offender.* New York: Plenum.

Knopp, F. (1984). *Retraining adult sex offenders.* Syracuse, NY: Safer Society Press.

Malamuth, N., & Donnersteen, E. (1984). *Pornography and sexual aggression.* Orlando, FL: Academic Press.

Scacco, A. (Ed.). (1982). *Male rape, a casebook of sexual aggressions.* New York: AMS Press.

Because the treatment of offenders is a new and developing field, current journal articles such as the following are vital to keep the counselor informed:

Groth, A., & Burgess, A. (1980). Male rape: Offender and victims. *American Journal of Psychiatry, 137*(7), 806-810.

Rapaport, K., & Burkhart, B. (1984). Personality and attitudinal characteristics of sexually coercive college males. *Journal of Abnormal Psychology,* p. 93.

CONCLUSION

Counselors are sometimes called upon to work with current victims and offenders of sexual abuse, including those involved in sensational court cases and events which shock and enrage the public. More often, however, the helper will encounter people who have been offenders or victims in the past, or are presently undetected. They also will see family members and friends of victims and rapists who are upset and confused by present or past events. Many times the sexual abuse will be presented as part of something else, like general family problems, alcoholism, or work/school difficulties. The helper who is knowledgeable about rape/sexual abuse can provide a strong service by encouraging discussion of what happened, by identifying feelings and reactions, by focusing on the impact of the event(s), and by helping plan a program for improvement.

SECTION III
INTEGRATING SKILLS

CHAPTER 7

PRACTICE IN
ASSESSMENT
AND TREATMENT

The following two cases present sexuality issues as the counselor ordinarily sees them. People seldom come for counseling with an isolated sexual concern. These situations are intended to give practice in balancing the sexual aspects with related problems which frequently occur.

CASE 1. SORTING OUT THE ISSUES

Background

Mr. Emory Watkins, 44, is a coach at a state college who comes to a counselor for help with what he describes as "a potential drinking problem" and "lack of energy." He is living in the family home with his two younger sons, ages 16 and 17; his ex-wife lives in a nearby town and has an intimate relationship with a former friend of his. Mr. Watkins states that he and his wife of 23 years have just completed the divorce process (now that their four children are old enough to handle it), and that his membership in a church and community has been sustaining him.

> **INTERVIEW SEGMENT: Focus Phase, 15 Minutes into the 2nd Session**
>
> **Counselor:** *"You used the word 'depressed' without wincing this time. After talking last week, can you accept the idea that it isn't weak to feel discouraged by changes in your family? And it isn't a failure of faith to be hurt and angry?"*
>
> **Emory:** *"Well...it was kind of a relief to stop fighting my feelings. I know I can be hard on myself, and hate to fail. But I'm more down than ever, now that I realize what a dud I was."*
>
> **Counselor:** *"Grief and loss hurts..."* (Thinks of some of his/her own losses.) *"I wish I could take it away from you, although I can't. But Emory, is there another kind of struggle you are having? You used the word 'dud'?"*
>
> **Emory:** (Deep sigh, from his feet up.) *"Well, I guess I'm showing my age. But I was brought up to be disciplined...when Carol wanted more emotional talking and sex, it seemed weak to me."*
>
> **Counselor:** *"It was really hard, or seemed unimportant..."*
>
> **Emory:** *"It didn't seem right! When I first soiled the bedclothes around 14, my father let me know I was thinking about the wrong things. Then my coaches all along talked about V.D. and dirty girls. I put all my energy into doing what I was supposed to."*

Counselor: *"Can you believe it's not your fault that your up-bringing was so negative about sex?"*

Emory: *"I suppose so, but then why did I mess up and get Carol pregnant, or we thought she might be, in college? She wanted to wait to get married, but I couldn't, so we went ahead. That was in February and then she wasn't actually pregnant until May, and dropped out of school. I graduated and got a job and have done my best to be a good Christian father to our kids."* (Red face, almost tearful.)

Counselor: *"It's hard to remember all that pressure...trying to do the right thing but not having it work out..."*

Emory: *"You don't know how I've prayed, how I've pushed myself running and working, trying to make it up to her...but not the way she wanted. I can't do that soap opera stuff."*

Counselor: *"You're getting upset as you realize that even back in the beginning you and Carol couldn't talk about premarital sex, birth control, when to marry, her feelings and your feelings...somehow you just ended up feeling bad and guilty?"*

Emory: *"You're right, I should have known. Now that she is go-ing out with Sam, I wonder if she ever liked being married to me? I rushed her and then did all I could to make it work, but not the sex and emotional stuff."*

Counselor: *"It sounds as though stereotypes about men and sex and feelings had you stuck. No one ever really helped you ex-press yourself."*

Emory: *"For sure. Carol didn't say much either, but she began to cry a lot and have stomachaches and go to bed after me. She said she never got anything out of it..."*

Counselor: *"Did you know what she meant?"*

Emory: *"Later yes...lots of times I climaxed as soon as I touched her."* (His body language seems to go numb.)

Counselor: *"Many men ejaculate fast, and there is help for that. But instead of talking about problems for a moment, Emory, I'd* *like to take the pressure off by asking you to recall any good sexual experiences with Carol. I hear your pain and disappointment, but were there some better times?"*

Emory: (Hesitates.) *"Thanks, when I get like this all I see is Carol crying, and then I can't even get mad about her being with Sam. That's when only bourbon makes sense."* (Long pause.) *"Well, once on a couples' retreat we had to talk to each other quite a bit, on Scripture but about our feelings too. And the leaders even encouraged sex it seemed...we were all married couples. Carol liked that weekend a lot."* (Hesitated.) *"Then a few times on vacation or after a victory party with some drinking, I let myself fool around with her. But I usually didn't keep it up."*

Counselor: *"I'd like to ask you here, with my support, to look at how much of a factor you think problems with sex were in the breakup of your marriage? It's a rough issue, I know."*

Emory: *"Well, we kind of stopped getting upset about it. Every couple of weeks I'd think it was time and sort of let Carol know what I wanted. In a day or two she would go to bed early and lie there quietly until I was done. It never used to take me long, but then toward the end it did."*

Counselor: *"When Carol stopped crying about it, sex seemed less of a problem for you, but I guess there still were things that bothered her. I've heard you mention the importance of communication. What other things besides sex were hard for you two to talk about?"*

Emory: *"Let's see...Carol had a miscarriage after Bobby, and I was afraid she couldn't have more than one child. Carol was upset and tried to make me talk about it; she even threatened to go back home after a while. Finally our minister helped us talk it out."*

Counselor: *"I think it is important for the future to realize that it isn't only sex, but that you have a hard time expressing your own feelings and needs. In addition to the strained sexual relationship, there were probably many things which just couldn't be shared."*

Emory: *"It's too late for me and Carol. She looks like the guilty party who left home, but I'm to blame. I always wanted to be her big 'Mr. Nice Guy,' but I couldn't keep her. It's my fault..."* (Chokes, averts his face, and puts his head in his hands.)

Responding to Case 1

To provide an opportunity for practice, you are asked to formulate answers to Items A through D that follow. After completing them, read Item E and review what you have written. Then compare your answers with information supplied in Item F. No one response is the correct one. The purpose is to enable you to analyze your comments in light of those given by experienced sexuality counselors.

A. Formulate a **counselor response** to Emory, exactly as you would say it.

_____

_____

_____

_____

B. State the **reasoning behind your response.**

_____

_____

_____

_____

C. Write an **assessment** of Emory.

_____

_____

_____

D. Make an **issue focused treatment plan** for Emory.

_____

_____

_____

_____

E. Review your responses in Items A through D before reading Item F.

F. Analyze your responses in Items A through D in comparison to the following possible responses offered for the four items. They are offered to stimulate your thinking about this hypothetical counseling situation.

1. **Counselor Response.** _"The bottom line is that you feel terrible guilt and punish yourself every day. I'm sorry. But I think it is just the only way you know how to experience loss, Emory."_ (Pause to get his attention.) _"A sense of responsibility can be a good thing, but not if it replaces other emotions and results in harming yourself."_

2. **Reasoning Behind Response.** Emory needs empathy for his pain but also a way out of the cycle of self-blame. His "responsibility script" makes Emory more familiar with guilt than with emotions like sorrow or anger at someone else. Carol was aware of his limitations in sexuality and intimacy when they married, and Emory's failure can be redefined as their incompatibility. Not being able to understand his feelings, especially about sex and intimacy, contributed to the divorce, and is now resulting in Emory's blaming himself instead of simply grieving. His total sense of self need not be a casualty sacrificed to guilt.

   Clients with character disorders who directly harm others may need to have their sense of responsibility strengthened, but those like Emory who turn all blame inward need help identifying more constructive emotions. The sexual aspects are important to Emory's self esteem, but not much can be done about them until the failure and guilt lift.

3. **Assessment of Emory.** Sexual ignorance/misinformation. Premature ejaculation. Sexual inhibition. Adjustment reaction to divorce with feelings of depression. Reported abuse of alcohol. Value conflicts about sex. Low self worth.

4. **Issue Focused Treatment Plan for Emory.**

a. Emory will work toward developing a positive self image, moving from depression and the abuse of alcohol to letting go of the past and building a new life. The *means* will be as follows:

1) Further exploration of the sources of negative conditioning.

2) Positive, relevant problem drinker information, reading, AA, or men's support group. An alcohol counselor, sponsor, detoxification, or residential treatment could be necessary.

3) Techniques to build ego strength, such as: RET irrational statements about worth and masculinity; guided imagery dialogue with self as a lonely worried teen. Many counseling approaches are available to build genuine self esteem and lessen self blame.

4) Practice in communicating needs and feelings.

5) Later confrontation with the idea that his ex-wife was also involved in their lack of communication and sexual comfort.

6) Eventual assignments and contract for self forgiveness and letting go of the past.

b. Emory will become aware of sexual options as a responsible, single adult man and work on improving his sexual self image. The *means* will be as follows:

1) Sexuality education provided on a gradual basis during counseling, with the goal of positive pleasure rather than performance or pleasing someone else.

2) Appropriate reading and fantasy suggested.

3) Self pleasuring as a learning experience explored.

4) Both celibacy and the possibility of new relationships considered.

5) Information given about the role of anxiety in ejaculation, with nondemand pleasuring and the concept of "stop and start" understood. Practice if possible.

6) Referral made for a thorough checkup.

c. Emory will work toward an integration of his religious values and a mature, adult life style as he accomplishes Points a and b of the treatment plan. The *means* will be as follows:

1) Identify potential ethical conflicts during counseling.

2) Reading.

3) Discussion with understanding clergy and lay people.

4) Prayer and meditation from a seeking rather than a guilt orientation.

Skills Needed in Case 1

As Case 1 for Emory is studied, you can ask yourself what skills the counselor needed. Using five of the major topics discussed in this book, skills are listed for this case. You may want to ask yourself which ones you would list prior to reading the information provided, then compare you answers with those provided.

Chapter 1. Background Knowledge in Sexuality.

Midlife and couples issues
The pleasure curve, human sexual response
Alcohol abuse and sexuality
Values and life style counseling

Chapter 2. Counselor Attitudes and Values. The counselor may have to monitor his/her own values about sex roles, since Emory has traditional, benevolent-paternalistic-athletic views of men and little real knowledge of women. If necessary, this can be carefully addressed when he expands his social contacts after more painful issues are resolved. However, a sex role issue for Emory may not develop, depending on the values he encounters as his social circle develops. Counselors cannot impose their own views.

The counselor also will have to be careful to take a supportive role as Emory works through his religious/value issues. Unfortunately, some of the moral advice that Emory reports may seem to conflict with good mental health approaches. The counselor needs to encourage further exploration rather than argue interpretations of dogma. Emory may even ask for the counselor's beliefs, and then general human growth principles would be more appropriate than personal religious convictions. However some general concepts about love and letting go of guilt could be helpful if the counselor has philosophical-religious interests.

Chapter 3. General Counseling Skills. Exploring Emory's situation and building a relationship should not be problematic, but changing his "failure" focus will require considerable skill. An orientation toward responsibility and self blame is usually accepted by clients as a given, so good counseling is necessary for them to see guilt as only one way of perceiving reality. The counseling suggestion cards would have to be very specific in the area of building self worth and stopping the abuse of alcohol; general verbal recommendations which were not closely followed up would be slow going.

Once Point 4.a. of the treatment plan is underway, probably goals for Points 4.b. and 4.c. can be agreed upon jointly. Should Emory decide that sexuality and emotional intimacy are morally good and acceptable for him, the difficult part of focusing will be accomplished. The third phase of counseling, implementing plans for change, is likely to occur along with some of the focusing. This should go well because Emory is a responsible person who follows through and is also in so much pain that improvement will be rewarding.

Chapter 4. Professional Issue. Probably the most important point here would be having a good network of referral sources for Emory's various needs: alcohol education and counseling, a men's support group, medical referral, and religious-spiritual resources.

Crisis intervention could be necessary in this case if Emory became more depressed about the divorce and his alcohol problem worsened. The counselor should have another experienced professional in mind in case a second assessment is required.

Careful case notes will be helpful because the problem list and the number of aspects to the treatment plan will require attention to detail. They also will be useful for communication with other professionals, with Emory's permission, should it be necessary in the future.

Chapter 5. Sexuality Counseling Skills. Aspects of both sexual enhancement and remediation exist in this case. Information, encouragement and tactful confrontation of negative sexual language will certainly be required. The counselor will need ease with more than positive sexual words, however, because the real task will be to help Emory correct his legacy of "should's" and "can'ts." When Emory reaches a place in his life where sexual expression is of interest to him again, a treatment plan for premature ejaculation would be appropriate.

The question of religion will need to be sensitively handled when anxiety about sex builds, since Emory may use it unconsciously to block progress, as he apparently did in his marriage. The counselor cannot get into a power struggle about doctrine, but needs to respect values while pointing out that very few specifics about sex are in the Bible. Also, other people whose beliefs Emory respects are able to appreciate sexuality. The counselor can encourage Emory to take time to gain insight as he works toward a more positive belief system.

Emory will have to resolve conflicts about dependency, letting go, divorce, and possible remarriage as he becomes less depressed. The counselor can help a client consider a possible reconciliation with an ex-partner, but if doing so, the counselor must be reality based and not contribute to the client's false hopes. Avoiding wishful thinking could be especially important here with a socially insecure client who would prefer not to make real changes in his life. Should his divorce remain final, the counselor can help Emory find his own "center" before making a new commitment.

Probably the greatest difficulty will be Emory's conviction that he is a "failure," with subsequent slips into drinking, when he encounters anxiety while rehabilitating his sexuality and self esteem. His problems with sexual expression are likely to be extremely threatening to Emory, and yet his moral/emotional reservations will make resolving his difficulty much slower. The counselor will need patience, alertness, and firmness to help Emory strengthen himself as he moves ahead.

INTERVIEW SEGMENT: Five Weeks Later

Emory: *"So it just seems too much at times."*

Counselor: *"It isn't surprising that a decent, single guy like you has several dinner invitations, as soon as you let yourself be more sociable. Do you notice that you are more uncomfortable when you like the woman than when you don't?"*

Emory: *"Well, there isn't anyone I don't like. But yeah, there is this one woman, Sara, that I've always thought was special...she has two teenage daughters though. I was a half hour late getting to their house for Sunday dinner, and that isn't like me."*

Counselor: *"It's progress when you have feelings instead of just depression, Emory, even if they are mixed feelings. Let's talk about them. Remember you don't have to rush or feel pressure. Your goal now is to have more friends, not drink alcohol, and learn to feel automatically good about yourself."*

COMMENTS: As the counselor helps Emory express his mixed emotions, sexual or other conflicts, the important teaching will be for Emory to work through real feelings, rather than withdraw or act on "shoulds."

Possible Intervention Points in Case 1

Childhood. A sound, positive sex education, integrated into loving family values could have prevented this pain. At the very least it would have helped Emory be ready to learn to express feelings, communicate, and accept his sexuality.

Adolescence. A teacher, coach, minister, or counselor who would have validated Emory's developing masculinity and sense of self, and offered good information and communication models could have helped prevent much of the later problems.

College. Some premarital counseling and sex education would have begun to remedy the negative messages and inadequate communication between Carol and Emory. They could have made choices about where sexual activities fit in their relationship, about contraception and intercourse, and about being able to come to a joint decision about marriage.

Adulthood. Couples counseling would have been helpful anywhere in the first 20 years of marriage, before their roles had become so rigid and Carol had given up. A good prognosis would have been possible, especially if Emory had owned his part in their problems without being required to do so by a crisis.

Present. Often people do not acknowledge a problem until they are forced to do so; it seems too late for this marriage. However Emory can build a positive self image, with sexual activities in a place appropriate for him, and very likely will find a compatible new wife if he decides to do so.

Later. If Emory doesn't continue with counseling now, he could become further depressed and alcoholic, feeling tremendous guilt, failure, loneliness, and perhaps eventual impotence. The more entrenched this become, the harder it would be to change.

Concluding Case 1

Discussion of the preceding case is recommended. Other helping professionals will have additional insights, and agree or disagree with aspects as presented. Write a series of counseling suggestion cards for Points 4.a., 4.b., and 4.c. of the Treatment Plan for Emory. Review your thoughts and work related to Case 1 in regards to your viewing the sexual issues as an integral part of the totality of human experience.

CASE 2. MORE THAN THE COUNSELOR EXPECTED

Background

Jeannie, age 16, is referred to her high school counselor by the attendance officer because "she doesn't seem to get herself to school." On the telephone Jeannie's mother said, "It has been a problem off and on for years, but Jeannie got on the bus more willingly before her boyfriend dropped out." All of Jeannie's teachers say that she is quiet, does her work well, and seems content when she is in class.

INTERVIEW SEGMENT: Establishing Relationship, 1st Session

Counselor: *"So I have been trying to get to talk to all of the Sophomores, Jeannie, because this is an important year. How do things seem to be going for you?"*

Jeannie: *"All right."* (Smiles shyly.)

Counselor: *"Could you tell me some of the things you like or don't like about our school?"* (The counselor then spends 15 minutes drawing Jeannie out on non-threatening topics and giving her an opportunity to bring up criticism in an accepting atmosphere.)

Jeannie: *"...and the main thing that I don't like is gym, but I know a lot of girls who don't either."*

Counselor: *"Would you say that worrying about gym keeps you from wanting to come to school in the morning?"*

Jeannie: (Silence, squirms, looks cornered.)

Counselor: *"You can tell that I know about your absences, Jeannie...I want to be honest with you all the time. And I called your mom to see if she has any idea why you don't come to school sometimes."*

Jeannie: *"She doesn't realize...there's nothing she can say..."*

COMMENTS: The counselor tries a number of open-ended questions including, *"Can you think of any reason why you might want to stay home?"* and *"Could it be that school just isn't the same without Billy?"* and even *"Do you sometimes wish that you had more clothes and things like so many kids have?"*

Jeannie: *"I just can't tell you any more, but I feel better when I'm at home with Mom...it isn't bad in school, but I hate to leave the house."*

COMMENTS: At this point the counselor is thinking in terms of Jeannie being a dependent personality, and after talking a while longer gives her a popular book entitled *Becoming a Woman*. Then the counselor continues the session.

Counselor: *"Could we meet weekly to sort things out and maybe look ahead to the future?"*

Jeannie: *"That would be good...this is a big school and I'd like someone to talk to."*

COMMENTS: The counselor is busy and can give Jeannie only twenty minutes every week, but after several sessions they begin to talk easily. Jeannie reveals some interests and more spunk and color than were apparent at first; she follows through on counseling suggestions focused on assertiveness. The counselor notes that she speaks protectively of her mother, warmly of her three older sisters, briefly about her teasing twin brothers, but becomes rigid and non-communicative about her father.

Counselor: *"So it seem that school is in a better-than-average place for you right now, Jeannie. I'm glad! But I've noticed that when you mention your boyfriend Billy, that you kind of frown sometimes?"*

Jeannie: *"Well, Billy can be a pain. He wouldn't come over to see me all weekend, or go out anywhere. He just wanted me to come to his apartment and clean up all the grease in the stove and the stuff his friends leave. I don't mind doing it for him, but those other guys are messing Billy up."*

COMMENTS: The counselor doesn't especially want to talk about Billy's friends' parties but knows it is necessary to help Jeannie express her concerns. They spent a while talking about how things had been going, and how Jeannie would like them to be.

Counselor: *"It seems as though you aren't asking too much, from all you've told me Jeannie, but that you would like a little respect, attention, and less cleaning!"*

Jeannie: *"I know, everyone tells me that I shouldn't put up with the way Billy treats me, and he won't keep a job...but I think that he depends on me."*

Counselor: *"That feeling of being important to Billy...being needed...makes it hard for you to speak up for yourself?"*

Jeannie: *"Well, I couldn't do that. I have to either break up with him or leave it this way. I'm not going to argue all the time. I can't stand any more of that."*

Counselor: *"You look almost sick Jeannie. It makes me wonder if you've already heard too much arguing in your life?"*

Jeannie: *"Well, I have. My father yells all the time. But he keeps at us to get my mother and sisters to admit things."*

Counselor: *"Your father gets upset about things you all do?"*

Jeannie: *"No. He gets weird about stuff we never did."*

Counselor: *"Could you give me an example, please?"*

Jeannie: *"Well, I'm not supposed to talk about it. But he accuses us of sex things, especially my sisters and mother."*

Counselor: *"You know I never quote anything, Jeannie. The only thing I would have to report is if a person is in danger."*

Jeannie: *"Well, we are sometimes. My mother is used to it, and she says he mostly squeezes her and she bruises easily. But lately he gets yelling and really hits her."*

Counselor: *"I think I have an idea what you are talking about. Your mother is very thin and looks kind of nervous sometimes."*

Jeannie: *"It got worse when Molly was living with us. She and my brother had to get married two years ago—she's my age—and my father wouldn't leave Molly alone."*

Counselor: *"Are you saying that your father hit Molly, or had an unhealthy relationship with her?"*

Jeannie: *"Yes. What you said last. Molly told my sisters the sex things my father made her do when my brother was at work, before they moved out. And my mother was real worried that something would happen, and maybe my father would leave...or get in trouble."*

Counselor: *"So you know something wrong was going on then? And they still argue a lot, and you are terrified that the family could break up or your mother get hurt?"*

Jeannie: *"To tell you the truth, it wouldn't bother me or my sisters if my father did leave, except that my mother says she'd die."*

Counselor: *"Your father has bothered you too?"*

Jeannie: *"For some reason he leaves me alone. I think my mother said I was the baby of the family and she'd kill him if he laid a hand on me. And when he gets down on her, it's better if I'm there."*

Counselor: *"So that is really why you stay home sometimes?"*

Jeannie: *"I told you school was OK. People are pretty nice here."*

Counselor: *"You have mentioned so many hurtful things. What worries you most? Do you think your father has a problem with being mean, yelling, or sex, or what?"*

Jeannie: *"Well he does really hurt my mother. And he always yells about sex. None of my sisters will be alone with him* *because of things he used to do to them. They can pretty much avoid him now, but he is after my mother 2 or 3 times every night. He's mad all the time."*

Counselor: *"It sounds awful. What do you wish would happen?"*

Jeannie: *"That's my problem, I just don't know what to do."* (Huddles over, seems to shrink.)

Counselor: *"Jeannie, I didn't mean that any of this family stuff is your responsibility."* (Puts arm around her shoulder gently to help her sit back up.) *"You are just a young girl growing up where you see so much confusion, and your father taking advantage of people. None of it is your fault."*

Jeannie: *"My mom keeps talking to me about what to do. I can't stand it because she won't take my advice anyway."*

Counselor: *"You know, there is some risk here, Jeannie. Your mother has been under such a strain lately and could feel desperate. Has she seen a doctor?"*

Jeannie: *"She weighs only 95 now and can't sleep. She told the doctor that she has troubles, and he gave her medicine and said to make up her mind to get a divorce."*

Counselor: *"From what you've told me it seems that your mother really needs some help. I believe it is my responsibility to talk to her so that she doesn't lean on you so much, and also to find out whether your father is a danger to anyone at present."*

Jeannie: *"I think he has bothered some other girls...but I don't know for sure if he is now."*

Counselor: *"It sounds as though he really has a problem. We may be able to get him some help too. But in the meantime I want you to know that you did the best possible thing. You waited until you decided that we were friends and then told me the painful family secret. Now I promise you that something will be done about the accusing and hitting and sexual threats."*

Jeannie: *"Please don't get my father arrested! My mother would be worse off than ever then. She just wants him to straighten up, she says."*

Counselor: *"That is a really good goal, Jeannie, and I promise that I will look into this considering the best interests of all the family. What I plan to do is talk to your mom and encourage her to confide in me...It sounds as if she could use some understanding right now."*

Jeannie: *"I'm glad you believed me. I tried to talk to somebody a couple of times and they didn't want to hear about our family problems. What will happen now?"*

Responding to Case 2

To provide an opportunity for more practice, you are asked to formulate responses to Items A through D that follow. After completing them, read Item E and review your answers. Then compare your responses with information supplied in Item F. No one answer is the correct one. The purpose is to provide you with practice and then to enable you to analyze your comments in light of those given by experienced sexuality counselors.

A. Formulate a **counselor response** to Jeannie, exactly as you would say it.

_____

_____

_____

_____

B. State the **reasoning behind your response.**

_____

_____

_____

C. Write an **assessment** of this situation.

_____

_____

_____

_____

D. Make an **issue focused treatment plan** for Jeannie.

_____

_____

_____

_____

E. Review your responses in Items A through D before reading Item F.

F. Analyze your responses in Items A through D in comparison to the following possible responses offered for the four items. The ones offered are to stimulate your thinking about situations similar to this one.

1. **Counselor Response.** _"Things have to get better, Jeannie, so you and all the family can relax and stop being afraid. Please don't expect total change overnight, but just know that some careful people will be helping. Why don't we get together tomorrow at this time?"_

2. **Reasoning Behind Response.** Jeannie needs to be reassured that she did the correct thing by telling, and that responsible action will be taken. A detailed plan is impossible at this point; more information is needed from the mother before a

plan is made. Jeannie simply needs to know that the counselor will see her regularly, keep her informed, and begin to get help.

3. **Assessment of the Situation.** This would appear to be a multi-problem family, requiring investigation by the Department of Social Services. The statutes in most states protect helpers who have reason to suspect wife or child physical or sexual abuse. The counselor could simply report what Jeannie has said and then focus only on Jeannie as a client. However, a pledge was made to contact and help the mother, so following through immediately is a necessity. Careful referral and coordination with investigative services would be extremely important in order to help the family rather than deliver a "knockout blow."

The earlier assessment of Jeannie as a "dependent personality" could be revised to something like "anxiety reaction to continued stress." Because the traumatic family situation has existed during most of Jeannie's development, one can reasonably expect that it has affected her significantly. The counselor will be able to do a better evaluation of the impact on Jeannie's mental health after the disclosure and readjustment period is passed.

Other individuals in the family will have to be assessed by different professionals to determine their needs. For instance, to what degree are the two sons affected by their father's alleged battering and incest behavior? Is the mother anorexic, a possible borderline personality, or simply a totally overwhelmed, battered wife with no awareness of alternatives? And what are the needs of the sisters who grew up in this threatening, abusive atmosphere?

4. **Issue Focused Treatment Plan for Jeannie.**

a. The safety and health of the family members must be provided. The *means* could be as follows:

1) An investigation of reported abuse will be conducted by appropriate legal/human services personnel, and all necessary steps taken to protect individuals.

2) The counselor will call on whatever resources are available, public and private. In some areas model programs will be available while in other areas almost no child/family protection services exist.

3) Assessments of the family system and of individual needs will be conducted by qualified professionals.

b. Rehabilitation and treatment must be provided for the family. The *means* will be as follows:

1) The father will be evaluated as a potentially rehabilitable batterer and sex offender, and a program arranged. The details will depend on the results of the investigation and the involvement of the justice system.

2) The mother will need her own case worker, therapy, battered women's group and health services.

3) Family and individual counseling and other services will be provided for all family members as efficiently as possible.

c. Jeannie's personal growth must receive immediate and long-term attention. The *means* will be as follows:

1) Clarification of Jeannie's role in the family. Through individual work, and possible joint sessions with her mother, Jeannie can be seen as a teenager in a family in transition.

2) Jeannie is at that time in her development when individual identity is the important task. The counselor can help her look ahead and plan for her life beyond the family (this would be true even if the family were not so destructive).

Some kind of work-study, PROVE, or CHAL-LENGE program, supervised by interested adults, could help Jeannie find a sense of herself in the larger world.

3) Relationship and sexuality education and counseling. Jeannie is at risk for developing the same kind of submissive, sex-object role she sees in her mother. Her views of sexuality must certainly be skewed. The counselor can consider her emotionally sexually abused and do remedial and preventative work as time goes on. Helping Jeannie develop positive relationships with men and women, and integrating sexuality in appropriate ways, will be very important.

Skills Needed in Case 2

As Case 2 for Jeannie is studied, you can ask yourself what skills the counselor needed. Using five of the major topics discussed in this book, skills are listed for this case. You may want to ask yourself which ones you would list prior to reading the information provided, then compare your answers with those given.

Chapter 1. Background Knowledge of Sexuality.

Sexual development over the lifespan.
Interpersonal and family dynamics.
Sex roles and stereotypes.
Sexuality education.

Chapter 2. Personal Attitudes and Experience.
A knowledge of the degree to which men are victims of sex role stereotyping may help the counselor work with feelings about the father. Possibly, the father is a survivor of an abused childhood too, and while neither of these excuse any of the abusive behavior, it can help the counselor channel rage and denial. The counselor may feel very protective of Jeannie and angry at the amount of abuse that emerges through investigation. Pity and impatience toward the mother who stayed in an abusive situation also may be difficult to handle. Condemning the roles played by the women or the men in this family will not be helpful.

Courage will be required for the counselor to work within all the conflicting needs and demands and follow his/her own best professional judgment. Pleasing everyone is impossible in these abuse situations, so the counselor will need a focus such as helping Jeannie emancipate herself from a damaging family role. Even after many services have poured time, attention, and help to this family, possibly some members will continue to be oppressors or victims. The counselor must have a philosophy of life which expects improvement but does not dictate how others will live.

Chapter 3. General Counseling Skills. Building the relationship, keeping Jeannie in treatment, and maintaining contact with the family are likely to be difficult. The mother may not cooperate, even Jeannie may vacillate and change her version of events several times. The closed, nontrusting habits won't change just because secrets are revealed.

If the family accepts help and the counseling continues, the focusing stage probably will be fairly smooth with Jeannie. The longer she is with the same counselor the more likely she is to want goals of being less responsible for Mom, to be more independent, and to enjoy planning for the future. Depending on how the rest of the family proceeds, however, the counselor may be in the position of a reality-testing person who has to caution Jeannie to take care of herself.

Other people will be carrying out the treatment stage with the family, but the counselor may find that Jeannie needs a great deal of help during the action phase of counseling. Carefully graduated counseling suggestions will be needed, such as: "Talk to one person you know from English class for a few minutes in the lunch room every day this week," and "Bring in three questions about the menstrual cycle from this book on women's health." Jeannie has not been rewarded for competence and is likely to find "being the baby" is safer, and she may remain content if things are less tense at home. The counselor will have to balance the fine line between Jeannie's right to adopt a passive life style and her capacity to do more with encouragement.

Chapter 4. Professional Issues. The counselor will need knowledge of the law and ethics as they relate to child sexual abuse and spouse abuse, confidentiality and responsibility. Conferring with other professionals will be necessary but must be well planned out. A child protection team would be ideal since they would have worked through many of the options for other cases.

Crisis management may become an issue. For a time anger, blame, and denial may exist within the family, with threats of rejection and separation. Jeannie will have to be supported through this until the family (and individuals within it) are far enough along in treatment, or the criminal justice system, for some kind of stability to be established. The counselor would need to know a variety of referral sources so that the various family members receive support and treatment. Finding services which the family can afford could be a serious problem. Often in cases like these, contradictory statements are made and the offenses do not quite meet legal standards of proof for incest or battering. The emotional damage is just as real, however, and civil remedies like separation may be necessary even if criminal charges will not hold. A team approach to treatment is usually best in these complex situations, so an in-depth knowledge of resources is vital.

The counselor may need continuing professional education and networking to become more skillful in working with people in families like Jeannie's. This is true not only for the period of crisis and disclosure, but also for the long haul, when various services may have different approaches to the clients.

Chapter 6. Sexuality Counseling Skills. Much of the counseling will be remedial, although any positive education will facilitate Jeannie's growth and perhaps prevent further damage. The counselor's main client in this case is a young person who was exposed over a long period of time to the physical, emotional, and sexual abuse of other family members. Exactly how this has affected Jeannie is not clear as yet, but most likely she will have mixed feelings and confusion about her role and worth.

The counselor will need to be aware of the tendency of women in abusive households to adopt a rescuer or victim role in their own relationships, and make Jeannie aware of this without interfering with her normal style. The counselor will need to watch for depression when Jeannie is no longer highly anxious about protecting mom. As in other trauma situations, when the strain of the siege is over, the person is forced to make changes for which he/she may not be prepared. The counselor is likely to have to mobilize resources for Jeannie until she can feel less lost and empty. The caretaker role may have served to cover Jeannie's own pain and unmet needs, both to herself and others.

Possible Intervention Points in Case 2

Childhood of the Parents. Adults do not abuse or remain abused for years unless they were deprived or damaged themselves. If this mother and father had more nurturing models, and good sexuality/sex role education, the tormented family situation would not exist.

Early in the Marriage. Had the wife gotten help when she was first battered or had knowledge of the husband's sexual interest in young girls, much of the later damage to this family could have been prevented (either by removal of the father or by rehabilitation). Financial and other problems could have existed, but life with a non-abusive single parent would have been less traumatic for the children than the damage caused by incest and physical abuse.

Present. Since the children are largely grown and the parents are older, this can be an excellent time for intervention. Simply the pressure of possible court action may be enough to keep in the family in active treatment. If not, other legal and social courses of action can be taken which will re-balance the family and protect individual members until they are more self sufficient.

This is also a good time for the father to see the isolation and risk of incarceration which further abusive behavior will cause; that is a perfectly good motivator for treatment. Elements of paranoia in his abusive yelling and accusations suggest that treatment for distorted thinking could decrease his tendency to act out.

Future. If nothing is done, Jeannie is likely to be under increasing pressure to stay home and support her mother rather than progress in school; in the process she would more thoroughly learn maladaptive patterns. How long the mother can stand the present stress is questionable, and the possibility is present that the batterer/abuser with poor boundaries will become more destructive. Unless acknowledgement of the problem occurs and treatment of some kind is provided, the other children will carry their burdens into their own family lives.

Concluding Case 2

Discussion of this case with others is especially recommended. What kinds of resources can be found in the trainee's locale to help with this kind of problem? Would some people ignore cues of abuse and wait for a definitive picture before acting? The counselor must remember that the duty to report, investigate, and protect lies with professionals not only when certain but also if any reason exists for suspicion of harm. The reality is that most cases come to light through subtle inference rather than dramatic proof.

Contact counselors who are experienced with children and adolescents and discuss Case 2 with them. They have much to contribute, and those counselors who see adults can discuss how they would work with Jeannie if none of this came to light until she was 30.

Also ask a person, who has worked with men like Jeannie's father, to discuss treatment programs available in the state and their effectiveness.

Consider the entire family during these discussions, from a systems point of view. Unfortunately, many people grow up with learning histories which are as troubled as Jeannie's.

FURTHER PRACTICE

Even the most expert sexuality counselor needs to have perspective and see all the client's issues in context. Very often the most effective procedure is to work with other aspects first, before focusing on the sexual ones. However the counselor must pick up cues to sexual problems, acknowledge them, and begin to lay a foundation as the counseling develops.

CLIENT STATEMENTS

The following very brief quotations made during counseling sessions illustrate typical presenting problems, which are expressed once rapport has been established. Read each statement provided and respond as the client's counselor. Expand statements into counseling exchanges based on the limited information provided. Then make a treatment plan for each case and list the most necessary skills. If possible, use the statements that follow as microcounseling roles in a group. This will provide you with input of different viewpoints to help you expand your scope.

1. *"My mother doesn't think 17 is old enough to have sex, but my friends all do. You have to compromise to get along."*

2. *"Doing it seems to really hurt my wife, and I feel terrible. Her old doctor said she might need a hysterectomy some day. Would that take care of it?"*

3. *"There are some sore bumps down there, but I couldn't show anyone. It's hard for me to think about how it might have happened."*

4. *"My parents think that I pretty much agree with them about sex and it's great I'm not girl-crazy. Wonder what they'll do when they find out I've been reading about the operation to become a woman?"*

5. *"Even after two divorces I seem to attract the wrong kind of guy. You wouldn't believe the number of times I've been raped."*

6. *"I thought that abortion was the only option when I was alone in my first job last year. Now I'm not so sure I did the right thing, and don't seem to have any interest in going out on dates."*

7. *"We have to find a home for him—he's 15 years old and beating off in public. I could put up with a lot, but not that."*

8. *"My best friend made me come here. She hates my husband for how he hits the kids. He forces himself on me, even now after change-of-life. But mostly when he's mad."*

9. *"So maybe my losing interest in sex is a punishment? No one knows that I did some things to young girls when I was at Fort Myers—and even to a boy once. But he was willing."*

10. *"It scares me to try to get pregnant but my husband keeps pushing for a family. We almost decided to have a baby last year, but lately I can hardly stand him touching me."*

11. *"Ever since I caught my wife calling that guy from work, I've been having more and more trouble in bed. I feel fine but when she gets turned on, I lose it. I've thought of shooting myself."*

12. *"Probably I'm pregnant but there was no other way to be sure he'd stay with me. He's going away anyhow and I have to decide what to do. I can't have a baby now, but I've heard you may never get another one. I just don't know."*

13. *"Every other guy on the team has made it lots of times. My acne is the pits...or maybe it's because I'm small?"*

14. *"My husband left a note around from his lover and I found out for sure they're gay. He's been irritable and we haven't had much sex lately. I've been dying inside."*

15. *"But the test can't be positive! I've never even known anyone who has herpes. And I'm a virgin."*

16. *"Sex hurts since I had cervical cancer but I wouldn't mind that so much. Except that lately I make my husband lose his interest a lot too."*

17. *"Every time I go downtown I swear I won't let anyone pick me up. But it doesn't work. I was even a sleeze with my uncle."*

18. *"My boyfriend says something's the matter with me—that it's not normal for me to want sex so much and be so slippery. Anyway, that's the only time he holds me. I don't know if I want to see my 33rd birthday next week."*

19. *"Most of my life I've enjoyed and...well...idolized...had feelings for...other women. Now that I'm single again it seems that guys turn me off. Oh, I have plenty of men friends, but I wonder what it means?"*

20. *"If I tell my sister what her husband has been doing with me since I was 13 it could break them up. I don't go over there, but he finds me and makes me. I have to be quiet because he's the only other guy in the family who knows I'm gay."*

21. *"So I'll stay inside another 5 to 6 years before parole, and there's no way I can be sure my wife will wait. What difference does it make what I do in here?"*

22. *"My 16 year old cousin says she was raped and I believe her. I used to work in the garage with the guy who did it, and she isn't his first. The family doesn't want any trouble but boy is she acting weird."*

23. *"There's been a lot in magazines about men's fantasies, and I'd be arrested for mine. The older I get the harder it is not to try to make them happen. Would it be OK to pay a woman?"*

24. *"My best friend isn't old enough to quit school so she's going to take off to get away from stuff at home. She got an ad for dancers in Chicago, where they make a lot of money."*

25. *"We're getting married next month and I want it to be perfect. I don't have much real experience with sex—what should I know?"*

Discussion of Client Statements

All preceding statements can be expanded into numerous human situations. Practice giving an immediate response and jot it down, before analyzing all the possibilities. By looking for patterns in the replies, one possibly can note whether the responses support the client, ask for further facts, give information too bluntly, jump to conclusions, or help the client explore further. The key point is to support the client's experience while beginning to move in a genuinely helpful direction.

After expanding a sample of the preceding statements into plausible situations, an excellent practice is to make a treatment plan for each and list the skills which would be especially important. Writing out counseling suggestion cards leads to thinking about possible goals and how to bring about positive changes. For those statements which are particularly difficult, more study and experience are needed.

The helping professional then can go on to write original practice dialogues focused on sexuality counseling, and treat them in ways similar to the two cases and brief statements presented in this chapter. After a time, replying therapeutically to cues about sexual difficulties will become so automatic that the counselor hardly realizes the high level of skill achieved.

IMPROVING THE SYSTEM

As stated earlier, sexuality counseling is highly rewarding. When individuals or couples improve the sexual aspect of their lives, the gain is reflected in their overall effectiveness. The results are even more significant, however, when professionals take the experience learned from sexuality counseling and apply it to a larger unit.

Most human service training programs stress the importance of improving the system as well as providing service to individuals. This is especially true in sexual areas, since taboos, ignorance, and uneasy silence often allow negative conditions to continue. Sometimes confusion about "confidential material," concern about teaching "values," or worry about possible "adverse publicity" conspire to block efforts to improve a system. These are significant issues, but confidentiality, public relations, and values can be addressed directly and not remain as obstacles in problem situations.

Question

What if an advisor to a neighborhood center, a camp, a freshman class, or a staff member of any human service program finds that a number of residents/students become pregnant, are abused, contact STDs, or experience some other negative sexual event? How long will he/she go on providing assistance to individuals before developing a program to intervene earlier? Will the professional be indirect or hesitant because the problem is sexual? How will the larger system (community, parents, board, staff, administrators) respond?

Answer

Working with a system is to viewed as a process which requires time and energy, and which will necessitate the cooperation of others. Experience has shown that a competent health or human service worker can set up a support system of colleagues, develop awareness about an existing sexual problem, and then be part of a group which implements a constructive program.

Without attempting to improve the larger system it is very likely that a counselor will eventually become discouraged and "burn out" through the process of picking up the pieces for people after damage has been done. Broad change occurs only by working with the larger picture, and not only with individual clients. However, one must be realistic and set reasonable goals, because rigid expectations produce their own problems.

EMPHASIS ON PREVENTION

The literature on prevention of mental health/social problems has grown into a distinct professional discipline during the last decade. In the volume *Promoting Sexual Responsibility and Preventing Sexual Problems,* by G. Albee, S. Gordon, and H. Leitenberg (Eds.), The University Press of New England, 1983, the editors summarized the proceedings of a conference which applied the concept of prevention to the sexual arena. Programs to address specific problem areas were described and evaluated, with the intention that others will adapt them to varied situations.

The many outstanding presenters at the Primary Prevention of Psychopathology Conference (The University of Vermont, 1981) offered a wide range of significant insights which the counselor can use, starting with the causes of the current sexual problems in society. More applied sections covered the development of sexual values and problems in male and female sexuality, childhood sexuality, sexual life styles, research on the effects of pornography, rape, child sexual abuse, and work with the mentally and physically disabled. The reference sections are especially helpful to the counselor because the focus on prevention instead of remediation with sexuality is new.

EARLY INTERVENTION

If prevention is not possible, then finding ways to intervene before a problem becomes critical is the next best solution. The counselor can look at national trends in counseling systems about sex, and apply selected aspects to his/her local situation. For instance, excellent group programs exist in some areas to support individuals with herpes, ostomies, or other difficulties and to assist couples with infertility concerns, or adolescent populations. By attending conferences or sending for material, the counselor can transfer others' experiences and can help design a sexuality program for a local need. Having several counseling clients with the same unmet need is often the necessary trigger to work toward improving a whole system.

Strides have been made recently in recognizing the importance of sexuality education for human service professionals, in helping parents become better sexuality educators, in the presentation of sexual safety education in schools, and in the provision of more comprehensive help to victims and perpetrators of sexual crimes. An interest in preventing unwanted pregnancy and in educating men to take greater responsibility for contraception is ongoing. Everyone involved with abortion continues to seek ways in which this choice will not have to be made. In addition, considerable concern exists about the effect of aggressive pornography on the attitudes and behavior of people. Finally, some growth seems to be occurring in understanding and tolerance toward a variety of sexual life style choices.

Counselors are encouraged to survey health and human services in their area and assess where progress is being made in encouraging positive sexuality and preventing negative sexual behavior. For instance, excellent programs may be provided in reproductive health by some providers but not by others, or respect for human sexuality for the residents of some local institutions (hospitals, foster care, correctional centers, homes for the elderly) but not for others. In these instances the counselor does not have to go far to find good models, and can be creative while helping to improve the units which are deficient.

UTILIZING THE CONSULTATIVE ROLE

One of the important contributions which an experienced sexuality counselor can make is to be a consultant to groups. Sometimes the role is minor, as in advising a coed high school exchange program on preventing possible sex-related problems abroad. At other times the role is critical, such as when testifying before committees that are writing legislation in sex-related areas like rape or child sexual abuse. All consulting is important because many well trained human service groups have no staff specialist in sexuality.

Steps for Systems Intervention

To gain experience in improving the system by utilizing skills in a consultative role, the trainee will find the following practice beneficial.

> 1. Survey and define a sex-related need or problem. Data can be gathered through a structured needs-assessment program, or by more informal interviews and the collection of existing information.

2. Discuss the issue with friends and colleagues in order to test and focus it. Then develop a definite group to work on the problem and generate ideas.

3. Start in small ways to raise awareness (i.e., circulate reprints of fact sheets or articles about the specific problem to interested others). Gather more information about the specific problem.

4. Discuss the target problem informally with administrators, significant persons, or others in a position to help. Give them a mix of good, factual data and the human side of the sexual problem. Obtain their ideas.

5. Locate funds, grants, space, resources, services, staff time, free publicity or whatever practical help can be found.

6. Begin to design a program with representation from everyone affected by the need or problem. Notice how the input to planning would vary if the counselor were working on issues around AIDS, sex education in a cardiology unit, boy victims of incest, or teenagers with multiple unwanted pregnancies.

7. Present a concrete plan to those who can authorize it, fund it, or help with its implementation. Be sure to include Goal, Specific Objectives, Outline of the Plan, Timeline, Budget, Resources, and Related Material. Obviously some mini-projects will fit on a single page, whereas other programs require a formal proposal. Plans can always be modified and improved. While this seems like considerable effort, the process actually makes the project work; it is much easier once a plan is laid out.

8. Look for already established groups which may have an interest in the sexual need or problem under consideration. A committee of Parents of Learning Disabled Children might help sponsor a general sexuality education series if special learning problems are addressed; a Battered Women's Shelter might allocate valuable staff time to assist in writing legislation on sexual abuse. Some marketing skills may be

needed to convince the larger organization to become involved with the sexual issue, and to see its relevance to their mission.

9. Utilize the media, if applicable, for educational aspects, to raise consciousness about the need or problem, and to obtain participants, audiences, funds or cooperation.

10. Contact groups in order to obtain an already established audience for training. Good example of this would be to arrange for a county-wide staff in-service on "A Sexual Assault Protocol for Emergency Rooms," or a pilot program, "A Curriculum for Training in Adolescent Sexuality for Sheltered Workshop Staff." These professionals then help carry the work of the project out into the community.

11. Approach the local Bar Association, the Rotary/Lions Club, the Visiting Nurses Association, or a School Administrators group and offer to give an educational (rather than a training) presentation at one of their meetings. You can relate the sexuality topic to the lives or general practice of those in the group, and possibly receive their support for a project.

12. Work with planning, government, or regulatory boards to implement change in sexuality-related policy. Examples of this would be putting a course on human sexuality into a physical therapy curriculum, drafting legislation which limits the distribution of violent pornography, training state-wide child protection teams in the prevention as well as the treatment of child sexual abuse, or writing fair labor practice guidelines which include a strong grievance process for sexual harrassment.

The resultant intervention, based on the consultative role, may be large or small. Not every sexual need or problem in the larger society will require all twelve of the preceding steps, nor be completely remedied by them. Often a few people can see a problem, locate a sexuality specialist in a nearby area, put on a workshop or program for the right group, have the presenter continue as consultant, and accomplish a measurable change in a reasonable period. At other times a start is made, obstacles are uncovered (that's progress but painful), and more time and projects are needed to continue working on the problem. In any case, whenever interaction with the larger society is attempted, the counselor will need to set clear, objective goals, gather data where possible, implement a program, and evaluate results.

Often a clinic, correctional center, or a college will obtain a consultant to set up an excellent program to address a sexual problem or need, but when the leader moves the program dies. This is sad because when the problem recurs and reaches a painful level, someone else has to reinvent the wheel. Allowing for continuity and cooperation as sexuality programs are developed makes the most of the hard work accomplished in remediation, prevention, and early intervention.

Another role which a consultant can take is that of *mediator,* when sex-related concerns divide people. The kind of training received for doing divorce mediation, pioneered by C. Coogler and J. Haynes, is helpful in working with couples, adolescents, and families, especially when acting out or sexual abuse is an issue. Any mediation training is useful for the "turf" problems which prevent cooperation and the sharing of resources among education, health, criminal justice, and human service professionals in sexuality-related programs. Mediation overlaps with counseling in important respects, although some of the goals and many of the techniques are different. Mediation skills are useful for a sexuality counselor to have as a consultant when working with any group or system.

ROLE OF SEX EDUCATOR

Sexuality counselors are excellent sex educators because they become familiar with the most common questions and problems of specific groups. One can understand why a medical social worker who counsels many mid-life women after surgery on an oncology unit will make a fine presenter on "Lovemaking for People Recovering from Cancer." In a similar way, someone who works with sex offenders could be very effective in helping high school groups understand the difference between "pressured" and "pleasurable" sexual behavior.

The resources presented in Chapter 1, under the effects of sexuality education, contain sections on methods and techniques which the counselor can use. Researchers have summarized data from many excellent sexuality programs and have shown conclusively that information alone seldom affects behavior. For instance, asking social studies or English classes to compare two excellent booklets on the prevention of pressured sex, in order to select which is better, will get the students into the material in an active, respectful way. A workshop format, rather than a passive "classroom" type of learning, encourages the participants to see, hear, express, and apply what is presented.

Most education departments offer courses or other training on "The Design and Leadership of Effective Workshops," and this is an important skill for sexuality counselors to develop. Booklets such as *Small Group Workshops,* published in 1983 by the Center for Population Options, 2031 Florida Ave., N.W., Washington, D.C. 20009, contain workable suggestions and models. Some of the best material for a trainer's use are put out by large city or state groups and can be located in the newsletters listed in Chapter 1. Small group education workshops require counseling skills since the leader must listen at a deep level during the interactions, assess the needs of the participants, and focus while interacting to accomplish good education.

One of the most important skills in sexuality education is drawing out and answering questions. Here again counseling techniques are helpful, although it is important not to turn a question into a counseling dialogue in front of a whole group. Experienced counselor/therapists like Eleanor Hamilton can be highly supportive of the questioner, even when totally disagreeing with the question.

EXAMPLE: Supporting While Disagreeing

Question: *"Don't you think that all this sex education has brainwashed girls into wanting sex? My daughters and I grew up without that and our best teachers were our husbands!"*

Counselor: *"It's wonderful that it worked out for you and your family. But we know that the biggest sexual complaint that women had a generation or two ago was that their husbands didn't know how to satisfy them or show affection. Also, 80% of women in the 1940s and 1950s did not reach climax, whereas now 80% do. The right sex education can result in both normal pleasure and responsible behavior."*

Many audience questions are actually embedded opinions, so that the counselor must be selective and choose how to respond. Also, everyone will be confused by exhaustive studies and statistics, because both the question and the answer will be lost. The counselor can be more effective by focusing on those aspects of questions which are particularly related to the topic under consideration, give salient background facts, and not debate each implication.

EXAMPLE: Pre-hysterectomy Couples Education Group

Question: *"How can we know...since there's no purpose to it afterwards...what to expect? You know...after the operation? She never was all that interested, and had the bleeding as an excuse this year, and maybe will be sore from now on?"*

Counselor: *"You are absolutely right that women with pelvic pain and GYN disorders aren't very interested in sex. However, the hysterectomy should really take care of the physical problems. For some people it has been a while since sexual intercourse resulted in any real physical pleasure. Let's break up into couples for ten minutes, so the women can say privately to their husbands what they would like lovemaking to be like after the operation. Then in the whole group we can talk about ideas and ways to bring about good feelings."*

One other important education skill is to maintain a supportive counselor role toward all the participants, even if they are abrasive or hostile. Rather than debating the "rightness" of one's own values, the counselor-leader can refer to conclusions drawn from study and experience, and continue to be clear that each person has a moral responsibility to make decisions for self but not impose them on others. Resources, A-V material, and group exercises are a great help because the leader is then in a position to process reactions rather than defend only his/her presentation.

For instance, if *What About McBride?* (a low-key film on homosexuality), or *An Abortion Clinic* (a documentary which gives time to varied opinions) are shown, the counselor-educator can supply correct information based on solid research as needed, and then turn the discussion back to the issues.

EXAMPLE: Responding to Personal Attack

Question: *"This program shows how easy it is to kill a baby, and if you agree with that you must be one of those people. Everyone knows that a woman can never get over it, but you picked the video because it skips over that part."*

Counselor: *"You know, our guilt and negative reactions are very much shaped by the beliefs of people around us. In places where abortion is accepted as a positive act, people do not have many negative mental health reactions. Here in American research shows that the outstanding emotion afterwards is relief, although approximately 10% of women do have other, noticeable negative reactions. One of the worst causes of bad emotional reactions is to be pressured or forced to continue a pregnancy or not, rather than deciding for oneself. Does anyone else have a comment or question about the videotape?"*

EXAMPLE: Using Film to Stimulate Questions and Discussion

Counselor: *"So now that we've seen the McBride film, what facts about homosexuality were familiar and what surprised you?"*

Question: *"Why did they make the guy who resented having a queer on the trip a heavy? I think the film is slanted pro-gay."*

Counselor: *"Maybe it is hard to portray hate and fear as attractive? Can others come up with some observations about the film which show its politics to be biased against heterosexuals or for homosexuals?"*

Designing and leading a workshop and handling group process are a lot like conducting massed bands and choruses who play together only one weekend a year. The counselor needs excellent listening skills, quick recall, and the ability to utilize the group to teach one another.

The counselor can volunteer to participate in training which is not focused on sexuality, in order to include sex-related aspects which would otherwise be over looked. General topics such as child development, anxiety and stress, or recovery from alcoholism have important sexual components. Some conferences on low school achievement, absenteeism, and school dropout would not even mention the key factors of adolescent sexuality and teenage pregnancy unless that is brought to the attention of the committee. Solid research reports are appearing, such as *Trauma and Its Wake* edited by Charles Figley (1985), Brunner/Mazel, which provide excellent examples of sexual problems integrated with a broader topic.

While counselors cannot be booked up constantly, it is satisfying to be selective and offer sexuality education where it seems especially needed. The fact that this is also good public relations for the counselor's practice, institution, or agency is simply a bonus. Some potential clients are reached through an educational approach who would never present themselves for help otherwise. Finally, the research, organization, and people-contact which go into planning sex education further improves the professional's counseling skills.

ROLE OF TRAINER

A specialized form of sexuality education is training presented to other professionals. Most people now practicing in human services and education have little formal training in human sexuality. Yet their work requires these same people to make policies and judgments, teach and counsel in sex-related areas.

The following are only three examples of the types of training which the counselor can offer to other practitioners:

1. information about sexuality to use in their jobs,

2. help in designing and presenting sex education to their clientele, and

3. basic counseling skills on sex-related topics to use with their students, patients, or clients.

For instance, being asked to present a panel or sexuality workshop at a conference for clergy, junior high counselors, or rehabilitation nurses is a privilege rather than as a burden. In a similar way, a significant contribution can be made by participating in continuing education for judges, especially those who work with runaways, delinquents, battering, divorce, rights of minors, rape, incest, child sexual abuse, pornography, and reproductive/public health decisions. The counselor-trainer must clarify beforehand the focus and scope which can be covered in the time allowed, considering the practitioners involved.

Any professional who deals with human services is likely to encounter sexually related issues in some way and is a possible candidate for training. Why should the counselor wait until a tragic scandal occurs in a day care center before offering sexuality-related training to local preschool teachers? In this specialty, volunteering is necessary rather than being invisible. A sexuality counselor can take note of all the nearby agencies (public and private) who work with every age level, from Scouts to Senior Citizens, and at least offer staff training.

Throughout the training activities undertaken, the counselor must remain within his/her particular areas of expertise. To extend one's scope, a co-presenter who is familiar with the specific population treated by participants in a training group is very helpful. Having the trainees work out exactly what the sexual issues are which their clients face is a vital part of the training. Much of the trainers' skill is not just in presenting information, but getting out hidden assumptions, encouraging group communication, and helping participants problem solve.

CONCLUSION

This training program has now come full circle, back to the basic purpose of sexuality counseling. The hope is that the counselor has added many skills and areas of knowledge during the journey. In the process of continuing to learn and practice sexuality counseling, the professional can expect to be of immeasurable help to many people. Much of counseling is very private and the helper cannot expect constant, positive feedback, but considerable enthusiastic appreciation can be and is a reward when providing sexuality counseling.

APPENDICES

APPENDIX A

SEX HISTORY

DIALOGUE FORM

Modify as appropriate for the client and situation

1. Can you put into words some things about sex in your life so far? Has it been serious, funny, stressful, relaxing, a problem, or unimportant? Anything you have to say about it is fine.

    (Listen, draw out, supply a word, note the tone, and remember any specific content to return to later.)

2. Why don't you look at the sex education you had? For instance, who explained any "facts of life" to you? How else did you learn them? What was mom's attitude? Dad's? Who else was important? Any classes in school or church? What did you learn from books, TV, movies, magazines? How did you learn about puberty? What did your early periods (wet dreams) mean to you? What sex-related experiences with other children or young teens can you recall? What sex information do you wish you had had earlier?

    (Empathize. Show interest, humor is fine. Summarize: "So your information came from..." to encourage completeness.)

3. Adolescence is so important to anyone's self image. What was yours like? Did you feel accepted or different? How were junior high and high school? Do you remember some conflict between your sexual experience and what you were taught? You may have been more aware of self pleasuring (masturbation) then. Was it comfortable?

Since half of adolescents have intercourse and half don't, it is fine to be in either group. Can you remember how sexually active you were in your teens? How was that for you?

(Focus on feelings as well as behavior: "You seemed to hesitate about...?" If the topic changes, tactfully return to sex-related issues, indicating that time will be available for other aspects later.)

4. Can we talk about how your sense of being female (or male) developed? Did you like being a girl (or boy)? Who was important to your sense of femininity (or masculinity)—in either a positive or a negative way? How did that effect your sexual behavior? What stereotypes influenced you? What were your reactions to the other sex while growing up?

(Some mild coaching based on earlier answers may help: "Did being the only boy..." or "Since you got your period late...?")

5. Would you mention the first names of people that you had a relationship with? Some were probably more sexual than others. You may want to think of both women and men, and both emotional and sexual relationships. And now, looking back, what did you learn from knowing...? (Mention each person.)

(Listen for who was important rather than simply genital sexuality. Ask: "Can you think of any others?")

6. As people mature they are exposed to a greater range of sexual expression. I'll read the usual list and you can answer yes, no, or pass if you like. If your answer is yes and you hold feelings about the activity, indicate whether or not the activity was satisfactory. Okay?

Activity	Yes or No	Satisfactory?
a. fondling with clothes on	_____	_____
b. fondling with clothes off	_____	_____
c. bringing partner to climax with hands	_____	_____
d. being brought to climax manually by partner	_____	_____

e. intercourse   _____   _____
f. orgasm during intercourse   _____   _____
g. giving oral sex   _____   _____
h. receiving oral sex   _____   _____
i. anal sex play   _____   _____
j. using vibrators, other sex toys   _____   _____
k. group sexual experience   _____   _____

(Low key overview here, rather than extensive discussion of each.)

7. Every person has an absolutely unique history of attitudes and experiences with birth control. How has that been for you—from the earliest to the present?

(Again humor. Uncovering attitudes, myths, and stress periods is important.)

8. Most people also have a reproductive health history. How often have you been pregnant or thought you were (or were involved in a pregnancy situation)? What was the outcome? Can you describe any health problems which have affected your sexuality? (Mention sexually transmitted infections, premenstrual tension, prostate problems, etc., according to the person's age and comments so far).

(Take time to explore what is mentioned and to relate it to sexuality.)

9. Of course we are not machines. Many people have some occasions when their sexual behavior is disappointing to them. Can you recall times when you felt unable to control your sexual behavior, or were disinterested in sex? Have you had difficulty becoming aroused, or reaching a climax? When, how long, is this still a problem for you? What seems to help or make it worse?

(Note whether a problem seems consistent or situational, and is apparently increasing or decreasing.)

10. We all know that forced sex is common. Can you recall times when you pressured someone else for sex, or they pressured you? How did

you feel about it them, and now? Circumstances? Was the person a family member, a stranger, or someone important to you? What has been the effect on you? Other experiences of pressured sex?

(Sensitivity is required here. If the counselor senses the possibility but meets resistance, it is best to go on.)

11. Every person is different. Are your sexual fantasies or behavior unique in some ways? Do you have an unusual or special "turn on" or partner pattern? What have we left out? What worries you...what pleases you, about your sex life?

(Inquire here about any atypical sexual expression which may have been alluded to, or anything left out.)

12. Last question: What part has sex played in your life so far? What would you like to change or improve? If you think of additional things before we meet again, please jot them down and remember to refer to them next time. A complete picture will help both of us.

(The client is the expert during history taking. Being thoughtful and letting all the material "settle" afterwards is important. The counselor must guard against becoming analytical, making guesses, and overinterpreting after a history. Because a person is willing to answer questions does not mean that he/she is ready to be confronted by all of it. Work the material and impressions gathered in the history into the ongoing counseling in a supportive manner.)

APPENDIX B

KEGEL-TYPE EXERCISES

Pubococcygeus Muscle (PC)

GOAL: To become aware of and exercise a neglected area of the body. You can expect to increase sensitivity, develop more strength and control, and thus enhance well-being and sexual pleasure. The Kegel-Type PC Exercises also will help with urinary incontinence, if that is a problem, and strengthen the pelvic floor.

LOCATION: Contract the long muscles between your legs, which extends from around the penis or clitoris in front to circling the anus in back. Notice its continuous, unitary feeling. Then start to urinate with your legs apart; the muscle that you squeeze to stop the flow is part of the PC muscle. Woman also can put a finger in their vaginal opening and feel part of the PC muscle contract there.

RESULTS: After doing the simple exercises daily for six weeks, you should be able to feel an increase in strength, sensitivity, and control. There is good research evidence that PC muscle strength is closely related to women's ability to experience sexual pleasure. In a parallel way, one would expect men to benefit from PC exercise, both in terms of arousal and timing.

Exercise 1

> Contract the PC muscle for 3 seconds, then relax for 3 seconds, then tighten briefly. Do ten of these at three different times each day.

Exercise 2

Rapid exercise: contract and relax the PC muscle continuously without pauses between. Do ten of these, three times a day.

Exercise 3

Bear down with emphasis on the front of the PC muscle, hold for 3 seconds and then contract strongly for 3 seconds. Then do the same for the center area (between the penis and anus for men, around the vagina for women), and then the back anal area. Do five of these three times a day. At first it may be easier to do five with one focus and then move back; later you can sequence easier.

Note: These exercises can be done while watching TV, driving, sitting in a meeting, or falling asleep. A good procedure is to change your position at different times, between sitting, standing, and lying down. You need not stay with rigid numbers since they are only a guide, but repetition and regularity are the keys to any good muscle tone. Once you have the basic work done, it is pleasant to vary the exercises or keep time to music.

APPENDIX C

SEXUAL ASSERTIVENESS

Assertion is the expression of one's feelings, beliefs, opinions, and needs in a direct, honest, and appropriate manner.

Assertiveness is self dignity but not tyranny.

Assertiveness is owning your rights as an individual human being and standing up for them without violating the rights of others.

A *request* is assertive, a *demand* is aggressive.

Communicating *consequences* is assertive, *threats* are aggressive.

Submissive	Assertive	Aggressive
passive	clear	threaten
"doormat"	firm	demand
indirect	independent	accuse-blame

You Feel	You Feel	You Feel
"I'm not O.K. You're O.K."	"I'm O.K. You're O.K."	"I'm O.K. You're not O.K."

STEPS IN THE PROCESS

1. Develop a Belief System
    a. What do you want sexually?
    b. You have a right to sexual expression.

    c. You can ask directly for what you want and need.

    d. You have a right to refuse both reasonable and unreasonable sexual requests.

2. Distinguish for *yourself* what is submissive, assertive, and aggressive sexual behavior.

3. Pinpoint your own blocks to assertiveness (e.g., sexual ignorance, constant desire to please, past negative experiences, and so forth.).

4. Develop reasonable sexual assertiveness goals and practice.

POINTS TO CONSIDER

Everyone has the right to construct his/her own sex life and individual sexual expression. There is no one kind of "normal" or "correct" sex.

Women have been socialized to focus on pleasing their partners and trading sex for security, attention, power, status, approval, or recreation.

Men have been viewed as the sex experts but are ill prepared for that role by society; they often feel pressure for performance and achievement.

Women are bombarded for years with negative sexual messages so that many become out of touch with their erotic potential. Men may be focused on genital sex.

Assertion interacts with other human relationship and communication skills (empathy, persuasion, confrontation, decision making). You need *not* always choose to be assertive but should be aware of the consequences of alternate behaviors.

Build changes in sexual assertion gradually. Choose small things at first before approaching more central areas.

Assertiveness in sex cannot always get you everything you need, or force others to change. In the long run it has a better chance than submissiveness or aggressiveness and you have your self respect.

INDEX

INDEX

A

AASECT 185-90, 199, 229
  code of ethics 190
Abel, E 359
Abortion 64-7
  counseling 349-50
  resources 67
Abuse, sexual
  adult victims 397-9
  assessing 389-91
  child 385-408
  defining 387-9
  factors to consider 390-1
  resources 399-401
  treating victims 391-9
Academy of Certified Social Workers 185
Accuracy in focusing 139-40
Accuracy in listening 133-5
Activities
  resources regarding health sexual 53-4
  type of sexual 290
Adler, A 32
Adler, L 366
Adultery 92
Aggressor, sexual
  counseling 426-35
  resources 435
Aging 271-2
Aging and sexuality 271-2
Aging, health, and sexuality 271-2
AIDS 134, 241, 281, 360, 471
  fear of 282-4
Alabama State Department of Health 192-3
Alan Gutmacher Institute 280
Albee, G 469
Alcohol/drugs and sexuality 271
Alter, J 39, 336
Alternative
  exploring 347-8
  partner preference 305-7
Alternative Lifestyles 72
Ambivalence
  pregnancy 335-6

resources for assistance 336
American Association for Counseling and Development (AACD) 181, 230, 303
American Association for Marriage and Family Therapy (AAMFT) 181, 185, 186
American Association of Pastoral Counselors 186
American Association of Sex Educators, Counselors, and Therapists (AASECT)
  39, 183, 197
American Jewish Congress 352
American Psychiatric Association (APA) 181, 195, 230, 303
Andrews, L 341
Androgyne
  definition 376
Annon, J 328
Ansbacher, H 30, 32
Ansbacher, R 32
Anthony, W 117
Applebaum, E 336
Approaches to offenders
  counseling 405-7
Areas
  development, *figure* 260
  potential problem 264
  problem 252-3
Arms, S 352
Arousal 48
  phase 325
Art and movement therapy 122
Asbury, F 117
Ashford, J 63
Assault, sexual
  classification 430
  counseling 409-35
  prevalence 410
  rationalizations 411-4
  social factors 411
Assertiveness
  sexual 487-8
Assessment 259-64
  framework 310-22

Miser, K v
Mitchell, J v
Molloscum contagiousum 281
Monat, R 367
Money, J v, 28, 87, 91
Monilia (yeast) 281
Moore, B v
Moore, T v
Moses, A 303
Mostel, A 63
Motivation
  of goals 152
Mrazek, P 400
Munjack, D 51, 54, 359
Muscle
  pubococcygeal 485-6
Mutual goal 138

N

Nadelson, C v, 329
Napiv, A 33
NARAL (National Abortion Rights
  Action League) 352
National Abortion Rights Action League
  (NARAL) 352
National Association of Social Workers
  230
National Board for Certified
  Counselors (NBCC) 184, 185
National Center for Health Education
  272
National Certified Counselor (NCC) 184
National League for Nursing 181
National Sex Forum 102
Necrophilia
  definition 371
Neebs, L 39
Nelson, J 94
Neumann, H 287
New Women/New Men
  definition 376
NGU (nonspecific urethritis) 281
NLP anchoring 122
Noffsinger, A 117
Noncompliance 157-8
Nonspecific urethritis (NGU) 281
Norbach, J 280

O

O'Brien, P 425
O'Donnell, S 28
O'Neill, M v
Oakley, A 87
Objectives
  realistic 158
Offenders
  antisocial 404
  credentials for treating 402
  incest 405
  insights about 428-34
  juvenile sex 404
  pedophile 405
  resources regarding treating 407
  sadistic 405
  stepfamily incest 405
  subgroups 404-5
  treating 401-8
  types of 403-4
Okun, B 118
Olds, S 265
Olsen, M 32
Ooms, T 347
OPERN 380
Organizations
  professional 181-2
Orientation 298
Outreach Newsletter 380
Outwater, A v
Oziel, J 51, 54, 359

P

Pacing 130-3, 151-2
Pain 357-8
Palinski, C 345
Parcel, S 39
Parents and Friends of Gays 299
Parker, J 425
Parkhill, N 118, 132
Parkinson's disease 356
Parrinder, G 94
Parrot, A 91
Parsons, R 118
Partner
  timing 299
Partner choice 291

prevention 195-6
Problem area 252-3
  potential 264
Problems
  attitudinal 315-20
  caused by lack of correct information 245-330
  counseling 119-26
  pregnancy 333-53
  rooted in guilt 316-20
  rooted in relationships 320-2
  rooted in self concept 315-6
  sexual expression 308-30
  sexual variations 373-5
  training 107-9
Process
  judicial 434-5
Product of Phase II 138
Program
  training, use of 7-8
Progress
  evaluating 329-30
  evaluation 167-70
  lack of 219
Psychotherapy
  vs. counseling 123-4
Pubic lice 281
Public Relations 232
Pubococcygeal Muscle (PC) 485-6

Q

Quinn, J 39

R

Ramey, J 38
Rapaport, K 435
Rapist 430-34
Rational-emotive approach 122
Rational-emotive therapy 30
Rationalized incest 405
Reality Therapy (RT) 122, 185
Rebirthing exercises 122
Record
  summary 213-14
Record keeping
  reasons for 214-15

Records
  case 207-15
Refer 165-6
  decision making 218-20
  facing failure 222-3
  major considerations 218-20
  process of 216-24
  successful 220-4
  types 216
Referral 383-4
  assessment 383
Relationship
  client-counselor 174-7
  issues 320-2
  personal 109-12
  problems 320-2
  quality of 291
Relaxation 48
  phase 327-8
Religion
  values 92-4
Religious Coalition for Abortion Rights (The) 352
Renshaw, T 400
Resnick, P 425
RESOLVE organization 341, 342
Response
  biological basis 51-2
  case 1 441-4
  case 2 454-8
  counselor 441-2, 454, 455
  human sexual 47-54
  reasoning behind 441-2, 455-6
  sexual 50-1
Revitch, E 375
Richards, D v
Richardson, M 336
Risks
  professional 112-3
Roberts, E 28
Robinault, I 365
Robinson, S 375
Roe vs. Wade
  Supreme Court decision 347
Rogers, C 33, 116, 118, 145
Role
  sex educator 473-7
  utilizing the consultative 470-3
Rosen, I 365
Rosenzweig, N 91
Rowland, J 426

Rush, F 385, 400
Russell, D 426
Russo, R 265

S

Sado-masochistic (S-M) behavior
   definition 370-1
Safilios-Rothschild, C 87
Same-sex partner
   timing 299
Same-sex preference 296-303
Sanford, L 400
SAR (sexual attitude restructuring)
   7, 187, 189
SAR-type training 102-5
Sarrel, L 28, 265
Sarrel, P 28, 265
Satir, V 30, 33
Scacco, A 435
Scales, P 28
Schiller, P v
Schlesinger, L 375
Schmidt, C 375, 379
Schur, E 375
Schwartz, M 376
Schwartz P 72
Segal, J 39
Seibel, M 341, 345
Self assessment 124-6
   foundation skills 239-242
Self exams
   health 270
Sex
   coerced 203
   for sale 370
   forced 203
Sex Background Knowledge Quiz 20-2
   answers 95
   form 21-2
Sex education 1-2
   resources 253-4
   skills 22-4
Sex educator
   role 473-7
Sex Information and Education Council
   in the United States (SIECUS) 39,
   183
Sex therapy 1-2

Sexual attitude restructuring
   (SAR) 102
   training 102-5
Sexual concerns
   figure 256-8
   life stages 255-65
Sexual development
   resources 265, 271-2
*Sexual Dilemmas for the Helping
   Professional* 200
Sexual education
   resources for 38-9
Sexual Experience Overview
   questions 104-5
Sexual health counseling 266-88
Sexuality 266
   education about 159
   questions 81-7
   resources 87, 272-3
   stereotypes 79-87
Sexuality and disability 365
Sexuality and health 266-73
   resources 272-3
Sexuality counseling 1-2
   cautions 6, 126
   during illness 355-60
   during disability 360-8
   encouragement 126
   facilitative 243-330
   value of 3-5
Sexuality counseling skills
   form 244
Sexuality development
   over the life span 25-8
   resources for learning 27-8
Sexuality education
   effects 34-9
   methods 34-9
   timing 34-9
Sexuality history 481-4
Sexually transmitted diseases
   (STD) 281-7
   resources 287
Sgroi, S 400, 425
Sha'ked, A 365
Shaping
   gradual 162
Shore, D 359, 399
Shostak, A 67
SIECUS, Sex Information and Education
   Council of the U.S. 254

Weisberg, D 400
Wells, C 347
Wells, H 76
Whitaker, C 33
Wicks, R 118
Williams, G 375
Williams, J 401
Wilson, P 39
Wirsens, C 63
Wise, T 375, 379
Wolf, T 76
Wolman, B 28
Women Against Pornography 385
Wooden, W 425
Woodman, N 303
Woods, N 359
Work
  pro bono publico 236

Work load 226-8

Y

Yeast (monilia) 281
Young Women's Christian Association
  (The) 352
Young, B 39

Z

Zilbergeld, B 54
Zoophilia (bestiality)
  definition 371

ABOUT
THE
AUTHOR

ABOUT THE AUTHOR

Kay Frances Schepp talks about counselor education with enthusiasm, even though she did not grow up with this vocation in mind. The first counselor she ever met, at age 21, told her to withdraw her plans for a Fullbright scholarship and social work or medical school, since she was engaged. This was the 1950s, so Kay Frances was graduated with honors from the College of New Rochelle, NY, married a month later, and had three children in four and a half years. While her husband, Ron Schmucker, attended law school in the early 1960s, Kay Frances earned a master's degree in counseling at Syracuse University.

In 1968, Kay Frances received a doctorate from the University of Tennessee with part of her course work in counseling and the rest in clinical psychology. Sexuality issues were frequently referred to her during graduate training and internships, perhaps because she was one of very few women in the program and being married added to her "credentials." Finding that more training was needed caused Kay Frances to study sex education, counseling, and therapy as these fields were developed in the 1970s.

Another branch of professional interest was counselor education and supervision, which became a major responsibility at the University of Vermont. Therefore, she logically combined these two interests during the 1980s and expanded into activities in the area of counselor training in sexuality. As people asked for materials and supervision, too much was available to deliver verbally or in fragments, this textbook emerged. Additional professional interests are helping make audio-visual materials for early intervention in mental health problems, working with resistant clients and psychological emergencies, and consulting with varied areas of the university.

Kay Frances and her husband have a divorce mediation practice with two associates; she is past president of the Vermont Psychological Association and makes regular presentations at state, regional, and national conferences. Kay Frances, Ron, and their children have raised most of their own food in the Champlain Valley of Vermont and enjoy cross country skiing in winter and visiting the Maine seacoast in summer. But at work, Kay Frances continues her sustained interest in counselor training, and finds the subspecialty of sexuality counseling very rewarding.

Dr. Schepp serves as resource review editor for *Journal of Sex Education and Therapy* and is certified as a Sex Educator and Sex Therapist by the American Association of Sex Educators, Counselors, and Therapists. She is a member of American Association for Counseling and Development, Association for Counselor Education and Supervision, and American Psychological Association. She is a licensed psychologist in the state of Vermont.